FREEDOM
of the PRESS
in SMALL-TOWN
AMERICA

My Opinions

STEVE HOCHSTADT

for Jim
with best wishes

Steve

FREEDOM OF THE PRESS IN SMALL-TOWN AMERICA: MY OPINIONS

Library of Congress Control Number: 2020911066

Printed in the United States

PROJECT MANAGER: Katie Cline
INTERIOR LAYOUT AND JACKET DESIGN: Nicole Sturk
COVER PHOTO: Cheryl Kelly

Table of Contents

Preface

I grew up in Levitt suburbia on Long Island, went to college and graduate school in Providence, RI, and taught history and published books on the Holocaust in central Maine until I was 58. Then we moved to Jacksonville, in the heart of Illinois corn and soybean fields, in 2006. Until that moment, my knowledge of the Midwest, of the "heartland", of America between the coasts, was only theoretical. Luckily, I had been married for nearly 30 years to Liz Tobin, born in Normal, Illinois, an inspiring teacher about the silliness of Eastern ideas about most of America.

In Jacksonville, we found a good life. People were different from the urban and suburban Easterners I knew well, but were equally humane, generous, and thoughtful. Personal religion is much more public than in more reticent and private New England, but neither version of spirituality is more heartfelt. Coming from Maine, we found the fears about snow amusing, although seeing someone trying to clear ice from a sidewalk with a blowtorch at Illinois College was alarming. We felt comfortable and welcomed. It is distressing to hear so many people assert deep social and moral differences between urban and rural America, between red and blue America, differences among Americans that make some better and some worse.

My life in Jacksonville touched the public space in ways new for me. I wrote weekly opinion columns for the local daily paper, the *Journal-Courier*, for nine years. That was an extraordinary opportunity for me, provided by my editor David Bauer, to freely write during remarkable times. The "freedom of the press" in my title captures the sense of intellectual and political freedom I enjoyed towards the end of my working life. An example of that freedom is the word limit within which all op-ed writers must operate. David let me gradually push the length of my articles from the standard 650 to nearly 900, as you will experience here.

I cherished that freedom, because I needed those extra words. I tried to use them wisely in these essays.

More important, for me and my readers, was the freedom of subject I was given. Although I was a local columnist, I could write about any place or any subject. Over nine years, I never heard a negative word from my editor about my subjects or my opinions on them. Like the extraordinary freedom that professors have in our classrooms, I could go wherever I wanted in my Tuesday columns.

My most frequent subject is America. I rarely wrote directly about Jacksonville, but my Midwestern home was always on my mind. What could I say about America, or Germany or China, or any global subject, that might inform, interest or even fascinate my local readers? So much happens and so much is written every day. Once a week, I decided to tell my readers about something I cared about and thought they should know more about. That's freedom of the press. My ability to write about anything and get it published in the local newspaper was a personal liberation.

The *Journal-Courier* gave me an audience of my neighbors. We shared Jacksonville and central Illinois. We kept seeing each other in stores and sports contests and restaurants and concerts all over town, but mostly had no idea about the other's politics. While I wrote, the paper evolved slowly from moderate conservatism towards moderate liberalism, but nothing to frighten away even the most right-wing readers, of whom there are many in the rural Midwest. Except me. I was an argumentative liberal voice in the only paper every week.

Readers saw my little photo next to my columns on the editorial page on Tuesdays. I took that as a challenge to draw as many as possible into considering what I had to say, without alienating potential readers with nasty language. I was not writing for an in-crowd, but thinking about a crowd who had rarely ventured very far beyond Republican orthodoxy. Each week, I tried to write a few initial paragraphs without revealing where I was going, hoping that curiosity and logic and information would lead some local people to see that they could agree with something I wrote.

I was easily recognizable, with a big gray beard and long dark hair, so eventually people in town would ask whether I was that guy who writes for the paper. My minor local renown brought me into personal contact with people at many places on the political spectrum. In all those years of writing and living in Jacksonville, nobody approached me with hostility.

I should not have been surprised, however, that some local people thought it was a scandal that I was allowed to have my say in the newspaper. Over the years, nasty right-wing outrage never disappeared; it continues to be hurled at every writer to the left of Trump. But I only encountered verbal violence in my mailbox or on the internet. The mirror image of those who wanted me banned came from many among Jacksonville society, who said to my shock that I was helping them come out of a political closet. All my personal encounters encouraged me to keep writing, even if our opinions turned out to be very different.

I expect that many of my opinions printed here are different than yours. The only way to find out if they are worthy of your attention is to turn the page.

May 2020

CHAPTER 1

An Introduction to Me and My Writing

This book presents a selection of my political opinions over the past 15 years. Why read what someone wrote about politics and American life last year or 15 years ago? Why read old op-eds?

While the issues I write about are of long standing, each column offers a glimpse at that moment in our history. This collection of columns and commentary describes American history over the past decade, demonstrating that our present problems began long before Donald Trump came on the scene.

Writing down my opinions for so many years has forced me to be clear with myself and on paper about who I am and how that connects to how I think. I don't practice identity politics, a charge leveled at liberals, which actually better fits the narrow racial and religious politics of the right. My politics do come out of my identity, as I demonstrate in many of these essays. That doesn't make me sure that I am always right, but I feel that my judgments are right for me.

The frame of this collection is freedom of the press. Every week, I practiced a craft defined by the state of that constitutional freedom in the 21st century. At the most local level, these columns display how one writer in a small town enjoys and employs and reflects on this privilege. To make my case, I begin with an old column.

Before we moved to Jacksonville, we lived in Lewiston, Maine, and taught at Bates College. I took an apprenticeship in the guild of opinion writers by writing irregularly for the *Lewiston Sun Journal*. The following was published in the *Sun Journal* in February 2006. Except for the names and places, the essay could be written today, with even more emphasis. At that moment, in that historically Democratic town, it also tested the limits of my freedom of the press.

What a Good Man Does

FEBRUARY 19, 2006

A good man takes responsibility. For men born in the baby boom, as I was, that message was a fundamental part of our education. Men were supposed to do and be other things, too. Just taking responsibility was not enough to make you a good man. But taking responsibility was necessary. All the good looks, big muscles, self-confidence, and courage could not cover up the fatal flaw of irresponsibility.

For a man raised in the 1950s, taking responsibility meant taking leadership, making good decisions, accepting the weight of responsibility for knowing what is necessary and doing it. But it's not enough just to be a leader. You also have to accept the responsibility for what you do. Without prompting, without demands from those whom you may have hurt, by accident or by intent.

Responsibility was a crucial part of the mantra, "Be a man!" I don't see this phrase the same way as I did decades ago. I know now that another, sometimes hidden part of that command was "Don't be a woman!" Don't be a woman, because men are better. Don't be a woman, because that means being gay.

I don't believe that any more. In these things, life has been a better teacher than all my childhood instructors. But I still believe that being a good man means being responsible. I expect the same of a good woman.

Maybe the news about Dick Cheney's and Harry Whittington's hunting accident puts responsibility on my mind. The injuries to Harry Whittington appeared at first to be minor, so it was possible to focus on what this incident shows us about our leaders as men.

The first official word from the White House was that Harry Whittington himself had some responsibility for being shot last Saturday. The danger of the pellets to Whittington's heart remained undisclosed for days. Cheney said nothing until Wednesday, letting his good friend Whittington take the blame.

I don't hunt myself and am uncomfortable with guns. I do live in a hunting state and have learned something about the reasons for hunting and its rules. I am sure that one of the fundamental rules is "Look before you shoot". Shooter takes responsibility.

George Bush, Cheney's boss, does not set a higher standard. Bush is dealing with much more important problems than a bit of birdshot. He constantly tells us that our national security is at stake in almost every decision he takes. But he and his administration have avoided taking responsibility for their actions or decisions.

Crises, even minor ones like the shooting, force us to act quickly, without thinking about how things will play, before speechwriters can cover up what we say with something palatable. Katrina's waters washed away New Orleans and washed away the layers of protection around our President, so we could see him as he really is. Bush's behavior at the beginning of the crisis was so appalling that a Republican-dominated House committee now criticizes the White House response. We know that hours after the levees burst, Bush was playing a guitar and having a good time. He didn't lead. It took days before he did anything.

Since then, the real problems that the Bush administration has caused have come out into the light: the politicization of FEMA, the indifference to disaster preparation even after 2001, the waste in spending recovery funds. We have heard no responsibility taken by George Bush or those who speak for him, for Katrina, or for lost lives in Iraq, for so misleading the American public about Iraq, for torture.

Cheney is simply following the official White House policy on taking responsibility.

You do not have to believe that we should leave Iraq now or that tax cuts are bad or any other partisan claim to see what kind of men are leading us. Being a good man is not a party issue; it does not favor liberals or conservatives. It is not about what you believe. It is about how a man acts and what he says about those actions afterwards, as their consequences become clear.

I lament that political parties and partisan positions have drifted so far apart that nearly all of our politicians put party before responsibility, defending the indefensible rather than telling us the truth. It is surprising that in these times of military crisis, even the virtues of taking responsibility by fighting for one's country are attacked, if the man comes from the wrong party or criticizes administration policy. Our current leaders prefer to attack the patriotism of their critics than to accept responsibility for their own actions.

I think that we all suffer from our irresponsible leaders. We don't get the information we need to make good decisions. Our emotions get deliberately stirred, but our analytical abilities are not encouraged. Our politicians, beginning with our President and Vice President, do not respect us.

They believe that they don't have to be good men to remain as leaders, they just have to act tough. "Being a tough guy" wasn't necessarily a bad thing when I grew up. Just being tough on other people, though, made you a bully. And being tough, whether for show or for real, was not the same as being good.

STEVE HOCHSTADT
Lewiston ME

That was my last editorial for the *Lewiston Sun Journal*. Soon after it appeared I was notified by the editor that my writings were no longer printable. The conservative owners had enough of my opinions.

Rejection can be useful, if always painful. I quickly learned the truth of A. J. Liebling's remark in *The New Yorker* in 1960: "Freedom of the press is guaranteed only to those who own one." Cynics of all political persuasions repeat some version of that. In that paper, I was no longer free to criticize the President. Writing has consequences.

I offer that piece as a sample of my writings that follow. It displays an element of my identity that reappears throughout this book, an emphasis on a personal moral structure that has nothing to do with the Moral Majority. I seek out goodness in people, as I seek goodness in government.

Before I offer pieces from my career in Jacksonville, here are two earlier Maine essays from 2005, published in the *Sun Journal* under the rubric "A Different View". They display where I was when I began to write opinions, in terms of political perspective and column construction. Because I'm a historian, I always back away from the present moment, whatever its flash, to understand the background, the context, the history of my subjects. I am also willing to criticize both sides: I am not a partisan, whose beliefs are determined by tribal loyalties. I am a liberal, whose perspective emerges from deeply felt moral judgments, humanitarian instincts, and observation of the world I live in.

As I write this in 2020, the coronavirus wreaks havoc across the nation, and Puerto Rican society still struggles to deal with the destruction by Hurricane Maria two years ago. Are we any better at dealing with natural catastrophes than we were 15 years ago?

What Katrina Reveals About Our Government

SEPTEMBER 14, 2005

The disasters in the wake of Hurricane Katrina reveal some glaring weaknesses in our political structure. These weaknesses usually mean dollars wasted or bureaucratic inconvenience. This time thousands of lives were lost because our governments could not be relied upon to do their job.

Many people these days are pointing a finger at the top, at the decisions of George Bush's administration. The facts I have learned about how this government has acted since his first election have convinced me that he and his closest advisers should be held to account. Right after his election in 2000, the Bush administration began to remake FEMA by cutting its budget and reducing its role in preventing damage from natural disasters. The Bush budget severely cut the Army Corps of Engineers 2005 funding requests for the New Orleans district; especially hard hit was the Southeast Louisiana Urban Flood Control Project. Bush himself was woefully ignorant of the dangers of flooding in New Orleans, saying on ABC's Good Morning America, "I don't think anyone anticipated the breach of the levees." That was three days after the levee collapsed, when a responsible President should have been better informed.

But some of the other weaknesses in the federal response should not be blamed on Bush alone. The men in charge of FEMA since Bush took office have been political appointees, who have no business leading a federal agency. Joe Allbaugh was Bush's chief of staff when he was Governor of Texas, and a central campaign organizer in 2000, who was appointed to head FEMA in 2001. He had no emergency experience. He stayed less than two years, replaced by his college friend, Michael Brown, who not only had no experience, but had been asked to leave his previous job, where he was commissioner of judges and stewards for the International

Arabian Horse Association. A current article in TIME magazine alleges that Brown padded his resumé in several places.

The fact that the national agency designated to help people whose lives have been catastrophically disrupted was led by an incompetent manager with no experience is a result of the American system of political patronage. Both Democrats and Republicans at the local and national level treat crucial public jobs as political plums for friends and supporters. The result is wasted money, unresponsive bureaucracy, and government incompetence. That all translates into suffering for Americans who need government programs. In this case, it meant needless death and destruction.

In the nineteenth century, our government was plagued by a corrupt patronage system which distributed important jobs as political favors. Over one hundred years ago, a professional civil service was created, in which government jobs are given out based on merit. Yet the most important positions, the heads of agencies, are still filled by political appointees rather than professionals.

The functions of our government are too complex to be handed out to political supporters. We should demand that managers in government agencies be professionals with significant experience and a record of success. It matters less whether they are Republicans or Democrats than that they can do the jobs we require.

Those who most need an efficient government tend to be our poorest citizens. They depend on responsive federal and state bureaucracies to meet immediate and pressing needs. Treating the work of government as a prize for political support means ignoring the plight of our neediest citizens.

It will not be easy to force our elected officials to give up the power they derive from their ability to hand out high-paying jobs. The disastrous response to Katrina and its basis in political patronage may wake up some politicians to the importance of efficient and professional government services. In the end, only an outraged electorate can take back our government from those who abuse it for their own selfish purposes.

STEVE HOCHSTADT
Lewiston ME

Every natural crisis is unique. But all the elements of the disastrous federal response to the coronavirus pandemic were present and obvious in 2005. Neglect of the government agencies whose task is to understand and react to emergencies at the national level. Dismissal of the scientific work which provides the crucial knowledge about what is happening and why. Critical delays in response by oblivious government leaders, who thought about politics as Americans died. Resistance to helping victims in the name of financial stinginess. This was the Republican playbook in 2005 for dealing with a localized disaster, and it reappeared in 2020, with Trump as its spokesman.

Will his criminal negligence finally create an outraged electorate?

The second early piece shows my reverence for elections as the ultimate performance of democracy. I always hope that elections can be used to do good for everyone, not just the winners. This column illustrates both a political fight in Maine 15 years ago that continues to rage across our country and how my politics developed out of my family's background. The Maine legislature passed a law in 2005 banning discrimination on the basis of sexual orientation. The so-called Christian Civic League of Maine immediately gathered signatures to put a repeal on the ballot. Their director, Michael Heath, said the vote would be about "defending society itself" against the immoral forces that threaten to destroy the family.

Why I Can't Support Discrimination
OCTOBER 12, 2005

My family was driven out of Vienna by the Nazis. My relatives were killed in gas chambers. What began as discrimination grew into persecution and ended as mass murder.

The Nazis also persecuted homosexuals. Making the argument that homosexuality was a disease that could be cured, they arrested thousands of gay men, put them in concentration camps, and tried to "re-educate" them by forcing them to have sex with female inmates. But because discrimination is always also based on hate, homosexuals were beaten, shot, drowned, starved, and worked to death by camp guards, men who had learned to hate homosexuals.

The Nazis are gone, but discrimination against homosexuals continues. The Maine Legislature has courageously gone on record as opposing such discrimination. Now we the people have a chance to demonstrate our belief that discrimination is not compatible with democracy by defeating the attempt to repeal this new law.

Those who wish to deny equal rights to gays have used three strategies, here in Maine and across the country. First they have tried to confuse the issue by making false claims about what ending discrimination means. For many years, they claimed that anti-discrimination laws gave homosexuals "special rights". This was an effective tactic: when I walked around my neighborhood in 2000 talking to people about the attempt to repeal an earlier anti-discrimination bill, I heard the phrase "special rights" many times.

There are no "special rights". The anti-discrimination law gives to homosexuals the same rights as other laws against discrimination have given to blacks, women, Jews, and other groups who have suffered from prejudice. The text of the law says only that it is "to prevent discrimination in employment, housing or access to public accommodations...in the extension of credit...and in education on account of...sexual orientation." Such laws have been very important in my lifetime in ending discrimination against Jews, which was common here in Maine and everywhere in the US when I was young. I have no special rights. I just have the right to be an American. Gay people should also have that right.

Now the repeal lobby has brought up a second tactic of confusion. They say that it's not this law that's so bad, but that it will lead to gay marriage. Like the claim about "special rights", this is just not true. There is nothing in this bill about gay marriage. Certainly some people are in favor of gay marriage, while others are opposed. If that issue ever comes up as a legislative proposal, it should be discussed. Discriminating against homosexuals does not become acceptable because one is opposed to gay marriage.

Finally, the repeal lobby relies on its most powerful argument: the Bible. Repealers constantly quote those passages in the Bible which say that homosexual sex is evil. These passages are pretty clear. So are some other passages from the King James Bible which used to be quoted quite often. For example, in "The Gospel According to St. John," Chapter 8:44-47, Jesus says to the Jews, "Ye are of your father the devil, and the lusts of your father ye will do....He that is of God heareth God's words: ye therefore hear them not, because ye are not of God." In "The Revelation of St. John the Divine," 2:9, Jesus told John to write, "I know the blasphemy of them which say they are Jews, and are not, but are the synagogue of Satan."

These passages were used for centuries to justify Christian discrimination against Jews. Right into the 20th century, Christian leaders, like the Popes, quoted these biblical passages as proof that it was right for Christians to discriminate against Jews, to hate Jews. Then came the Holocaust, in which Christians all over Europe participated in murdering Jews. Now every Christian faith has rejected the intent of these words in the Bible. Lutherans disavow the words of Luther when he advised his followers to raze Jews' houses and burn their synagogues. Catholics disavow the words of Pope Paul IV, who ordained the creation of ghettos for Jews in 1555. Lutherans and Catholics and Baptists and Presbyterians can be good Christians while ignoring the meaning of some Biblical passages.

Discrimination is wrong. The United States of America was founded by people who believed it was self-evident that "that all men are created equal, that they are endowed by their Creator with certain unalienable Rights." Our founders still discriminated against women and blacks, but their ideology of equality and democracy led later to laws which prohibited such discrimination as against our founding principles. The new law which prohibits discrimination on the basis of sexual orientation is one more link in this proud chain.

I know how hurtful discrimination is, and not just to the victims. We can see in Maine how inhumane the repealers have made themselves by their arguments. I value the rights that came at such a high cost to me and my family. I will vote NO on 1.

STEVE HOCHSTADT
Lewiston ME

In that election, the people of Maine rejected discrimination 55% to 45%.

You don't have to read very carefully to see my cautious comments above about gay marriage. In 2005, when Massachusetts had just become the first state and only the sixth jurisdiction in the world to legalize same-sex marriage, I could avoid confronting that subject directly. Read on in later chapters to see how I have "evolved".

I had no idea that what I wrote in 2005 could be read usefully 15 years later. The family festivals and the political issues I have written about since then haven't disappeared. My approach hasn't changed either. I am a fact-finder and fact-checker. My essays offer to be your source of information on some political and personal subjects. I want to understand why and then give that understanding back to anyone who will listen.

These columns are not news reports. They are questions and answers, big questions and my answers, around important parts of our daily lives. One of the chapters here collects what I wrote and thought about the 2012 election. Like all modern American elections, much changes and much remains the same. I believe those 2012 writings are instructive about the election we face now with great apprehension.

Do I need to say that I'm not crazy? In the age of Trump, bombast and hoaxers rule. When lunatics can adopt the most appealing disguises, when clever combined with deception can be turned into millions of dollars, when it's hard to tell fact from fanaticism, I need to assert my sanity, and more, my rationality. These essays are rational arguments based on carefully researched facts with the logic out on the open. That's what I say, anyway.

I don't seek "likes", but I hope for "understands". In 800 words, I believe I can inform. Putting together many of my essays, I might be able to persuade. The op-eds reproduced in this book can inform our discourse today, tomorrow, and possibly for years to come. In my opinion.

As Dr. Seuss's Sam-I-Am said, "Try them! Try them! And you may. Try them and you may, I say."

CHAPTER 2

Jacksonville: A Yankee on the Illinois Plains

Jacksonville is a small town. There were many papers here for nearly all of its two centuries, but the morning *Journal-Courier* has been the only survivor since 1983. When we arrived in 2006, the ownership and editor were almost reflexively conservative. Not only was there no liberal media here in central Illinois, there was no liberal voice at all. The editor allowed me to write a few columns as a guest, but he published them as long letters to the editor, not as op-eds.

Without making any programmatic decision, I began just before an election by trying to define my political identity, which does not fit the usual left-right categories, if those actually fit anyone. When I read this now, I still see myself.

Why I Am a Conservative
OCTOBER 21, 2006

I believe in traditional values. I think that values from our heritage as Americans need to be more powerfully expressed in our society. On those aspects of social life in America where I feel like I stand outside today's norms, people call me conservative.

I was raised in the 1950s, when traditional values dominated in America. We were taught to respect teachers and government, that families should eat together, and that being a good sport was more important than winning.

I married a conservative. Elizabeth Tobin's values come from deep within her family: regular family gatherings, staying close to family members that other people call distant, emphasis on the Christian holidays, and ways of behaving at the table. There is no line between inlaws and outlaws. Instead family friends become family, creating long explanations about how we are not actually related. All blood kin are important, but being related goes beyond blood. My family was more scattered and much more narrowly focused, like other immigrants and refugees. I love being part of the large warm family my wife's values create.

We had no trouble agreeing to be strict in the lines we drew for our children and our unwillingness to abandon them. Our children called us conservative, and complained mightily by comparing us to more liberal families they knew. That prompted heated but ultimately useful exchanges about our values and their belief that we were enforcing outrageous discipline. Since I am heavily influenced by my children's ideas, I was happy when their arguments became half-hearted, because they came to share our family values. We could all agree that Dr. Spock screwed up by encouraging permissiveness at every crisis.

Our family attitudes toward television were considered so neanderthal, we had trouble finding babysitters in our working-class city. Our children had to learn by hearsay what was going on in the popular shows so they could pretend to have a normal home life. Now they laugh at us for having bought a large-screen TV so we can watch sports.

I feel very protective of my family. I get steamed up when people try to get inside my family circle to promote their own interests. I just think that my family is nobody else's business. It seems like every day somebody I don't know asks for my home phone number. I know that my response is unusual, because so many of those people get confused when I refuse to provide it.

Of course, my children are pleased to point out each way that I lag behind in contemporary telecommunications. It doesn't bother me a bit to be so unmodern.

I believe in regulation. My natural response to bad behavior is to think about better rules. Rules are the opposite of freedom, but I want to make rules for children, for students, and for employees. Good rules protect society. Unregulated freedom encourages selfishness.

I like old things. We live in an old house which we are restoring to its old look. It is filled with old furniture. I keep old tools in the basement, and save used nails and screws in case they come in handy later. My father-in-law's favorite phrase has become our family's byword: waste not, want not.

I like the one Latin phrase I know, although the habit of quoting Latin has gone out of fashion: "*de gustibus non est disputandum*". There is no disputing taste. I can't defend my taste for old things and it's far better not to argue about it. I know that because my arguments with my children about revealing clothing, low slung pants, and contemporary music accomplish nothing. I do draw the line, though, on things that some people want to say are about taste. I think some men's taste for children is criminal. I think Hollywood's taste for violence is sickening. People with illegal tastes should be put in jail. I don't think our society's penalties for stealing, lying, conspiring, or abusing are severe enough. I don't accept the defense that we just have different tastes. How conservative is that?

I smile when someone calls me a conservative, to show me how wrong I am. I like that. I have come to my principles over a lifetime and I'm proud of them. What I miss are more people who call me a conservative to show how right I am. I don't seem to get any conservative credit for my traditional values. Our very public citizens who have decided they represent conservatives don't talk to me. I hear them talk about traditional values, but I don't see them stand behind them.

Family values are supposedly a conservative idea, but today's conservatives are not protecting my family. They refuse to keep poisons out of our food or our air, which could ruin the health of my children or grandchildren. They shut their eyes and ears to the reality of global warming, which could devastate my children's world. They are always talking about the right to life, but have done nothing to protect women's lives from the men who brutalize them.

I want to conserve the beauty that makes America unique, but that doesn't qualify as conservative today. Every effort to preserve our national parks, to limit suburban sprawl, or to save endangered species is labeled liberal by today's conservatives.

I want to limit government, but that's no longer a conservative value, either. Today's conservatives want to listen to my phone calls, look at my bank account, and read my email. But they sure don't want me to know what they are doing, hiding behind the kind of government secrecy that our founders hated. Maybe it's because they are so busy spending my tax dollars to support their private interests rather than the public good.

Today's conservatives try to keep those without power or money quiet, but where are their values when it comes to the rich and powerful? Every effort to get giant corporations to follow our laws is labeled liberal. Why do the biggest crooks in history, stealers of billions of dollars from private citizens and public coffers, seem to be buddies with today's conservatives?

Probably the most traditional value of all is my feeling about the truth. I hate lies and the liars who tell them. Public lies are the worst lies, for they are meant to deceive the most people. Honesty no longer seems like a traditional value, just an inconvenience when the truth is hard to take. Today's conservatives have brought our political standards of honesty to a new low. Can we even imagine one of our current leaders voluntarily telling us an inconvenient truth before everybody already knows about it?

I feel nameless. When they harken back to simpler times, I feel a kinship with intellectual and political leaders who name themselves conservative. But they spend much more time attacking me, not just when I take positions they call liberal, but when I try to defend my conservative values.

Not all my values are traditional. The founders were heroes of their time, but I'm not a principled strict constructionist because I don't like all of their principles. Racism in public life, sexism and paternalism in private life are values I reject. The founders were far ahead of their time, but also products of it. The popular forces for equality have won great victories since then, often relying on the underlying ideas of the founders, but then going further than they were willing to.

One of the things I learned in the fifties was that homosexuality was bad. Eventually I found out that the evidence for this idea was made up, that many of its most vocal proponents were hypocrites, and that homophobia was just a nasty prejudice with deadly consequences.

So I support a mixture of values, traditional and liberal. I don't think that makes me middle-of-the-road, however. People who know me remark on my strong opinions and the strong way I express them.

I am not a moderate.

Now I have to vote. That is both a responsibility and a privilege, which I am grateful to use. Out of all those mathematically conceivable combinations of values here in America, there seem to be only two choices in every race, sometimes with a dark-horse third. Often there is really just one choice, the incumbent, whose powers to influence elections would astound our founders.

This year, wherever I have a real choice, I'm voting for the candidate who is called most liberal. I don't agree with everything liberal politicians do. I wish they would pay more attention to some of my traditional values. But if I want to ensure my family's health and future, preserve the principles that make America unique, and solve the real problems that modern life creates, then conservatives don't offer me anything except loud talk.

It was scary during those years when liberal became a curse word. Liberals ran away from being liberal, and found other words, or just kept running. People with the most unpleasant manners and least willingness to change their minds have been screaming at me for years that liberalism is a sickness. Fortunately I can regulate what I hear on the radio, and by now you should be able to guess where I turn the dial: oldies stations.

Now liberal is making a comeback. It turns out the party that prides itself on being conservative, led by its most self-congratulatory of conservatives, is not even competent to do most things that a government should do. Liberals will make gains, and some will even dare to embrace the word.

I want to rescue the good human values packed into that word: generous, open, free-spirited.

I am a liberal.

I guess.

STEVE HOCHSTADT
Jacksonville IL

I soon discovered how deeply conservative my central Illinois surroundings were, which was reflected in the official positions taken on the editorial page of the *Journal-Courier*. Policies I had taken for granted as good government my whole life were viewed as dangerous here in the early 21st century.

I don't like labels, and liberal is a dangerous label. For most of the past 40 years, liberal has been a curse word for Republicans. Their Party platform in 1992 said, "Liberal Democrats think people are the problem." Liberals were anti-family promoters of drug use and immorality, godless lovers of big government, greedy for taxes and soft on crime. The word liberal and its traditional meanings of generosity, tolerance, and freedom were "turned up on its head" as Hillary Clinton said in the 2007 Democratic debate, when she avoided claiming "liberal" for herself.

Many Americans have accepted this Republican redefinition and retain a deep hatred for liberals. I searched for a voice that could express liberal ideas as American ideas. Now in 2020, that equation is still not widely accepted in rural and small-town America.

The editor of the *Journal-Courier* refused my repeated offers to write regularly, citing the obstacle of his usual $15 weekly payment for local op-eds. When I said I would do it for nothing, he twisted around into asserting that some set of bureaucratic rules prevented him from doing that. I don't know what role my politics played in his thinking. So I was only able to occasionally interject my thoughts into the local public discourse.

I got frustrated by my inability to gain a regular audience for my perspective on American politics. In Maine, my contributions to the public conversation were one piece of the public liberal discourse, to the left, but still within bounds. In central Illinois, there was no public liberal discourse. If I didn't express those ideas, nobody else would. Since Obama's election, our politics had descended into the gutter, and the local paper was not interested in my civil, but outraged reactions.

I dealt with that frustration by seeking my own audience in summer 2009. I compiled a list of email addresses of family and friends, which included many former Bates College students. What I told them has become the backbone of my writing since then: Take Back Our Lives.

Taking Back Our Lives

AUGUST 20, 2009

I am sending this message to many people I know. It is my experiment with your interest in what I have to say.

I feel a broad despair gripping people who, like me, thought that the campaign and election of Barack Obama meant something inspiring about our nation's politics. Glenn Beck said on "Fox and Friends" late in July that Obama was a racist and hated white people. Lou Dobbs wondered on CNN if Obama was really an American. Sarah Palin's early August invention of "death panels" in the health care reform legislation was the final push of our public politics into the screaming chaos of ignorance and lies. This was not the change we hoped for.

Paul Krugman responded to the "death panel" fantasy with a plea to Obama in the NYT on August 14 to "rise to the challenge of unreasoning, unappeaseable opposition". I hope Obama does find an effective way to present his ideas. But it's time to stop looking to Obama or to anyone else. I think that people like us need to find our own way to influencing the kind of politics we live with. Despair comes from believing that you can't do anything to stop its cause. It's time to take back our lives.

The development of the "death panel" claim is exactly where national media politics makes the politics we hoped for impossible. It didn't start with Palin. Right after Obama was elected, a *Washington Times* editorial urged readers to expect a budding T4 policy out of the White House. T4 was the Nazis' program of murdering disabled Germans by developing an efficient gas chamber. Earlier this year, a few well-known conservatives used misrepresentations of provisions in the stimulus bill to claim that Democrats supported government-induced euthanasia.

Then Republican Senator Johnny Isakson of Georgia introduced an amendment to the big reform legislation in the Health, Education, Labor and Pensions Committee giving people a new benefit "to obtain assistance in formulating their own living will and durable power of attorney." Many in my generation have been doing exactly that in recent years, as our parents age, get sick, and die. It would have been helpful for me to have had some assistance when my parents and I were forced to explore these painful issues and deal with the impenetrable private and public insurance bureaucracy.

That's when the big lie machine got cranked up. Betsy McCaughey, who made her name as critic of the Clintons' health care proposal 15 years ago, said on radio that the bill in the House "would make it mandatory - absolutely require - that people in Medicare have a required counseling session that will tell them how to end their life". That was only one month ago. Since then Palin coined the phrase "death panel" and extended the death fantasy to include "my baby with Down syndrome". Senator Charles Grassley said last week that "We should not have a government plan that will pull the plug on Grandma!"

Now our neighbors and fellow citizens are screaming about T4 to every politician who dares to face the public. I would be happy that more people show knowledge about the Holocaust if they actually demonstrated that they understood the difference between Nazi Germany and their own country. Mr. Isakson's comment that anyone like Palin who confuses a living will with euthanasia is "nuts" is irrelevant. So is the history of Republicans' support for end-of-life counseling. In 2003, 204 House Republicans and 42 Republican Senators voted for the Medicare prescription drug bill, which provided funding for counseling on end-of-life issues. Governor Palin proclaimed April 16, 2008, Healthcare Decision Day for Alaskans, a statewide effort to provide information about advance directives. The truth doesn't matter. Neither does our society's need for real help as we deal with increasingly difficult decisions about our elderly relatives and our own futures.

All that matters is I win-you lose politics, with ignorant and outraged people as pawns. When that's the game, we are always the losers. That's what I have learned from Holocaust deniers, the spiritual ancestors of today's conservatives. Krugman was right to call Obama's opponents unreasoning and unappeaseable. Like Holocaust deniers for whom no document or photograph, or millions of them, can be accepted, the conservatives who call the tune for the Republican Party don't really want to see a birth certificate when they demand one. No certified birth certificate, no newspaper article, no scientific fact can stop their public campaign. Arguing with them on their terms is already their victory.

We need our own terms. Unlike most of the stuff that politicians do, health care reform could change our daily lives. Let's have our own discussion and make it so truthful and useful that we win. That would be just one step in taking back some control over our lives. If you think that's worthwhile, please send this on to others you know. And get ready for more. Or let me know to leave you alone.

best wishes,

STEVE HOCHSTADT
Illinois College

That tentative step into regular opinion writing was welcomed by most and rejected by hardly anyone. I hit a nerve among many people, who appeared to share my optimism, which in hindsight appears naive. My selected audience responded positively, so I was encouraged to think more positively about where we were and where we could go.

I resolved to rely exclusively on the weapons of facts and logic, and to be critical of the way my own assumptions emerged in my writing. Carrying out that resolution is not easy for any opinion writer, and I believe I have gotten better at the task over the past decade.

That work means examining every word, the detailed discipline of the writer. My subject also frequently turned out to be the examination of other people's words, a fundamental practice of any history teacher, reading thousands and thousands of student words every semester. I can coerce my students to write with attention to evidence and truth by threatening failure. I can do little about the reckless words of politicians beyond exposing them.

I struggle every day between "it's not enough" and "let's keep going". Four years after Trump's election, I would reply to the standard polling question that the country is on the wrong track, along with the majority of Americans since 2002. One unavoidable theme of my writing is that conservative politicians have been loudly pointing us in the wrong direction. I might have confined my writing to academic prose had not my need to show how wrong they were pushed me into op-ed writing.

Words are important. It has been important to me to underline the public words that public people say and to ponder their significance.

Taking Back Our Lives

SEPTEMBER 8, 2009

White House Press Secretary Robert Gibbs said that conservatives had entered "silly season" with their complaints about President Obama's address to schoolchildren today. I think it's much worse than that. This is just the latest tactic in a concerted and radical crusade to delegitimize Obama. This campaign is deliberate, unprincipled, and dangerous for our country.

It is not surprising that some fringe cranks attacked our first black President as not a real American, by focusing on the illegitimacy of his birth. Latently racist attacks surfaced throughout the 2008 campaign at the edges of Republican events. Sarah Palin never had the courage to denounce the death threats to Obama voiced by some of her supporters, but John McCain, closer to the Republican establishment, eventually did. After the first few months of the Obama administration, however, Republican leaders began to react to their stinging November defeat by tolerating and then supporting the Birther movement. Senator Richard Shelby and Missouri Congressman Roy Blunt offered doubts about Obama's American citizenship, and roving video reporter Mike Stark caught Representatives Trent Franks (AZ), Cathy Rodgers (WA), Charles Boustany (LA), Greg Harper (MS), and Nathan Deal (GA) giving credence to the Birthers.

The usefulness and limitations of these attacks on Obama's legitimacy as President are demonstrated by recent polls, which show how the official Republican silence about the Birther mythology has helped spread it among their rank-and-file. A July opinion poll by Research 2000 showed that 28 percent of Republicans believed Obama was not born in the US, and 30 percent were not sure. In the poll, three-quarters of Southern whites doubted the official account of Obama's birthplace. A Public Policy Polling survey in August found that only 32% of Republicans in Virginia thought that Obama was born in the US.

The latest manifestation of the effort to deny our President legitimacy is the feigned outrage over Obama's address to schoolchildren, normally a non-partisan staple of Presidential leadership. The Florida Republican Party chairman characterized Obama's speech as trying to "indoctrinate America's children to his socialist agenda."

No need to pile up more examples here, because the effort to delegitimize Obama is so public that everyone can see and hear it. We need to discuss what it means for us and for our country.

We know that the place of America in the eyes and hearts of the world depends significantly on their perception of our President. The sudden boost in favorable ratings of the US by countries across the globe when Bush was replaced by Obama shows how focused other peoples are on our President. This is true in democracies, for whom the election of a black man in an historically racist society brought admiration for our institutions, and in dictatorships, where attention is always concentrated on the leader.

By tearing down the honesty and humanity of Obama, by spreading doubts about his legitimacy, by encouraging the violence at the fringes of American politics to focus on him, conservatives are hurting America's position in the world. No matter what our foreign policy is or will be, the unrestrained conservative attacks on Obama as unworthy to be President weaken its effectiveness. Need I say that this comes at a time of war?

Encouraging comparisons between a health care plan closely identified with Obama himself and Nazi mass murder is treason. I'm not exaggerating here: "a violation by a subject of his allegiance to his sovereign or to the state" is the first definition in my dictionary. A more descriptive phrase there says "giving aid or comfort to the enemies of one's government." Today's public conservatives in the media and in Congress are themselves the enemies of our government. That's why South Carolina Senator Jim DeMint used the metaphor of Waterloo to describe his hopes to play Wellington to Obama's Napoleon.

Because I think our daily lives are much more determined by what happens here at home, I think the domestic effects of the campaign against Obama are even worse. Obama's opponents created the myth that his supporters were rock star fans, out of our minds about him. If he is a fascist and a socialist and doesn't care about Granny and may not be American, then those of us who voted for him, who were enthusiastic about his politics and a new politics for America, are stupid, deluded, and possibly evil. We all are being delegitimated daily by the Republican onslaught against our political choices.

It doesn't matter that we are the voting majority. It doesn't matter that we represent more people and more kinds of Americans. The real treason here is that conservatives have declared most Americans the enemy. By violating their allegiance to their democratically elected leader and the government which he represents, conservatives show they have no allegiance to the actual Americans who are their neighbors.

They are wrong. We are America. We just need to say it more often.

STEVE HOCHSTADT
Illinois College

Right after I wrote that, Rep. Joe Wilson from South Carolina shouted "You lie!" in the middle of Obama's address to Congress. That was 2009, long before Trump dove into the "birther" controversy, when he had just changed his registration from Democrat to Republican. He could not have taken over a party that believed in respect for others and standards of behavior other than the purely partisan. His extreme ideas and extreme personality found a comfortable home.

By September 2009, I had found a groove, writing twice a month to a small group of interested readers about politics as I saw it. This next piece exhibits my comfort in expressing a fear that was not uncommon then and is not uncommon today, fear that American politics will get much worse.

For my whole life, conservatives have portrayed liberals as un-American, using whatever contemporary lingo they could appropriate. You aren't a real American if you are a quiche-eater, an elitist, a socialist-communist, a libtard, a snowflake.

Now in 2020 it appears that these "real Americans" have taken power.

Taking Back Our Lives
Weimar America
SEPTEMBER 30, 2009

Dangerous political movements have threatened the peace and structure of democratic society throughout recent American history. Violent hatred has motivated groups on the left and right extremes, and sometimes these movements have gained considerable local power. I found Maine to be a most tolerant and peaceful place when I lived there for 27 years, but I learned to my surprise how pervasive the influence of the Ku Klux Klan had been in Maine during the 1920s, when it had 150,000 members.

The White Citizens' Councils were thoroughly integrated into the justice and police system in the South in the 1950s and 1960s. Both organizations were representations of social movements of like-minded, often violent people who perverted our political institutions for racist purposes. These movements threatened American citizens and American institutions, but their dominion was local and temporary. The dangers that such seemingly uncontrollable social forces pose to our lives and liberties should be one of the major lessons in the teaching of American history.

Perhaps I am especially sensitive to similar dangers in the present because of my professional and personal preoccupation with the Holocaust. In Weimar Germany, the Nazi fringe was tolerated, encouraged, and funded by mainstream conservatives, giving respectability to its brand of violent antisemitism and radical anti-government propaganda. When economic disaster struck in 1929, the Nazis' calls to overthrow the democratic system suddenly jumped from 3% of voters in 1928 to 18% in 1930 to 37% in 1933.

I think similar forces are at work in our country, and they frighten me. They are obscured by the ludicrous claim that the Democrats are today's Nazis.

The very commonness of Obama with a Hitler mustache at conservative events is a new and noteworthy feature of today's political life, duly reported by all major media. It functions as a visual prop for the much more serious insistence that Obama and the Democrats are planning a health care system which resembles the Nazis' T-4 program, in which they murdered at least 270,000 handicapped people.

The woman who asked Barney Frank in all seriousness why he was supporting an American T-4 program gave him a You Tube opportunity to show how irrational her beliefs were. But she was serious. Egged on by media voices that are reminiscent of Father Coughlin in the 1930s, but much more ubiquitous, she can also reasonably observe that her political beliefs are encouraged by Republicans in Congress, in governors' mansions, and in official Party posts. In a philosophy class I just attended, the professor said that large numbers of people generally do not support completely implausible arguments. Historically this only happens when people with power and influence make a concerted effort to propagate a big lie.

It is easy for intellectuals to laugh at the historical nonsense of charges that Obama is both a socialist and a fascist, a Nazi trying to bring Communist health care to the US. The official voice of the Republican Party, Michael Steele, may seem silly when he circulates the claim that Democrats want to deny health care to Republicans. But we should not laugh at the final step, thus far, of the movement unleashed by mainstream conservatives — bringing guns to Obama's public events. Conservatives say they are merely demonstrating their support for their threatened Constitutional rights. Would Republicans have allowed a known leftist to carry a weapon openly at a Presidential function after 9/11? Under the Patriot Act, and the illegal surveillance which accompanied it, American citizens couldn't be sure they could joke on the telephone about Bush being dead. Now the über-patriots are saying that our President is a racist who might try to kill your Grandma and simultaneously providing cover for crazies who might try to shoot him.

Our democracy is under attack. Men in high public office and with control over our national airwaves are deliberately stoking a potentially violent movement opposed to our democratic process. They challenge the legitimacy of the last election, they label our elected leaders with the worst political curse words they can think of, they encourage the purchase of weapons at local gun shops and talk of secession in the capitals.

You don't have to be a Holocaust-obsessed Jewish academic to see what is going on. Or to remember that German mainstream conservatives were so opposed to the liberal reforms pushed by the democratic Weimar system that they thought they could harness a violent radical and hateful movement to win political advantage. They were stupid. But we would be stupider the second time around.

STEVE HOCHSTADT
Illinois College

At that moment, a more difficult and exciting opportunity was presented to me. A new editor, David Bauer, had taken over at the *Journal-Courier* in May 2009. After publishing a few pieces as guest columns, he agreed to publish me every week as a regular columnist for that $15. His rules were simple: "No personal attacks, no defamatory statements, no vulgarities — in short, nothing that can get me sued." My first column came out on November 24, 2009.

My audience had now changed radically. No longer a hand-picked group, my readership expanded to 10,000 local subscribers and many more online readers. They didn't know me and would turn the page unless I offered more than shared assumptions. That was the beginning of my education as an op-ed writer. I was suddenly offered freedom of the press and the responsibility to use that freedom well.

The positive role of science and the distortions wreaked upon its development by rigid ideologies is one of my frequent subjects, because these distortions irritate and deeply trouble me. I proclaim allegiance to the scientific method broadly interpreted, which I have tried to practice as a social historian and a journalist. My irritation is provoked by those who choose evidence only to assure an outcome, make illogical leaps in reasoning because logic leads the other way, chop up history to select the few pieces which appear to confirm an ideology, and just plain lie. More troubling to me is the apparent success these dishonest methods enjoy in our public sphere.

My title here was shortened in the process of publication, a practice which led to intermittent arguments with the editor about my titles. Some were too long or too short, or too pointed. I restore my titles in this book.

Science and Politics (or The Politics of Science)
NOVEMBER 24, 2009

Ever since Pope Urban VIII condemned Galileo in 1633 for asserting that the Earth revolved around the sun, it has been obvious that what people accept as science is influenced by religion and politics. The Pope argued that Galileo's claims about the solar system, based on the most advanced astronomy, contradicted the Bible, and therefore could not be correct. The political power of the Vatican transformed Urban VIII's assertions about science into lifelong imprisonment for Galileo.

Science is one way of explaining our universe. The methods of science can be extremely complex, but they are guided by a few simple rules: gather the best evidence; create explanations based on all available evidence; do not allow forces outside of scientific evidence to influence conclusions. No human being can be a perfect scientist. Every step in a scientific investigation is human, meaning inevitably imperfect in design, implementation, and understanding. Scientific method is an admirable goal, impossible to reach.

But scientists have gotten quite a bit better since the 17th century. Relentlessly doubting every discovery, improving every instrument, and broadening their inquiries to cover every facet of the material world, scientists have transformed human society. Science has not just gotten better, it has triumphed over other ways of explaining what we experience, consciously and unconsciously. Magical, mythical, and religious explanations of physical reality have retreated in the face of modern science. If we want to know whether we will recover from an illness or how to feed a baby, we don't ask a priest or a medium; we seek the scientific consensus.

Political forces, however, can distort science and encourage popular ignorance of the truth. Both the Soviet Communists on the far left and the Nazis on the far right made politics the sole judge of what was acceptable science. To a much lesser degree, every American administration has used political ideology and political muscle to push science in a particular direction. Even considering this history, the Bush Administration politicized science to an unprecedented extent. Scientists outside and within the government ceaselessly complained about the misuse of scientific evidence that characterized Bush's two terms.

There is nothing new here. Conservative political leaders have been using government power to obstruct scientific progress for decades: they denied that pollution of our air and water was dangerous and that tobacco caused cancer. George Bush killed legislation to give the FDA power to regulate cigarettes by threatening to veto it, and Republicans in Congress continue to be the main opposition to the effort to control the sale of tobacco. Conservatives have repeatedly refused to accept the best science about threats to our public health, because only government could then offer remedies. They have fought significant efforts to improve public health, from Medicare to our current health reform debate, in order to prevent the growth of government. And every time their "science" was wrong.

Now we discover that the Republican candidates for governor of Illinois reject the worldwide scientific consensus that humans have significantly contributed to global warming. Conservatives in Illinois and across the country once again line up against the best science, because they fear the political consequences. I use "fear" deliberately. Ask any of our Republican candidates which country is the world leader in science. I doubt that any would name Germany or China or Japan. But they are afraid to accept the conclusions of American science. They fear that if Americans believed that the health of the Earth we will leave to our children and grandchildren is threatened, the populace would demand that we do something about it.

So once again politics trumps science, and our health is the casualty. I wonder what they say when their children come home from school with F's in science.

STEVE HOCHSTADT
Jacksonville IL

That essay was also published in "LAProgressive", an online magazine based in Los Angeles that had been started the year before by Dick Price and Sharon Kyle. My potential readership expanded much further geographically, but only to people who chose to go to a "progressive" website. Like countless websites with a clear political orientation, the conversation is inward, towards and with those who like the label progressive. Headlines, jokes, and cartoon assume a shared politics. I was very pleased to have my writing get more attention, but my primary responsibility was to my Jacksonville readers.

I wanted to encourage local people who shared my political perspective, but I also tried to turn my face toward an imagined reader who would pay attention to uncomfortable information I thought they should consider. I never knew how many such readers existed or what they thought of me.

The Republican Party in Disguise
JUNE 15, 2010

The Tea Partiers are not what they seem. They say they're about freedom, not party, that they just want government off their backs. They appear to attack incumbents of both parties. So why are they all Republicans?

Americans have just suffered through eight years of escalating government intrusion into our lives. The Bush-Cheney version of Republican government violated constitutional rights with impunity, especially in their first term, when Congress was also controlled by Republicans. Once their secret surveillance programs became known, even the Republican-nominated Supreme Court rejected these Bush policies.

The only consistent critics of these infringements on our liberties have been Democrats, notably Barack Obama. The transition in Congress from Republican to Democratic majorities in the election of 2006 and the election of Obama in 2008 have meant a reversal of Republican violations of the Bill of Rights.

Why doesn't this matter to the Tea Partiers, whose arguments all appear to end with anger at "big Obama government"? Here's why: both Democrats and Republicans believe in using government intrusion into otherwise private matters to accomplish their objectives, but unlike the Republicans, liberals focus on the marketplace.

One of the 15 commandments on TeaParty.org is "Intrusive Government Stopped." The website of the Tea Party Patriots makes clear what they mean: "we oppose government intervention into the operation of private business." This is a familiar Republican idea, but as in everything else, the Tea Partiers are extremists. Rand Paul, Senate candidate in Kentucky, criticized the Civil Rights Act of 1964 for prohibiting private business from racial discrimination. Sharron Angle, who just won the Republican nomination for Senate in Nevada, wants less government regulation of off-shore drilling, as BP's catastrophic well keeps pumping oil into the ocean.

Another commandment is "Government Must Be Downsized." But this is not the libertarian mantra. The TPs demand more government control to achieve their goals: "traditional family values", English as the official language, pursuit of illegal immigrants.

Like many extremists, the TPs are blinded by ideology. They don't understand the relationship of government and big business. TeaParty.org demands more "pro-domestic employment", which means restrictions on the export of our jobs by global corporations. They want "Political Offices Available to Average Citizens", which cannot happen without government restrictions on corporate political contributions.

The Tea Partiers won't admit that big business is on their backs and everyone's back. Despite their concerns about taxes, they don't seem interested in where the rest of their money goes. They are obsessed with their property, but they don't want to think through the complex economics which determines what their property is worth. If Obama and the Democrats prevent big banks from ripping them off through credit card fees, they won't talk about it, because it might confuse their ranting about big government.

The Tea Partiers really are only interested in getting government off *their* backs. They don't care about our backs or anyone else's backs. They don't care about people who look or sound like they might be recent immigrants — they want the whole country to follow Arizona's new immigration and anti-ethnic studies policies. They don't care about people whose lives are endangered by corporations. Even faced with the deaths of 29 miners in West Virginia and 11 oil workers on Deep Horizon, they continue to attack regulation. They don't care about our safety, as long as their "sacred" right to carry guns wherever they go is unlimited.

The Tea Partiers are wrong. The people they support will increase government intrusion into our private lives, under the guise of protecting us from enemies all around, and will help big business exploit our private resources.

In any case, they won't change American politics. Despite putting pretty faces like Glenn Beck and Sarah Palin on their posters, they're way too unattractive. Like the guy who strolls into Starbucks with his gun, they might get a lot of attention, but they'll make no friends.

STEVE HOCHSTADT
Jacksonville IL

I was certainly wrong to make that prediction. Now we have a Tea Party President.

The Tea Partiers constantly cited Waco as a symbol of their own martyrdom at the hands of a police state, and suggested their respect for the Oklahoma bomber. In neither case did the threat to our civil liberties come from "big government". It was the Bush-Cheney administration which threatened our civil liberties in the name of the war against terror. They orchestrated the initial bailout which the Tea Partiers linked only with Obama. How could Cheney have been the voice of Tea Party ideology?

I see evidence for two different answers to this seeming contradiction. One has been made often under the label of Astroturf politics. The Tea Partiers presented themselves as average citizens beyond partisanship, but like many groups who espouse conservative causes, they might have been a front for big private organizations, including the Republican Party. The apparently earnest men and women, mainly mature adults, who speak so forcefully about freedom from government and who have entered organized politics so passionately, were just shills and dupes of the powerful interests who call the shots.

Big right-wing money flowed to the Tea Party since its beginnings, but its millions of adherents across America were not merely shills. The Republican establishment certainly cheered on the Tea Partiers and tried desperately to penetrate and take over their movement. But there was plenty of resistance, as in the dumping of Utah Senator Bob Bennett for more conservative and completely inexperienced candidates.

Maybe the Tea Partiers were honest advocates of their rights and not just the loud and frightening face of the latest Republican scare tactics. But I didn't respect them, because they were ignorant and selfish. They made themselves into the dupes of the moneyed power of conservative Republican politicians, who follow a different ideology.

When Rand Paul claimed that his disagreement with civil rights legislation is about "government intrusion", I heard white supremacy and I thought about my family. I was raised, not by my family, but by my culture, to be an unthinking racist. I had to learn how to think about race from the silent but firm models of my parents, the social realities of American life, and the history of millions of families who suffered from racism.

I learned about the concept of "white privilege" in my narrow academic life and then observed how appropriate it was in naming what I saw in real life. One of my fellow local columnists got angry about Attorney General Eric Holder's insistence that we talk about race, and then issued a pronouncement that the whole country should "shut up about race".

Why I Will Keep Talking About Race
SEPTEMBER 4, 2010

Jay Jamison writes that everyone should "shut up about race". But I won't.

I will keep talking about race because Jacksonville's history is permeated by race. While slavery dominated the South, Jacksonville had a significant free black population in a section of the city called Africa, south of College Ave. Before the Civil War, abolitionists, many at Illinois College, clashed with defenders of slavery. But race as a defining element of social life in Jacksonville was not only an issue of the 19th century. Well into the 1960s black people in Jacksonville were openly discriminated against in downtown stores. Racism is a living memory for many black and white residents of Jacksonville.

I will keep talking about race because we keep learning more about how racism in the United States operated. James Loewen's eye-opening book, *Sundown Towns* (2005), describes how small towns all across America kept African Americans out by passing laws that non-whites had to leave by sundown. These communities remained segregated into and past the 1960s. In Illinois, according to the 2000 census, Scott County and Mason County still had no black households, and Stark County had one.

I will keep talking about race because my students cannot understand American history without knowing the role played by racism. Official and unofficial discrimination against virtually every ethnic and religious group who were not Anglo-Saxon Protestants determined social and economic life in America for most of our history.

I will keep talking about race because my life is a product of racism. My father came to the US at 18 because he had to flee his home in Vienna or be killed by the Nazis. He found a haven in America and within a few years

Lt. Ernst Hochstadt, US Army interrogator

was back in Europe wearing a US Army uniform. Thousands of other German and Austrian Jews, including my grandparents, were denied entry by antisemitic immigration laws and practices of the US government. After I was born in 1948, antisemitism still determined where Jews could live, what colleges we could attend, what organizations we could join, and where we could work. I have seen antisemitism gradually dissipate in America, but not disappear. Within the past few years, I heard a speaker talk about being "Jewed" at a public gathering here in town.

I will keep talking about race because my brother, George, who lives in eastern Pennsylvania, tells me that "nigger" is common parlance among white people he meets. Racism is still widespread in America. A survey conducted this year by the University of Washington found that more than half of whites agreed with the statement: "It's really a matter of some people not trying hard enough; if blacks would only try harder they could be just as well off as whites."

I will keep talking about race because a candidate for Senate in Kentucky has said that he thinks it is wrong that the Civil Rights Act of 1964 makes racial discrimination by private businesses illegal. Unless one agrees with Rand Paul, it is important to defend the civil rights won in that hard fight against racism in the 1960s.

I will keep talking about race because that is what prevents and eliminates racism. If young people in America are less racist than the older generations, it is because they have heard open and truthful talk about race in schools, in film, in the media. They have learned that racist stereotypes are lies, that discrimination is illegal, and that racism must be fought not only in bad foreign places, but here at home.

It is a remarkable day when a white man tells our black Attorney General Eric Holder, as well as black and white "scholars, activists, and others" to shut up about race. It is a remarkable argument to blame racism on the words of those people who have been and still are discriminated against. It is remarkably ironic to say that the targets of racism are obsessed with race.

Those of us who have felt racism are not obsessed with race. But we know that pretending racism will go away by itself is a privilege of those who have never felt its sting. And we won't shut up.

STEVE HOCHSTADT
Jacksonville IL

I didn't want to get into arguments with another local columnist, but I couldn't allow his comment to go unchallenged. The conflict between my ideal image of myself as a regular commentator and what drove me to make public comments characterized my career as a journalist and everything else I have written.

In late 2010, I was searching for the positive as politics became more negative. Perhaps that quest describes me at all times. But optimism, like pessimism and all of our deepest impulses, can lead our analytical thinking astray. At that time, my summary of the midterm elections seemed persuasive to me. I was wrong about much of it.

Do We Have Common Ground?

NOVEMBER 9, 2010

The election last week, and the intense campaigning throughout 2010, seemed to me to be the most contentious, nasty, negative manifestation of American politics that I have experienced. Both sides predicted the end of life as we know it if they did not win: either the Tea Party would take us back to the Stone Age or the liberals would inaugurate socialism in America. Sharron Angle's comment about "Second Amendment remedies", which might have lost her the election in Nevada, was representative of how both sides demonized their opponents, crying "wolf" so loud and so often that it was hard to keep paying attention.

The extreme partisanship of this election, and of the actions and inaction of Congress in Washington and the Legislature in Springfield, represent a major problem for our country. In fact, neither Democrats nor Republicans command a majority of the electorate. Although every poll shows slightly different results, the Politico-George Washington University poll in mid-October revealed a typical portrait of the American electorate: 42% Republicans, 41% Democrats, and 17% Independents. Yet this weight in the center of the political spectrum was ignored by campaigners this season, as they pushed their extreme agendas.

If we tune out the shouting, we might find that we American voters are not at war with each other. Tuesday's results included several messages about national policy that most Americans agree on. Here they are:

1. Americans are concerned about the deficit. Since the year 2000, the national debt has risen from about 5.5 trillion to 13.5 trillion dollars. The two wars, exploding health care costs, and the near depression all contributed to the accelerated growth in debt. Economists do not agree about how this level of debt will affect our economy over the long term, but it seems certain that the government cannot keep spending so much more than it takes in.

2. Getting more taxes from the rich is not popular. Democrats and Republicans split very forcefully on what to do about the Bush tax cuts for the wealthy. The Republican desire to maintain the tax cuts for households earning over $250,000 does not appear to have hurt them at the polls. In Washington state, where the Democrat Patty Murray won reelection for Senate, voters rejected by a 2 to 1 margin a ballot measure to impose an income tax of 5% on people who earn more than $200,000 and of 9% on those who earn more than $500,000.

3. Voters did not support broadly cutting taxes. In Massachusetts, voters rejected cutting their sales tax in half; in Colorado three measures to restrict state and local borrowing, to cut motor vehicle and other taxes and fees, and to limit property taxes were killed by voters with 2-1 or 3-1 mar-

gins. A few specific taxes were voted down, for example, on alcohol in Massachusetts.

4. Cutting back entitlements, like Social Security and Medicare, is an election loser. Most conservatives refused to include Social Security in the programs they would cut. Sharron Angle's intimations that she would raise the retirement age contributed to her defeat.

5. Congress is not working. An overwhelming majority of voters disapprove of the way Congress has performed, with approximately equal criticism for both parties: only about 30% approve of Democratic or Republican performance. This is a non-partisan verdict. Many more Americans approve of Barack Obama's performance in office, with poll numbers hovering around 45%. So the verdict on Congress is not mainly a disapproval of liberal policies, but of gridlock, lack of cooperation between the parties, and flagrant use of congressional perks, like earmarks.

These messages are clear, although many politicians pretend they have received a mandate to enact extreme ideas, that in fact are unpopular. Unfortunately, it will not be easy to turn these popular ideas into legislation. It will not be possible to control the growing deficit without doing something about entitlements and about military spending. Without more tax revenue, the federal government and many state governments, like Illinois, will go further into debt.

The deep recession has created a political crisis across America. But getting the major parties to work together in the middle has become less and less likely in recent years. We need statesmen on both sides to offer serious long-term visions and to embrace practical political compromises. I wish I knew who they were.

STEVE HOCHSTADT
Jacksonville IL

Thinking about those 5 messages in 2020 is sobering. Trump recognized that Paul Ryan's open advocacy for cutting Social Security, Medicare, and Medicaid was a loser, so he just proposed that on the sly, while promising he would never do such a thing. The Republicans presented a small tax cut that middle-class families had not demanded, in order to enact a giant tax cut for the wealthy, which only they thought was necessary.

On number 1, I was just wrong. Americans don't care about the deficit. Those who most loudly proclaimed the overriding importance of reducing the deficit throughout Obama's presidency are delighted with Trump's doubling of the deficit. It turns out they were driven by much less admirable impulses. Writing about American politics in the 21st century kept interfering with my natural optimism. The politics of race over the past few years have gone backwards.

Color Blindness
NOVEMBER 23, 2010

Ever since race became a dominating political issue across America in the 1960s, some Americans have claimed that they have transcended race, they have learned to be color blind. These claims have mainly come from conservatives, who were lukewarm about or openly opposed to civil rights legislation, affirmative action plans, school desegregation, or other policies which attacked racial discrimination. For example, the Texas-based Campaign for a Color Blind America is a conservative organization whose purpose is "to challenge race-based public policies".

Claims about being color blind are not personal statements. I don't think I have ever heard a friend say that they are blind to skin color. I hear public assertions of virtue, made to support policy. In April 2008, when a controversy broke out over Sarah Palin's attitude toward hiring African Americans in her Alaska administration, her spokeswoman said, "Governor Palin is totally color blind."

These claims typically go further, like this: "I am color blind. My organization, my party, my church, my business, we are all color blind. Good Americans are color blind. So we don't need to think about race any more. The need for government concern with discrimination is over." When the Supreme Court in 2007, under the new leadership of John Roberts, decided that plans to desegregate schools in Seattle and Louisville were unconstitutional, this was applauded by conservatives. They especially liked Roberts' statement, "The way to stop discrimination on the basis of race is to stop discriminating on the basis of race."

I don't believe the claims of individuals that they are color blind, and I certainly don't think that the issue of race in America is a thing of the past. Here's why.

I was raised by a family that passionately believed in racial equality. My father had been given lessons in racial persecution by the Nazis, escaping with his life and most of his family before all those left were murdered. When he returned to Germany with the US Army, he and other interrogators heard some of the first claims of color blindness, as Nazi prisoners denied everything they had just done.

By the time I was born in New York City in 1948, Jackie Robinson had just broken the color barrier in baseball in Brooklyn. In my family the Brooklyn Dodgers stood for moral goodness, even if their baseball was hapless. When I was young, discrimination was still a live issue for Jews as well as blacks in America.

I learned to believe in the goal of equality, equal treatment of everybody by everybody, even if I have come to suspect that it is a utopian dream.

But I am not color blind. I see color very well. I notice instantly the color of the person I am looking at. Then out come all the things that I carry around in my head about race. That includes my desire to get to color blindness, my experiences in communicating and trying to understand people who look different than I do, my feelings about fellow minorities. It also includes other ideas that I absorbed from my American surroundings, whether I wanted to or not: the idea that blacks and whites are different; that blacks are potentially dangerous; that race matters.

No matter what my rational self thinks, those racist ideas deep in my consciousness never disappeared. I still see myself flinch as a big black man ran towards me on a street in New York many years ago. He was in a hurry, but I only figured that out after he was already past. I saw color and reacted.

That experience tells me how far I still have to go to get to color blindness. Our nation also has far to go. Claiming that we are color blind, that whites no longer have privileges in America, that we need no longer worry about preventing discrimination is nonsense. One need only have observed the reception of our first black President to know how important skin color still is in America.

STEVE HOCHSTADT
Jacksonville IL

Color blindness is a biological condition, not a social reality, except as a concept promulgated by people who are anything but color blind. Closing one's eyes to real life results in total blindness; pretending that one doesn't see what's right there is faking blindness.

Some fakers elicit my admiration — magicians, actors, comedians, fiction writers, and others who readily acknowledge that they present alternative but non-existent realities. The fakers who claim to be truth-tellers outrage me — con men, telephone scammers, and celebrity purveyors of alternative facts.

What's With the Pipe, Glenn?

NOVEMBER 28, 2010

A few days ago, Glenn Beck accused George Soros, a Holocaust survivor, of turning in Jews to the Nazis. Now some people want his head, calling him an antisemite. I don't agree. His head is worth nothing. Beck's history lesson shows exactly why.

Beck doesn't like Soros. Soros is one of the world's biggest donors to liberal causes, and he has lots to give. He reportedly made $1 billion in an English currency crisis, by correctly predicting that the pound sterling would be devalued. The organization that Soros created and leads, the Open Society Institute, promotes democratic ideals and liberal practices in countries with authoritarian governments. Beck hates the causes that Soros funds.

But that's all irrelevant to what happened to Soros in 1944 when the Nazis occupied Hungary. He was a Jewish teenager trying to avoid being sent to Auschwitz, where over half a million Hungarian Jews were murdered that year. To survive, Soros had to do some unpleasant things. He once told a journalist that he and other kids were called to the Jewish Council, a group of Jewish leaders forced to transmit the Nazis' orders to their fellow Jews. The kids were given slips of paper to deliver to Jews in town. When he went home and showed them to his father, he found out they were notices of deportation. His father sent him back out to tell the recipients not to go. Soros was 13 years old.

When he was 14, he took on a Christian identity and found protection in the home of a sympathetic Hungarian bureaucrat. Once, when that man was sent to inventory the property of a Jewish family who had already fled the country, he took young Soros with him for 3 days, rather than leave him alone in Budapest.

Like most Holocaust survivors, Soros has not talked much about his narrow escape from death. His writings are all about his current political interests. So we don't know much more than what I wrote above. But Glenn Beck claims he knows a lot more. Beck said Soros "used to go around with this anti-Semite and deliver papers to the Jews and confiscate their property and then ship them off....It was frightening. Here's a Jewish boy helping send the Jews to the death camps."

Beck's comments about Soros are a perfect window into his mind. More than other conservative media personalities, Beck uses historical information to prop up his political ideas. In his attempt to play the TV historian, he appears in disguise, dressing up as one of the academics he constantly mocks. Decked out in a tweed blazer, writing on a chalkboard, a pipe in his mouth, he tells his viewers stories about World War II, Franklin Roosevelt and the writers of the Constitution. And about Adolf Hitler — Beck constantly brings up Hitler and the Nazis.

Real historians try to create a story that could explain as much evidence as they can find. Like everyone else, we bring our own prejudices and assumptions, interests and experiences to this task. About historical eruptions like the Holocaust, every historian and every survivor creates a personal narrative.

No historian would transform the evidence into the nasty claims about Soros, and the Baumbach family who saved him, that Beck broadcast to his 2.6 million FOX News viewers. Beck is not a historian at all. He doesn't hate us for our "elitism"; his suits cost more than my yearly salary. He worries that we will expose his act.

His antisemitism isn't the main issue. Our American problem is that Beck the entertainer pretends to be teaching history. Beck's TV lectures have the same truth value as Jerry Seinfeld's jokes or Tina Fey's impersonations.

Maybe less value, because Seinfeld and Fey are honest about what they are doing. Beck isn't — perhaps he is deluding himself, too, as most successful con men do. FOX News presents him with a straight face. But we are supposed to laugh, not believe.

I won't be watching, though. I don't get Beck's sense of humor. I can't laugh when I hear someone call Katrina victims "scumbags", and I never liked Holocaust jokes.

STEVE HOCHSTADT
Jacksonville IL

Beck lost his FOX News show, but not his dishonest flame-throwing. In February 2020, he told the conservative Political Action conference that electing Bernie Sanders would lead to another Holocaust.

Writing weekly columns changed me. If I didn't want to be an opinionated pontificator, I had to learn quickly and think carefully about my subject for next Tuesday. That is a peculiar discipline. It's not at all like writing a book or creating a film, which take years to develop. An article in a scholarly journal takes much more time. Like other journalists, an op-ed writer has a short deadline.

Preparing an op-ed essay is most like writing a lecture in a college course that meets three times a week. Even when I pulled some pages out of a file drawer from a previous course, the same discipline held: what do you know? what can you find out that's new or different in a couple of days? how can you present what you know in the clearest way? I happily believe that I have gotten better at this.

I have changed in other ways, too. I read more political and environmental and economic news than I ever had, with greater intensity. I have gradually been able to make my essays more personal, not about me, but from me. It took me years to realize how much I had been downplaying what I thought would make me unacceptably radical in Jacksonville in order to get conservatives to read me. At the time, that was good for me, and maybe for certain readers.

One fundamental aspect of my political and personal perspective that I never revealed in my writing was my religious viewpoint. I knew that I was out of step with my surroundings because of my Jewish background: the nearest synagogue was 30 miles away in Springfield. But more fundamental was my distance from all organized religions. In modern parlance, I am not a "believer". I do not believe in a supernatural being, the power of prayer, or the coming of a Messiah. I am an atheist.

I am a very moral person, however. I need to say "however", because the religious right in America always argues that following their religious politics is equivalent to good morals, and always condemns the political beliefs of the left as immoral. The way that those who have and defend abortions are demonized is only one example.

I come back to religion and politics many times in my writing, because they are so intertwined in American life, despite the fact that we were the first nation founded on the separation of church and state. I finish this chapter's survey of my early Jacksonville writings with two pieces written in the Christmas season of 2010. They represent two subjects I think about constantly, politics and family, how those may become intertwined with religion, and two ways of writing about them.

A Christian Nation
DECEMBER 14, 2010

Many Americans are saying that America should be a Christian nation. I wonder exactly what they mean.

Do they mean a Christian nation like the ones from which the Puritans and most of our early settlers fled? In those countries, the King was also the head of their state Church. All citizens had to worship in the prescribed manner or face persecution, jail, or even death. Our founders created a new nation without a king and without a state church, the first nation in which the government "shall make no law respecting an establishment of religion".

Do they mean a Christian nation like that demanded by the Ku Klux Klan during the decades when the Klan was a powerful force in American politics? Klansmen called themselves defenders of the Christian faith, but they meant only a narrow form of Protestantism, which used violence to exclude Catholics, Jews, blacks, and other non-whites.

Do they mean a Christian nation like the one I grew up in, in which Jews and blacks were excluded from living in many communities, excluded from belonging to important social organizations, excluded from attending or teaching at the best universities? Or do they mean a more tolerant version, where we can go everywhere and do everything, as long as we are quiet when an organizational meeting or a government function begins with a Christian prayer?

Do they mean a Christian nation in which laws are created out of a narrow interpretation of certain Biblical passages, which many other Christians dispute? Many who claim that America is a Christian nation then go on to demand that laws about the teaching of science, the legality of contraception, and the treatment of homosexuals be determined by their version of Christianity.

Do they mean a Christian nation "where we are tolerant", as Sarah Palin said on Bill O'Reilly's show earlier this year? I don't want to live where I am tolerated. I want to live where my religion or lack of it makes no difference, where public money is not spent on promoting Christian beliefs and practices, while the rest of us watch from the outside. And there are a lot of us: one of every four Americans is not a Christian, including over 6 million Jews, over 2 million Muslims, and millions of others.

Those who claim that the Christian nation in their minds is based on the founders' ideas are silent about how much more Christianity has been added to America since our founding. "In God we trust" was first added to currency in the 1860s, and our pennies and nickels did not say that until the 20th century. The words "under God" were only added to the Pledge of Allegiance by an act of Congress in 1954.

Conservatives who promote more Christianity in public life also appear to believe that America has been going in the wrong direction for many years. Do they mean the decline in the proportion of the adult population who identify themselves as Christian, from 86% in 1990 to 76% in 2008? Barely more than half of Americans tell pollsters that they attend religious services more than once a year. Now that there are relatively fewer Christians, should the nation be more Christian?

I don't want to live in any version of a "Christian nation". I want to live in the United States, in which religious ideas are a private matter, in which my government plays no role in my spiritual life, and denominational beliefs play no role in government. The 18th-century founders were not able to fully divorce their politics from religion, but they went further than anyone else had gone before. In many ways, such as race, their vision was clouded by traditional prejudices. Since then we have created a more perfect union, although not yet perfect. Perfection will be closer when whites no longer insist on retaining the privileges they have built up over centuries of supremacy, and when Christians stop saying that they specially represent America.

A few nights ago I attended a wonderful Christmas concert in the chapel at Illinois College. The music was beautiful and inspiring, like the soaring building itself. The freedoms to create and perform all kinds of religious music, to sing religious songs with our neighbors, are just as beautiful. Those freedoms are only guaranteed as long as America is a nation in which religion is a personal choice, not a public prescription.

STEVE HOCHSTADT
Jacksonville IL

Christmas has been a part of my life since childhood. Although my parents celebrated only Hanukkah for a few years when I was very young, eventually they decided to include a Christmas celebration, too. Jewish celebration of Christmas is one element in the assimilation of Jews into American life, which well into my adulthood recognized only Christmas as a legitimate December holiday.

Yet I love Christmas. I learned to appreciate Christmas as a unique celebration of family by participating in the holiday celebrations of my wife's family. Although I did not take a formal survey, I believe that many in her family are also non-believers. Their Christmases represented a long pause in normal life to bring a growing family together to shower love, and gifts, on each other. My writings about Christmas were one of those gifts, to all members of my family.

The Gifts of Christmas

DECEMBER 28, 2010

Our family exchanged a lot of gifts this Christmas. Fifteen of us sat in a big circle, so it took hours to open all the presents, one by one, everyone commenting as each package was unwrapped. It's fun to see your family express themselves in the presents they want and the ones that they give. This year Santa brought photographs and other works of art, scarves, cooking utensils, and many books. My dogs got new leashes and I got pajamas from the Three-Legged Dog. There were many squeals of delight as we got exactly what we hoped for or were surprised by the thoughtfulness of our relatives.

We love our family rituals. We all went out to brunch on Christmas eve and sang carols that night. We teared up watching "It's a Wonderful Life", while we did last minute wrapping. Yet just as we try to preserve the familiarity of Christmases past, each holiday is different. No longer do our children wake up with wide-eyed anticipation and run screaming down the stairs to see what Santa has left for them. The youngest this time was 24 — she baked a coffee cake, but she still puts on a Santa hat and distributes the gifts from under the tree.

That younger generation brings new celebrants into the circle. This year we initiated my niece's boyfriend to our fun and seriousness. The reading of "The Night Before Christmas" and "The Polar Express" has passed to that generation. Now they listen to our political discussions, and sometimes lead them. I am a bit envious of my two friends who celebrated new grandchildren this Christmas. I look forward to a time when there will again be little children in our family, who make Christmas a time of wonder and mystery for everyone.

It wasn't a perfect Christmas, though. The Post Office failed to deliver some gifts on the day they had promised. Not all of us were healthy. My father-in-law, who has presided over dozens of these family gatherings, was not there.

His Alzheimer's would have transformed this happy event into confusing frustration. We stopped our gift-opening a few times, so smaller groups could go visit him in the nursing home, bring a present or two, and show him that his family would stay with him, no matter what.

There is no perfect family and no perfect Christmas. Every year brings challenges, even to the happiest family. Material goods can't make problems go away.

We can't prevent minor disappointments from intruding on Christmas celebrations. But we can watch our children pass new milestones of maturity or take over more responsibilities for family meals or find appropriate gifts for their family.

We can't produce good jobs for the young people in our family who seek to take on responsibilities in an unforgiving marketplace. But we can encourage them to have patience, to see how much they already have, to keep getting better at finding their niche in the working world.

We can't bring my father-in-law back from the Alzheimer's fog which limits his understanding. But we can teach each other how to deal with the sadness of aging.

We can't create a perfect Christmas. But we can use this once-a-year moment to exchange gifts of love, to celebrate what we have and what we are.

I hope you all had a merry Christmas.

STEVE HOCHSTADT
Minneapolis MN

CHAPTER 3
Struggling with Non-Partisanship in 2012

Race has been on my mind since a group of African American students at Brown University, which I had entered as a very unpolitical scholarship student in 1966, walked off campus to protest racism in admissions and curriculum in 1968. After teaching in Maine, where public history meant the American Revolution, coming to Illinois meant shifting focus to the Civil War, to Abraham Lincoln, and to slavery. For the first time, I began to research American race relations, inspired by the ambiguous racial past of Jacksonville, whose history was dominated by a color line drawn much more generously toward African Americans than its surroundings, but drawn clearly nevertheless. Finding a way to talk about race as a white person but a Jew, as a scholar of racism in Europe rather than America, as an outsider and an insider, is not easy. I don't know how well I succeeded, but I kept trying.

The subject of this chapter is the 2012 presidential election between President Barack Obama and challenger Mitt Romney. But I begin with a context of race, which played an understated role in that election, a role I did not sufficiently recognize at the time. I now realize that issues of race lurk deep in the psyche of Americans when we vote, whatever the apparent issues. This essay represents my thinking about race and ethnicity. Before I jumped right into the 2012 election, I wrote it to express my optimism about racial progress in America at that moment.

★ ★ ★

I'm Not a Racist

APRIL 24, 2011

"I'm not a racist." How often I hear and see that statement. I wonder if it's ever true.

Ideas have much longer lives than people. The simple idea that skin color matters in the worth of human beings might be as old as society itself. But the complex ideas of scientific racism, that ranked skin colors and heredity from super-race to inferior beings, were created at the end of the 19th century, and then elaborated in the 20th. Racism was a mélange of sciences, a truly interdisciplinary theory that used what passed for scientific evidence 100 years ago to demonstrate conclusively that northern European white people were the finest people of all. The Nazis turned this certainty into a program of genocide, but neither did they invent it nor did it die with Hitler in his bunker.

Throughout the first half of the 20th century, American scientists, philanthropists, and political leaders agreed that people of any color but white were inferior and that their lives were not worthless, but worth less. The discriminatory immigration laws with national quotas, the experiments on African Americans at Tuskegee from 1932 to 1972, the 1920s growth and then post-World War II reemergence of the Ku Klux Klan, the Jim Crow laws and sundown towns across the country, the treatment of Native Americans by governments at all levels, were supported by a clear set of ideas that biological scientists and social scientists "proved" were true again and again.

The racist consensus was visible in every public space in America. Every major newspaper, every radio and, later, TV station, every legislative body, every private club and every classroom taught, repeated, and reinforced the racial rankings that had been developed. Even if one refused to swallow this ideology whole, it was impossible not to be affected by its constant repetition.

I was born into this American racist consensus and I have lived to see its demise. The greatest proof that we are nearing the end of this idea is the constantly repeated claim, "I am not a racist." Until the 1960s the overwhelming majority of white American leaders and white American citizens proudly proclaimed their racism and insisted on its continuation as the determinant of public life. Being racist is no longer socially acceptable.

But it is not so easy for a society to just forget every aspect of an all-encompassing racial world-view. The battles over ending open, public, legal racism stretched into the 1970s, and the remnants of less visible racism in mortgage loans, hiring practices, and history books persist into the 21st century. Powerful ideas cannot be waved away with a magic wand.

There are too many recent manifestations of these racial ideas for anyone to argue persuasively that we have reached the end of racism. Not merely at the fringes of responsibility, but in the center of public life, racism is still being practiced. Orange County GOP Central Committee member Marilyn Davenport just circulated an email picturing President Obama as a chimpanzee. She wondered what all the fuss was about, because those seemingly defeated ideas still resonated with her and with those with whom she exchanged the message. Mississippi Governor Haley Barbour can't understand what was so bad about Jim Crow.

I know that phrases from my past, images that I remember from long ago, and beliefs which I was taught still rattle around in my head. I try to keep them inside, out of my speech and away from my behavior. But they haven't disappeared, for me or anyone else who had them implanted in our minds.

Racism isn't an either-or, yes or no, 100% or 0% issue. All of us, of all colors, carry images and stereotypes of ourselves and others, which can be overcome, but never eradicated. Maybe there will be a society in the future where race doesn't matter at all, where skin color is like eye color, where heredity is like shoe size, an interesting but inconsequential fact. A society where people can say, "I am not a racist," and be believed. We aren't there yet, and we won't get there until we examine how the lingering racial idea that was so powerful just a lifetime ago still affects our public lives. We just have to look at the nasty debate about immigrants or current discussions about Muslims as terrorists to see the continued power of that idea.

Yes, you are a racist. So am I. Let's hope today's children are better. It all depends on what we teach them.

STEVE HOCHSTADT
Jacksonville IL

The most vociferous declarations that one is not racist appear to come from the most committed racists. I don't believe that anyone aside from Trump has ever publicly bragged that he is "the least racist person in the world". Certainly he has been the most racist President in my lifetime, and is personally responsible for encouraging the eruption of public racism that has characterized the past few years. We will be confronting that racism for the rest of my life.

The election in 2016 was the most important of our lives. The midterm election in 2018 was the most important ever. The 2020 election has overwhelmed everything since the middle of 2019 and threatens to unleash a tsunami of media noise until November.

National elections are always important and always revealing about our nation, about all of our citizens who vote and don't vote, about what is important at that moment and long after. But I fear the coming presidential election more than the other 13 I have lived through. Already in May, the campaign is unbearably nasty from Trump's side, far from the clash of political visions that should take place in a democracy. Harsh words will ring in our ears far into the future. A divided America will become more divided. And the most dangerous man ever to be President could get four more years.

I believe and I write as if the best therapy for fear is with facts. Like my fellow historians, I look back, seeking facts from history to help me understand today's blur of news and opinion. The 2012 election presents one chapter in a historical guide to modern American elections, past and future. For a few months, I was an intensive student of American electoral politics.

By that time, I was a more experienced writer than when I began, and America was a different place. We had a black liberal President and a remarkably intransigent conservative Congress, as the Tea-Party-infused Republican majority in the House utterly refused to discuss anything liberals proposed, because liberals were effectively traitors.

The Presidential election between Obama and Romney would be a fascinating collision of two parties, two ideologies moving rapidly apart. In the summer, I made my editor a new offer: I would write twice a week about the election until it happened. Here is what the Jacksonville *Journal-Courier* published on August 7, 2012: "There are 13 weeks until Election Day. Many people say this is one of the most important elections in recent history. Because voters need clear and objective information to make good decisions, the *Journal-Courier* will publish twice weekly factual articles in which columnist Steve Hochstadt looks at some of the issues at stake in these elections."

For me the most important words in that preface were "twice weekly factual". I had actually written "non-partisan", but the editor substituted "factual". I would have to speed up my processes, devote more time each week. Much more difficult, I had to restrict political judgment, those judgments about right and wrong that are an inevitable feature of op-eds. That made this exercise more like writing a college lecture, where I believe it is the professor's job to leave such judgments to students.

Of course, judgment colors all actions. I presented information which could be easily verified. Phrases like the one above, "intransigent conservative Congress", were banned. But the context for every article was my judgment about subject and approach. I wrote 24 columns, with the final "At Last, It's Over" a few days after the election. The backstory of our 2020 predicament and opportunity lies in the columns gathered in this chapter.

Perhaps it was not my best choice to begin the series with a wonky subject, the regulation of banks. But it was a typical choice for me — how government regulates our daily lives and how politics shapes those regulations. It's about how the fine print matters.

Federal Regulation of Banks
AUGUST 7, 2012

I got an official notice from my bank the other day, concerning government regulation of banks, a major issue in the November elections. "Financial companies choose how they share your personal information. Federal law gives consumers the right to limit some but not all sharing. Federal law also requires us to tell you how we collect, share, and protect your personal information."

"Personal information" includes my Social Security number and credit history, information about my account balances, about payments I make, even about my income. Big US banks can find out what and where we buy, how much we spend every month and how we pay our balances.

Farmers State Bank and Trust, my local bank with local owners for 100 years, chooses not to share any of this financial information with anyone, except where it is necessary to do my business and serve my banking needs. What I do with my bank stays with my bank.

CitiBank, the giant bank which handles my credit card and millions of others, sent me the same notice, but with a different message. CitiBank spreads my personal information all around. They use it to market their own products to me. They also give it out to other financial companies and to their "affiliates". I can't stop CitiBank from doing that; it is their legal right by law.

CitiBank also discloses my transactions and account information and credit scores to all kinds of other companies, affiliates and non-affiliates. By law I could limit that sharing, but I have to make a special request.

As the statement from Farmers Bank says, all of those provisions about my financial privacy come from federal laws about banks, a political issue that clearly divides the two parties.

When I visited my bank this week, I noticed a sign about another major element of federal regulation of banks: the Federal Deposit Insurance Corporation guarantees my deposits up to $100,000. In the midst of the last great depression, Congress passed and Franklin Roosevelt signed the Glass-Steagall Act of 1933, the first major federal regulation of banks. That law created the FDIC so that customers at banks which went bankrupt would not lose their savings. Millions of Americans have been rescued from financial disaster by the FDIC.

Glass-Steagall also prohibited commercial banks from simultaneously being investment banks or insurance companies. The Republican Congress in

1999 passed the Gramm–Leach–Bliley Act, which repealed that wall of separation. Most Democrats voted for it, some opposed it, and President Clinton signed it. A special provision that Democrats insisted upon was the basis for the notifications these banks sent me, and thus for my ability to opt out of some sharing, but not all.

Republicans and Democrats are now arguing about more recent federal legislation, the Dodd–Frank Wall Street Reform and Consumer Protection Act of 2010. Dodd-Frank provided the first federal regulation of hedge funds, limits risky investments by banks, and requires public corporations to allow shareholders to vote on executive compensation every 3 years, among many other complex provisions.

Dodd-Frank also created the Consumer Financial Protection Bureau. Since Republicans took over the House later in 2010, they have tried to prevent the CFPB from coming into existence. The NY Times wrote, "In May 2011, 44 Republican senators signed a letter saying they would refuse to vote on any nominee to lead the bureau. They argued that the agency had too much power."

During a Congressional recess, President Obama used his executive authority to appoint Richard Cordray as director, so the CFPB could begin work.

Last month the young agency demonstrated what these federal regulations mean for consumers and voters. In the first enforcement action by the CFPB, Capital One Bank, which has clever commercials ("What's in your wallet?"), but misleading marketing, will have to refund $210 million to its credit-card holders, because it tricked them into buying costly add-on services. According to USA Today, "The bank's phone-sales operators told customers that services like payment protection and credit monitoring were free or mandatory or offered more benefits than they did."

At the same time, the CFPB began to investigate the home mortgage process, hoping to make it easier for borrowers to understand the kind of loan they are getting and its cost.

Dodd-Frank was passed by Democrats when they controlled Congress. Nearly every Democrat voted for Dodd-Frank, and nearly every Republican voted against it. In August 2011, Mitt Romney said, "I'd like to repeal Dodd Frank." In January, he said, "Now, the banks aren't bad people, they're just overwhelmed right now." He called the CFPB the "most powerful and unaccountable bureaucracy in the history of our nation". While he was in London last week, Romney continued his attack on Dodd-Frank, calling it "unnecessary" and "overly burdensome".

President Obama and the Democrats defend these laws, and want the CFPB to continue its work.

Every banking transaction you perform is regulated by federal laws. Democrats and Republicans strongly disagree about how much regulation should restrict banks' behavior.

How do you want your personal information treated by banks who participate in your daily lives? How actively should the government investigate banks who cheat their customers? Your vote matters.

STEVE HOCHSTADT
Jacksonville IL

That was factual. If it was not "non-partisan", that's because the facts were not kind to Republicans.

I grew up believing in science as the highest calling of the human intellect. Eventually I turned to history as a similarly scientific inquiry focused on people. My life has been devoted to respecting, encouraging, and employing the work of scientists, physical and social.

Republican dismissal of science baffles me. Science is useful only if its conclusions conform to their prejudices. Go to the doctor, listen to the weatherman, read about dinosaurs to your children, but don't talk about rising temperatures, rising seas, rising dangers. Mitt Romney's official Republican position in 2012 was uncertainty, well to the left of his Party, dominated by certainty that global warming hadn't happened.

Scientific organizations of all types offer increasingly anxious warnings about how warming is already making life more difficult and more dangerous. As the evidence has piled up and the effects of climate change become more apparent, the Republicans have gone backwards to Donald Trump's assertions that it's all a hoax.

Will conservatives still deny science when Miami is underwater?

It's Not Just Warm, It's Hot

AUGUST 30, 2012

Here in central Illinois, it's been a hot year. Compared to records since 1895, the first half of 2012 was the hottest ever measured. July was the hottest month ever recorded in the lower 48 states.

One hot summer does not mean the globe is warming. Temperatures fluctuate widely, from day to day, season to season, year to year. The summer of 1936 was about as hot as this year. Climate change means a shifting long-term pattern.

The science behind global warming covers three separate ideas. One is concrete and measurable. Temperatures calculated across the globe, in Illinois and in the Arctic, over land and sea and up in the atmosphere, by cheap thermometers and delicate instruments, all show the same thing — the Earth has gotten warmer over the last century. Not much, by about one degree since 1980, barely noticeable at any moment. But enough to indicate a new pattern.

The United States is on track for its hottest year ever in 2012, and 6 of the 10 hottest years since record-keeping began have occurred since 1998. The heating up of our climate is not a theory — it is a measurable fact.

The effects of slight changes in temperature are enormous. Since 1990 the border between zones 5 and 6 on the plant hardiness map of the Arbor Day Foundation has shifted more than 150 miles northward. Central Illinois was in zone 5 and now is in zone 6. The amount of sea ice in the Arctic has reached its lowest point ever measured, and is shrinking even faster than scientists predicted a few years ago.

The second element of global warming science cannot be shown by simple measurements: that the cause of warming is the production of greenhouse gases by human activity. Yearly global emissions of carbon dioxide have increased about 50% in the last 20 years. Here scientific experimentation, testing of hypotheses, and synthesis of differing arguments are ways of creating the most plausible explanation. That warming is caused by our behavior in industrialized societies is not a fact, but an idea supported by at least 90% of climate scientists. This theory is as well supported by science and by scientists as the atomic theory that led to the creation of nuclear weapons and nuclear power.

The third element is the least certain and the scariest: that warming increases the number of extreme weather incidents, such as heat waves, storms, and droughts. This is a matter of uncertainty among scientists who agree on the first two ideas. It will take many years of collecting data before anyone can be sure one way or the other.

The debate about climate change is mainly political. Republican politicians generally attribute the evidence about warming to a world-wide conspiracy. Senator James Inhofe of Nebraska has often said that global warming is a "hoax", based on his religious beliefs. In March he said: "The arrogance of people to think that we, human beings, would be able to change what He is doing in the climate is to me outrageous." Ron Paul called global warming "the greatest hoax I think that has been around for many, many years." Rick Perry attributed evidence of warming to "scientists who have manipulated data so that they will have dollars rolling into their projects," and Paul Ryan agreed that "leading climatologists make clear efforts to use statistical tricks to distort their findings and intentionally mislead the public on the issue of climate change."

Mitt Romney has shifted his position on global warming. As Governor of Massachusetts, he moved to reduce greenhouse gases until he decided to run for President. In June 2011, he said, "I believe the world is getting warmer, and I believe that humans have contributed to that." In October, his words shifted: "My view is that we don't know what's causing climate change on this planet."

The Obama administration has accepted evidence about warming. In 2009, the Environmental Protection Agency moved for the first time to reduce greenhouse gas emissions. Obama's National Security Strategy of 2010 says that "climate change" is a "severe" national security threat. In April he spoke of his "belief that we're going to have to take further steps to deal with climate change in a serious way."

Among voters, according to a poll in 2011, party affiliation also determines scientific belief: 80% of Democrats and 47% of Republicans say that warming has been occurring.

What happens if you take the politics out of the debate? The nation's insurance companies, through the National Association of Insurance Commissioners, reported in September 2011 their concerns about the effects of warming on the properties they insure. The report's author, Sharlene Leurig, said, "Climate change will inflict damage across the U.S....Unfortunately, science is telling us that more years in the future are likely to look like 2011."

American businesses do not think that spinning tales about conspiracies and doing nothing now is the best policy. They recognize that means even greater costs for future generations.

STEVE HOCHSTADT
Jacksonville IL

That piece's title, "It's Not Just Warm, It's Hot", was changed by someone in the machinery of publication into "Global warming no hoax", thereby violating my promise not to take sides, but just to print facts. Nowhere did I make such a definitive statement. I only offered information about temperature measurements and the conclusions of scientists, being careful to address uncertainty directly. The media business does not profit from such care, so my freedom to be non-partisan disappeared right at the beginning of my article.

But I kept trying. No single political issue has been more important to more people and more divisive than health care. In the eight years since I wrote the following op-ed, Republicans have tried countless times to repeal Obamacare without having any replacement. Because it was the signal achievement of Obama's presidency, Trump made it a priority to get rid of it. Now the whole discussion has shifted toward even more expansive coverage under the slogan Medicare for All. I have found it remarkable that Republicans have disavowed their own health care proposals, which became the basis for Obamacare, in order to score partisan points against Democrats. Perhaps more remarkable is the lack of conservative concern for the financial and medical effects of their political positions on millions of Americans, evident in 2012 and 2020. My mother, Lenore Hochstadt, didn't mind my writing about her, she minded the indifference of some politicians.

Who Will Pay for Health Care?

SEPTEMBER 4, 2012

My mother is slowly losing her hearing. Hearing aids allow her to talk with us, if we are close and speak loudly. Pretty good for 90, I could say, but that's not much consolation to someone who is 90 and going deaf.

Modern medical science has created amazing devices to perform functions our bodies can no longer do. Here's one you may not know about, if holding back deafness is not part of your family life. A cochlear implant is an electronic device which replaces the normal process of sound transmission to the brain with a series of electrodes. Cochlear implants have been used successfully in infants born deaf and in older people who have lost hearing.

These tiny devices are expensive, at least $45,000 each. So insurance providers restrict the circumstances under which they will pay. My mother can understand words now at 70 decibels, but not less. Only when her hearing gets worse will her doctor recommend an implant, unless she pays herself. So we have an appointment for another test a year from now. The same is true of the more common and much cheaper operation to save eyesight from cataracts. Sight must deteriorate to 20/40 before insurance will cover an artificial lens.

In both kinds of operations, private insurance companies and Medicare have similar thresholds to determine when they will pay. That's the meaning of rationing care. People at the top of giant organizations decide when and where and by whom health care is provided to all of us. Health care is already rationed and private insurers also specify which doctors they will pay.

Where do the parties stand on cochlear implants? By her next appointment with her ear doctor, we could have a Republican or Democratic President, implementing their party's platform. The trouble is, it is very difficult even for experts to figure out the long-term effects of the Democrats' Affordable Care Act, usually called Obamacare, or the Republicans' proposals contained in Paul Ryan's budget plan. Factcheck.org says: "The presidential campaign is overflowing with claims from both sides designed to scare seniors into thinking Medicare is being gutted or about to end altogether."

The Republican proposal for cochlear implants, and for the whole Medicare system, is to do nothing to the system for my mother and me and anyone over 55, and to completely change it for everyone under 55. Instead of Medicare's specific benefits, like payment for cochlear implants or prescriptions, younger people would get a voucher from the federal government to pay insurance premiums when they retire. Would the voucher pay for insurance plans as good as current Medicare, or would seniors have to pay much more out of their pockets? Since this would not take place for a very long time, nobody knows.

But there are some hints in their party platform."Medicare...is the largest driver of future debt....Without disadvantaging retirees or those nearing retirement, the age eligibility for Medicare must be made more realistic in terms of today's longer life span." Since Republicans emphasize reducing the debt by spending cuts alone, younger people will be "disadvantaged", most obviously by raising the age eligibility.

Obama's Affordable Care Act envisions considerable cost savings in Medicare over the next 10 years by reducing payments to hospitals and insurance companies. Democrats propose no reductions in benefits or eligibility. The hope for these future savings may be wishful thinking, because nobody knows how much medical costs will rise.

For all the hullabaloo about Medicare, however, the real difference between the parties is on Medicaid, the health care program for the poor. The Affordable Care Act would expand Medicaid coverage from about 60 million people to 77 million by 2016, as part of the Democrats' effort to provide health care insurance to everyone. Costs would be shared be-tween the federal and state governments, and it is not clear how that would be financed.

Republicans want to end the federal program and have the federal govern-ment give grants to the states for 50 different Medicaid programs. The Ryan budget plan would make cuts of $1.4 trillion to Medicaid over the next 10 years, although that is not mentioned in the party platform. According to the non-partisan Kaiser Family Foundation, that "would almost inevitably result in dramatic reductions in coverage."

Those cuts would mainly affect the poor, typically invisible in American politics, and completely invisible in the Republican Party platform. During their working lives my parents saved well more than the average for peo-ple who are retiring now. But that nest egg is being spent on nursing home care for my mother. Modern medicine has brought about 1.4 million se-niors like my mother into nursing homes, because they need 24-hour pro-fessional care. In a couple of years, her savings will be gone, and then she will qualify for Medicaid. Right now about 60% of all nursing residents get Medicaid, which also assists paying for one-third of all babies born in the US.

By that time, the Republicans might have severely cut Medicaid, as the Ryan budget foresees. That would certainly disadvantage her and millions of seniors like her.

STEVE HOCHSTADT
Jacksonville IL

Governments represent voters, so people with power in a society try to use that power to determine who votes. For most of our history, democracy applied to a minority of Americans. Although women had already been voting for decades, "One man, one vote" was a slogan from my childhood, still unrealized in the 1960s. Its eventual acceptance in theory is still violated in practice across America. The promise of democracy remains unrealized.

The over-representation of rural districts, enshrined in the founders' creation of the Senate, was replicated in many state legislatures until a variety of federal court cases forced the drawing of districts more equal in population. In recent years, Republicans have developed other methods of distorting election results, notably by creating new ways of excluding groups of voters who tend to vote for Democrats. While the requirement for official identification might seem reasonable at first glance, it has become clear that African Americans and the poor, likely Democratic voters, are the most likely to lack such ID. Because the Republican justification for these new requirements is to prevent voter fraud, which is virtually non-existent, and is combined with other Republican tactics to impede Democratic voters, the label "voter suppression" is justified.

Modern technology enables another form of electoral distortion to take extreme forms. Gerrymander is an old word, first used in 1812 to refer to the redrawing of Massachusetts state election districts under Governor Elbridge Gerry to benefit his party. One of the new districts resembled a salamander. Even though Gerry's Democratic-Republican Party lost the next election to the Federalists, the contorted districts remained in Democratic-Republican hands. Since then, gerrymandering has been used successfully by both parties to maximize the number of seats they could win. Since the 2010 census, Republican state legislatures have employed computer-assisted schemes based on big data to develop the most advantageous possible district lines, which the Associated Press called "the most extreme gerrymanders in modern history," some of which have been overturned by the Supreme Court.

Who Gets to Vote?

SEPTEMBER 6, 2012

The key to democracy is voting. White colonists in America insisted on voting as the basis of government. But voting in America has always been limited. The Massachusetts Bay Puritans only let settlers vote who conformed to their religious doctrines. Only men could vote, with a few exceptions, until the 20th century. African Americans were excluded from voting by slavery and the law, then by violence and local Jim Crow laws, until the 1960s. Eliminating voter discrimination required constitutional amendments, congressional legislation, and federal enforcement.

Throughout our history there have been other forms of discriminatory voting restrictions, serving local partisan purposes. In New York City in 1908, the Democratic administration tried to suppress the Jewish vote by picking Saturdays, the Jewish sabbath, as voter registration days. They feared that many Jews would vote for socialists. The official justification was, of course, to prevent fraud.

In 2008, a number of attempts were made to limit access to the polls. Between January and October 2008, 666,000 Ohioans registered to vote, and 200,000 of them provided driver's licenses or Social Security information that did not match government records, for example, in the spelling of their names. Five weeks before Election Day, the Ohio Republican Party asked a federal court to require the state to list all these people, so they could be purged or their votes challenged.

The Republican Party of Montana challenged the registrations of over 6,000 voters in 6 Democratic-leaning counties based on change of address information. Many were service members and students eligible to vote in Montana, who had their mail forwarded to where they were serving or going to school. The Republican Lieutenant Governor criticized these challenges. A federal judge found them frivolous.

Election 2012

This year, who can vote has become an even more contentious national discussion. Many state legislatures have passed laws requiring voters to show a government-issued ID. These state laws have much in common. Their proponents all allege that the purpose is to prevent voter fraud, even though there have been very few cases across the country which such an ID would prevent. ID laws create hardships for those who do not have a driver's license, do not have easy access to birth records, cannot drive to distant government buildings to procure IDs, or have recently been registered. Such people are disproportionately poor, African American or Hispanic, groups who tend strongly to vote for Democrats. The new laws were passed by Republican legislative majorities and signed by Republican governors.

Republicans say they are protecting democracy. But the partisan nature of these efforts peeks through. In June, the Pennsylvania House Majority leader, Mike Turzai, was videotaped at a Republican gathering saying that the new voter ID law "is gonna allow Governor Romney to win the state of Pennsylvania." Turzai's comments produced loud applause.

Judges have not looked favorably on many of these laws. In July, Wisconsin Circuit Court Judge David Flanagan ruled that the new Wisconsin voter ID law was unconstitutional. Flanagan had been appointed by a Republican Governor.

In August, a federal court rejected the new Texas ID law. All three judges, two appointed by Democrats and one by George Bush, agreed that the law imposes "strict, unforgiving burdens on the poor" and noted that minorities in Texas are more likely to live in poverty.

The number of voters who could be disenfranchised by strict voter ID laws is staggering. The Brennan Center for Justice estimates that 21 million Americans do not have current government-issued photo IDs. They are disproportionately African Americans, working poor, and students — exactly the groups which won the 2008 election for Obama.

Laws about when voting may take place also affect who gets to vote. More than 20 states have sought to restrict early voting and Sunday voting. In Ohio early voting was greatly expanded in 2008, including Sunday voting. On the Sunday before Election Day many black congregations came out of church and went straight to the polls to vote for Obama. Republicans in Ohio then passed a law to restrict early voting, and eliminate Sunday voting, except for members of the military. Last week a federal judge ordered the previous rules reinstated.

One more method of distorting voting through partisan politics is in determining who is on the ballot. Gary Johnson is the Libertarian Party nominee for President. He was Governor of New Mexico from 1995 to 2003. Republican party officials in Ohio, Michigan, Pennsylvania, Iowa, and Oklahoma have tried to get Johnson's name off the November ballot by mounting legal challenges to petition signatures.

Johnson is a Republican, and took part in the early Republican primaries. He is trying to appeal to libertarian-minded voters who had favored Ron Paul's candidacy. Paul drew over 10% of the vote in 29 of the 40 Republican primaries. Sizable numbers of voters for Johnson in November could make the difference in the race between Romney and Obama. In August, the Republican Secretary of State of Iowa rejected these challenges.

For years Democrats have tried to make voting easier. Republicans in many states are trying to restrict voting. The only bipartisan agreement about voting has been among judges and state officials who have struck down these laws as unconstitutional limitations on our most fundamental right.

STEVE HOCHSTADT
Jacksonville IL

What can justify depriving some people of their participation in our democracy? Vote suppressers have always justified their actions with claims about the lack of responsibility among those people whose votes they try to suppress: people without property, women, and blacks were all alleged to be too irresponsible to decide about American government. Mitt Romney updated this prejudice in 2012, revealing what's behind Republican voter suppression.

These "secret" words by Romney may have sunk his campaign. In 2016, secret words by Trump appear to have had no effect on voters. I can't explain that.

Republicans at Home, and at Heart
SEPTEMBER 20, 2012

Mitt Romney was in a good place in May. His dinner host was Marc Leder, who made a fortune, just like Romney, by founding a private equity firm, Sun Capital. Mitt stood in front of about 30 people of his own small class —

very rich, very important, and very conservative members of America's real elite. Rich enough to spend $50,000 a plate for dinner with Romney, because he had just clinched the Republican nomination. Rich enough to give lots more money to any politician who might make America an even better place to be rich, important, and conservative. And they were giving it up for Mitt, their messenger, their mouthpiece, their leader. Mitt was at home.

Here is what he said, to them and now to us all, since video of that dinner can be seen on your computer: "There are 47% of the people who will vote for the President no matter what. All right, there are 47% who are with him, who are dependent upon government, who believe that they are victims, who believe that government has a responsibility to care for them, who believe that they are entitled to health care, to food, to housing, to you-name-it. That that's an entitlement. And the government should give it to them. And they will vote for this President no matter what.... These are people who pay no income tax. 47% of Americans pay no income tax.... So my job is, is not to worry about those people. I'll never convince them they should take personal responsibility and care for their lives."

Romney made a lot of mistakes that night. It is not true that 47% of Americans pay no income tax. That many pay no *federal* income tax, but many fewer pay no state income tax. Everyone in politics knows that only 18% of households pay no taxes at all; two-thirds of households who pay no federal income tax still pay payroll tax.

That is a serious mistake, because Romney and his campaign advisers know that he was not telling the truth. But a bigger mistake was to put into the same basket all the people he doesn't like. The 47% of Americans who pay no federal income tax are, for Romney, the same 47% who vote for Obama "no matter what". Those people feel entitled to everything they need from the government because they see themselves as victims, and those same people will never take personal responsibility for themselves.

Who are these people that Romney will not worry about, who will never be convinced to act responsibly? They are millions of retirees on Social

Security, students who are no longer their parents' dependents, the unemployed, poor families with children, and working families whose Earned Income Tax Credit eliminates their federal tax liability. And thousands of millionaires who used our tax code to pay no federal taxes.

Most of the people who use the EITC to reduce their federal taxes soon pay taxes because their economic situation improves. Romney knows that, and he knows something else: his father George "was on relief, welfare relief for the first years of his life," as Romney's mother said in an interview when George was running for governor of Michigan in 1962.

Where do these people whom Romney dismisses live? Even Whoopi Goldberg knows, as she said on "The View", that of the 10 states with the highest percentage of people who do not pay federal taxes, Republicans are governors in 9. She's wrong, though: all 10 governors are Republican.

The contempt for Obama voters could not be clearer. I think that is the source of the much more focused Republican hatred of Obama. Obama is the opposite of this characterization of Obama voters. He is an even better all-American story than the anecdotes that conservatives tell to prove that any American can get anywhere with hard work. But Obama has turned his back on the American Dream. Instead of being grateful for everything America has given him, he put himself at the head of the rabble, the non-tax-paying 47%, the won't-hold-a-good-job welfare abusers, the whining masses who feel sorry for themselves. For that, conservatives hate him.

Once he found out that his remarks were being broadcast to the nation, Romney held a hasty press conference on Monday. Here he told the truth. "This is, of course, something I talk about a good deal in rallies and speeches and so forth...Well, um, it's not elegantly stated...I'm sure I can state it more clearly in a more effective way than I did in a setting like that.... but it's a message which I'm going to carry and continue to carry."

No mistake here, no correction of any of his false statements. That's because it is not just Romney's message. The other Republican candidates, as they each took the lead in the primaries, said the same disdainful and untrue things about half of Americans. A staffer at FreedomWorks, Dick Armey's huge organization behind many Republican campaigns, got excited: "A new video that makes me like Mitt better than I did."

Romney does not want to be President of these Americans. He said on Monday that he approves of that message. So does the Republican establishment.

STEVE HOCHSTADT
Jacksonville IL

That was true and fair, but not exactly non-partisan. The more closely I listened to what Republicans said, the more difficult it was for me to avoid taking the side where I saw compassion, truth, an America for all Americans.

I kept trying, though, in this piece about foreign policy. Nearly all lines of Trump's foreign policy were clearly drawn already by Republicans in 2012, except for his sycophantic attitude toward Russia. A sinister undercurrent appears here, the shaping of our foreign policy for purely domestic purposes, again presaging both Trump's America First rhetoric and the exploitation of Ukraine's vulnerabilities to serve his re-election efforts that led to his impeachment. The foreign policy professionals who testified in the impeachment hearings harkened back to a time which it was possible to be non-partisan. In 2012, I thought that was important.

Partisan Wars Over Foreign Policy
SEPTEMBER 23, 2012

Mitt Romney is inexperienced in foreign policy. Much attention has been paid to his recent verbal blunders, from criticizing English Olympic preparations while visiting London in July, to calling American diplomats' efforts to deal with hostile crowds in Cairo "disgraceful". Many presidential candidates are inexperienced in foreign policy, as Barack Obama was in 2008. If Romney is elected President, he would improve at enunciating his policies. More important is to know what those policies would be.

Republican foreign policy under George Bush was a disaster. The war in Iraq was unnecessary and unwinnable, and the war in Afghanistan was going nowhere. Osama bin Laden remained alive and Al Qaeda was spreading. No progress had been made on peace talks between Israel and the Palestinians. World opinion about America, even among our allies, reached a low point.

Republican leaders do not mention Bush, and have not discussed what went wrong and why. Many of the neoconservative experts who orchestrated the Bush foreign policy are now advising Romney. They have been very critical of President Obama's foreign policy, without clearly outlining one of their own. What would they do differently?

Republican foreign policy can most easily be described in the negative. In March, Romney called Russia "without question our number one geopolitical foe." Republicans spend more time talking about China: Romney repeatedly says that punishing the Chinese for unequal trade policies will happen on Day One. Mexico and the rest of Latin America are the sources of all those illegal immigrants who should deport themselves back home.

The vast Muslim world is dangerous, populated by a religion which many conservatives label as morally deficient. They attack those, like the Muslim Brotherhood in Egypt, who might apply Islamic ideas to government, while arguing that our government should be ruled by their version of Christian fundamentalism. In the section of their Party platform about foreign policy "Islam" appears twice, both times as the threat of "radical Islam".

Western Europe used to be our closest allies, but today's Republicans only criticize Europe. In campaign speeches, Romney calls Europe "a social welfare state" and an "entitlement nation." He describes the coming election as a battle for "the soul of America", because voters must choose between "a European-style welfare state" or "a free land."

Whom do Republicans like? Israel. But only the most extreme politicians there, who refuse to limit settlement activities on the West Bank. Any effort to move Israel toward compromise is equated with "throwing Israel under the bus." Republicans appear ready to let Israel draw us into a war with Iran on Benjamin Netanyahu's timetable.

A frequently used Republican word about Obama's foreign policy is "feckless", meaning weak and ineffective. That reflects the overall Republican strategy of projecting more strength, more power. The Democratic administration has been reluctant to use power, especially military power, compared with the ostentatious use of military power by their Republican predecessors. There is not much difference between the parties on the wars in Iraq and Afghanistan. Both are widely unpopular among American voters. Partisan interpretations of the withdrawal of troops from both war zones notwithstanding, the pace of withdrawal has been cautious under Obama.

Obama has pursued the broader war on terror as vigorously as did George Bush. He has not closed Guantanamo and uses drones to kill enemies, even if they are American citizens. He ordered the pursuit and killing of Osama bin Laden, although Republicans appear peeved at his success.

In the turbulent Middle East, Obama has been reluctant to intervene in unpredictable situations. Each country touched by the Arab Spring has followed a different path away from dictatorship. Egypt was a major ally, whose government was dictatorial and unpopular, so there was little American interference in the rebellion there. Libya was ruled by a sponsor of terrorism, for whose overthrow international approval, especially from NATO, was immediately forthcoming, so limited American military assistance was offered to the rebels. Syria sits in the center of the Israeli-Arab conflict, and Obama has refrained from anything beyond verbal support of the revolutionaries.

Republican foreign policy is really driven by their domestic effort to unseat Obama and the Democrats. The *New York Times* reported in July that European leaders who felt slighted by Romney's words had been told by his advisers not to read too much into statements made for a domestic political audience.

The Democrats offer a known quantity, the continuation of this cautious foreign policy of the previous four years. What Romney would do in office is much less certain. The aggressive and risky proposals that Republicans advance in the campaign, like openly arming the Syrian rebels and threatening Iran with air attack if their nuclear program is not stopped immediately, may just be for show. But the nationalist arrogance of Romney's "American century" rhetoric, the wholesale distrust of the world's Muslims, the disinterest in seeking allies, and the support of the most belligerent section of the Israeli electorate are likely to continue to determine the foreign policy choices of Republicans, in or out of the White House.

STEVE HOCHSTADT
Jacksonville IL

That last sentence may seem prophetic. I would not have guessed how each of those four approaches to the rest of the world would reach the most extreme positions under Trump: America First; the Muslim ban; deliberate distance from European allies; and unprecedented policies on Jerusalem and Israeli settlements. In 2012, no senior Republican advocated those positions.

Party ideology is always shifting, slowly or suddenly. President Nixon had created the EPA and many 20th-century Republicans interpreted conservatism as favoring preservation of the environment. Now that's ancient history. As in every issue, Trump proclaims absurdly extreme positions — modern light bulbs are no good; low-flow toilets don't work; wind energy is unreliable. But the direction of his energy policy is nothing new — drill, baby, drill.

Running Out of Energy

OCTOBER 2, 2012

When you drive through northern Illinois near Peru, 50 miles southwest of Chicago, hundreds of tall windmills appear on the horizon, slowly turning in unison. They produce electricity with no pollution.

Forests of windmills also change the rural landscape. Their clean white industrial lines seem out of place in the cornfields, among the wooden barns. But we need their output and every other productive energy source, because we are the world's energy hogs.

The US is the second greatest producer of oil and natural gas, just behind Russia. But we are the fourth largest importer of natural gas, and by far the largest importer of oil. We account for about 20% of the world's total energy consumption with 5% of its population, more than twice as much per person as other highly industrialized countries. We rely on oil, natural gas and coal far more than other fully modern nations, who use more power from water, wind, and sun.

The only bright spot in our energy picture is that we use a bit less energy per person than 20 years ago. But in China and India and a host of other nations energy usage is increasing at an accelerating pace, as they raise their standards of living. The price of our imported energy can only go up as demand multiplies. Staying in place means a very expensive energy future.

The two parties approach that future very differently, because energy and environmental politics are intertwined. The clash of energy philosophies has been symbolized for decades by the huge Arctic National Wildlife Refuge in Alaska. Republicans have pushed to open the ANWR to oil drilling, while Democrats have resisted. Bill Clinton as President vetoed a bill passed by the Republican-controlled Congress. Democrats in the Senate and Republicans in the House clashed during the presidency of George Bush, who supported drilling there. The latest vote in the House in February saw nearly 90% of Democrats vote against drilling and 90% of Republicans vote for.

New energy sources have transplanted this conflict to new locations. In the controversies over offshore oil drilling in the Gulf of Mexico, retrieving gas in the shale under the Midwest states through fracking, and the proposed Keystone pipeline from Canada to Texas, the same argument remains unresolved. Democrats want to lessen the threats to the environment, and study the health of people who live in affected areas, while Republicans want to forge ahead, repeating their mantra "Drill, baby, drill."

While Republicans stress increased production of oil and gas, Democrats favor using government funds to encourage renewable energy sources. Republicans have gleefully used the failure of Solyndra, a solar manufacturer supported by the Obama administration, to criticize the idea of shifting to renewables. But nobody wants to keep government out of energy production. The US government, in our names, from 2002 to 2008 gave $72 billion in subsidies to fossil-fuel based sources and $29 billion to renewable sources, according to a study by the Environmental Law Institute.

Shifting this balance cleanly divides the parties. A Democratic bill in the Senate to reduce the subsidy to the 5 largest oil corporations by about $2.4 billion per year came up for votes in May 2011 and March 2012. Both times nearly every Democrat voted for it and nearly every Republican voted against it, so there were not sufficient votes to prevent a Republican filibuster. To put those numbers in perspective, those corporations made $134 billion in profits in 2011.

How much energy do we need? What would reducing our energy usage as a nation look like?

The reduction in American per capita energy usage comes from a major increase in the gas mileage of automobiles and trucks, which has already saved billions of gallons of oil imports. When the Corporate Average Fuel Economy (CAFE) standards were first enacted by Congress in 1975, in the wake of the Arab oil embargo, cars averaged under 13 miles per gallon. Mileage was doubled by 1985, but then Republican presidents or Republican congressional majorities blocked further legislation proposed by Democrats. However, the rise in gas prices and the competition from highly efficient Japanese cars forced American car manufacturers to raise their fuel efficiency without government regulation.

In 2007, the Democratic Congress passed and President Bush signed legislation to raise CAFE standards to 35 mpg by 2020. One of President Obama's first legislative successes was to move that forward to 2016. This August, the Obama administration announced that the U.S. auto fleet will average 54.5 mpg by 2025, a goal endorsed by both industry and environmentalists. Mitt Romney has said that he would repeal these standards.

Regulations and subsidies are not the only governmental actions that could help solve our energy problems. Communicating useful information could also contribute. For example, few people know that three-quarters of the electricity used by home electronics is consumed while the products are off. Unplugging appliances or using power strips between electronic devices and power sources could save us all money and reduce electricity demands.

Maintaining our wasteful national lifestyle and relying on underground sources of energy means watching other nations take the lead toward an affordable energy future. With the right policies, the US could eventually become an exporter of both fuels and energy technology. Doing nothing now means falling further behind over the next ten years.

STEVE HOCHSTADT
Jacksonville IL

I planted trees on the first piece of land my wife and I owned, and I built a compost bin out of scrap wood on Earth Day. Those were physical expressions of my feeling of closeness to the Earth, of my joy when I'm on my knees in the dirt. I was happy to call myself a gardener in the blurb printed under my columns every Tuesday. Our Jacksonville home is surrounded by flowering trees and perennials.

Professional gardening is guided by science, experience, and skill; my gardening is motivated by the pleasures of physical labor and the beauty of botanical fertility. Those simple but powerful emotions guide my approach to everything environmental — energy and food production, pollution, forest preservation, and habitat protection. My environmental advocacy might stem from atavistic proclivities, but it's based on rational argument. Damage to the environment is, sooner or later, damage to human life. That's a fact. So is the politicization of environmental issues by a Republican Party that now wants to get rid of Nixon's EPA.

I find it difficult to understand people who support pollution, just as I wonder what makes people litter our neighborhoods. The link between environmental policy and government spending is one powerful explanation for conservatives against conservation. So much of conservative policy depends on getting maximum money from corporations, giving minimum money to help Americans in need, and not being open about either.

As I read this again, it appears that non-partisanship was beyond me. But since my newspaper only promised that I would be "factual", I still think I kept that promise. How can a person remain both non-partisan and truthful, when one side lies all the time? That was a problem in 2012, which has only gotten much worse by 2020.

The belief that I grew up with and that became the foundation of my work as a historian, that seeking and telling the truth was the highest calling, now seems hopelessly outdated. I am no longer certain that the truth will out or that it even matters to many Americans and many American politicians. Concepts like "spinning", promoting a misleading message by carefully massaging the truth, are no longer appropriate to an age of blatant fabrication, outright lying, the replacement of Walter Cronkite with Alex Jones. I began writing with the certainty that my adherence to verifiable information made a difference. These essays reflect that determination. I keep writing that way today, because I can't do anything else. But does it matter? Is ideology more important than evidence?

For some people, it certainly is. The day after another article of mine appeared highlighting the lies that Mitt Romney told in the second presidential debate, a local man wrote to the principal fund-raiser for my employer, Illinois College. He highlighted his allegiance to Illinois College since his graduation and his annual donations. But lately he has refused to make any donations, for reasons which he summarized in three words: "Professor Steve Hochstadt". He was upset that someone who was not "a creditable representative of the College" was publishing views which he considered "radical and far outside the mainstream".

As I explain throughout this book, my views are outside of the mainstream, perhaps radical on some issues. But nothing that I published in the *Journal-Courier* was radical. They only appeared radical to readers who had never been faced with standard liberal political writing. My critic's message that I was bad for my employer's fund-raising efforts reveals the nature of the media landscape in small-town America. Liberalism is out of the mainstream. Its appearance provokes outrage and attempts to shut it down. That message is part of the standard conservative rhetorical repertoire, culminating these days in Trump's attacks on the Democratic majority in the House, and thus the majority of American voters, as traitors.

I felt in no danger from this infuriated critic. My freedom to keep writing was protected by people with greater allegiance to the value of diverse opinions. But the presence in conservative ideology of the false belief that liberalism itself is radical is dangerous for us all.

Ideology and Politics

OCTOBER 23, 2012

The ideological differences between Democrats and Republicans are deeper now than at any time I can remember.

Everybody has their own political ideology, created from life experiences, family traditions, and personal beliefs. Although pollsters, journalists and academics like to group people into a few simple categories, the variety of such political belief systems is unlimited.

For that reason, political parties usually include a wide range of political positions. Although the job of party leaders in Congress is to convince every member to vote the same way on legislation, strictly party line votes are rare. When the House approved the North American Free Trade Act in 1993 under President Bill Clinton, about 40% of Democrats voted for it and 25% of Republicans voted against it. In the Senate, Democrats split right down the middle for and against. The voting was similarly split for the U.S.-China Relations Act of 2000. Even the Senate vote to impeach Clinton showed the Republicans divided: one-sixth voted not to impeach.

Under President George W. Bush, there were many such divided votes. His signature education legislation, the No Child Left Behind Act of 2001, attracted more Democratic than Republican votes in the House, where one-sixth of Republicans voted against it. Late in his presidency, the Comprehensive Immigration Reform Act of 2007 was written by a bipartisan group of Senators, but eventually failed because of a Republican filibuster. In the key cloture vote, about one-third of Democrats sided with two-thirds of Republicans to kill it.

Not all votes showed such crossing of the party lines. Clinton's Omnibus Budget Reconciliation Act of 1993 passed Congress without a single Republican vote.

Since Barack Obama was elected President in 2008, the Republican Party has become more ideologically uniform. Obama's first piece of legislation, the Lilly Ledbetter Act of 2009, allowing women to more easily sue for equal pay, passed the House with only 2 Republican votes. No House Republicans voted for the Stimulus Act in early 2009. In 2010, only 5 Republicans voted to repeal "Don't Ask, Don't Tell". The most controversial piece of legislation under President Obama, the Affordable Care Act, received only one Republican vote in the House and one in the Senate, even though Massachusetts Republicans had supported a nearly identical bill when Mitt Romney was Governor.

The Democratic Party continues to include a wide variety of political positions on every possible issue.

Considerable pressure has been brought on Republicans at the federal level to make ideological promises which exclude political compromise. The most notable is the Taxpayer Protection Pledge not to raise taxes ever on anyone, promoted by Grover Norquist. As of May 2011, all but 7 Republican Representatives and 7 Republican Senators had signed on, as well as other leading Republicans, including Romney and Paul Ryan. When the many Republican primary candidates for President were asked during a debate in August 2011 whether they would accept a hypothetical legislative compromise that included $1 in tax increases for every $10 in spending cuts, they all said no.

The increasing ideological purity of the Republican Party at the national level has pushed moderates away. Senator Olympia Snowe from Maine, one of the Tax Pledge non-signers, announced this year that she would not seek a fourth term. She cited the "dysfunction and political polarization" of the Senate, and in particular, "the overly rigid language on abortion in the GOP platform". Another Republican non-signer, Rep. Richard Hanna from New York, complained about being "frustrated by how much we — I mean the Republican Party — are willing to give deferential treatment to our extremes".

Republicans considered too likely to make compromises with Democrats have been challenged by more conservative candidates in primaries. John McCain, who had worked in bipartisan fashion more than most Republicans, survived such a challenge in 2010. Senator Richard Lugar from Indiana was defeated this year by Richard Mourdock.

Yet the ideological purity of the national Republican Party is not reflective of their own voters. Two polls in August showed that one-third of Republican voters believe the rich should pay more in taxes, and nearly one-third believe that abortion should be permitted beyond just cases of rape, incest, or to save a woman's life.

The ideological purification of the Republican Party led Mitt Romney to reject his long moderate history on issues of abortion, climate change, health insurance, and taxes, in favor of ideological commitments to "severe conservatism". Since his nomination, Romney has been veering back to the center.

But the problem for voters is not whether Romney is a flip-flopper, or whether he has any ideological commitments at all. With virtually all national Republican politicians rejecting any possibility of compromise on key issues, the gridlock in Congress, which has caused its approval rating to stay below 15% for the past year, will continue. Rigid adherence to ideology makes practical politics impossible.

What is practical politics? In a candidates' debate for local office, I recently heard a Republican incumbent say that the biggest problem was insufficient revenue to accomplish what needed to be done. That was an honest, frank, and hopelessly non-ideological statement.

STEVE HOCHSTADT
Jacksonville IL

Now the ideological gap between Democrats and Republicans has become a chasm. Moderate Republicans and Democrats have lost primary races to more extreme challengers. Compromise seems to be a dirty word, especially on the right. I like the new leftist Democrats, like Alexandria Ocasio-Cortez, just as I liked and still like the old-timers, Bernie Sanders and Elizabeth Warren. But I recognize that they and I rest at an extreme of the American political spectrum. They can push the middle further towards what I consider social justice, equality, and democracy, but the middle is where things get done. When there is no middle, progress is stalemated. I support the left, but fear for demise of the middle.

I waited until the last moment to make an electoral prediction. I was right about the Presidential race and about little else.

Why the Democrats Will Win This Election
OCTOBER 30, 2012

Next Tuesday, Obama will win. The unemployment rate will still be nearly 8%. The housing market and the construction industry will still be depressed. A record number of people will still need food stamps to feed their families. An unpopular war will still be killing Americans.

Even though he's black and intellectual, and some people still say he was born in Africa, Obama will beat a blue-blood son born into politics and wealth. He'll beat billions of billionaire dollars poured over the past four years into an unending campaign of vilification of himself and his policies, and then unleashed in unfathomable amounts during this election, with the blessing of a Supreme Court appointed by Republicans. He'll defeat an unprecedented congressional campaign of intransigence and obstruction led by a coalition of party leaders and Tea Party newcomers.

How did he manage that? Barack Obama deserves much credit for his first four years as President. Eight years of Republican control of domestic and foreign policy had left the United States in its worst shape since the combined oil crisis, stock-market crash, and Vietnam defeat back in the early 1970s. Two wars raging with no end in sight, an economy beginning to free-fall into an almost great depression, and worldwide opinion horrified at the arrogance, dishonesty and incompetence of American foreign policy.

Each of these crises had taken years to develop. Now all three have been reversed. In two years we will no longer be fighting in the Middle East. The economy is recovering, not as fast as anyone would like, but the last great depression took a decade to recover from. Our standing in the world has rarely been higher — our few enemies are everyone's enemies.

But I don't think Obama's successes will be the deciding factor in this election. It's Republican failures.

I don't mean the Republicans I see every day in my small town in central Illinois. There are plenty of them, enough to dominate local elected offices. They are normal people who advocate normal policies. When the state government tried to shut down a historic facility for the mentally ill with which Jacksonville has identified for over 150 years, our local legislators, all Republicans, have pushed back. Although such closings are precisely what would happen everywhere if the congressional Republican budget were passed, here they have fought for the well-being of the patients, the employment of the staff, and the spirit of the town, even if it costs more.

A series of Republican mayors backed by a Republican city council have spent millions and asked the federal government for millions more to make the downtown work again, investing now in our collective future.

My local Republicans are nothing like the cartoon Republicans who have dominated our TV screens for over a year. Their extreme ideology is the big loser. American public opinion has moved on, past gay-bashing, past shoot-first, think-later foreign policy, past the condescending racism of self-deportation, past conspiracy theories about socialists and scientists, past the tried-and-true Republican political tactics of the 20th century.

When someone stands up at a party and says that global warming is a hoax perpetrated by evil scientists or that gays will go to hell or that a woman must deliver her rapist's baby, people start edging away. The cartoon Republicans haven't grasped that yet.

The blind wrath that brought a few Tea Party zealots into federal and state offices in 2010 is gone. The economy is getting better. The angry men in Congress and in governors' houses have accomplished nothing but get other people angry.

Mitt Romney has tried hard to erase the cartoon image he created for himself, in order to defeat the wacky line-up of extremists he faced in the primaries. He almost made it, replacing the "severe conservative" persona he has been working on since 2007 with a reasonable Romney in the last few months. In this final week, I expect him to lurch again in some direction, either to the middle to win some undecided voters or to the right to energize the extremists.

But why vote for a man who just reentered the real world from far right Fantasyland since the Republican convention in August, when the other man on the ballot had been struggling with real-world problems for the past four years with some success?

Obama's victory is not Romney's personal failure. The country is moving away from the extreme form of Republican conservatism which has come to dominate the party since Ronald Reagan's presidency.

Obama's victory in 2008 meant only that the failures of Republicans under Bush were too obvious to ignore. Now, despite the continuing economic disaster, despite lingering racism across white America, despite the daily uncertainties of the world outside our borders, Barack Obama wins again. His victory in 2012 means that Republican ideology is a failure.

STEVE HOCHSTADT
Jacksonville IL

Ha! What nonsense. Obama won and cartoon Republicanism is now stronger than ever. Mitt Romney now represents a glimmer of rationality among Republican Senators. Obama's legacy has been systematically dismantled by Republican politicians. Although a small group of anti-Trump Republicans cry out that he has abandoned true Republican ideology, they get no support from Republican voters, who line up behind extreme positions that the Tea Partiers of 2010 did not approach.

My defense for poor prophecies: nobody guessed all that in 2012. The lesson for me was to forget prognostication and stick to history. Explain the present. The future is unpredictable.

At Last, It's Over
NOVEMBER 6, 2012

Since the first Republican primary debate in May 2011, we have endured 18 months of constant campaigning. Perhaps this campaign actually began earlier, in October 2010, when Mitch McConnell said, "The single most important thing we want to achieve is for President Obama to be a one-term president."

Presidential campaigns in the US last far longer than in other democracies. Spending here is vastly greater. What do we citizens get out of it?

We get repetition. Obama and Romney boiled down their political visions into a few bite-sized slogans, which they repeated a thousand times. Even in their debates, they fell back on slogans, instead of explanations. Over the final months of this campaign we learned very little new about either candidate.

We get polls. The media devotes far too much money and column inches and screen time to constant polling. The Pew Research Center calculated that only 22% of news coverage concerned the candidates' policy positions in the last 2 months. Instead we get poll after poll telling us how other people might vote in the future. Nate Silver, whose 538 website provides the most interesting daily commentary on the polls, wrote last week that the polls just before the election looked like the polls in June. After four months of relentless campaigning, hundred of millions of dollars in ads, and four debates, few voters have changed their minds.

We don't get what we need to know about the candidates. They tell us what makes them look good. Occasionally we get a peek behind the scenes, in unguarded moments, when candidates say what they really believe. Still it's all talk.

Only in real life can we get the information we need to make good judgments about candidates and policies. "Superstorm" Sandy gave us a frightful dose of real life. The East Coast, where I lived most of my life, and New York, where I grew up, were hit hard. Like the people in Joplin, Missouri, in New Orleans, and everywhere else where freakishly destructive weather wreaks havoc on human life, the Easterners will recover and rebuild. They will look out for each other as much as they can. They will be thankful for the prompt and professional help of charitable organizations.

And they will look to governments to do the rest. Local governments are the first line of public defense, but they are still trying to get the water out of their offices. The power, resources, and reach of state governments and especially the federal government have been crucial in saving lives, limiting damage, moving supplies in and water out, and restoring transport and commercial life. The photos of President Obama and Governor Christie together on the ground and in the air represent the response to disaster that a modern democratic nation must provide.

Now we see clearly what this campaign has been about. The Republican budget plan, authored by Paul Ryan, envisions drastic cuts in the Federal Emergency Management Agency, and in other agencies like it. Mitt Romney wants the federal government out of the business of disaster relief. His philosophy says private enterprise can do everything better, so in the June 2011 Republican debate he specifically said about FEMA: "Every time you have an occasion to take something from the federal government and send it back to the states, that's the right direction. And if you can go even further and send it back to the private sector, that's even better." Moderator John King asked once more if Romney was referring to "disaster relief". Romney said, "We cannot afford to do these things without jeopardizing the future for our kids."

George Bush put a hack in charge of FEMA. Romney wants to make public disaster relief into an opportunity for investors to make money.

Those opportunities will increase in the future. Although Republicans continue to put politics above science, a growing majority of climate scientists believe that global warming is increasing the frequency of extreme weather events. Capitalists agree: the giant German reinsurance company Munich Re issued a report in October titled "Severe Weather in North America". It said that global warming "particularly affects formation of heat waves, droughts, intense precipitation events, and in the long run most probably also tropical cyclone intensity."

Republican policy will mean relief for profit, outside of public control, in a new age of deadly storms. Democratic policy will mean strong public control of relief combined with an effort to slow down global warming.

Which did you vote for?

STEVE HOCHSTADT
Jacksonville IL

Elections have consequences. Keeping Democrats in charge of disaster relief meant that lives and livelihoods were saved. Democrats in charge of health care policy meant that millions of Americans got health insurance. Democrats in charge of the safety net of welfare programs, from Medicaid to food stamps, meant that the poorest among us got help from the government, not enough, but something they could count on.

Obama was hardly a perfect President, but he modeled presidentialness. He was and is a good man, the subject of the first essay in this book. Looking back at 2012, just a few years ago, seems like an exercise in nostalgia for an America that worked, for a government that tried to be democratic, that tried to promote equality, that spoke in measured tones about serious problems. I don't hope to go backward. America in 2012 was in a better place than in 2020, but not as good as I keep hoping for our future.

Thinking about 2012 forces us to recognize how much more extreme Republican politics and ideological justifications have become in less than a decade. Trump is able to personify and steer this course, only because the vehicle was already speeding in that direction. The active support by Republican elected officials of Trump's acceleration toward the edge can only end badly.

After November 2012, I was relieved to be able to abandon a non-partisan stance that I was unable to maintain. I had dreamed that presenting the facts in an even-handed manner might break through some tribal party loyalties. Instead my loyalty to a politics based on both evidence and justice, on compassion rather than nationality, on rejection of all forms of discrimination, was strengthened. I wish I knew what the impact of my writing has been on the variety of my readers. That hidden knowledge extends to everything teachers do — how do we matter?

CHAPTER 4
No Storms on the Horizon: 2013

The elections of 2012 were good for Democrats, but not terrible for Republicans. Obama won the popular vote by nearly 4% and piled up a comfortable majority in the Electoral College. But his margin was only half of his defeat of the McCain-Palin ticket in 2008. Democrats gained 2 Senate seats, giving them a 55 to 45 edge. Democrats won the total popular vote for House candidates 49%-48%, and gained 8 seats, but the tilt of our electoral system away from urban representation, exacerbated by extreme Republican redistricting, meant that Republicans retained the majority 234 to 201. The ability of Republicans to blockade Obama's program with a majority in the House and the filibuster in the Senate was undiminished.

Obama's campaign had used the slogans "Change we can believe in" and the chant "Yes We Can" in 2008, but it was clear that the Republican determination to enforce "No You Can't" would prevent any significant change from being enacted.

As usual, I found peace and joy at a much more intimate level, among my family.

The Ghost of Christmas Presents

JANUARY 1, 2013

It's now a week after Christmas. Ornaments have been put away and trees set out by the curb. The stockings, hung by the chimney with care, are back in the closet. Acres of wrapping paper and miles of ribbon are in the garbage (or in recycling containers). What's left are the presents, the results of the biggest shopping binge of the year.

It's easy to decry the commercialism of Christmas, unless you are a retailer who depends on Christmas shopping for survival. My family, like many well-off families, spends too much money and exchanges more gifts than necessary. With 16 people sitting around a circle, there were lots of presents. But rather than focus on quantity, it is worth thinking about quality — what did we give each other and what does that say about us?

Our family likes to eat, make and give good food. Homemade jams, granola and pickles were exchanged; during frequent breaks in present-opening, we ate freshly baked coffee cakes, thanks to my nieces. There is always a cookbook under the tree, mainly directed at the younger generation. A box of chocolates is a tradition, provided by Santa for the family to pass around the circle.

Electronics are a much more modern gift. Ear buds and external batteries for smart phones appeared this Christmas, keeping the younger generation charged and connected for 2013.

At our Christmases there are always books. Everyone in our family is a reader and book giver. Fiction off the best seller list was prominent, like Louise Erdrich's latest novel. Some of the books came from common entertainment preferences, in particular, mysteries of murder in Russia, Iceland, and the US. Others reflected shared political perspectives — rejection of efforts at voter suppression, sadness about the history of white America's persecution of Native Americans, wonder at the irresponsibility of bankers in our recent recession. Other books were silly, like "How to Tell if Your Cat is Trying to Kill You". My oldest relative got 60 books at once, on a Kindle of course, transforming her into a thoroughly modern reader.

The new book that I have been reading since Christmas has been unexpectedly informative. My children got me "Jewish Jocks", which recovers the surprising history of Jewish dominance in early 20th-century boxing.

A surprise to me this year were some records, called vinyl by today's hipsters. Decades after turntables and records appeared to become extinct, they are experiencing a revival, because the sound quality still beats out digital music. Perhaps my collection of early Motown and Beatles will once again spin around, reminding me of those days when older people thought rock and roll was a sign of civilization's impending end.

Clothing is a favorite gift from parents to children. Now that the children in our family are all out of college with responsible jobs, clothing gifts have shifted from sports wear to items suitable for the office: dress shirts and nice sweaters, but no ties, as that formerly preferred gift has fallen into sartorial disfavor.

Arts and crafts are always well represented in our Christmases. Pottery old and new came out of well-padded boxes. Antiques from Roseville, Weller and Van Briggle competed for attention with pieces by modern potters. Metal flowers by Jeff Garland, a local artist who teaches at Illinois College, and a poster by a distant cousin from her graphic arts class reflect our common appreciation of the beauty of creation.

Christmas presents reflect the family which exchanges them. Much depends on financial circumstances — ours is comfortable enough that we can buy what we want to give, a circumstance for which we all are grateful. Three decades ago our Christmases were much simpler, although certainly not less joyous.

The quality of gifts is not inherent in the things themselves, which can be expensive but unwanted, finely made but unappreciated. Gifts at Christmas and other times reflect relationships; they tangibly connect givers and receivers. When the most successful gifts were opened, you could see smiles from both parties, whose emotional understanding of each other was momentarily embodied in a symbolic object. It might be consumed that day or treasured for years. Whether frivolous or serious, practical or beautiful, the gifts which were opened at our Christmas were thoughtful expressions of love and knowledge. The hose nozzle my sister- and brother-in-law gave me, the sponges from my other sister-in-law, the coffee grinder from my wife, son and daughter-in-law, and the heavy lined shirt from my daughter will remind me of our relationships with each future use. These prosaic objects have been infused with the spirit that brings us together each year to celebrate our family Christmas.

Happy New Year!

STEVE HOCHSTADT
Springbrook, WI

Not everyone responded to my good wishes with equally good wishes. On Christmas Day, my newspaper essay had been about guns, in response to the massacre of 20 children and 6 adults at the Sandy Hook Elementary School on December 14. I ended it with this: "Let's ban assault weapons and high capacity magazines now." On the spectrum of opinions about gun rights and gun control, that's moderate. That article was an example of my effort to meet my readers halfway, to advocate for positions I believed in, but not for everything I hoped for.

I never will know how most readers responded. Like few issues in modern America, guns bring out extreme emotions, meaning extreme internet nastiness.

Why Some Americans Want Big Guns

JANUARY 8, 2013

Two weeks ago I urged a ban on assault weapons and high capacity magazines, because I argued that there are no reasonable civilian uses for them. But there are unreasonable ideas about why Americans need big guns, which are clearly displayed in some of the not very friendly responses I received, like the following, printed in its entirety: "Go f**k yourself and take your Liberal opinions with you. As a history prof why don't you tell me about the Nazi's, China, Mexico, etc...How's that working out for the millions of dead that were oppressed by their government ??????"

I'm not sure what this respondent thinks about Mexico, but his argument for guns is clear: American civilians need powerful military-style weapons to defend ourselves against our own government, which he compares with Nazi Germany and Communist China. The opposition to gun control goes well beyond the National Rifle Association and has deep roots in right-wing extremism.

Exaggerated fears of our government have a long history. After World War II, the John Birch Society brought together extreme conservatives who saw every policy put forward by the federal government, both Republicans and Democrats, as proof that communists were controlling politics in Washington. They saw communist conspiracies behind every movement they didn't like: in a 1965 flyer title "What's Wrong With Civil Rights?", they argued that the civil rights movement "has been deliberately and almost wholly created by the Communists".

The Birchers were welcomed by conservative Republicans, and they were enthusiastic about Barry Goldwater's candidacy in 1964. They were repudiated by more moderate Republicans, like Richard Nixon, but they lived on, warning about fluoridation, the United Nations, the Federal Reserve system, and "one world government".

Although the Birchers eventually lost influence, the conspiratorial right continued to spawn organizations dedicated to fighting the federal government. Often called the "patriot movement", loosely organized extremists and tightly organized militia formations argue that our government is the greatest enemy of Americans' constitutional freedoms. The feds were behind Timothy McVeigh's 1995 bombing of the Murrah Federal building in Oklahoma City; the Federal Emergency Management Agency (FEMA) is building concentration camps to detain patriotic Americans; politicians are conspiring to subordinate the US to a "New World Order".

The election of Barack Obama as President has brought out the latent racism which was always part of this movement. Obama has become the lightning rod for ever more hysterical theories about the federal government as the enemy of the people. A major focus of the "patriot movement" is the United Nations Arms Trade Treaty, an attempt to control terrorists' use of the international arms trade to gather weapons. It is instead perceived as a conspiracy by liberals and foreigners to take away Americans' guns. These ideas have little to do with political reality, but that makes no difference to the spinners of conspiratorial nightmares.

The sudden "secession movement" is another expression of this anti-government sentiment. Within weeks of Obama's reelection, about 700,000 people from every state put their names to online petitions to secede from the United States. While Americans of the left and right, often with silly motives, have joined this meaningless exercise in virtual secession, there is powerful anger in the depths of this movement.

This imaginary patriotism of right-wing extremists has been translated into a surge in demand for assault weapons, not for hunting or for protection against criminals, but to make war against our government. Offering far-fetched interpretations of the Constitution, demonizing immigrants, feminists, and liberals, and justifying their accumulation of weapons of mass destruction with reference to the Second Amendment, extremists of the far right dream of destroying our democracy, not protecting it.

They are angry and irrational. They are impervious to political discussion. They don't care what the majority of Americans think. And they are buying big guns.

STEVE HOCHSTADT
Jacksonville IL

The day after I wrote this and the day before it was published, Piers Morgan's TV interview with Alex Jones, talk radio host of "InfoWars", exemplified the paranoid rage lurking behind the defense of "gun rights". Jones, whose show is syndicated on 140 channels, had previously accused the US government of being behind the Oklahoma City bombing and the 9-11 World Trade Center attacks.

Morgan displayed remarkable patience, persistently repeating the key question about assault weapons: "Why do people need them?" Jones finally interrupted his own repetitive and irrelevant ranting to say this: "They need them to protect us from the number one killer in history, government in the 20th century".

Jones then made himself and InfoWars over the next 7 years into the primary loudspeaker for the fantasy that the Sandy Hook killings were faked, that the parents of the dead children were in on a government conspiracy, that this was one among many "false flag" operations by the US government. Only at the end of 2019 did he begin to pay a price in court judgments for his slanders of the families of the victims. The connection between the far right, gun politics, anti-government movements, and the conspiracy theories of fake news remains a volatile and dangerous mix in America.

Few issues break through our daily routines like guns. I am always startled when I see a gun in Jacksonville not carried by the police. The stakes of any miscalculation suddenly jump through the roof. Other issues in our popular culture, just as important, remain out of sight until some courageous and perceptive soul points them out in a memorable way. They may not be dangerous to life and limb, but merely to an unreflective understanding of the world we live in. Alison Bechdel's comic strip invention shook up my interpretation of culture and played a pioneering role in the broader questioning of Hollywood's role in preserving male supremacy. The #MeToo movement had already been founded in 2006, but had not yet caught public attention.

Putting Movies to the Test
FEBRUARY 5, 2013

We saw a nice movie the other day — "Silver Linings Playbook". The people on the screen were attractive, sympathetic and believable. There were no devils or angels, but real people struggling with their past, making the same bad decisions again and again, yet learning from experience how to give and find love.

"Silver Linings Playbook" rivets our attention on Bradley Cooper as the crazy good guy, so thoughtful, so compassionate, despite his obsessive fantasy about why his marriage broke up, occasionally exploding out of his control. As in real life, crazy isn't so easy to tell from the rest of us. Then crazy good guy meets crazy good girl and off we go on an exciting ride to Happyland. We smiled at the ending, the one designed to tug our heartstrings right into the theater. But that's not always real life.

It's not just the happy ending that makes this a fantasy. If you step out of the dark theater back into the real world and think about this film, and all the other films we can see, a big question pops up — where are the women? and what are they doing?

In 1985, one of the dykes in Alison Bechdel's comic strip "Dykes to Watch Out For" explained to her friend how she rates movies: "I have this rule, see. I only go to a movie if it satisfies three basic requirements. One, it has to have at least two women in it, who, two, talk to each other about, three, something besides a man."

This Bechdel test is not about feminism, or any political ideas, unless wondering where the women are is being political. It doesn't matter what the women talk about or think about, as long as it's not always about some man. Lesbian porn, if there's any dialog, and alien invasions can both pass the test. Hundreds of great films fail the test and some terrible ones can pass it.

The Bechdel test is just a reality check. Does a film portray life as we know it, where even if women don't have half the power, they are half of life itself? Or does the film present some imaginary world, where every scene, every action, every conversation, is mostly about men?

The Bechdel test sets a pretty low standard — one conversation, however brief, between any women, even if they are not named characters, gives a pass. One website that allows people to rate movies shows 91 of 155 films from 2012 passing the test. But if you just raise the bar to two different scenes with women talking to each other, many more films fail.

More interesting than finding out if one film passes or fails is to examine the film industry. So let's look at the Oscar nominees. Of the 9 films nominated for best picture, 2 failed the test. Most of the 7 which passed, however, just barely passed. "Silver Linings Playbook" has one conversation between women. In "Les Miserables" only unnamed female characters conversed. "Lincoln", "Argo", and "Zero Dark Thirty" are dominated by male characters, passing the test by one or two brief conversations.

The 5 best actor nominees all starred in films in which they were the main characters. But men were also the main characters in 3 of the 5 films nominated for best actress. All the best director nominees were men; only one woman has ever won that Oscar.

Thinking about the Bechdel test, and other measurements of how men and women are portrayed in films, helps us think about Hollywood and which slice of life it shows us. For example, Hollywood often borrows from best sellers, and loves suspense, action, and murder. Murder mysteries still sell millions of copies and offer great, usually flawed protagonists of both sexes. Female sleuths sell as many books as male sleuths: on mystery.com's list of the top 50 best sellers, 23 have female leads. But when Hollywood chooses which detectives to make into movie heros, it's nearly always the heros and not the heroines.

It's fine that films are fantasies — going to the movies means a brief respite from the daily grind. But why must it also be a vacation from women, a male-dominated zone, where films which have women talking to each other are derisively labeled "chick flicks"?

At the end of the strip which defined "The Rule", the two friends decide to skip the flicks, go home and make popcorn. If more us did that, perhaps Hollywood would get the message that men having fantasies about men is not the slice of life that we all crave.

STEVE HOCHSTADT
Jacksonville IL

Although the sexual abuse of women in the film and TV industry was nothing new, the accusations against Bill Cosby in 2014 kicked off a spiraling number of media-rich court cases against the biggest names in popular culture, which has transformed the line-up of men presented to us every day as paragons of virtue and accomplishment. Less likely to hit the front pages have been stories about the continuing subordination of women as media professionals. The proportion of women nominated for Oscars, for example, has crept up from 23% in 2016 to 31% for 2019 movies. The lack of any female nominee for director shows how much more needs to be done.

Discrimination has never been eradicated from any society. It has been attacked and defended, forced to retreat and then put back into place in new forms. The hopefulness in arguments about the arc of the universe may be mostly perception. The human history of persecution of minorities is one I know too well. My visions of social goals are radically different from what I experience, but my immediate prescriptions have tended to be moderate. I perceive that moderation as both a nod to my Jacksonville audience and an outgrowth of my reading of history's tendency toward gradual change.

Looking for Reason in the Middle

FEBRUARY 12, 2013

In the never-ending debate between liberals and conservatives over political issues, both sides present their positions forcefully. But not always reasonably. The extreme versions of proposals get in the way of finding the middle ground which is necessary for actually creating good policy. Only compromise between reasonable positions will satisfy the majority of Americans, who find themselves in the middle of the political spectrum.

So let's think about the Boy Scouts. After many years of insisting that boys who are gay could not be Scouts, the national organization is now reconsidering. Many troops are organized by churches who do not tolerate homosexuality among their members, so vocal opposition has arisen to any change in Scouting policy. I personally find any discrimination against homosexuals offensive, just as if church-led organizations said that they were not open to Jews, who commit a sin against their doctrines by not believing in the divinity of Jesus.

But it is unreasonable to demand that every Scouting organization be opened now to homosexual boys and leaders. If a church wishes to exclude homosexuals from membership or leadership positions at this time, I would accept that.

I also believe it is unreasonable to demand that no Boy Scout unit can accept homosexuals, which is the position advocated by many people today. That demand reflects the religious doctrine of some, but not all Christians. Thus it insists that the Boy Scouts officially retain a particular religious ideology of exclusion.

How can I call that position "unreasonable"? Who says what's unreasonable?

In the 1940s, when I was born, the demand that homosexuals should be able to enjoy the same marriage rights and privileges as heterosexuals was thought by most people to be unreasonable. It certainly was unusual.

Reason has changed. We have learned a great deal about homosexuality in my lifetime. We have heard the revelations about Nazi persecution and mass murder of homosexuals, and we have read about the physical abuse and sometimes murder of homosexuals in America. We know more about how socially stigmatizing a group makes it easier to believe myths about them, and we understand more about the biological causes of homosexuality and other behaviors that were traditionally thought of as sinful. We recognize how much like heterosexuals homosexuals are and how they are different. We see that our celebrities and leaders, our heroes and heroines, our friends and our relatives are gay.

It is not any more reasonable to discriminate on the basis of sexuality, than it is to discriminate on the basis of gender. Just because there is a long tradition of considering females and gays to be inferior and sinful, just because some of those traditions are religious, does not make that discrimination reasonable.

Until World War II, nearly every Christian tradition considered Jews to be inferior and sinful, preached those values unendingly, and asserted that they came from the word of God. Seeing the genocidal results of those beliefs and learning more about what Jews really are like, nearly every Christian tradition has changed its definition of reasonable. In the Catholic church, the moment when the Pope publicly said that previous Popes were wrong was 50 years ago, in the encyclical "Nostra Aetate", first written by Cardinal Augustin Bea for Pope John XXIII in 1961, considered by the Second Vatican Council in 1965, passed by the bishops of the world by a vote of 2,221 to 88, and then promulgated by Pope Paul VI.

What Catholics had considered reasonable, even mandatory to believe, had become unreasonable. There continued to be votes and voices against this change, but they were no longer persuasive.

Like the Constitution, the Bible also gets reinterpreted, as human society learns more about itself. Although Deuteronomy demands that a woman who is betrothed and then raped before marriage, and a woman who is not a virgin when she marries, both be stoned to death, now Christians criticize Islam for suggesting that women be stoned. What once was reasonable has become unacceptable.

So why don't I demand that every barrier to homosexuals, within the Boy Scouts and everywhere else, be immediately dropped? Why is a slower path to equality reasonable?

This is not mainly about changing rules. If the goal is equality, that must be created through persuasion. Those who argue against equality of man and woman, against equality of Christian and Jew, against equality of black and white, have lost the argument and have become unreasonable. That happened by changing people's minds. I believe this inequality of sexual identity will also succumb to reason. None of these changes have been easy or quick. Those of us who had to fight for our equality have suffered. But suffering won't be diminished by fixing only on the goal and not on the process.

Allowing individual troops to make their own decisions about homosexual members and leaders will be a big change for the Boy Scouts. Many will leave in a huff, shouting about tradition and morality. They will become the unreasonable ones, because the best human society has not only reached reasonable moral positions, but also is reasonable in how it gets there.

STEVE HOCHSTADT
Jacksonville IL

I try to ground my opinions on the foundation of my daily experience. I never met anyone who would pretend that their child had been shot in order to promote some government plan. I never met a scientist who would make up ideas about global warming just to get a grant. I never met an academic who sees the job as an opportunity to indoctrinate young minds. I never met a gay person who is trying to promote some "agenda" other than their own equality. I never met a feminist who hates men, although I have met some who hate the way men treat them.

I'm sure people like that exist, just like auto executives who cheat on emissions tests, financial managers who steal from their customers, and nurses who kill their patients. But they are rare. Basing general policies on such exceptional people leads only to extremism. Or to smokescreens, such as claiming that voter ID laws are needed because of the vanishingly small number of illegitimate voters or creating welfare policies founded on assumptions that "welfare queens" are everywhere.

I have come to rely on the most basic of questions: does that seem likely? It doesn't always work, but as a first response before investigation it is very useful. It eliminates spending any time worrying about whether the moon landing was faked or whether the Bush administration was behind 9/11.

Grounding myself in real life usually means that easy answers disappear. Evidence piles up that does not fit into ideological categories. I'm never happy to spend time in hospitals, but it does provide better information about the state of our health care system than reading dozens of diatribes.

Is Health Care Too Expensive?

FEBRUARY 26, 2013

I recently spent 36 hours at Passavant Area Hospital. A bad stomach pain, which I first attributed to eating too much clam dip while watching the Super Bowl, got much worse, so I arrived at the emergency ward at 1:30 AM looking for help. A day and a half later, my stomach pain was gone. I had received professional care from warm, friendly people, who restored my health and revived my spirits. I also had a bill for $12,074.

That's a lot of money. Median household income of Americans after taxes is less than $50,000. So my $12,000 bill for a common stomach bug would be a financial disaster for anyone without good health insurance.

I admit that I don't know how to think about the cost of my brief hospital stay. Was that too much? Or a bargain?

Here's what I got. In the emergency room, I saw an intake receptionist, two doctors and four nurses. Once I was transferred to a semi-private room, I saw three RN's, two CNA's, a nursing student, a dietician, an X-ray technician, a room cleaner, a chaplain, and my own family doctor. Also contributing to my successful stay were security personnel, food service workers, a billing department, and various administrators. The president of the hospital came into my room to ask that I fill out a survey, so they could find out what might be done better.

A portable X-ray machine was wheeled into my ER cubicle to see what was wrong. Later I had blood tests and a CAT scan, which were analyzed almost immediately, allowing the doctors to diagnose me quickly and correctly. Then I received an IV of antibiotics and fluids, which cured my bug and kept me functioning.

The technology was expensive. The CAT scan alone cost $5300, nearly half the total bill. The blood tests added another $1500. My room was billed at $1400 a day.

Hidden in those prices are the costs of all those people who cared for me. About 60% of total hospital costs nationwide are for people. I asked what everybody made at Passavant. The CNA's make $10 to $15 an hour, which comes to $20,000 to $30,000 a year. RN's make $50,000 or more. The ER doctors earn about $200,000 a year, family practice doctors up to $400,000, and surgeons (fortunately I didn't have to see any of them) upwards of $600,000.

To most people, I would guess, doctors' incomes seem enormous. Perhaps the huge gap between what doctors and nurses earn should be disturbing. In terms of caring for me, the whole patient, beyond my particular ailments, nurses tend to do much better than doctors.

But my doctors have been successful, so far, in keeping me healthy, and after my one serious injury as a teenaged touch football player, in keeping me alive. Who could say that surgeons make too much money, when professional athletes and stock brokers and bankers and corporate managers make many times more? Average compensation for CEOs at the 3000 companies in the Russell index was $5.8 million. Doctors' compensation is not too high — nurses' is too low, compared to the importance of their work.

Those are my subjective reactions to the financial side of our health care system. I'm glad that I have a good health insurance plan and that my employer pays part of that cost. I can't say that any of the care I received was unnecessary or too expensive. I think every American deserves that same quality of care.

Most people have an opinion about our health care system and its costs, but most people don't know any more than I do. In fact, wrong ideas about the Affordable Care Act ("Obamacare") are responsible for most of the opposition to it.

About 40% of Americans still believe in "death panels" of bureaucrats deciding whether patients get treatment, a nightmare invented by Republican politicians trying to defeat the ACA. More than half believe the law requires free treatment of illegal immigrants. More than one-third believe smokers will have to pay $1000 extra a year. These incorrect beliefs about unpopular ideas promote opposition.

On the other side, many people are sure that very popular provisions of the law are not in it: 20% don't realize that children under 26 can be included under their parents' insurance; nearly 30% don't realize that insurance companies will have to cover people with preexisting conditions; and 40% don't realize that insurance companies will be prevented from limiting the total amount paid for a person's health care.

No wonder opposition to "Obamacare" hovers near 40%. Here's what the researchers who conducted this survey said about the connection between correct knowledge and support: "If the public had perfect understanding of the elements that we examined, the proportion of Americans who favor the bill might increase from the current level of 32% to 70%".

Politicians could help us have that perfect understanding, so we could make good decisions about what system we would prefer. They don't, and they won't until we demand that they do.

STEVE HOCHSTADT
Jacksonville IL

Misinformation, and its cause, deliberate disinformation, fascinate and frustrate me. In 2016, another poll still found 29% believing that "death panels" would decide who received care and who should die, a lie propagated by Sarah Palin in 2009 after she and McCain lost the 2008 election, called by PolitFact the "Lie of the Year". Most Republicans could not say that the death panels were a political fiction.

How can we develop good policy about such a complicated subject as health care when so many people believe nonsense? How can government work in partisan times when one party deliberately disseminates lies? How can we have faith in government by the people, when so many people are misinformed and see it as in their interest to believe disinformation?

Efforts to counter lies and spread truth are not appreciated by those who live by fake news and extreme ideas. My lack of importance in the national conversation protects my ability to write my opinions more than my government's respect for freedom of the press. The self-proclaimed defenders of the Constitution are the most likely to call for dictatorial laws and persecution of dissenters.

My lifetime of opinions depends on the crapshoot of birth, the chance of geography, and the idiosyncracies of family life. Had I not been born into a Jewish family, I might not have understood discrimination in my bones. If my father had not been a refugee from the Nazis, I might not always sympathize with persecuted minorities. If I had grown up in Philadelphia, I might have been proud that the Phillies manager Ben Chapman had told Jackie Robinson in his first year that he should "go back to the cotton fields".

Identity means a lot, but not everything. I'm happy to have grown up in New York, not because I can exchange sarcasm with the best, but because I learned some things early.

Play Ball, Jackie
MAY 5, 2013

I grew up in a Brooklyn Dodgers family. I loved Duke Snider, Carl Furillo, and Pee Wee Reese. I rooted for the Dodgers when they were "Da Bums", when they lost three World Series before I was five years old, all to the Yankees. So of course I loved Jackie Robinson.

Robinson's historic first season in major league baseball was 1947. By the time I was born the next summer, Roy Campanella was catching for the Dodgers, and Larry Doby and Satchel Paige were playing for the Cleveland Indians. When I was old enough for my father to take me to Ebbets Field, when the Dodgers at last won their first World Series in 1955, the best black man on the Dodgers was the pitcher Don Newcombe,

1999 US stamp honoring Jackie Robinson

with a 20-5 record. The best black man in baseball was Willie Mays of the hated New York Giants, who won both National League MVP and the Hickok Belt as best professional athlete in 1954, and who led the league in homers in 1955.

They were great players, but Jackie Robinson was an icon in my New York Jewish home. I don't know for sure why my parents revered him. They rarely made political pronouncements. They didn't belong to any organizations. There were no black people in our all-white suburb to be friends with. It's too late to ask them why they hated racism.

Maybe it was my father's experience with Nazis in Vienna. Many Jews identified with African Americans as victims of brutal prejudice. Like Ben Chapman, the foul-mouthed Philadelphia manager, racists were usually also antisemites. "There are hundreds of stories that Jews have written about how important Jackie Robinson was to Jews in Brooklyn," said Rebecca Alpert, professor of religion and women's studies at Temple University, who wrote "Out of Left Field: Jews and Black Baseball," and who grew up, like I did, near Ebbets Field. Robinson returned the favor and later condemned the antisemitism of some black nationalists in the 1960s.

The new film "42" shows us many hard truths about how Robinson broke through baseball's color line. Both he and Dodgers' general manager Branch Rickey, who was 66 in 1947, had spent years preparing for the April day when Robinson took the field for the Dodgers. Robinson was a mature married man of 28, who had already experienced and fought against discrimination in college sports and in the Army. Rickey was one of the remarkable white men who risked their careers, and were threatened with death, because they believed in equality for blacks. He had played professional baseball and football, coached at two small colleges, and become the most innovative baseball executive by creating the farm system and the first real spring training facility. Rickey had been talking with the Dodgers organization about drafting a black player since 1943.

But "42" leaves a lot out. Other African Americans helped Jackie get through that first year. He had met Joe Louis, the boxing champion, in the Army, and Louis' protests helped him gain entrance to Officer Candidate School. Robinson and Doby often spoke on the phone during their first year in baseball. Robinson fought for the rights of African Americans on the field and off. He stole home 19 times and criticized segregated hotels and restaurants.

Some political leaders stuck their necks out, too. New York Mayor Fiorello LaGuardia created a Committee on Baseball which pushed the Yankees, Giants and Dodgers to integrate their teams.

The film leaves out Bill Mardo, a white sportswriter for "The Daily Worker", a Communist newspaper in New York, who had waged a public campaign to integrate baseball since 1942, asking New York fans to urge their teams to sign Negro League players. Mardo was also there in Florida as Robinson tried out for the Montreal Royals in 1946.

Watching "42", it's easy to hate racism and racists. The director of "42" made the unusual choice to include the entire national anthem: Jackie Robinson and Branch Rickey become the real Americans, who are "decent-minded", while Ben Chapman and the white fans who screamed at

Jackie are the un-American villains. Like black people, Jews and other minorities in the 1940s, racists are now the despised "other". Even racists deny being racists before spewing some stupid, hateful remark about Michelle Obama's clothes or her husband's birthplace.

Hollywood makes everything simple, but racism is never easy to deal with. American racism wasn't defeated in 1947, or in the 1960s, or with Obama's reelection. Many racists are obviously jerks, like Ben Chapman, but some of our neighbors, and some of our political leaders, have never been cured of the racist disease.

I don't know how my parents' political views, our family's history during the Holocaust, rooting for the Brooklyn Dodgers, and Jackie's own nobility and fearless civil rights activism mixed together to make me hate racism. We all have our own trajectories of fate and chance and education, bringing us to important decisions that define our character. Jackie Robinson, like Rosa Parks and many others, endured terrible injustice to make our nation more just. They challenge us to find the better angels of our nature.

STEVE HOCHSTADT
Jacksonville IL

Racism was different in 2013. It made sense to me to say that racists are now the despised "other". The long-delayed process of social reversal had taken off when I was young and seemed to continue inexorably. Racism was not defeated, not eliminated, not fully conquered in any part of our lives, but was in retreat.

Great leaders played a memorable role, but change is a social process. As I entered graduate school in 1973, the traditional "great man" perspective was under attack by younger historians. In my practice of history, I have emphasized in writing and teaching the need to understand the whole society.

Donald Trump did not reverse this process, but he has pushed the needle further by himself. He did not create racist Americans. I think he is unlikely to make people more racist in their thinking, because he offers no thoughts worth considering. By performing the racist in his speech, his policies, and his carefully crafted image in the most public of ways, he has told racists they should be out in the open, like him.

My gratitude for "42" was immense, but my self-congratulatory feeling that another corner had been turned has not lasted. I hoped that the evils of racism had been confined, were under control, like the evils in Pandora's box. That box has been pushed open by white conservatives and their extreme cousins, white supremacists. Trump calls encouragement to those who escape. Will we be able to put them back where they belong?

I think of Pandora, because I read mythology avidly as a kid. One of the sparse clues to the intellectual side of my father was his gift to me of *Bulfinch's Mythology*, first published in 1867, ancient Greek religion distilled into stories for everyone. In the absence of religious practice and religious dogma in my home, the myths filled the space for the fantastic, the superhuman, stories about gods. I have come to think about religion as a kind of mythology, not history, filled with wonderful stories to inspire and instruct us, characters impossibly good or bad, lessons for the world. I think we humans are on our own.

The insane Christian attacks on all Jews that make up a important part of the history of the last 1000 years, whether they thought like me or studied the Torah daily, also made me more skeptical of those religious claims, and then all such claims. From that attitude comes my distrust of those who say, we should pray as they do, whether they are Jews or not.

Pray Like I Do

MAY 12, 2013

A few days ago, a group of Jewish women gathered to pray at the most sacred place in Jerusalem. The Wailing Wall surrounds the ancient Temple Mount, where Jewish tradition says God gathered the dust to make Adam, where Abraham bound his son Isaac, where two Jewish temples stood for hundreds of years, where the Divine Presence rests. The women were surrounded by other Jews, who tried to prevent them from reaching the Wall, who cursed them, and threw water and chairs and stones at them. Three of these ultra-Orthodox Jewish protesters were arrested.

Last month the praying women themselves had been arrested. Their offense? They had not been praying the right way. The Women of the Wall are non-Orthodox Jews who wear prayer shawls that Orthodox Jews believe should only be worn by men. Until last month, Israeli police prevented women in these garments from praying at the Wailing Wall, because Israel enshrines Orthodox religious practices into state laws. Over the past few years, Jewish women have been arrested and put in jail for wearing a tallit, the prayer shawl, under their clothes, for holding a Torah scroll, and for praying out loud, all activities which the Orthodox believe should be reserved for men.

On April 11, the Jerusalem District Court ruled that the violent Orthodox protesters, not the praying women, were the ones causing a disturbance, and that the women should be allowed to pray as they wish.

The discrimination against women in Israel goes much deeper than disputes at the Wailing Wall. On bus lines serving areas where Orthodox live, women are forced to sit at the back. Recently some women have protested this discrimination, bringing references to the actions of Rosa Parks over 50 years ago. Israeli authorities have reacted in ways reminiscent of the reluctance of American leaders to challenge segregation: in 2011, the Israeli Supreme Court ruled that segregated buses were illegal, but allowed them to continue to operate.

These arguments among Jews about how to be Jewish are common to other religions. Sunni and Shia Muslims have disagreed about the nature of Islam since the prophet Muhammed died in 632 and a dispute developed over his successor. Sunni and Shia continue today to kill each other in the Middle East. The split among Christians during the Reformation in 1500s led to a century of violent conflict across central Europe, during which Christians killed other Christians over religious differences. When the leaders of the Russian Orthodox Church instituted reforms in ritual practices in the 17th century, many Russians refused to allow any changes. The so-called Old Believers were then persecuted by the dominant Orthodox clergy and by the Russian state. Old Believers use two fingers to make the sign of the cross, while the official Russian Orthodox Church uses three fingers.

Violence and persecution within religious faiths occurs when state power takes one side. The French Catholic monarchy organized the massacre of French Protestants, called Huguenots, in 1572, killing at least 10,000, and probably many more. Saddam Hussein's regime in Iraq was Sunni, and although a minority among the population, persecuted and murdered members of the Shia majority.

The religious disagreements in Israel are not violent. The Israeli government has allowed the Orthodox minority, estimated to be only about 10% of the population, to control significant elements of national life, notably marriage and divorce. There is considerable controversy in Israel about the outsized power of this fundamentalist religious minority, who avoid military service and receive state support for men to study religion all their lives.

Americans typically know little about the nature of the Israeli state that we support so generously. Would Americans so willingly support a state that discriminates against women? Or that makes rules about how one must pray?

In fact, American support for Israel is most powerful among the most fundamentalist Christians. A 2004 poll asked Americans "Should the U.S. support Israel over the Palestinians?" Although more Americans disagreed with that question than agreed, among evangelical Protestants the split in favor of supporting Israel was over 2 to 1.

All too frequently, religious fundamentalists of various faiths demand that everyone must follow their rules. The controversy across our states about marriage equality is a home-grown example. Citing their interpretation of the Bible, American fundamentalists want our government to enshrine their views of homosexuality into secular law.

Everyone should have the right to determine their own religious preference and beliefs. Nobody should have the right to demand, "Pray like I do."

STEVE HOCHSTADT
Jacksonville IL

A different upbringing in a different household would certainly have given me other perspectives with which to understand the world. We are all shaped by so many influences at home and in the world that we end up with an infinite variety of people, none exactly like another, every one a puzzle of origin and development.

I will always wonder in what ways my father shaped my idea of fatherhood. I can now look in the other direction, and try to figure out how I shaped my children's approach to parenthood. Either way, the questions overwhelm the few answers we can create.

Fathers are Forever

JUNE 16, 2013

I'm writing this on Father's Day. Father's Day is an afterthought. The second Sunday in May was officially designated Mother's Day in 1914 by Congress and President Woodrow Wilson. The first presidential proclamation honoring fathers was issued by President Lyndon Johnson in 1966, over 50 years later.

Until recently fatherhood itself was an afterthought. In men's lives, fathering was not the top priority. Men were breadwinners. Men were considered the heads of the household and people gave lip service to "Father Knows Best", but women cared for children.

The women's liberation movement of the 1960s and 1970s finally made an issue of fathering. If women were going to get out of the house and into the workplace, men had to change their roles, too. By the 1980s, fathers were allowed into the delivery room, present at that magical and painful moment when fatherhood really begins. A few couples shared jobs and child-rearing, and thought this was the wave of the future.

But changing cultural assumptions and family dynamics was not easy. I still remember being the odd man out when I brought my son to a play group in the 1980s. The mothers didn't know what to do with me, even though we all knew each other. Did I have any interesting things to say about paper vs. cloth diapers? Did I know how to play with children? Would I act like a man among women, that is, superior and condescending? Father knows best?

Women today still struggle with workplace discrimination and unequal pay. Paternity leave policies are far from universal. Stay-at-home fathers face social stigmas about their choices. Although fathers spend much more time taking care of their children, they are still far behind mothers. Since the

1960s, fathers have tripled the amount of time with their children, but that amount has risen from 2.5 hours a week (20 minutes a day?) to 7.3 hours per week, barely an hour a day. On average, that's not really fatherhood.

There is much public concern about inadequate fatherhood. Many commentators on fathers and their absence, such as the National Fatherhood Initiative, claim that "Today, one in three children are growing up without their father." This is an unfortunate error: one in three children live apart from their biological father, but many live with a step-father or adoptive father. Still, the number of fatherless children is very high, a bit more than one in four. That compares to only one in thirteen who live with no mother.

Furthermore, fathers raising their children without a mother tend to have it easier than mothers alone, according to the Census Bureau. In 2011, fathers alone cared for 5% of 12- to 17-year-old children, but only 2% of those 2 years old or younger. Fathers alone took care of 6% of children with no siblings, but only 2% of children with 3 or more siblings. About 21% of fathers caring for children with no mother lived below the poverty level, but that was true for 44% of mothers alone. The median income for mothers alone was about $25,000, while it was over $40,000 for fathers. On each of these measures, women take the tougher parenting roles.

Some of the blame for men's insufficient attention to fatherhood can be attributed to our sexist culture. Girls are still given dolls to practice with, while boys play video games where strong men save sexy women. One of today's Father's Day TV programs is the Miss USA pageant.

But men themselves have to shoulder most of the responsibility for their lack of responsibility. Too many men help to make children, but then fail to help raise them. Raising children means not doing other things, including participation in the family-unfriendly work culture of corporate and professional life. Men have let women be the advocates for flexible hours, leave for child care, and other reforms which make it easier to combine family and work.

Being a parent is difficult. Fatherhood has been my most demanding, but also most rewarding accomplishment. There were no days off. Sometimes the work was literally shitty, but I liked changing diapers, because it was a moment of tender touching. (I'm a fan of cloth, by the way.) Every decision seemed momentous, with no obvious answers. Should we let our baby cry a bit longer? Is it time to replace the crib with a bed? How late can they stay out?

Fatherhood is about taking responsibility. You only earn a say in big deci-sions by getting up in the middle of the night, by missing meetings to stay home with a sick child, by replacing a social life with a home life. That investment is worth every second. Long after the rigors of parenting are over, children who are no longer children reflect back the love they have received. On Father's Day, and every other day, fatherhood is the best thing to which a man can aspire.

STEVE HOCHSTADT
Jacksonville IL

I was living then in a temporary phase of fatherhood: father to married children with no children. There were no diapers to change or struggles over eating to endure. It was easy to forget that parenting is a physically demanding, inherently repetitive job that extends through day and night. Now that I have 4 grandchildren under 3, I am frequently reminded of both the hard realities and the unique joys of child-rearing. Fatherhood isn't just an attitude. You only get there by working hard.

Now I'm a grandfather. All the other grandparents I know agree with me that it is wonderful. The label itself has become my name, but in German slang, Opa. So I embrace the label.

That's how identities shift in real life. My geographical identity has changed a few times, from New Yorker to New Englander to small-town Midwesterner. Native Wisconsinites might object, but years of summers and winters in northern Wisconsin have also remade my thinking.

Hooray for Nature

JULY 6, 2013

Wisconsin has beautiful rivers, curving through thick forests, running over boulders left by glaciers hundreds of thousands of years ago. Last week, as we canoed down the Namekagon in the northwestern corner of the state, we enjoyed some natural encounters uncommon in central Illinois. Turtles the size of serving platters sunned themselves on dead logs until we approached too closely, then slipped into the water. A bald eagle watched us approach and then swooped overhead for a closer look. Most of the time the loudest sounds were leaves rustling and water rushing past rocks. During two hours on the river, we saw only a group of three kayakers.

At the other end of the state, the Wisconsin River runs through a sandstone gorge, also created by glaciers, called the dells. About 5 million people every year visit this area, which calls itself the Waterpark Capital of the World. To keep these millions coming back, new attractions are constantly being invented. For 2013, you could forget you are a thousand miles from the ocean by surfing an artificial wave at Noah's Ark Waterpark, the largest outdoor waterpark in America. For more thrills, you could ride 70 miles per hour on the Hades 360, billed as "the world's first upside-down, underground, wooden rollercoaster." To relax, you could jump into the 1000-square-foot hot tub at the Kalahari Resort and swim up to the bar at the Mud Hut.

The Namekagon and the Dells represent two different approaches to the interaction of humans and nature. Namekagon is derived from an Ojibwe word meaning "the place abundant with sturgeons." It is part of the St. Croix National Scenic Riverway, whose mission is to "preserve, protect, restore, enhance, and interpret the riverway's exceptional natural and cultural resources for the enjoyment of present and future generations." This and many other protected areas were created by the Wild and Scenic Rivers Act, signed by President Lyndon Johnson in 1968. The system preserves 12,600 miles of 203 rivers, less than one out of every 400 of the nation's rivers.

The rivers are protected from us, from the kind of human intervention which created the Dells. Not only is building not allowed along these rivers, but existing buildings have been purchased and removed. Campsites along the Namekagon are accessible only from the river. Entertainments are provided by nature itself.

It is all too easy to romanticize nature. In northern Wisconsin nature can be intrusive and annoying. Swarms of tiny insects, often called no-see-ums, just hatched on July 4 and covered every white surface they could find, including our sinks and bed sheets. More dangerous are the much larger animals with which we share this region. Recently encounters between black bears and people have increased, as the bear population of Wisconsin more than doubled over the past 25 years, and their range has moved into the more populous southern part of the state for the first time in a century. Although bear attacks on people are rare, they can be devastating. If we want to coexist with nature, we must exercise caution and discipline.

The contrast between the Namekagon and the Dells is not only between natural and artificial, but also public vs. private. Preservation of wilderness as a public good requires political will, which was manifested throughout the 20th century by the gradual creation of our system of national parks. That bipartisan will remains strong among Americans: 92% of Democrats, 90% of Independents, and 81% of Republicans believe it is quite or extremely important "for the federal government to protect and support" our national parks.

But much of that will has disappeared in Washington. The last Congress was the first since 1966 not to protect a single additional acre of wilderness. Even after the sequester cut the budget of the National Park Service by 5%, Congress cut another $30 million in March. That means more cuts in staff, longer lines to get into parks, shorter seasons, fewer campsites and nature programs, locked restrooms and overflowing trash cans. Our national parks are a bargain: while 5 million tourists spent a total of $875 million in the Wisconsin Dells area in 2011, the 280 million visitors to our 401 national parks, memorials, lakeshores, parkways and historic sites cost the taxpayers only three times that much, $2.6 billion.

Some people prefer waterslides to watching bald eagles, riding artificial waves to spotting a snapping turtle. It's less effort to swim up to the Mud Bar than to carry a canteen of water in a canoe. That's fine, but we also need the less commercial, more natural experiences. Anti-government ideologues say they want to protect future generations from a debt disaster. In fact, posing as deficit alarmists, they are destroying our children's chances to enjoy America's unique natural heritage. Instead they will only be able to ride the world's tallest looping waterslide, and see eagles in the zoo.

STEVE HOCHSTADT
Jacksonville IL

In northern Wisconsin, the helpful hand of federal government is mostly absent. Democrats in my lifetime have not spoken persuasively to rural Americans, poor or not. It has not been enough to say, "We don't give you much, but it's more than the Republicans." Even though it's true.

Poverty is hidden in the woods, at the end of long driveways. Countless studies show that the poorest rural places in America are reliable reservoirs of Republican votes. My whole life Democrats have tried to alleviate poverty against Republican opposition. Yet the white Republican disdain for offering public help remains strong. Republicans have been politically successful among the rural poor, partly because Democrats have been so unsuccessful.

Tough Luck for the Poor

SEPTEMBER 22, 2013

Republicans in the House just voted to cut food stamps for poor Americans. They say the program is too large, because so many Americans need food stamps to help them buy groceries. Too large means too many tax dollars are being spent to feed poor Americans. The Republicans want to cut taxes, and they mean to do that by cutting programs that spend money on the poor.

Why does rich America have so many poor people? The answer cannot be found in the recent economic disaster from which we are slowly recovering. The problem of the American economy is much older.

The typical American household, right in the middle of the economic spectrum, is making the same real income as in 1988, 25 years ago. The per capita size of our economy has grown 40% in that time, but none of the gains have gone to middle Americans. Even worse, the real net worth of the middle American family has fallen 6% since 1989.

Over the past 15 years the number of full-time year-round workers has barely changed, as more and more corporations offer only part-time work in order to reduce the need to pay benefits. Even for those with full-time work, like factory workers, real wages have fallen since the 1970s. Adjusting for inflation, the minimum wage has fallen steadily since the 1960s; it is now only two-thirds of the value it was 45 years ago.

In fact, the vast majority of Americans, the real 99%, have seen little improvement. Since 1993, real income for the 99% has grown only 6.6%, about one third of 1% a year, barely noticeable.

For the top 1%, on the other hand, the past 35 years have been a bonanza. In 1978, the top 1% made 9% of the total income in the country; last year their share was 23%. In the last 20 years, their incomes nearly doubled. The top one-hundredth of 1%, the richest 16,000 families, have increased their share of total income from 1% in 1978 to over 5% now, the highest it has ever been. These 16,000 families make about the same each year as the bottom 16 million families.

While the very rich have been increasing their share of the American economy, the number of poor Americans has been rising. Although the social programs and economic expansion of the 1960s reduced the number in poverty from 40 million to under 25 million, the number began to climb again after 1978 to over 46 million in 2012. But the so-called poverty rate of 15% of Americans for 2012 is misleading about the nature of American poverty. Over the three years 2009 through 2011, nearly one-third of Americans experienced a spell of poverty lasting 2 or more months. Only 3.5% of the population were poor for that entire span. So the spending on anti-poverty programs like food stamps works to help the millions of Americans who fall into poverty to stand back up again.

You wouldn't know any of this from listening to Republican politicians. They blame poverty on the poor. Of course, they don't actually make that argument openly, because nobody could really believe that the poorest Americans have caused the rich to get richer and the rest to stagnate. They make the argument behind closed doors, like Mitt Romney did when he was caught on videotape during the 2012 campaign.

In public, they talk a lot about the national debt, and then try to reduce it by cutting every program that helps the poor. Here's how they connect the dots. The biggest problem in our economy is the national debt. That is caused by too much taxation and too much government spending, but not every big government program needs to be cut. The programs that need to be cut are the food stamp program, unemployment compensation, and Head Start. Programs that need to remain or even grow are tax breaks for the rich, tax breaks for corporations, and subsidies for agribusiness.

None of those programs can possibly help the poor, or the sinking middle class. And that's the whole idea. The Republicans are not trying to use government to make life better for most Americans. They don't believe that government should help most Americans.

The Republicans don't even have to pretend that they care about the economic plight of the majority. In Owsley County, Kentucky, over half the population gets food stamps, but this nearly all-white county voted 81% for Romney. Of the 254 counties whose number of food stamp users doubled since 2007, Romney won 213.

So tough luck for the poor. Republicans are trying to slash the programs which have allowed most people who fell into poverty during the recession to get out of it. And for the rest of the middle class, whose incomes are going nowhere, they can watch the very rich eat up more and more of our national wealth.

Maybe the trickle down will start tomorrow.

STEVE HOCHSTADT
Jacksonville IL

The Republican House leadership's shutdown of the federal government in 2013 was another data point for most Republican voters to ignore. Hoping the move would hurt Obama, they ignored how much it hurt the 2 million federal employees who received no pay and the countless citizens who received no services. There had been shutdowns of individual federal agencies or parts of the government before as the parties could not come to an agreement, but like many recent manifestations of partisan hostility, this was the biggest and baddest.

Republican attempts to eliminate Obamacare are another example of how they reject programs which primarily benefit poorer Americans without paying a political price. In 2017, *Newsweek* counted over 70 Republican attempts in Congress to get rid of Obamacare since its inception. In that year, their seven-year campaign finally failed, when the Health Care Freedom Act failed in the Senate, despite Republican control of Congress. Since then, Republicans have used civil suits initiated at the state level to try to gut Obamacare. The Supreme Court will no doubt issue a final decision, but that may not come before the 2020 election.

Republican myth-making about health care continues, as they try both to repeal Obamacare and take no responsibility for the consequences. Trump uses his familiar playbook. He tweeted in January 2020, "I was the person who saved Pre-Existing Conditions in your healthcare."

In our looking-glass world, truth is irrelevant and the purveyors of fake news accuse fact-checkers of fake news. As a believer in the liberal arts, I am supremely frustrated by the claims of propagandists that the liberal arts is propaganda. The conservative assault on higher education has been supported by circular reasoning: we don't like what you do, few conservatives sign up to be professors, so you are discriminating against us, therefore we don't like what you do.

All of our social, economic, environmental, and political problems require knowledge for their solutions. When assailing the creators and disseminators of knowledge becomes a premise of a major political party, I sense a long-term catastrophe.

I feel that assault in my small town. The newspaper allowed anyone to send vile anonymous email comments to "Open Line". The best way to raise the temperature and lower the value of any kind of comment is to publish them anonymously. But one value of Open Line is that it reveals what some people really believe.

The Beauty of the Liberal Arts

NOVEMBER 3, 2013

Some critical comments about Illinois College have appeared recently on Open Line. While much of what is said on Open Line is not worth discussing, those comments reveal a much wider issue.

The comments began on October 25: "A student cannot speak up in a classroom that is run by a left-wing radical. There is no freedom of speech with radicals." There was escalation the next day: "If Illinois College actually discourages open discourse and debate, then it's really not a college at all. It's more like the re-education/indoctrination camps of the former Soviet Union." The next day these claims were generalized: "Freedom of speech doesn't apply to the college campus. Students are indoctrinated with socialist ideology." Finally, on October 29: "It is the left-wing liberals at the liberal arts colleges that do not tolerate a difference in opinion."

We don't know who wrote these comments, or if it's all the same person. Although there is nothing to prevent a commenter from signing their name, these critical voices always hide behind anonymity. It's clear that they have never been in an Illinois College classroom. Their fears about what happens on campuses come from somewhere else: right-wing fears of liberal arts colleges.

Liberal arts colleges compare favorably with business organizations. Colleges are less hierarchical, with power being distributed horizontally: faculty, even newly hired professors, have extraordinary control over what they do every day. Colleges are more democratic in their decision-making, as students and faculty enjoy unusual powers of self-government through egalitarian institutions. Colleges offer more protection against arbitrary firing of employees. Colleges are less likely to engage in corrupt financial practices, which is clear from the comparative histories of higher education and big business. Perhaps most important, colleges emphasize learning for its own sake, pay attention to the progress of individual students, and constantly seek to improve the delivery of knowledge.

Colleges are partnerships among trustees, administrators and faculty, who each play a crucial role in creating a safe place where students can mature, question, and discover themselves. Trustees bring financial experience and fiscal responsibility; administrators develop the mechanisms which ensure that the enterprise runs smoothly; faculty provide specialized expertise in every possible subject.

Liberal arts colleges are remarkable islands of discovery and democracy in American society. Young adults grasp responsibility for the first time — they organize their own education, they create and run organizations of the most varied kinds, they vote for and lead their own governing bodies, they publish their own newspapers.

So why does the right wing hate institutions of higher education? One reason is that many courses deal with subjects that make extreme conservatives uncomfortable. Biologists teach evolution, not creationism. Scientists believe that global warming is caused by human action. Men and women are treated equally in the content of our courses.

Topics like race, class, and gender upset conservatives. Dealing with those subjects inevitably means discussing our history of slavery and segregation, and of the dispossession of Native Americans. It means studying how women have been subordinated by law and custom until very recently. It means looking critically at the darker sides of our history, alongside the idealism of the American revolutionaries and the triumph of democracy, addressing both the good and the bad.

I admit to having taken particular positions on race in my own teaching. In the course on the 1960s which I team-taught with another professor, we were clear that we thought that segregation was wrong, morally and constitutionally, and that the civil rights movement was justified. Should we be teaching our students something different than that?

Here's an example of the "indoctrination" that occurs at Illinois College. In a classroom used for political science courses hang several posters urging our students to vote. During the Presidential election, students were encouraged to see the primary debates, the Party conventions, and the election night reporting. I have never heard any professor tell any student how to vote.

In fact, the right wing is not against indoctrination, it is against institutions that do not indoctrinate students with their own ideas. William F. Buckley, Jr., argued in his 1951 book, "God and Man at Yale", that higher education in America was hopelessly liberal, and then turned around and suggested "banishing from the classroom" all professors who did not advocate the ideas of Adam Smith.

Conservatives, according to their own words, prefer colleges which stress political indoctrination: Young America's Foundation (motto: "The Conservative Movement Starts Here") only approves institutions which "emphasize principles including smaller government, strong national defense, free enterprise, and traditional values", which "proclaim, through their mission and programs, a dedication to discovering, maintaining, and strengthening the conservative values of their students."

The Open Line writers imagine that everybody believes in substituting persuasion for teaching. I invite anyone who thinks that open discourse is discouraged at Illinois College to attend a class and see for themselves. We don't try to strengthen either the liberal or conservative values of our students. We try to help them think about what their values are, test those values against the widest variety of human experiences, and realize that other good people have other values.

STEVE HOCHSTADT
Jacksonville IL

My feelings about teaching at a liberal arts college are right there. If it seems I am describing a higher calling, I feel privileged to have been able to follow that calling at institutions that have encouraged it for over a century. History cannot be taught truthfully by emphasizing "smaller government, strong national defense, free enterprise, and traditional values". History teaching is about getting students who have not thought much about these issues to ask questions about the size of government, the nature of military force, the role of government in the economy, and the consequences of social values. I am discouraged to see how much effort and money is being spent trying to trash those values.

Once again, however, the end of the year helps me focus on more encouraging thoughts. The holidays are special times when family takes precedence in our daily consciousness.

Thanksgiving in the Kitchen

DECEMBER 1, 2013

On Thanksgiving morning, five of us bumped into each other in our kitchen, as we prepared an elaborate dinner. Janet, my mother-in-law, made creamed onions, a casserole combining several jars of onions, cubes of bread, a cream sauce, and some cheese. I had never seen that dish before it was served to me at the first Christmas after our marriage. It is a traditional dish in my wife's family, which has evolved over many decades. "Know your onions" used to mean that we should understand the differences among local varieties of onion. But interstate commerce, made possible by big capital and better methods of preservation, has standardized onions across America, as it has potatoes, apples, and most fruits and vegetables. Our daily foods have changed in ways we can no longer grasp.

When Janet married into a family which had generations of connection with Wisconsin, she began to scout the offerings of antiques and foods along the journey from northern Illinois to northwestern Wisconsin. For years, she, and now her daughters' families, have bought cheese at one store in Tomah, an intersection in the center of the state, which specializes in fine aged cheddar. I love the onions, but the younger generation is less interested, and that tradition is likely to disappear.

My son Sam and daughter-in-law Katie brought squashes and wild rice for a vegetarian "salad" (they couldn't agree on what to call it). They haven't eaten meat for years. So they developed together a daily menu of foods I had never known and rarely eat except with them. Among the many traits they share are an appreciation for good raw foods prepared by hand and the willingness to spend time every day shopping and making dinner. Some of these dishes are so good, I have looked at Katie's food blog to copy the recipe.

Many people, vegetarian or not, feel they can't spare the time that such attention to healthy, tasty food requires. But Katie and Sam also have busy professional lives, often climb rocks and mountains, and generally do just as much as anyone else. Although they may not think about it this way, I would say they have swapped television for eating. According to Nielson, Americans average over 35 hours a week of TV, more than 5 hours a day. Instead they entertain each other in the kitchen and have learned much more about food than if they had been watching the Food Network.

My wife Liz made the turkey. It was probably the first turkey she made this year. She only cooks big birds on the biggest family holidays, and never orders turkey in a restaurant. The lengthy prelude that a turkey requires is as much a family ritual as the final presentation of the platter of fragrant meat, the moment when preparation ends and eating begins. Turkey is a symbol of the celebration of family and family history, made possible by national holidays, repeated every year through our mutual desire to be together. We are hardly a "traditional family", in the mythological sense often given to that phrase, but we are bound by our traditions.

My contribution to the Thanksgiving meal was a cranberry bread, mostly according to the recipe printed on the bag of cranberries. Liz's sister Pat makes a cranberry bread at family gatherings that I can't get enough of. I connect cranberries with Maine, where I spent 27 years, and with Sam, who remains the only person I know who likes raw cranberry juice and is proud of it. Katie suggested that I don't chop the cranberries, as the recipe suggests, with the result of bursts of cranberry scattered through the bread.

No family gathering brings everyone together. Someone we all remember has died, everyone is connected to more than one family, distances are no longer manageable without expense and planning. But I thought of Pat while I made the bread. Sharing recipes is like sharing love: it makes everyone happy today and in the future.

I did make another contribution to this holiday's events. Although my own family paid little attention to Jewish holidays, like Passover and Hanukkah, Liz and I incorporated Jewish holidays into our new family's invented practices. She probably had never seen a latke before she met me, and maybe never heard the word. On Friday, Liz made plate after plate of potato pancakes, onto which we all spooned apple sauce that had just come off the stove. The food processor eliminates the hardest task; latkes are no harder to make than hash browns. The only difference lies in the histories of the families who make them.

Family foods change gradually with each generation. Cooking and talking, bumping into one another constantly, checking each other's dishes, cleaning up and making a mess again — it brings us all together with a common purpose and a shared understanding of who our family is, what we believe in, and what we want to eat.

For that I am thankful.

STEVE HOCHSTADT
Jacksonville IL

That's the family side. Now for the retail side. Few among the uncounted gifts we exchange are self-made. I mention some homemade gifts here in my annual essay about Christmas, but most of what we gave had been purchased. I may imagine the value of a less commercial Christmas, of fewer gifts under the tree, but much of our retail economy would collapse if we all decided to do that. If this is a flaw in our society, I don't see much downside in people voluntarily buying unnecessary gifts for other people.

Is There a Perfect Gift?

DECEMBER 29, 2013

Christmas is over. Gifts have been given and received. Our family is lucky — everyone has a job they like and we can afford to give each other gifts. Since many of us gather to celebrate together (10 this year, an unusually small number), there were many presents to open. We open one by one, with lots of oohing and ahhing, taking time to appreciate each gift.

That made me wonder — what makes a perfect gift?

A perfect gift might be on your Christmas list. I hoped for a hand-held Dremel tool for my home refinishing projects. My daughter Mae put books at the top of her list. Much to our delight, both were under the tree. Not much surprise, but Christmas wishes fulfilled.

My wife Liz had put warm pajamas on her list, and was very happy to receive a pair. But much better was the photograph of a Wisconsin barn from our children and their partners, framed in barn wood, bought in Indiana and transported to Minneapolis. It was wrapped in the biggest package under the tree, which occasioned much comment and anticipation. Even before it was opened, the gift was already a hit. Since Liz loves pictures of barns, that present was pretty near perfect.

There might be something that you haven't put on your list, but for which you have your fingers crossed. Maybe it costs more than you could ask anybody to spend. Or it would be best as a surprise. Mae's grandmother Janet gave her a cast iron pot, too expensive to put on a list or maybe even to hope for, but perfect for a young household where cooking is important.

Perhaps perfection lies in the effort of the giver. My nieces Jane and Helen and my sister-in-law Pat pickled peppers and made flavored mustards. Long after Christmas, even into warm summer days, I will taste their love and generosity.

Practical gifts can be perfect, too. Marti, my brother-in-law's mother, gave me LED light bulbs, still expensive but the wave of the future. They'll last for years and perhaps shift my bulb-buying habits.

One of the first gifts opened was a book on making pies for Jane, a talented and enthusiastic baker. Every time I looked at her, she was reading another recipe, lost in an imagined world of sweet smells and beautiful desserts. She didn't ask for it, nor need it. When we taste one of those pies some time in the future, we'll all remember that gift, how it united two people in the shared joy of Christmas giving.

These thoughtful gifts, and many others, brought us all together in appreciation of our good fortune and of each other. Perfection does not require expense or size. The best gift might be anonymous. Dropping coins into the Salvation Army bucket or writing a check to another charity which supports the poor is especially important this season, when more Americans are in great need than at any time since the Depression. Charitable givers just have to imagine the joy of those who might be able to buy a warm coat for a child or put a festive meal on the table.

Unfortunately, a recent poll showed that Americans plan to give less to charity this holiday season, due to the economy. Perhaps that attitude is reflected in the recent Congressional decision not to extend unemployment benefits for the long-term unemployed. Christmas giving can be selfish, too.

Marti gave me a tiny book of Chinese wisdom. More than two thousand years ago, before Christmas and Christ, Lao Tse wrote about the perfect gift: "Kindness in giving creates love."

STEVE HOCHSTADT
Minneapolis, MN

That was 2013, the first year of Obama's last term. There was little in 2013 that might have predicted 2016 and what has come since. That's why Donald Trump has been such a shock — he mobilized people I did not think existed, he encouraged them in ways I thought publicly impossible, and he gathered support from many big institutions and powerful people who had been dismissive of just that possibility. He defied all of our expectations.

Now we look backwards to find the origins, the causes, the clues about the reversal of that course and the large minority of Americans who desired it. I was as clueless as everyone else.

CHAPTER 5

A Liberal Life in Conservative America: 2014

Oklahoma!

JANUARY 7, 2014

We spent the final days of 2013 in Oklahoma City, celebrating the wedding of a "nephew", son of a family to which my family has been closely related for generations, in friendship if not in DNA. It was my first time in Oklahoma.

When we're in a new city, we walk around and go to museums. Walking around is not so easy in many American cities. There were no sidewalks on the busy road near our hotel. But we could drive to a small park in the center of Oklahoma City. There is a wide grassy field, a ring of trees, and a broad reflecting pool at the former site of the Murrah Building. There are also jagged concrete walls, the few pieces still standing 19 years after it was blown up by Timothy McVeigh on the morning of April 19, 1995, with the help of Terry Nichols and the encouragement of thousands of Americans in white supremacist, Christian Identity, government-hating organizations. In carefully planned rows facing the pool, within the footprint of the Murrah Building, sit 168 empty chairs with the names of everyone killed that day.

The park was peaceful. A park ranger answered our questions with clear and thoughtful stories. But we had even more questions, the pool had floating ice and the National Memorial Museum stood just a few feet away, in the damaged and repaired former *Journal Record* newspaper building.

We sat in a small room and listened to a recording of the Water Resources Board hearing that had begun at 9:00 on April 19. Unlike the woman, the "bureaucrat", who was explaining the proceedings to all the participants, we knew what was coming. The explosion was still a shock, but it prepared me to see the hundreds of photographs of American faces, amidst fire and rubble, that the Museum uses to convey the human disaster that followed. In one room, a photo of each of the victims is displayed.

The park looked different when we came out of the museum. The chairs now had faces and personalities. The whole city looked different. We knew something more, felt something more, about the buildings in downtown Oklahoma City, about the people who lived in and near the city, about violent things that even a wedding can't make you forget.

We visited another unique museum, the National Cowboy & Western Heritage Museum, at the top of the list of the state's top museums. It used to be the National Cowboy Hall of Fame, and great cowboys are all around, real ones and Hollywood imitations, statues and paintings and artifacts from 200 years of the Western cowboy experience. The name has been changed and now both cowboys and Indians are honored. Towering above visitors as they enter the building is James Earle Fraser's gigantic sculpture of a muscular Plains Indian, at "The End of the Trail". The colorful, varied, and intricate art of and about Native Americans mingles with cowboy themes, just as they lived next to each other for hundreds of years.

Most of that history was violent. Cowboys and Indians might have mostly been competitors, but it was soldiers who drove Native Americans westward across the country, on behalf of the US government. Those who didn't die were confined and their culture was attacked, to be replaced by the superior civilization of the whites.

For Native Americans, the US government was the enemy. It carried out the popular wishes of white America, against Natives, against Africans and their descendants, against immigrants, especially if they were not white.

Now all those excluded people are part of America. White America and non-White America have been coming to terms my whole life, and that process will continue.

Some people oppose the full and equal inclusion of all Americans. Timothy McVeigh was the deadliest in a long line of Americans who have used public terror to attack "the government". By "government", McVeigh and people who share his ideas actually mean the whole American society whose government has changed so much in the last half century. McVeigh followed the bible of right-wing fanatics, the "Turner Diaries", which claim that there is no way to destroy "the Jewish-liberal-democratic-equalitarian plague...without hurting many thousands of innocent people."

When McVeigh planned his crime, he set out to kill the government employees who help the elderly get their Social Security payments, who recruit for our armed forces, who enforce our laws. McVeigh said, "I believe we are slowly turning into a socialist government. The government is continually growing bigger and more powerful and the people need to prepare to defend themselves against government control." You can hear similar words from a whole flock of conservative politicians. You can read in your local paper about "government bureaucrats" who are responsible for America's decline.

Government can be the enemy, as it was for the Native Americans. But it isn't any more. Those who can't tell the difference create the atmosphere for fanatics to take up violence against people who do our public work, people like us.

STEVE HOCHSTADT
Jacksonville IL

I don't think of myself as part of "white America". My skin is darker than those who proclaim the importance of whiteness, typically Christians from northern Europe, but not dark enough to be mistaken as non-white. My heritage lies in southeastern Europe and southern Russia, lands that were never at the top of any white supremacist's list of worthy places. More important is my Jewish background. My family experienced violent antisemitism in Europe and a much quieter antisemitism in America. Jews in America, like the Irish and Italians and other groups whose skin color did not matter but origin did, had to become white to become American.

As I lived what I thought was a normal life from the 1950s onward, I kept being told that I was among the first Jews to do this or that. Much has opened that was closed before, including nearly every organized body of people or resources or power. When I experienced each of those openings, I felt less liberated than disappointed in the behavior of the people who had kept them closed.

So I see "white America" as an outsider, as if I'd just been invited to join after a long time outside. I recognize that I benefit and have benefitted my whole life from my skin color. The accepted victimization of Jews in America has retreated much further than for people of color. But I remain attuned to all the manifestations of "white is better".

Whiteness and poverty are closely aligned, not so much in demographic fit as in popular perception. Poverty afflicts every American group. Blacks and Hispanics are more than twice as likely to be poor as whites, but there are more than twice as many poor whites as blacks. Nevertheless, the political forces of the right who argue that poverty is the fault of the poor, who consistently try to reduce government help for poor Americans, have succeeded in convincing many white Americans with low incomes to vote for Republicans. The poorest states, Mississippi, Louisiana, West Virginia, and Alabama, and especially the poorest rural counties in America, are the biggest Trump supporters. Much of that persuasion was accomplished by racializing poverty, from Ronald Reagan's welfare queen to Trump's hostility to non-white immigrants.

The Wealth and Poverty of Nations
JANUARY 14, 2014

Poverty is America's greatest problem. We're not being attacked by any foreign powers. Our infrastructure, although aging, still works well. The national economy has rebounded from deep recession, and signs point to a continuing upward trend. We don't have a civil war as in Syria, Iraq and Libya, or a national war of criminals against society as in Mexico or Venezuela.

But we have too much poverty. According to a UNICEF report from 2012, we have the highest poverty rate among 35 economically advanced nations. Only Romania rivals the US in the percentage of children who live in poverty. About 23% of American children live in households whose income is less than half of the national median income. That's much higher than Greece or Italy or Spain, countries which have been suffering from serious economic problems. Nations we like to think of as comparably well-off, like Norway or Austria or Germany or France, have rates under 10%.

Poverty is relative. To be poor in countries like Zimbabwe, Afghanistan or Haiti, where the per capita gross domestic product is less than $1500 per year, means a totally different life from poverty in the US, with a per capita GDP 30 times that amount. Many poor Americans have cars, televisions and washing machines, which would be luxuries only the wealthy could afford in less developed nations.

But it is meaningless to tell an American family trying to survive on $10,000 a year that they would be rich in Vietnam. Poverty is really economic inequality. The poor anywhere are poor because their income is far below what average people in their own country make. So to say that we have a poverty problem in America is to say that we have too much economic inequality.

We have enormous wealth. One-third of the world's billionaires live here. Credit Suisse estimates that over 40% of the world's millionaires are Americans, and that number is now rising faster than anywhere else: 95% of the world's newest millionaires were created in the US in the past year. Yet we also have widespread poverty.

Poverty is structured differently across nations. In many countries, like Australia and France, most people defined as poor cluster just below the poverty line. But in the US most poor people are far below the poverty line. In most developed nations, the rate of child poverty is about the same as the overall poverty rate. But in the US, child poverty is much higher, indicating that households with children are much more likely to be in poverty.

The UNICEF report is discouraging for an American. On every measure of poverty, we rank far below other nations. On some measures we take last place among the 35 nations surveyed: the overall poverty rate; the poverty rate among families with one child or with a single parent; the poverty rate among high school graduates without a college education. The US has one of the developed world's highest poverty rates for unemployed households.

And that is about to get worse. Republicans in Congress have insisted that the government should stop giving benefits to the long-term unemployed. More conservative Republicans, like Rand Paul, do not support unemployment benefits beyond 26 weeks. That approach ignores the new reality of unemployment. Since 1969, at any time only about one-third of the unemployed had been out of work for more than 14 weeks. Since the recent deep recession, however, more than half have been out of work for more than 14 weeks, and about 40% for more than 26 weeks. Cutting off benefits to families who can't find work is cruel.

What makes a great nation? Perhaps we could compare nations to people. What makes a great person? Not being the strongest, although we give awards in competitions of strength. Not being the toughest, although boxing champions make millions of dollars. Not having the most money, although many people associate wealth with virtue.

Human greatness is about compassion, helpfulness, a willingness to serve others. The Christian Bible, often cited as the ultimate source of wisdom, offers a clear definition of greatness. In Matthew 20:26-27, Jesus said: "… whoever desires to be great among you, let him be your servant. And whoever desires to be first among you, let him be your slave."

If the United States is the greatest nation on Earth, as so many people claim, then why do we allow such misery to continue generation after generation? If the total number of billionaires made a country great, the US would be the undisputed world's champ. But if we look at how nations treat their poor, how they ensure that their children have enough to eat, how they help those who cannot find jobs, then we are among the world's chumps.

STEVE HOCHSTADT
Jacksonville IL

Economic inequality is the tissue connecting the twin 2020 upheavals, to reform structural racism and to survive the global pandemic. Poor Americans have a right to be angry with our government. But electing conservatives will ensure they stay that way.

How do we locate the connection between poor white support for Trump and his uniquely polarizing political speech? It is not simply true that poor whites support Trump. Among whites, the lower the income, the less likely is support for Trump. But within any income group, lack of college education translates into doubled support for Trump. Does that segment of Americans thrill at Trump's language? Maybe less educated Americans are the most unhappy about the new rules for speaking about others they consider unworthy and thus the most attracted to Trumpian rhetoric.

By modeling the ugliest behaviors and then labeling criticism of them as left-wing political acts, he has spawned a movement of imitators. A decent conversation across partisan lines is difficult. But it was not impossible in 2014.

Talking with Another American

FEBRUARY 11, 2014

I met Jim Watson at the grocery store. Watson served in the Illinois House of Representatives from my district for 11 years, 2001-2012. I don't think he'll mind if I describe our conversation.

He laughed when he told me that he didn't agree with most of what I write every week. Yet he and I are more alike than he might think, besides being two men food shopping on a Sunday morning. We agree that family is center of life, that we want to make life better in the place we live, and that we believe America can be a better nation. We disagree about exactly what better means and about what to do next.

Jim laughed even more when I asked him what he was doing now. He said I would hate his work: he is executive director of the Illinois Petroleum Council, which describes itself as representing "the institutional interests of Illinois' large integrated oil companies". His job is to maintain good relations with governments, in Springfield and in Washington, that is, to lobby. But he demonstrated the congruence of our interests by bringing up the pet-coke mountains which have recently spread black dust in Chicago neighborhoods. He thinks what I think — they need to be taken care of. That means his employers need to do something different.

I don't hate his work. I don't agree with Watson's public arguments that this is all just normal business. His job is protect the interests of and thus keep costs down for petcoke producers. But he recognizes the problems they cause. Exactly what to do and how soon are certainly more subjects Jim and I disagree on.

Jim Watson and I agreed on one fundamental idea: we could talk together. He takes seriously ideas that he doesn't share. I believe Jim implied that something I wrote stays with him and affects his thinking today. That's something every writer wants to hear, which is why I express some uncertainty. Maybe I was just dreaming.

But I wasn't dreaming about our interaction. It was friendly and open, accepting of our disagreements, and we eventually found a place where we could agree and shake hands warmly. There shouldn't be anything noteworthy about that, but in today's politics it is no longer the norm.

The new normal, at least for conservative Republicans, is to argue that liberals are hateful traitors, that our President is a foreign socialist Muslim, that a government in the hands of Democrats should be shut down.

Barack Obama is a middle-of-the-road Democrat. You can tell by the opposition to every one of his major policies from within the Democratic Party. The more liberal wing criticizes him for not having pushed a national health care system, for spying on Americans, for being too slow about gay rights. More conservative Democrats want him to reduce regulations and balance the budget. The Affordable Care Act is no more radical than Bill Clinton's proposals, and Clinton was most definitely a middle-of-the-road Democrat. Yet Obama has been treated to unprecedented vilification by leading Republicans, and especially by Tea Party members.

The uncompromising right wing does not attack only Democrats. Republicans like Jim Watson are reviled as Republicans In Name Only by the new angry conservatives. The raging Americans who have gathered under the banners of the Tea Party attack politicians more conservative than Jim Watson. Senators Mitch McConnell of Kentucky and Thad Cochran of Mississippi are being challenged by even more conservative Tea Party candidates, who criticize them for every inch they have budged from rigid obstructionism in Congress.

These self-identified real Republicans can't talk with anyone who doesn't totally agree with them. You can see in their media rants, in their online comments, in their books and articles how unable they are to have a normal conversation, to listen to people with whom they disagree, to learn anything more about anything. Nothing changes their angry minds.

Parties of anger are dangerous. We saw that in the 1960s, when angry white political establishments used government authority to justify violence against people and their political formations they hated.

There hung a lesson — the marchers and protesters and strikers were right. Segregation was wrong, discrimination was wrong, the Mississippi Sovereignty Commission, Governors Ross Barnett and George Wallace, Birmingham's police chief Bull Connor were all wrong. Their fury at those who wanted equal rights blinded them to human truths.

Today's angry Americans and the radical politicians they vote for are also wrong. Not because of their political principles, but because they won't listen to those with other ideas, won't accept facts they don't like, won't treat political opponents with respect. If they can't talk with the great majority of Americans who don't share their ideas, how could they possibly govern us, except with violence?

STEVE HOCHSTADT
Jacksonville IL

There is considerable resistance to the very concept of white skin privilege from people who want to think of their whiteness as normal, not privileged. But real American life demonstrates that it has been a most valuable privilege and continues to be one.

I wouldn't ask my students to believe on my say-so that white privilege is a historical fact. I asked them to consider that white privilege is a useful concept and to examine what real difference skin color made and makes. That's an enlightening exercise.

The Privilege of My Whiteness

FEBRUARY 25, 2014

My nephew just got married in Boston. The celebration was beautiful, and I especially liked hearing all his relatives, old and new, saying how much they appreciated our coming from "so fah away". You can hear a Bostonian a mile away.

I am a New Yorker. Everywhere I have lived in the United States, people nod their heads when I say I'm from New York. I don't say "New Yawk" or talk like Jerry Seinfeld and his friends, but I guess regional identities go much deeper than that.

I'm Jewish. That puts me in a distinct minority nearly everywhere I go, except in synagogue and at some of my friends' children's weddings. In this part of the rural Midwest, Jews are more noticeable than where I grew up, or even in Maine, where I have lived the longest.

But more than any of these characteristics, I am white. Before anyone I meet learns about my regional origins, religion, education, or personality, my white skin is apparent, even if I rarely think about it.

When I walk down a city street or into a store, when I stand in front of a class or an audience, when my photo appears next to my name online, I am obviously white. In America, that mainly means not black. We whites don't usually think about our whiteness, because it has been defined as the American norm. When Thomas Jefferson wrote, "All men are created equal," he meant white men. Two centuries later, as I was growing up, any deviation from whiteness was still exceptional in every position of authority, wealth, and status.

Whiteness was not just the American norm, it was an American privilege. White skin was a universal passport into businesses, restaurants, clubs, universities, and neighborhoods. Black skin was a handicap. Not only in the South, but in towns like Jacksonville all across the US, barriers were constructed to keep black skin out. Golf clubs and banks, college admissions departments and restaurant owners and real estate agents accorded white skin the privilege of respectful treatment and black skin the handicap of refusal.

Because whites were the great majority, most barely noticed that they enjoyed the privilege of decent human treatment. Blacks couldn't help but notice their handicap.

That contrast of privilege and handicap continues today. When Oprah was told by a Swiss sales clerk that she couldn't afford an expensive handbag, it made worldwide headlines, but more serious incidents happen every day to ordinary people of color. Earlier this year black Illinois College students were falsely accused of shoplifting by a clerk with color on her mind.

The so-called "stop and frisk" policy of the New York City Police Department, in which pedestrians were stopped by police officers only on the basis that they looked suspicious, was declared illegal by a federal judge last year, because of its racial implementation: of the nearly 700,000 people stopped in 2011, 84% were black or Latino. The NY Police Commissioner Raymond Kelly told state legislators that blacks and Latinos were purposely targeted "to instill fear in them" that they could be stopped by police any time they left their homes.

The dangers of driving while black are not exaggerated. The Kansas City police were three times more likely to stop a black driver for "investigation", not traffic safety, than a white driver, and five times more likely to search their car.

I have been thinking a lot about my whiteness lately. The Illinois College campus is suddenly much more diverse, because the first-year class is one-third minorities. There are African and African American students in my small class on political writing. My department is searching for a specialist in African American history, which has never been taught at IC before. There is no reason to believe that black people see these encounters with me in the same way I do.

The privilege of having white skin in America is that I will be treated as any person should be treated: with respect. I am not assumed to be deviant or dangerous, to be a criminal or a drug addict. That's a privilege that can easily be forgotten. It takes a trip to China to remind me what it is like to be considered weird just because of the way I look. Outside of a few cities like Shanghai or Beijing, white people are rare in China, and the Chinese have no social prohibitions on staring. It can be unnerving to have everyone you encounter on a busy street turn and stare, to have bicyclists crane their necks to look at you, to have drivers risk accidents to get a better view.

But that's still not enough to fully understand how blacks continue to be treated in America. The Chinese are not hostile, just curious. The police don't stop me. Nobody fears me because of my skin color.

My white skin is an unearned privilege, one which I hope eventually disappears.

STEVE HOCHSTADT
Jacksonville IL

Oprah's incident in Switzerland speaks to everyone who has been singled out as undesirable, essentialized as inferior. The targeting of some young people I knew based only on their visual identity tells me things about the society around me that I wish I didn't need to know.

"Stop and frisk" is back in the news, seven years after it was abandoned as normal policing in New York City. Michael Bloomberg spent billions of dollars in advertising to try to get beyond his lusty defense of "stop and frisk" as New York mayor. His very recent recognition that the policy was both wrong and racist didn't go far enough. "Stop and frisk" was one element in a theory of race with deep roots in the American past. An admission that Bloomberg and many others believed this theory and that it was racist would help to demolish that theory altogether. That's particularly important in 2020, as racist theories are resurfacing in presidential politics.

Compared to my childhood, there is so much more talk about racism now. We are more aware of the impacts on minorities of what was normal white behavior. We talk far more with our children about racial issues than my parents did. I wondered why, but never asked. And then the opportunity disappeared.

As they aged, my parents' world got smaller, something that happens to us all at the end of our lives. The din of politics, seemingly so noisy, faded as their hearing and their interests diminished. Eventually all that mattered were the same basic functions that interest a baby — food, warmth, comfort.

The inevitability of shrinking consciousness doesn't make it any easier for anyone.

My Mother's Choices
MARCH 18, 2014

My mother usually reads these columns. The newspaper is delivered to her room at Jacksonville Skilled Nursing. She doesn't comment on my work, but I think she's proud of her son, the writer.

She won't be reading this column. After two years of ups and downs at the nursing home, I think she's finally dying. I say finally, because she told me long ago that she had had enough. Life held only the faintest of joys to balance her deep miseries: loss of memory, feelings of constant confusion, lack of ability to help herself. Then came incontinence and its attendant shame. Next her food had to be ground up.

Lately she is not interested in eating or drinking. She stays in bed with her eyes shut, sleeping most of the day. Nothing left to live for.

If she could take a pill and pass away, would she? I don't know and won't ask. Probably not, because she has always let others make the big decisions for her. So she's waiting for natural processes to run their course.

But other people face much more difficult circumstances at the end of their lives. Some are in constant pain. Some know they will die very soon from incurable diseases. How much control should they be allowed to have over their own lives and deaths?

Christianity, Judaism and Islam all frown on suicide, but religious authorities have shifted their positions on whether it is prohibited. For example, the Catholic Church labels suicide as a sin. The Catechism of the Catholic Church says: "We are stewards, not owners, of the life God has entrusted to us. It is not ours to dispose of." Further, "Voluntary co-operation in suicide is contrary to the moral law." But Catholic views on suicide have changed: a funeral mass and burial are now allowed for suicides, and whether they must go to hell is left uncertain.

None of these religions accept suicide as a rational means of avoiding suffering at the end of life. Those religious prohibitions have until very recently determined laws about the possible role of physicians in helping patients end their lives. Just as the Catholic Church has shifted its position, so have lawmakers. Some European nations, like Switzerland, now allow assisted suicide. In 2011, 84% of voters in Zurich rejected a ban on assisted suicide.

Dr. Jack Kevorkian brought the issue of physician-assisted suicide to national attention in the 1990s. He helped 40 people in Michigan commit suicide. That prompted several ballot initiatives to allow this practice in other states. Such a vote narrowly failed in California in 1992, then barely passed in Oregon in 1994. A second vote in 1997 was not close, as Oregon voters confirmed the right to choose death. In the state of Washington, a ballot measure failed in 1991, but passed easily in 2008. Other states have recently had mixed outcomes. A ballot initiative was narrowly rejected in Massachusetts in 2012, while the Vermont legislature passed a law allowing patients to administer life-ending drugs to themselves.

Suicide, assisted or not, is an extreme response to a hopeless medical condition. Much more common is the attempt to ensure that a dying person can have a "natural death", meaning not being subjected to heroic medical measures to prolong life. The commonly used phrase is "do not resuscitate" (DNR). That is a medical order by a physician which excludes CPR or a tracheal tube in case a person's heart stops or they stop breathing. Because the phrase implies that a procedure will be withheld, the words "allow natural death" (AND) are becoming more popular.

Patients do not create DNR's, doctors do. A person may create an advance health care directive, sometimes called a living will, which specifies how they would like to be treated in a health crisis. Their purpose is to avoid situations where aggressive medical efforts to prolong life produce unwanted results. People who are kept alive through feeding tubes or, worse, in a vegetative state, generally would not have wished to survive that way. These medical practices are enormously expensive: families can lose their entire savings, even if they have insurance, keeping someone alive when they no longer want to live.

Yet it is difficult to write out a directive that adequately covers most likely medical situations. Living wills have become more complex to offer specific guidance to both family members and medical professionals.

What does this have to do with my mother, or with yours? I want my mother to have the best possible life. That doesn't just mean a minimum of suffering, but also as much control as possible over the biggest decisions about life and death. But how do I know exactly what she wants? Will my feeling about what is right for her be colored by what I imagine I would want if I were near the end of my life?

I have no answers. Even thinking about these questions is painfully guilt-inducing.

I think my mother has made her choice. But what should I do? Prevent the nursing staff from feeding her? Encourage her to drink water, which will prolong her life, possibly by weeks?

What is right? I don't know.

STEVE HOCHSTADT
Jacksonville IL

My mother's life had been active, but she enjoyed quiet hours with a book. When she could no longer get out of bed and couldn't understand the printed pages, her life had ended. Her body took some months to catch up. Those months were hard for everyone.

We decided to let her be. She had no interest in food or anything else in the world around her. I spent quiet hours with her every day. She died peacefully. She and my father had made arrangements for cremation long ago. The local funeral home was kind and efficient. We sat in the small room next to the oven — they had to bring in chairs.

I have a long interview with her on tape, so her grandchildren can grasp her life more clearly, and her great-grandchildren can hear her voice.

I was quietly influenced by my mother, who ran a small business, wore pants, played pool, and could throw a baseball. I am grateful that I was old enough in the late 1960s and early 1970s to grasp the significance for society and for me of the feminist and civil rights movements. In my youthful optimism, I would never have guessed that 50 years later, the battles still needed to be fought.

My mother was the first flower gardener I knew. Her ambitions were modest, but always colorful. As she passed away, flowers appeared in my garden. Life is finite, but constantly renews itself. Spring can be so beautiful that it overpowers the bad news about politics and government. Concepts that irritate, like hypocrisy, cold-heartedness, dishonesty, have no place in the garden. A perennial garden is nature at her most creative and colorful. Seemingly by magic, green shoots push out of dark soil, buds swell on woody branches, and soon flowers appear, so desirable that every society uses them as gifts.

Spring engenders optimism that the impossible can be achieved, hence all the revolutionary springs, from 1775 in Massachusetts to the Arab Spring in 2011. Gardening is not a revolutionary activity, but it is nourished by the same hopefulness for warmer days to come.

Springtime in the Garden
MAY 6, 2014

For a gardener, spring is the most exciting season. One day, what looked dead shows signs of life. As long as humans have understood the natural world, spring has meant rebirth. Easter, the celebration of resurrection, and Passover, the re-creation of liberation, have their origins even further back in human social development, as do Holi, the Hindu festival of colors, and Nowruz, the first day of the year in ancient Persia. Human nature celebrates nature itself.

Springtime means cleaning. Things pile up during winter, inside and outside the house: leaves, boxes, twigs and branches, dust, mud. When the house is finally opened to the air, when warmth opens dormant plants, the big mess that winter leaves becomes apparent. Once the ground thaws, the most pressing garden work is spring cleaning. One garden after another gets a face lift, a hard scrubbing, a close shave. Removing all that wrinkly brown dead stuff reveals what has already begun. Smooth bright green sprouts are pushing through to the light.

Springtime means repair. Winter is harder on material objects than on the resilience of people. Although we may come back in the spring with more weight and a painful back, the warmth and movement of spring allow our bodies to repair themselves. The roof can't repair itself. Garden objects that stand up during the winter take a beating and need our help. This winter a small pergola that we acquired with our house many years ago finally listed too far to ignore. Broken branches on our biggest tree, a sugar maple that has never been tapped, needed pruning. Stones and bricks that mark our gardens mysteriously twist and glide a bit each winter, until they no longer look the way we want. By repairing winter damage, we impose our constructive will on the forces of nature.

Springtime means anticipation. The shoot poking through the soil and the bud swelling on the branch mean flowers will soon appear. Eight months after we first moved in, our inaugural spring displayed the gardening dreams of past owners. Pointy sprouts became daffodils, the carpet of bright green shoots grew into lilies, while magnolias, viburnum and dogwood blossomed. Since then, I have added a dozen flowering trees and spread bulbs across many gardens. Now, well before flowers open, I relish the anticipation of their color and smell. I know they will be lovely, but exactly when will it happen? Although we've seen it all before, the final opening of protective leaves, unveiling flowers of many shapes and sizes, is always new and renewing.

Springtime means hope. Will there be more blossoms than last year? Will life get better? Unexpected blooms and unforeseen popular movements erupt in spring. The gathering of armed rebels in Lexington and Concord in 1775, the meeting of the Estates General in Paris in 1789, and the liberalization of communism in Prague in 1968 were encouraged by the hopes of spring.

By the time spring ends, many of these hopes have disappeared. The sweet spring flowers have dropped onto the garden, leaving dead heads that call for more work. The ubiquitous garden undesirables threaten to drown their weaker neighbors that we insist are the real plants. Many of winter's messes are still all around; humans have not repaired all the things we have broken.

We keep trying. Nature and human nature cannot be reduced to our arbitrary rules of good behavior and proper breeding. When we try too hard for perfection, we make the worst mistakes: the 19th-century passion for perfecting human society became sterilization, mass deportations and genocide in the 20th. But still we must seek improvement.

Gardening takes patience. Planting some seedlings this year won't make a garden next year or the year after. A clear vision of the future must be combined with the patience to keep tending immature plants. Even more patience is needed to nurture the immature children, the immature organizations and programs and systems we create. Not every plant will survive, nor look right if it does. Not every political reform will produce the desired results. Gardening and politics require constant correction.

Maybe we can do more than produce good gardens. Maybe we can produce better societies, if we keep trying.

Spring always comes back. We get another chance.

STEVE HOCHSTADT
Jacksonville IL

Science often remains invisible behind the technology it invents. The magical procedures of medicine were developed through years of research, hypothesizing, testing, arguing, and around again. The science of today stands on the shoulders of the sciences of yesterday, each new certainty spawning new questions and possibilities. Doctors trained to put science in the service of human health have saved my vision more than once. It's hard for me to imagine a greater gift than sight.

Blindness and Science

JUNE 24, 2014

I almost went blind. Vision in my left eye started clouding about two months ago. After waiting too long, I went to my eye doctor. Dr. David Sutton diagnosed a partially detached retina, and the next day Dr. Lanny Odin in Springfield operated. Now I'm almost back to normal vision.

The retina coats the back of the eye, changing light into electrical signals sent by the optic nerve to our brain, which forms pictures of reality. With age and chronic near-sightedness, the liquid that fills the eye can begin to dry up, peeling the retina away from the eyeball. It looks like a dark curtain covers the field of vision. When it all peels off, the eye is blind.

Until the 1960s we could do nothing about that. As more people lived beyond age 65, millions went blind in one eye, some in two. By the 1970s doctors had developed a remarkable procedure that fixes the retina and saves vision. Here is what WebMD says about the vitrectomy: "the surgeon inserts small instruments into the eye, cuts the vitreous gel, and suctions it out. After removing the vitreous gel, the surgeon may treat the retina with a laser (photocoagulation), cut or remove fibrous or scar tissue from the retina, flatten areas where the retina has become detached, or repair tears or holes in the retina."

Poking around in my eye for an hour, Dr. Odin reattached my retina with lasers. He also injected a bubble of gas. I had to look down all day for 10 days, keeping the bubble floating at the back of the eye, so it would properly press the retina in place. Now the bubble has been absorbed and I can see again.

The day before, when he first examined my eye, Dr. Odin offered me a choice. I could let him perform a vitrectomy as described above. Or I could go blind in that eye. He offered no guarantees. His diagnostic belief that he could fix it might be wrong. Although operations are very safe, they still are not completely predictable.

I didn't understand half of what Dr. Odin proposed. I remembered the models of the eye in my optometrist's office, incredibly complex organs depending on a series of biological, electrical and physical processes to allow me to see the world. How could someone poke around in there and restore my vision?

In our daily lives, we often must rely on the advice of experts. From doctors to electricians, insurance agents to plumbers, we need help to understand our complex bodies and a complex world. The experts, Drs. Odin and Sutton, were in agreement about my eye — I had a detached retina and it needed to be fixed right away, or it might peel right off. Their consensus would cost me money and cause me inconvenience, a lot of both. I would have been a fool to ignore these scientific opinions.

Yet that is exactly what millions of American voters are doing when they vote for Republicans who ignore the expertise of the world's climate scientists. You can get a second, third, or hundredth opinion about whether we need to do something now to prevent future environmental disasters, and they would all agree. Our National Climactic Data Center offers a variety of evidence about air temperature, ocean temperature, rising sea levels and glacier shrinkage. The warming of the Alaskan Arctic threatens a way of life dependent on fishing, hunting, and ice. Our National Academy of Science and the British Royal Society have produced a booklet which answers basic questions about climate change In May, Miami Beach Mayor Philip Levine said, "We are past the point of debating climate change."

But we're not. Why do people in responsible political positions assert that the experts are all wrong? Why do so many Americans say the same thing, more than in other industrialized countries? Why are those voters and politicians who don't believe in the need to deal with climate change so overwhelmingly Republican?

I think the answer is fear. I was afraid when my doctors talked about cutting into my eye. I once fainted when an eye doctor described how a cataract operation was done. If I had given in to the fear, I could have created lots of rational-sounding explanations for why I was ignoring the experts. I might have searched until I found someone who might be labeled an expert who would say I didn't need an operation. But I would have been a fool.

Conservatives are afraid that if they admit that global warming is happening and that we can do something about it, that would mean more public spending, more public regulations, the American public operating through our government to save the future of our society. That is correct, unless they can develop workable non-governmental methods to accomplish the same goals. They don't think they can, so they close their eyes and repeat "la-la-la-la" as loud as they can.

I'm happy I didn't go blind. Why are they embracing blindness?

STEVE HOCHSTADT
Jacksonville IL

A glance around the small world of opinion columnists reveals that most columns are critical of something the other side does or says or maybe believes. That's because it is much harder to come up with positive proposals more specific than "be less partisan", "seek compromise", or "reach across the aisle". Tea Party conservatives and their descendants, most vocally Trump, don't even agree with those bromides.

Hence we do not have a useful discussion about even the most obvious and significant issues, like taxes. I offered some positive steps here to improve our tax system. The essay is still useful, because six years later, none of these things have happened.

Let's Cut Our Taxes

JULY 15, 2014

Many Americans would like to pay less in taxes. That desire is a major motivating force behind the Tea Party revolt at the right end of the political spectrum. I'm sure many liberals would also like to have their tax burden reduced. In the interest of bringing these two sides of our partisan political debates closer together, I propose that everybody get behind the following three ways to reduce the tax burdens of most Americans.

1. Do a better job of collecting the taxes that Americans owe. Every year about $385 billion in tax revenues are not paid. During fiscal year 2013, the US government collected $2.77 trillion in tax revenues, meaning that about 12% of what should have been collected wasn't. Those uncollected taxes would considerably reduce the budget deficit and the resulting federal debt.

Who doesn't pay their taxes? Most Americans would be easily caught if we cheated: our income is reported by employers on W-2's. Joe Antenucci, professor of accounting and finance at Youngstown State University, offers this profile of the typical tax cheat: "male, under age 50 in a high tax bracket with a complex return." The most common method of cheating is to overstate church donations. But the most profitable methods involve hiding big incomes illegally. This year, Swiss bank Credit Suisse pleaded guilty to helping wealthy Americans hide billions of dollars from US tax collectors in foreign bank accounts, and will pay $2.6 billion in fines. These methods are open only to the wealthiest Americans.

How can we stop such cheating, increase legal tax collections, and reduce the burden on the rest of us? Not by decreasing the enforcement budget of the IRS. Cuts in the IRS budget demanded by Congressional Republicans have reduced its staff by about 8000 people over the past four years, and thus reduced its ability to catch cheaters. As the IRS budget has dropped, so have the number of audits. I have read many different estimates of how much new revenue each additional dollar invested in IRS enforcement brings, ranging from $4 to $10. But it's clear that increasing the IRS enforcement budget decreases the deficit and thus could contribute to lowering our tax rates.

2. Reduce some tax loopholes. There is always discussion about "tax loopholes", legal ways that people avoid paying taxes. Congressional Republicans have recently talked about ending the loophole that allows homeowners to deduct mortgage interest. That would significantly increase the taxes paid by most middle-class Americans. But they haven't talked about ending some amazing loopholes that benefit only the very wealthy. For example, in 1993 Congress passed legislation designed to prevent corporations from deducting giant salaries for their executives as expenses. But a loophole in the law exempted so-called "performance pay", including stock options. Over the past 6 years, Walmart has claimed a deduction for $298 million in "performance pay" for its eight top executives, reducing its tax burden by $104 million. Multiply that by all the giant corporations that employ this loophole, and the result is a lot of money that must be made up by the rest of us.

Here's another loophole. The biggest American pharmacy chain, Walgreens, is considering becoming the biggest Swiss pharmacy. If Walgreens, currently located in Illinois, reincorporates in Switzerland, its tax rate would be considerably reduced. In 2012, Illinois gave Walgreens $46 million in corporate income tax credits in exchange for a pledge to stay here for 10 years. Walgreens may not make the jump, but many other big US corporations have "moved" to tax havens like Switzerland and Ireland. Profits from American consumers end up as taxes elsewhere.

3. Make all income equal. Unlike the great majority of ordinary taxpayers, people whose income consists mainly of capital gains pay a much lower tax rate. Capital gains are taxed at 15%, or 20% for those who make above $400,000, while their rate for other income is 39.6%. In 2011 it was

reported that billionaire Warren Buffett paid the lowest tax rate of anyone in his office, including his receptionist. Nearly all of the capital gains tax benefit goes to people with annual incomes over $1 million. Here's the result: in 2007, the richest 400 households by income, who each made over $340 million that year, paid the same tax rate as those earning $50,000 to $75,000. The annual cost in tax revenues is about $40 billion.

We could have the same governmental services that we have now and pay less taxes if just these three changes were implemented. Or we could have somewhat more services (like better roads), and still pay less. We might feel better, too, because all Americans would be treated more equally.

What's in the way? Each of these changes would benefit only 90% or 95% or 99% of Americans. The extra revenue from catching tax cheaters, closing those loopholes, and treating all income equally would mostly come from the richest 1%. They are a tiny minority, but they have the greatest influence. Their fellow millionaires in the Senate and the House are easily persuaded by the trickle-down economic theories which defend these tax breaks. Their personal connections to Congress through big donations and lobbying groups magnify their voices. That's not going to change unless the rest of us speak louder.

STEVE HOCHSTADT
Jacksonville IL

The Republican tax cutters in 2017 did not listen to my suggestions. Some kinds of income especially enjoyed by rich people are still better than the kind most people get in a paycheck. While the presidential campaign slogans of Richard Lugar in 1996 and Ted Cruz in 2016 to abolish the IRS have not been realized, the decades of Republican attacks on the IRS have severely weakened the ability of government auditors to catch tax cheats and evaders. "Strengthen the IRS" is hardly a catchy slogan, but the increased revenues that stronger enforcement bring in would benefit us all, except for the cheaters.

Laws matter and so does enforcement. Look at a society's laws and how they are implemented and you see into that society's soul. One of the less noticeable, but most revealing aspects of "stop and frisk", and the "war on drugs" that preceded and informed it, was its contrast to the permissive governmental attitude toward white-collar tax cheating, an overwhelmingly white crime.

I don't like tax cheaters, who imagine they are only cheating "government", but are actually cheating all of us. I try to write as if I didn't matter, but I know that my personal values constantly inform my political opinions. Like any scientist pursuing some truth about reality, I don't really know how objective I am or how much my identity affects my results.

I know it does. And I know that who I am affects how you, one reader among all the readers I write for, will react to my messages. Here is a column where my own experiences matter. Even something as universally applauded as fatherhood can mean contradictory things to different people. So I'll just offer my version of fatherhood without any prescription, except that it works for my family.

Father of the Bride

AUGUST 12, 2014

My daughter Mae got married this weekend. That gave me a special status as father of the bride. But exactly what that means is not so clear.

The 1991 comedy "Father of the Bride" starring Steve Martin, and its predecessor from 1950 starring Spencer Tracy, portrayed these men as foolish protectors of their adult daughters, only slowly reconciled to losing them to their future sons-in-law. That wasn't an attractive model for me, but it was based on widely accepted ideas.

For centuries fathers have given away their daughters to new husbands. That ritual reflected the idea that women were not independent beings, but for their whole lives dependent upon men. Marriage represented a moment of transition, when a father handed over responsibility for his daughter to her husband.

This transfer of responsibility for a woman was also symbolized by changing her name from her father's to her husband's. The question of whether women should change their names at marriage became controversial in the 1970s, when many women influenced by the feminist movement decided to keep their names.

It's hard to find out how frequently women have kept their names since then: you can read quite different percentages from different studies. An academic paper says around one in five over the past couple of decades, with a slight decrease since 2000, while a Facebook study estimates about one third. When women talk about making that decision, they often describe the social pressure to change their names. The phrase we use to label a women's birth name reveals the ancient thinking behind this tradition: the words "maiden name" imply women's virginal state before marriage.

Mae is 30 years old, and didn't need or want anyone to give her away. She and Ben had developed pretty definite ideas about how their wedding should be celebrated. They wanted to get married in the woods of northern Wisconsin, to eat homemade foods, to have wedding pies instead of a cake, to dance to a musical playlist they put together. They wanted every element of the ceremony to display the equality of their relationship. They wanted fun rather than formality.

The weekend was a family event. Not only did third cousins and third cousins of third cousins come from all over to celebrate their wedding, but they also baked and cooked and set up and cleaned up. Their friends created silly games to play outdoors on the wedding afternoon. In fact, weddings are two-family events, when groups of people, who may have never met, find themselves joined together by matrimony. Members of both families pitched in, inspired by this do-it-yourself approach and joyous for their opportunities to participate.

Words of love and wisdom

My role as father of the bride, of course in tandem with my wife, was to facilitate those plans: arrange the food they wanted to eat; rent the tents they wanted so guests could eat outside; buy paper plates and plastic spoons and vinyl tablecloths; procure a generator to run lights and sound system on the lakeshore; and write a few checks.

Of course, that's not enough. The father of the bride is expected to address the wedding party and the guests with words of love and wisdom. There are countless websites offering advice to fathers on how to give a wedding speech. They are strong on well-phrased platitudes, and thus not very useful, except to display the many themes that a father could express.

Generic phrases were not able to express my feelings about this wonderful milestone in Mae's and Ben's life. Ultimately, my status as father of the bride depended for its meaning on my daughter. For her, as for me, following traditions is less important than making her own decisions about the role she wanted me to play. Being father of the bride is nothing more than continuing to be a father. That role doesn't end with a wedding. Nobody is lost or given away. Strong women don't need protection. I was delighted to support her thoughtful choices, to welcome a new set of relatives, to carry on being a father, a man's most joyous role.

STEVE HOCHSTADT
Springbrook WI

Republicans have not had much success finding inspiring people to showcase their ideas. Cliven Bundy was a bust. The earlier "average guy" Republican, Joe the Plumber Wurzelbacher, famous in 2008, didn't turn out so well either, later blaming both the Holocaust and the Armenian genocide on gun control legislation. But Republicans kept picking men who hated something as their spokesmen. In May 2014, Phil Robertson was the featured invited speaker at the Republican Leadership Conference. Most Americans knew his name because he plays a character on a reality show about hunting, "Duck Dynasty", the highest rated reality show on cable. He is rich now from decades of devotion to his duck call business, the extraordinary success of his TV show, and big paydays as a speaker.

Robertson's uncompromising hostility toward homosexuals, based on his devotion to a particular form of Christianity, recommended him to the Republican leadership. Since he has never hidden his views, they must have known of his belief about the ideal female partner: "Make sure that she can cook a meal.…Look, you wait 'til they get to be 20 years old, the only picking that's going to take place is your pocket. You got to marry these girls when they are about 15 or 16." Although few Republican politicians would offer that advice, they are more likely to promote Robertson's views on race, which fit nicely into the imaginary color-blind world of conservatism. So it's useful to check whether Robertson knew what he was talking about.

No One Was Singing the Blues

AUGUST 31, 2014

What do conservatives think about race in America? Phil Robertson, the new conservative hero, offered an argument about the history of race relations that is popular with conservatives: "I never, with my eyes, saw the mistreatment of any black person. Not once. Where we lived was all farmers. The blacks worked for the farmers. I hoed cotton with them. I'm with the blacks, because we're white trash....They're singing and happy. I never heard one of them, one black person, say, 'I tell you what: These doggone white people.' Not a word!...Pre-entitlement, pre-welfare, you say, 'Were they happy?' They were godly, they were happy, no one was singing the blues."

Robertson justified this version of race relations in Louisiana before the civil rights era by saying, "I'm with the blacks." But he wasn't with any blacks in school, because all the public schools in Louisiana were segregated long after the 1954 Supreme Court decision about Topeka, Kansas. In November 1960, when the first blacks were admitted to school in New Orleans, whites in Caddo Parish, where he grew up, burned crosses at the all-black high school and at the Parish School Board Office. Robertson was 14 years old. The first blacks were admitted to public schools in Caddo Parish in 1965, after he had graduated. School officials there kept delaying integration through the 1970s. So of course, he had no black teammates at his high school, where he was all-state in football, baseball, and track.

Robertson met no black people at any sporting or social event, due to the 1956 state law banning "dancing, social functions, entertainments, athletic training, games, sports or contests and other such activities involving personal and social contacts in which the participants or contestants are members of the white and Negro races."

When he went to Louisiana Tech in 1965, there were no black students. That year a federal judge ruled that Louisiana Tech finally had to admit African Americans. A photo of the football team where he played ahead of Terry Bradshaw shows no black players. Across the state at Louisiana State University, the segregation laws had made national news in 1956, when the University of Wisconsin's football team had rejected an LSU demand to leave their two black players home, and LSU then refused to play. LSU had no black players until 1971.

Louisiana had a long and violent history of racism. At least 27 African Americans were lynched in Caddo Parish alone between 1878 and 1923, more than one every other year. Perhaps the last black man lynched in Louisiana was R.C. Williams in 1938 in Ruston, home of Louisiana Tech.

Charles Blow of the NY Times said this about Robertson's claims about race: "Only a man blind and naive to the suffering of others could have existed there and not recognized that there was a rampant culture of violence against blacks. Whether he personally saw mistreatment of them is irrelevant."

Robertson's casual dismissal of racism in the Deep South fits well with conservative Republican mythology. His Governor, Bobby Jindal, calls himself one of Robertson's "loudest and earliest defenders". He said, "I'm tired of the Left, I'm tired of those that say they are for tolerance, they're for diversity, and they are, unless you happen to disagree with them. The Left wants to silence anyone who has a different view or a different perspective." Earlier this month, Representative Mo Brooks from Alabama said, "What is the one race that can be discriminated against? All whites." That echoes conservative Pat Buchanan's comment from a year ago.

Why are conservative Republican politicians blind to the history of American racism? Why do they make absurd claims about how good things were for blacks in the Jim Crow era? One reason is the widespread self-pity among conservative whites. A study in 2011 showed that whites believed that anti-white discrimination was stronger than anti-black discrimination.

White conservatives fear that diversity brings discrimination against them: in a recent poll, nearly two-thirds of white conservatives said that "discrimination against whites will increase due to rising diversity." A majority of white conservatives believes that "high levels of racial and ethnic inequality are a natural outcome of the economy." Thus they oppose "new steps to reduce racial and ethnic inequality in America through investments in areas like education, job training, and infrastructure improvement." Observing the events in Ferguson, Missouri, 61% of Republicans believe race has been getting too much attention.

In April, Rand Paul told students at Howard University that "the Republican Party has always been the party of civil rights and voting rights." Reince Priebus lamented at the Republican Leadership Conference that the party of Lincoln doesn't get enough credit: "We're the party of freedom and we're the party of opportunity and we're the party of equality, we're the ones with that history." Yes, once upon a time the Republican Party was the party of freedom for African Americans. But as long as conservative Republicans celebrate deniers of our racial history like Phil Robertson, nobody will believe that.

STEVE HOCHSTADT
Jacksonville IL

Phil Robertson doesn't surprise me. His views about race and gender and the Bible were common, even the norm, not very long ago. They have worked for him and he has led a successful life.

What is significant for every American is the Republican Party's continued promulgation of his views. Whether they believe them or not, their promotion of his color-blind racial narrative empowers those who don't believe in the goal of equality and do everything they can to impede it. The choice to deny racism is the choice to prolong it.

Do you believe that Phil Robertson is a useful authority about race? Whom do you believe? That's often an unexamined choice we make. Do you believe the state lottery officials who pretend you have a good chance of winning big bucks? Do you believe the "Nigerian businessman" who wants your help to bring $20 million to a bank in the US? Do you believe the news brought to you by the "mainstream media", or the dark theories of people like Alex Jones and Rush Limbaugh and Sean Hannity, which are constantly disproven, but never apologized for?

More pertinent perhaps is the prior question — how do you decide whom to believe? The internet makes it all too easy to propagate stupid theories, false facts, twisted narratives, and malicious accusations. I applaud the legal decisions that will make Alex Jones pay for his vile inventions. But shutting down Infowars will not solve the problem he exploited for fun and profit — too many people choose to believe what interferes least with their psychological comfort.

The Global Warming Hoax
OCTOBER 21, 2014

The history of scientific hoaxes is often amusing. In 1813, Charles Redhoffer created a "perpetual motion machine", a device that created more energy than it used. After hundreds of people paid a dollar to see it spinning around, Robert Fulton, inventor of the steamboat, grew suspicious of its uneven motion. When pieces of wood were removed from the wall behind the machine, a belt drive made of cat-gut was revealed, leading to an upper floor, where an old man was turning a crank with one hand and eating bread with the other.

In 1869, well diggers on William Newell's farm in Cardiff, New York, found an enormous petrified man, 10 feet long. Newell set up a tent over the "Cardiff Giant" and charged 25 cents to see it. People came in droves. P.T. Barnum offered to buy it for his traveling show for $50,000, but the owners refused, so Barnum secretly had a copy made and displayed it as the original, claiming that the other was a fraud. David Hannum, a member of the syndicate which was making money on the original, remarked, "There's a sucker born every minute."

The Cardiff Giant was actually a piece of carved and treated gypsum, created by the atheist George Hull, who wanted to embarrass a local minister who had quoted Genesis to prove that giants once walked the Earth. Hull confessed his hoax two months after the "discovery".

In 1912, a British amateur archaeologist claimed he had pieces of a skull belonging to an evolutionary link between apes and humans. Named "Piltdown man" after the gravel pit where these pieces were supposedly unearthed, most of the scientific community believed the find to be genuine. Only gradually were doubts expressed, until it was proved in the 1950s that the pieces were a human skull, an orangutan's jawbone, and fossilized chimpanzee teeth. By then it was too late to identify the hoaxers.

These hoaxes share some common traits. An unexpected "discovery" is accompanied by a plausible story about how it happened. The hoaxer has answers to initial objections, but eventually enough questions are raised by experts about the story's details that it falls apart. The hoax can fool the public, but not the experts.

Hoaxers thrive when political ideology influences science. Joseph Stalin hated the Western science of genetics. When the biologist Trofim Lysenko denied the importance of genes and claimed that acquired characteristics could be inherited, and that he could thus create strains of wheat which could withstand Russian winters, Stalin gave him the power to dominate Soviet biology. Lysenko purged anyone who did not agree with him and set Soviet scientific research back for decades.

So we come to the big scientific hoax of our time, the "global warming hoax". Put those words into a Google search, and you will find the major organizations which claim that there is no human-caused global warming.

In 2003, Nebraska Senator Jim Inhofe said before Congress that "man-made global warming is the greatest hoax ever perpetrated on the American people," and he has not altered that position. The politically correct view for any Republican running for national office is to agree with Inhofe.

It is a fact that every national science academy across the globe has endorsed the idea of global warming. Studies of thousands of scientific papers have shown that over 95% argue in favor of global warming.

So if there is a global warming hoax, it is being perpetrated by virtually all the world's scientists and governments. The following organizations must also be in on the hoax: the American Medical Association, American Academy of Pediatrics, the Presbyterian Church, National Geographic, Nature Conservancy, the insurance industry, Sierra Club, National Wildlife Federation, National Audubon Society, League of Conservation Voters, and too many others to name.

This would be the greatest hoax ever, because unlike every other hoax, it is being committed by all the world's experts, which is precisely what the global warming deniers are claiming. It is hardly coincidence that those who claim that global warming is a hoax, all have a significant financial or political stake in preventing any action against global warming. Behind the newspaper articles, the radio broadcasts, the tiny number of paid-off scientists, and the politicians are the major oil companies like ExxonMobil, the coal industry, Koch Industries, but also a much larger sector of "dark money" funneled through untraceable pass-through organizations.

The "independent" organizations which deny global warming, like the Heartland Institute, get their funding from these sources and from conservative political PACs. Before the Heartland Institute attacked the science behind global warming, it attacked scientists who said smoking causes cancer.

The political result is that the global warming hoax idea is believed by conservatives. In 2012, 71% of "very conservative" respondents, 52% of "somewhat conservative" but only 13% of liberals believed global warming was a hoax. As Bruce Sterling wrote at Wired online, "Wherever moral panic, hasty judgment, fear, brutal partisan ignorance, and spin-centric travesties of disinformation can flourish, Lysenko's spirit will never die."

Who believes politicians paid by ExxonMobil instead of scientists, doctors, and conservationists? Gullible people who want to believe. That's what makes hoaxes work.

STEVE HOCHSTADT
Jacksonville IL

Joseph Bast, head of the Heartland Institute, wrote to my newspaper on October 27 that my above article on the global warming hoax was "false" and "defamatory". I do acknowledge an error: Heartland is not funded by "conservative PACs", but by conservative foundations and other conservative organizations.

Heartland got its start arguing that smoking tobacco was not unhealthy, pushing seemingly earnest and detailed arguments that mimicked science writing. Long after the tobacco industry, Heartland's funders, admitted to itself that smoking caused cancer, Heartland's writers pushed their made-up "science". The purpose was delay, not persuasion. It was obvious that the truth about smoking would eventually knock through the wall of lies that those global economic giants had constructed around their profits. But postponing that reckoning was worth billions.

Now Bast's Heartland Institute has perfected the art of climate disinformation. It's worth examining that art in detail.

Bast wrote: "Tens of thousands of scientists who have studied the climate change issue believe the human impact is small and the likely effects not harmful. More than 31,000 of them signed a petition to that effect." Not true. In 1998, Arthur Robinson sent out a petition urging rejection of the Kyoto climate agreement, and rejection of the idea that human-caused global warming would lead to "catastrophic heating" of the atmosphere. Anyone could sign and list their degrees. There are 31,000 signatures, as Bast wrote, exchanging "not harmful" for not "catastrophic". Among the signers were characters from "Star Wars", Charles Darwin, duplicate entries, and corporate names. Even Bast's own publications list only 9000 as having PhDs. Of those, very few were in climate science. *Scientific American* tried to verify those people, and found that some did not agree with the petition and some did not remember signing. *Scientific American* estimated that the petition was signed by "about 200 climate researchers". What Bast says about the petition is a lie that is still promoted on their website.

Bast says that my claim that 95% of scientific papers argue in favor of global warming "has been repeatedly debunked". Who did this debunking? On Heartland's website, Bast's article "Global Warming: Not a Crisis" cites a study by Benny Peiser, who claimed to find 34 papers which "reject or cast doubt on the view that human activity has been the main driver of warming over the past 50 years". But when challenged, Peiser couldn't show that such papers existed. He retracted his claims and wrote the following email to Media Watch: "I do not think anyone is questioning that we are in a period of global warming. Neither do I doubt that the overwhelming majority of climatologists is agreed that the current warming period is mostly due to human impact." Peiser wrote this in 2006! That was long before Bast cited Peiser as the guy who proves there is no consensus.

Heartland's website displays their visual trump card, a graph entitled "No global warming for 18 years 1 month". This graph is based on data that NASA scientists use to show that 2005 and 2010 were the planet's warmest years since data have been collected, and that of the 13 warmest years since 1880, 11 were from 2001 to 2011. But you can't see that, because of the misleading way the data is displayed by Heartland. Most newspapers in the US published articles about how 2014 would probably be the warmest year ever, and every year since then has been hotter.

Bast and his funders want people to believe that science is political, that scientists "benefit financially from the global warming hoax by using it to justify government funding." He argues that all science is dishonest: during a FOX interview, Bast said that "peer-review has been corrupted, and we can't trust what appears in our most prestigious journals anymore." The world's scientists and scientific organizations and journals are engaged in a giant conspiracy. Instead we should trust him.

Heartland is paid to create a scientific hoax, an exhibit that can fool unwary onlookers. That hoax is designed to provide talking points to Republican politicians, when they are asked about our climate, especially when they are asked to support spending money to keep the changing climate from harming Americans.

Bast is no better than the people who call me up to say that my "Social Security account" has been compromised, so I should call their "IRS agent" in India to clean it up. But Bast is much more dangerous. His pseudo-science helps Republicans defeat the gloomy Democrats who insist that something drastic must be done about climate change.

What Happened on Election Day?
NOVEMBER 11, 2014

The obvious thing that happened was that Democrats got trounced. In races that were supposed to be competitive, Democrats lost. Republican governors who were supposed to be unpopular defeated Democratic challengers. In Illinois, a Republican newcomer, Bruce Rauner, handily defeated the sitting Governor, Pat Quinn, 49% to 45%. Republicans will control 59 of the 98 partisan state legislative houses, and 31 of the governorships across the country.

But that's not the whole story of the 2014 midterm elections. Where Republicans won, popular Democratic incumbents also won. In Illinois, Senator Dick Durbin defeated Jim Oberweis 53% to 43%, although Oberweis was a familiar name statewide because he had run several times before. That means that about 1 of every 6 people who voted for Rauner split their ticket to vote for Durbin. One out of every 4 Rauner voters split their ticket to vote for Democratic Attorney General Lisa Madigan, and 1 out of 3 voted for Democratic Secretary of State Jesse White.

Several ballot questions in Illinois addressed partisan issues: a new 3% additional tax on incomes over $1 million, raising the minimum wage to $10 an hour, and a requirement to include birth control in prescription drug coverage in any health insurance plan. These were all "advisory questions", meaning that they need legislation to take effect. They were all pushed by Democrats and all passed by a two-thirds majority.

Morgan County, where I live, is dominated by Republican voters. Rauner got more than twice as many votes as Quinn. But the tax on million dollar incomes also passed 60% to 40%, and so did increasing the minimum wage. Nearly half of those in Morgan County who voted to re-elect Republican Aaron Schock to Congress also voted to raise taxes on millionaires.

This ballot splitting between candidates and issues happened across the country. An amendment to the Colorado state constitution to define "person" at conception was defeated 65% to 35%, although Democratic Senate incumbent Mark Udall was defeated. A personhood amendment in deeply Republican North Dakota lost 64% to 36%. Minimum wage increases passed in Alaska (69% in favor), Arkansas (66%), Nebraska (59%), South Dakota (55%), all states where Republicans easily won Senate races.

Why did so many American voters select the Democratic side of issues and the Republican slate of candidates? Illinois may provide a partial answer. Illinois voters have been evenly divided in statewide races in recent years. Republicans and Democrats have alternated as governors during the entire 20th century. At the moment, Democrats control the state government, with super majorities in both houses of the legislature. But during the five years that Pat Quinn has been Governor, they made very little headway against the state's deep financial problems. An income tax increase from 3% to 5% was passed, which I believe was necessary given our deep debts, but nothing else has been done. Democrats have failed in Illinois. The responsibility for this failure must be shared across those in leadership, including House Speaker Mike Madigan and Senate President John Cullerton, and throughout the ranks of Democratic legislators. Despite their dominance, Illinois Democrats have been afraid to tackle the difficult problems of the state. And Quinn is at the top of the ticket.

I think there is one more reason. The Democrats lost the battle of public opinion. It is always easier to point to problems, and Republicans at the national level have done little besides that for six years. During perhaps the most challenging period of American foreign policy in decades, Republicans have relentlessly criticized every decision that our Democratic President has made. Without acknowledging their own responsibility for the mess in the Middle East or proposing any new principles to guide our foreign policy, they have feasted on the extraordinary difficulties in Iraq and Syria and Libya and Afghanistan and Gaza and everywhere else.

But the Democrats have also failed to present persuasive reasons to believe in them. After passing one of the most significant pieces of legislation in memory, the Affordable Health Care Act, they have been running away from its initial difficulties ever since. Instead of proclaiming how much good it has done for millions of Americans who previously had no health insurance, they have allowed the Republicans to persuade most Americans that it is fatally flawed.

Democrats have failed to explain why the economic recovery has mainly helped the rich and how they would change that. Raising the minimum wage is only a start, a necessary one, but not much help to those earning just a bit more or without a job at all. On Sunday, President Obama said, "We have not been successful in letting people know what it is that we're trying to do and why this is the right direction."

So Americans angry about the economy have turned to a party which forced an end to unemployment insurance for the long-term unemployed, which wants to cut both welfare programs and taxes on the wealthy, which opposes doing anything to prevent jobs and profits from going overseas.

We'll see how that turns out.

STEVE HOCHSTADT
Jacksonville IL

I hate hoaxers who seek personal benefit from victimizing people with lies. But what about Santa? Do we hoax our children? Let's see if I can make a persuasive distinction between pernicious hoaxers and stories about the mythical bearded philanthropist.

Yes, Virginia, There is a Santa

DECEMBER 30, 2014

At the family dinner table a couple of days before Christmas, my nephew, who is about to become a father, expressed reluctance to lie to his child about Santa Claus. That led to many stories around the table about belief in Santa.

My son Sam remembered that he was getting skeptical about Santa one Christmas when his great wish was for a Lego Monorail kit. He didn't have much hope, however, because in his 6-year-old judgment that toy was much too expensive for his frugal parents. Then the Monorail appeared under the tree on Christmas morning in his grandparents' house, after a long night of secret construction in the company of my similarly busy brothers-in-law. Sam's skepticism vanished for another season.

One year my daughter Mae told her slightly younger cousins Helen and Ann that she knew "the truth about Santa" and she would be happy to pass on this knowledge. They were not ready for "the truth", but the next year Helen went looking for clues before Christmas. She found some hidden gifts that then showed up in her stocking on Christmas.

Most Christmas movies, especially the older ones I love, like "Miracle on 34th Street", not only assume that Santa is real, but that all good people will eventually come to believe that. In the modern remake of "Miracle on 34th Street", when some military man testifies in court that it would be impossible to make billions of toys at the North Pole, Kris Kringle scoffs. Of course you can't see the factory — it's magic.

"Dear Prudence" on Slate recently argued that children don't get hurt by eventually discovering "the truth about Santa". She wrote that "one of the delights of being a parent is to spread a little fairy dust occasionally." But not everyone agrees. Philosophy professor David Kyle Johnson at King's College, a Catholic college in Pennsylvania, denounces the "Santa lie". His argument appears to be about the immorality of lying, while most psychologists say that parental tales of Santa do no harm.

The wonderful story "The Polar Express" directly addresses how belief in Santa gradually disappears as children get older. University of Texas psychologist Jacqueline Woolley interviewed children and found that belief in Santa peaked about age 5, when nearly all children believed, and then dropped off quickly, so that by age 9, only one in three thought Santa was real. Research by Occidental College psychologists Andrew Shtulman and Rachel InKyung Yoo showed that children gradually lose their belief in Santa's purely magical qualities as their understanding of the physical world grows. But to preserve something of Santa, they develop explanations for his impossible activities which are more plausible to them, such as that he has millions of elves as helpers to make all those toys.

My children are too old to have experienced the Elf on the Shelf craze, and I'm happy for that. Scaring children into proper behavior with stories about magic spies for Santa is, in my opinion, a perversion of Santa's magic into something that parents, not children, want. I might not go as far as Professor

Laura Pinto, who argues that the all-seeing Elf prepares kids to accept the controversial activities of the NSA and the surveillance state, but I find the whole idea creepy.

In a *New York Times* opinion column, Seth Stephens-Davidowitz writes that Google searches for "depression" and similar words are less frequent around Christmas. Gallup surveys show Americans' mood improves around Christmas, while the number of suicides drops. Maybe that's part of Santa's magic.

Can Santa really deliver toys across the world in one night? Can he squeeze down all those chimneys? Those are the wrong questions. Even in some Jewish families, Christmas is a magical time, when we all can dream of giving the perfect gift, of seeing our loved ones smile with delight as they discover what's inside those carefully wrapped packages. For me, as long as belief in Santa might fascinate another generation of children with images of magical generosity, I'll grin when Kris Kringle wins his case one more time.

STEVE HOCHSTADT
Jacksonville, IL

CHAPTER 6
I Meditate on Power: 2015

I grew up as a Jew on Long Island in the 1950s and 1960s. I was many other things, too, of course. The reduction of human beings to simple labels, like Jew or New Yorker or professor or Democrat, makes us less intelligent. We come to believe that all of those people are alike.

My first trip to Israel meant many unpredictable and personal things. The day I set foot in Israel in 1993 I had an entirely new feeling: everybody is like me in one important way. I did not have to wonder about what it means to everyone I meet that I am a Jew.

But Jews are only alike in our Jewishness, whatever that means, and in nothing else. The whole point of antisemitism is to say that we are all one thing, and the whole point of fighting antisemitism and other racisms is to show we are a diverse representation of humanity and there is nothing that we all are, do, or think. In one way, though, Jews in America are alike: what happens in the Middle East is both political and personal. But these personal feelings and political conclusions vary widely.

At the beginning of 2015, my wife and I and another academic couple from Illinois College went to Israel and Palestine. I don't think I'll ever fully sort out my feelings and judgments about Israel, founded in 1948, the year of my birth, and the conflict in the Middle East. But I left with indelible and unpleasant impressions.

A Rocky Separation

FEBRUARY 3, 2015

I have never seen such a rocky place as the West Bank. Among undulating hills and valleys, a small field of plowed soil is a rarity. For thousands of years, people have moved rocks so they could grow plants. The steep hills have been cut horizontally with terraces dug by hand and animal power. The terraces are supported by stone walls, some looking recent, some stretching back thousands of years. The olive orchards which line the layered earth look as old. These ancient walls blend into the landscape and support an agricultural economy sustained by the people of this rocky land for thousands of years.

Recently a new type of wall has appeared in the West Bank. Twenty feet high, sunk deep into the ground, topped with barbed wire, the Israeli walls of separation prevent movement, separate people and interrupt that way of life.

The official political separator between Israel and the occupied West Bank is the Green Line, drawn on maps in 1949 to separate Israel from its neighbors at the end of a year's warfare. In the 1967 Six Day War, Israel occupied Palestinian territory beyond the Green Line: East Jerusalem, the West Bank and Gaza. Nearly 50 years later, the conflict over this land continues.

The major separation wall generally follows the Green Line, but small and significant deviations reveal a long-term Israeli population policy of separating themselves from Palestinians and expanding their borders. The wall bulges out to encompass less inhabited hills and valleys. It bulges in to exclude Palestinian villages and urban settlements from the rest of Israel. Walls extend deep into the West Bank to surround the many Israeli settlements that have been created there.

Every Israeli wall separates Palestinians from their families, their friends, their customers, and their culture. Shepherds are separated from grazing lands and water supply. Villages are separated from one another. People are prevented from access to stores, hospitals, government buildings, and each other.

Walls keep people out and people in. From the Great Wall of China to more modern walls in Berlin and on our border with Mexico, if walls are long enough, they can control entire populations. Walls become security measures when the enemy is defined as everyone on the other side.

Walls mean control and control varies by the category of people. In 1977, I could negotiate the annoying checkpoints in Berlin, cross the Wall, and wander around a city that no longer exists. East Berliners could only watch.

The new walls of Palestine funnel all people through a network of gates, where privilege is doled out by religion and nationality. We passed all the checkpoints with ease. Once a young soldier bent over to talk to us in the back seat. Our role was to identify ourselves as Americans, and she waved us on. Israelis, identified by their license plates, drive through, barely slowing down. Cars with Palestinian plates, and the much more numerous Palestinian walkers, are stopped.

Some walls are impenetrable: many roads in the West Bank have been built only for Israeli settlers, connecting isolated enclaves back to Israel. Other walls are just difficult. A delay of hours, plus humiliating treatment, must be part of every Palestinian's plan for negotiating a checkpoint.

These walls are part of a larger scheme to shape the population of Jerusalem and the West Bank in Israeli interests. The walls operate in conjunction with colored identification cards to segregate Palestinians into exclusive categories. Those with blue cards are considered to be residents of Jerusalem, and can move more freely than those with green cards. These "West Bankers" can enter Jerusalem, which they have considered their capital for centuries, only with special permits. The entire system of walls, identification cards and checkpoints makes travel by Palestinians in the West Bank difficult and time-consuming.

The Israeli government is worried about the demographic future. What does a state that proclaims itself Jewish do with a Palestinian minority that threatens to grow? The wall is one answer — exclude some, prevent others from entering, encourage them all to leave.

Israel uses wall-building to promote ethnic exclusion. Other more coercive methods are also being used to reconstruct the population of the West Bank. In September 2014, new plans were revealed which would move thousands of Bedouins away from their villages just east of Jerusalem into one new "Bedouin township" miles north and east, near the border with Jordan. That expulsion would clear a large area for future Israeli settlements. Protests by Palestinians and some Israelis have interfered with these plans, which appear to violate the Geneva Convention about treatment of an occupied population.

Even the privileged have to submit to the power of the wall. We started on the ancient route from Jerusalem to Jericho, just over 20 miles, cut thousands of years ago into a rolling landscape of rocky slopes. But just outside of East Jerusalem, we ran into a wall, towering over us, turning the road into a parking lot. Go away, the wall said.

Walls are bad for both sides. These walls will eventually fall, too, but not until they have harmed the lives of all the people of Palestine.

STEVE HOCHSTADT
Jacksonville IL

I taught about the Berlin Wall all the time. My wife Liz and I and a Bates College German language colleague took students 3 times for a full semester in Berlin, and I led a shorter trip with an Illinois College colleague. The

Wall, which by then existed only as a historical artifact, was always a major subject. Memorials to the Wall are scattered across Berlin.

Every great wall, from China's to Trump's "beautiful wall", separates a privileged society from a much less privileged one. Usually they are built by richer to keep poorer out, but the Berlin Wall was constructed to keep the poorer, the less free, in. Long after the Wall's demise, the privilege of the West was obvious on any street.

The Israeli wall is much taller than the Berlin Wall. It struck me as a historical violation of that ancient place. The Israeli government and those Israelis who support it say the wall is for their protection against Palestinian violence.

Whose Violence in the Middle East?
FEBRUARY 17, 2015

In January, a man carrying an automatic rifle entered a market in Jerusalem's Old City, cursed the local merchants, assaulted a young man, and began shooting. Israeli soldiers arrived and protected Jewish citizens, arresting a Palestinian man. The soldiers then created roadblocks at the City gates and interrogated many young Palestinians.

If you assumed that the shooter was Palestinian, however, you would be wrong. The violent man was an Israeli settler terrorizing Palestinians. Israeli forces responded by targeting Palestinians.

This is not the usual news we hear about Middle East violence. Not because it is unusual. An Israeli newspaper reported last year that there have been thousands of Jewish settler attacks on Palestinians in recent years, with more than one per day in 2013. We hear little about them.

What we learn about the Middle East is too general, too simplistic, and too loaded with presuppositions. It's worth hearing much smaller stories. It takes a lot of small stories to reach any understanding. But if the truth lies anywhere, it's in hundreds of stories about people we can imagine in places we can envision.

Every story begins in the middle, and every West Bank story begins thousands of years ago. Here's one story I couldn't find anywhere, so I had to piece it together myself. We'll start with the establishment of the Jewish settlement of Shvut Rachel in 1991, in the middle of the West Bank, closer to Jordan than to Jerusalem. The Israeli government in the 1980s had declared Palestinian land to be "public" if it had not been fully cultivated over the past 10 years.

A group of settlers took some of this land to create Shvut Rachel, which the Israeli government considered illegal, but then decided it was legal in 2012. One of the Shvut Rachel settlers, Jack Teitel from Florida, began a reign of terror against local Palestinians after he arrived in 1999. Teitel was convicted by an Israeli court in 2013 of murdering two Palestinians. Other Shvut Rachel settlers pushed further out in 2000, occupying a nearby hilltop which they called Esh Kodesh, without any permission from the Israeli government, a mile beyond any Jewish settlement, on some private Palestinian land that had been declared "public" by Israel and some Palestinian land that was still private. Picture a dozen trailers on a rocky hill, called an "outpost".

Settlers create so many of these illegal outposts on the West Bank that the Israeli government has had to dismantle dozens which were not even inhabited. But not nearly all: a road was paved to Esh Kodesh and precious water lines were run back through Shvut Rachel.

Almost immediately there were confrontations between Esh Kodesh settlers and the local Palestinians. The settlers built a fence around "their land", and then demanded that the local farmers stay out of fields just outside of their fence, which the government enforced. They began ploughing land outside of the fence, which is fertile enough to support vineyards, unusual in that rocky landscape.

Violent incidents piled up. In March 2011, settlers invaded Qusra village, provoking a gunfight there. In July 2011 settlers attacked some herdsmen and butchered a sheep. Soldiers arrived and "dispersed" the Palestinians. The army set up a base in September 2011 near Esh Kodesh. In 2012 Palestinians' olive trees were vandalized.

A United Nations report in fall 2012 noted two consecutive weeks when "settlers from Esh Kodesh have attacked Palestinian civilians from Qusra village." 126 Palestinians and 32 settlers had been injured that year on the West Bank. Another report counted 10,000 Palestinian trees damaged or destroyed in 2011.

Finally at the end of 2012, the Israeli High Court of Justice ruled that Palestinians could no longer be barred from working their own land around Esh Kodesh. Israeli soldiers had to physically remove settlers who protested that decision. In December, Jews uprooted olive trees and stoned Qusra homes. In January 2013, Palestinians attacked settler vineyards outside of Esh Kodesh. In February, settlers with guns attacked Qusra and wounded 6 Palestinians. More uprooting of Palestinian olive trees, but also planting of trees on Palestinian land. Israeli officials uprooted those illegal trees in January 2014. Esh Kodesh settlers again went out to Qusra, but this time they were captured by hastily arranged security details of villagers, assaulted, and turned over to Israeli soldiers.

There is no reason to believe that the outward push of Esh Kodesh settlers, and whole settler movement, will stop. Since Shvut Rachel was founded in 1991, the number of settlers has tripled. In 2012, the Israeli general in charge of the West Bank characterized settler violence as "terrorism". The Shin Bet, Israel's internal security service, the Justice Minister and the Public Security Minister argued in 2013 for using that label for violent settlers, but nothing happened.

With great patience protesting illegal actions by Israeli settlers and government, with self-defense squads to protect their homes and fields, with occasional attention from Western media, West Bank residents will gradually lose their lands and livelihoods. Unless something is done to reverse decades of Israeli policy.

STEVE HOCHSTADT
Jacksonville IL

There is no justification here for any act of Palestinian violence. I don't think violence in response to violence, as is portrayed favorably in the Torah, read by Jews, Christians and Muslims, is justifiable. I do see that Palestinian violence is well-represented in the Western media. Despite some movement of popular opinion and media portrayals away from an unquestioning assumption of Israeli innocence and Palestinian terrorism, it still takes effort to discover that there is much more to know.

I was changed by our West Bank visit. I find no adequate justification for what I saw. Israelis live in a powerful nation practicing a form of ethnic cleansing against weaker peoples. Many protest and many demand harsher policies, and most go along. I don't feel any more that Israelis are like my siblings because they are Jews. But I also feel that I, as an American, cannot say that the politics in my country are a model to follow.

In the 60s, construction workers in New York City shouted at Vietnam War protesters that they should "love it or leave it". Those conservatives said protest equaled lack of love, and lack of love meant hate. That remains a conservative mantra accompanied by flag-waving at every opportunity. It's the source of the peculiar assertion by the right that liberals hate America, peculiar because the right routinely expresses hatred for the majority of Americans who don't agree with them, in terms that can't be found among liberals. There is no liberal equivalent of Trump accusing Democrats of treason, which he has done many times.

One of the labels employed by conservatives to designate people and behavior they most dislike is "hippie". From their sudden appearance in the buttoned-down early 1960s to today, hippies have been cast by conservatives as carriers of the worst social diseases. Given the right's proclamations of their love of freedom and their rejection of government power, anarchic hippies might be seen as allies. But conservative disgust for hippies and other free-thinkers reveals that they reject only certain types of government power and applaud only their version of freedom.

Hippies Were Happy
MARCH 31, 2015

Hippies have a bad reputation, especially among conservatives. In 1967, the "National Review" said that hippies were self-indulgent and had a "horrified rejection of work and production". Their thinking, "if indeed thinking it can be called, is more like orgiastic love-spluttering than coherent thought." They might cause "outbreaks of polio and typhoid".

In 2007, Ted Nugent remarkably blamed "stoned, dirty, stinky hippies" for "rising rates of divorce, high school drop-outs, drug use, abortion, sexual diseases and crime, not to mention the exponential expansion of government and taxes."

The most popular speaker at the 2015 Conservative Political Action Conference, Duck Dynasty star Phil Robertson, received a huge applause for claiming that millions of cases of STD's today are "the revenge of the hippies!"

Even less hysterical commentators still want to blame hippies for all of our ills: in 2010, David Brooks of the NY Times blamed the hippie "agenda" for the New York City crime wave of the 1970s.

Historians also saw hippies as scapegoats. In *The Unraveling of America* (1984, p. 277), Allen J. Matusow asserted that they did not believe in reason, progress, order, achievement, or social responsibility, probably because "Few hippies read much". More recently, Micah Issitt said in *Hippies: A Guide to an American Subculture* (2009, p. 64-5) that hippies were personally irresponsible, poor parents, and unwilling to contribute to anything more than their own pleasure, and he blamed hippie advocacy of free love for climbing divorce rates.

These stereotypes of hippies were created by people who hated them and didn't want to understand them.

Hippies utterly rejected the consumer life. They believed that watching the clock, dressing for success, and hoping for the next raise damaged the soul. Hippies put a lot of stress on stress. Unlike most people, they were willing to make big sacrifices to avoid stress. The anxieties of modern working life, the pressures of schedules, and the confrontations with authority were not worth the hassle. At a time when daily life was being compared to a rat race, hippies wanted to leave it all behind.

Hippies took spirituality seriously. They created lives far out of the mainstream in order to preserve and nurture their spirit. Traditional gods did not play a big role in hippie spirituality. Some remained with traditional religions, but tended to worship on their own. Many, perhaps most, hippies imagined their own spiritual worlds, blending the social gospel of Western faiths with the inward search of some Eastern beliefs. A love of nature often focused on the Earth as a living being and maternal symbol. In religion, as in every area of belief and behavior, hippies were independent spirits.

Hippies did not get in your face. They didn't send out mailers or make phone calls or knock on doors or shout into microphones. They didn't believe that their way was necessarily better for everyone. They wanted to do their own thing.

Hippies were peaceful. That attitude went far beyond signs and symbols, and was more profound than opposition to the Vietnam War. Hippies thought that peace is meant to rule our daily lives, from international relations to the family home. When they raised two fingers and said "Peace", they converted a plea for cooperation into a daily greeting.

Hippies abhorred violence. For trying to escape or end the draft, they were labeled cowards, but they were not. They stood up to the entire straight world, including every familiar figure of authority, to say "No," we don't want that life. The hippie approach to violence has been forever symbolized in the 1967 photo of a protester putting a flower into a National Guardsman's gun in front of the Capitol.

Hippies got high. That didn't distinguish them from normal folks. They used a different set of drugs — not depressants like alcohol or pills, but marijuana and psychedelics, including LSD, peyote and mushrooms. Their infrequent bad trips were only bad for themselves. They were less likely to drive drunk or get into brawls than the people who criticized them for using dope.

Hippies were ahead of their time. Their unconventional ideas about gender equality, their acceptance of a variety of sexualities, and their preference for organic products and vegetarian diets are now widely accepted. "Question authority" is now a bumper sticker, but few actually reject social authority as profoundly as did the hippies.

Hippies were less likely to cause trouble than most people. Hippie "crime" was typified by the illegal planting of flowers in People's Park in Berkeley in 1969. But that didn't stop people from causing trouble for them. They were called lazy, irresponsible and un-American. Hippie rejection of conventional American life made them pariahs in a country supposedly founded on individualism and freedom.

Conservative attitudes toward hippies demonstrate the shallowness of right-wing libertarianism. Rejection of authority only means rejection of government. Liberty means freedom from taxes. Politics is war.

Enough to make the real libertarians want to tune in, turn on, and drop out.

STEVE HOCHSTADT
Jacksonville IL

I wasn't a hippie, although some people think I look like one. I was never ready to reject conventional life as fully as they were. But I found their protests refreshing and inspiring, because of their courage, for which they are given little credit. In freedom-loving America, the loudest freedom-lovers don't appreciate people who refused to follow.

The right-wing attitude toward hippies was based on their ignorance, often deliberate, about what hippies were actually like. American conservatives often call their imagination into play when reality becomes bothersome. Obama as a Muslim, liberals as traitors, guns as safety devices, Trump "telling it like it is", are some of the fantastic tales proclaimed as truth by the right.

A particularly pernicious but characteristic intellectual invention of the right is a fable about American government. Trump supporters in all generations believe there exists a "deep state", government officials who secretly manipulate policy to thwart conservatives. In the absence of knowledge that Republicans enforce by attacking journalists, professors and scientists, the "deep state" conspiracy theory nicely fills in for reality. But belief in an unelected elite exercising outsized influence on American politics is not just a conservative nightmare. Dwight Eisenhower's warning that "the acquisition of unwarranted influence by the military-industrial complex" could lead to "the disastrous rise of misplaced power" fed not conservatism, but liberal distrust of government. Liberals, not conservatives, have pointed to the Pentagon Papers in 1971, the faulty justifications for the Iraq War, and the Afghanistan Papers today as evidence that the American government consistently lies to the American public about military matters.

It's always tempting to point the finger at shadowy forces promoting evil behind curtains of respectability. But is it crazy?

Who's Crazy?

JUNE 2, 2015

I have a friend I talk politics with occasionally. I'll call him Dan. He told me the other day that our country is run by an invisible government of bankers and other rich people. Obama and Reagan, and presumably most other politicians, are their puppets.

Dan is a good businessman. He owns my favorite diner, fighting off the big boys in our small town, the billion-dollar corporations who have surrounded him with industrial food products. Dan loves my articles about politics and he tells me every time I go there.

So was that crazy talk from Dan?

Other people do offer crazy theories about who is really in charge. No amount of evidence or logic could dissuade those who claim that the US, or maybe the world, is run by Jews, or the Illuminati, or the Trilateral Commission, or liberal fascists. They don't like facts which contradict their pet beliefs, formed out of paranoia and prejudice. Their wacko ideas are encouraged by politicians and media pundits who see an advantage in slyly promoting the irrational passions of their most extreme followers.

But Dan's theory is backed up by lots of evidence, and I'm not saying that so I'll get better service the next time I go out for breakfast. I get great service anyway.

The power of giant global banks over our daily lives is enormous. We don't think about how much power when we use their credit cards every day. We only hear about their ability to manipulate entire economies when they screw up and get caught. Big European banks manipulated world currency trading for their own profit. Big American banks played risky games with millions of our homes and caused a recession when millions of people lost their jobs.

Gigantic sums of money flowed up the economic pyramid to them and their friends, a small part of which was paid in fines, and the leaders of the corporations are right where they were before.

The influence of banks and other giant corporations on the political process has never been greater. Their armies of lobbyists influence, and sometimes even write legislation which is supposed to regulate their activities. They escape any personal responsibility for illegal actions, even when they are caught red-handed. Now the Supreme Court's Citizens United ruling has removed the limits from their contributions to political campaigns.

I don't think this makes our politicians puppets of the bankers. American politicians are independent actors. But they are remarkably dependent on rich contributors for their electoral success, and while in office they share the lifestyle of first-class travel, sumptuous meals, and luxurious perks. Even if they can't get rich in office, after their political careers, they join the economic elite.

The differences between the policies of Ronald Reagan and Barack Obama are enormous, but both the conservative Reagan and the liberal Obama allowed the giant banks to run the American economy in their own interests. Neither one made big bankers who broke the laws, thereby taking money illegally out of Americans' pockets, pay personal penalties.

Our system of taxation which allows rich people to pay a much lower rate on money they earn by investing, not working, while wage-earners pay a higher rate, was set up and supported by Republicans and Democrats.

Politicians aren't puppets, but they are the friends of the rich, not the poor, and lately not the middle class.

I could be picky about what Dan said. I think he made a complex situation too simple, seeing politics only in black and white. Don't we all do that in conversation?

He's not any crazier than the rest of us. Allowing our democracy to be hijacked by the wealthiest Americans, watching the gains from our economy trickle up, and then voting for the same people over and over again, expecting some different result. Isn't that the definition of crazy?

In fact, Dan has drawn the logical conclusion. He likes Bernie Sanders. Sanders is obviously not in the pocket of big bankers or big anybodies. He doesn't go around giving million-dollar speeches in front of the economic elite, stroking their impression that they are the most important Americans. He has been uncompromising in his efforts to rein in the power of billionaires and give it back to ordinary Americans, and he promises to continue that as Senator or President. Neither Hillary Clinton nor certainly any of the dozens of Republicans running for President have said anything like that.

Annoyed at the way our economy is steeply tilted toward the rich, but planning to vote for the same old candidates? So who's crazy?

STEVE HOCHSTADT
Shanghai, China

If crazy means doing the same thing when it keeps failing to have the desired effect, maybe I'm crazy to write about facts every week hoping to change minds.

The next month, my title was changed again. I wrote "Stay Out of Bad Wars", which I considered an obvious suggestion. It was published as "Bad Wars and Their Consequences", less pointed and certainly less catchy. Over the years, it became clear to me that the rewriting of my headlines mingled standard formatting conventions and subtle political censorship.

I have never fought in a war nor worn a soldier's uniform. When my college student deferment was eliminated in favor of the draft lottery in 1969, I was lucky that my birthday was selected as number 333. By that time, I and many in my generation had decided that we did not want to fight in a bad war in Vietnam. I'm thankful that I was not faced with a decision about what to do after being drafted.

Since then I've been faced with the less significant decision about how to think about American soldiers. Are all soldiers heroes, as politicians frequently assert? Do soldiers automatically deserve more respect than teachers? I'm sure of three things. Politicians, not soldiers, make the momentous decisions to start and prolong wars. The two soldiers I knew best, my Army father and my Marine father-in-law, were my models of how to think about honor and soldiering. And very few wars are worth the immeasurable sacrifices they entail.

Stay Out of Bad Wars

JULY 7, 2015

I went to see the model of the Vietnam Veterans Memorial when it came to the center of Jacksonville. "The Wall That Heals" travels across the country, bringing the cathartic effect of the larger wall of names in Washington to the hometowns of veterans and casualties of that long war. I did not serve, but I assume that this traveling reminder of the 58,300 Americans who died in Vietnam helps those who still experience the war's pain.

I was moved to think again of my friend, Paul Semplicino (1947-1971), who died on leave in Bangkok, while President Nixon claimed to search for "peace with honor", but secretly escalated into Cambodia and Laos.

What balances the national pain of all those deaths, over 150,000 physically wounded and many more psychologically scarred? What good did our intervention in Vietnam do?

Print by Sandra Ure Griffin, 2011

A few years later in 1980, Ronald Reagan, running for the presidency, claimed that "ours was, in truth, a noble cause." Individual men and women served with honor and demonstrated personal nobility. W.D. Ehrhart, just my age, writes of the unpredictable mixture of boredom, bravery, foolishness, disdain for the Vietnamese and willingness to die to save their lives.

But our country earned no honor in Vietnam, and our cause was not noble. The war was part of the global power struggle, ignoring the interests of the Vietnamese people fighting for independence from colonial domination. Hundreds of thousands of civilians were killed, including more children than American soldiers. We sprayed 20 million gallons of herbicides, mostly

Agent Orange containing dioxin, on 1/7 of South Vietnam's surface. Both American veterans and Vietnamese civilians, including babies born long after the war's end, have suffered from the effects of these chemicals.

That was a bad war in which America, represented by a succession of governments, acted badly.

There have been good wars. That phrase is misleading about war, but it expresses a truth about joining a war. American entry into World War II was almost a "noble cause", composed of self-protection, a response to aggression, and a fight between good and evil. Everything we have learned about World War II in the 70 years since its end demonstrates that our reasons were good, our fighting was good, and the results have been good.

One story I just heard from a new friend shows that. In the 1950s, his father took the family to France, where he had fought in 1944, but about which he said little. He drove seemingly lost among small villages. Suddenly he pulled into a little farm and stopped in front of the house and barn. The farmer came out shouting about this violation of his property, the father gestured and raised his voice that he had been here before, and the family of mother and children, including my friend, watched with dismay. The father knelt down and drew in the dirt the number "116". The farmer burst into tears.

As the Army had come through, my friend's father with the 116th had set up a hospital behind the farmer's barn. The farmer's daughter got sick. She was saved in the hospital. As the Americans and British advanced, they met joyous celebrations by the French people.

The German response to the Normandy landing was different. Six days after D-Day, a Waffen-SS battalion killed everyone in the village of Oradour-sur-Glane by herding them into barns and the church and setting them on fire.

American fighting in World War II liberated people who desperately wanted to be liberated. We even helped liberate the Vietnamese from the Japanese, only to support the reimposition of French colonial domination.

Since then we have engaged in wars around the world where we were not attacked, we were as aggressive as those we designated as our enemy, and our government lied to convince us that we were on the good side.

But I'm not making a moral argument. My point is that the results of justifiable and unjustifiable wars are different. We could have destroyed Vietnam, but we could not prevent its independence. We easily got rid of a murderous dictator in Iraq and have not been able to prevent the country from sinking into anarchy, with less security than before. We thought we could fix Afghanistan in our own image and kill those who had attacked us on 9-11, ignoring the earlier failures of the British and the Russians. The Taliban is still there, Al Qaeda has spread further, and a more deadly virus of fanatic destruction has arisen in the Middle East.

In Vietnam, in Iraq, in Afghanistan, and in many other places, our leaders did not know what they were doing. The result has been disaster for our soldiers, for the countries where we intervened, for our global image and our image of ourselves.

The political leaders who now demand that we commit more people and money to these mistaken incursions into other people's lands are the same ones who say we don't have enough resources to pay for schools or poverty programs or museums. They don't want to remember the lessons of the bad wars we have fought, perhaps because they sent us into them.

We need to learn those lessons.

STEVE HOCHSTADT
Jacksonville IL

Through the luck of marriage, I joined a family with roots in northern Wisconsin. A century ago, one of my wife's ancestors built a house on a small lake 50 miles south of Lake Superior. Generations later, dozens of relatives gather every summer. The nearest grocery store is 15 miles away. We were married there and so were our children. Living in the woods provides this suburban-raised, small-town academic with a fresh perspective on life in America. Fresh air, fresh water, and many fresh animals.

The Bears Don't Hate Us, So Far

AUGUST 8, 2015

Up here in northern Wisconsin, we talk a lot about bears. Everyone has seen a bear or bears wandering through the woods. These black bears are not dangerous to humans, although incidents are reported every year of accidental but tragic human-bear interactions in someone's backyard.

The bears aren't hunting us. What if they did?

Humans are generally murderous foes of animal life. We have hunted bears, and other impressive animals, for thousands of years all over the globe. The development and spread of guns changed the natural world in the 19th century. The enormous flocks of passenger pigeons, which once took hours to pass overhead, were killed off by 1900. Bison herds which covered the plains were wiped out as the frontier was pushed westward. Animal life was subordinated to political concerns: the government promoted the slaughter of bison by the Army to make room for cattle and to weaken Native American tribes by eliminating a major food source.

Every culture treats some animals with great respect, at times bordering on reverence. Pets have special status. But the idea of maintaining the permanent existence of certain wild animals by creating legal protections is a very recent idea. The shock to the popular imagination of the extinction of passenger pigeons and the near elimination of bison and whooping cranes turned the tide of public opinion in the early 20th century. The Migratory Bird Conservation Act of 1929, a 1937 treaty restricting the hunting of whales, and the Bald Eagle Protection Act of 1940 created legal protections for a few species. The Endangered Species Act of 1973 went much further — President Richard Nixon declared existing laws inadequate because they ignored the destruction of habitats. We extended protection to animals we barely knew, to animals we feared, to animals to be named in the future.

Today our society harbors deeply conflicting viewpoints about the treatment of animals. At one extreme is People for the Ethical Treatment of Animals (PETA), an organization which argues that animals also have the right to life. PETA focuses on situations where animal life is routinely abused for human convenience, such as on factory farms and in laboratories. But PETA also makes the radical claim that we should extend our concern for human life "to other living, feeling beings, regardless of what species they may be."

At the other end are people like Walter Palmer, who illegally killed a lion in Zimbabwe. His desire to kill animals has frequently violated the law. The international attention being given to his obsession with killing wild animals might cause further shifts in public opinion about animal life.

Daily life is more complex than the simplistic arguments of media and politics. What animals should I kill today? I set traps for the mice which live in our cabin. Should I feel bad about swatting the mosquitoes buzzing around my head? Can I save the daddy longlegs in my bed? We all express our hopes that the loon family, which never comes very close but whom we hear across the lake, will have babies that survive.

I found a garden snake the other morning and called out my family to see it. Pretty and fast, small and helpless against any human desire to kill it. I would have felt different about a rattlesnake sharing my yard with children and dogs.

Beauty helps. Who would crush a butterfly? They don't do us much good. Displays of dead butterflies have fascinated millions of museum visitors. But killing a butterfly appears to most people, I think, as undisciplined brutality.

It seems remarkable to me that only humans hunt for the pleasure of killing. Animals might attack us individually when they feel threatened. As of now, we have nothing to worry about from all the species which we routinely kill, which we hunt, which we render homeless, sick or dead by our profligate use of the Earth and waters. We are much more likely to be confronted with nightmares about a revolt of machines, from "I, Robot" to the "Terminator" and "Matrix" series, than we are to think about a revolt of the animals. The scary fantasy in "Rise of the Planet of the Apes" depends on a change in the chimpanzees' nature through human-developed drugs. Hitchcock's "The Birds" is a rare film about aggressive animals hunting us.

What if any of those physically powerful or very numerous, and potentially deadly species we go around killing decides they've had enough? That seems crazy. But thinking about it is useful. Do whales have a right to attack our boats?

I'm not against hunting. I like hamburgers made with domesticated, slaughtered beef and with wild hunted deer. I'm not against hunters, although I believe some hunters are thrilled by a murderous blood-lust that I find abhorrent. I'm not a vegetarian.

But I think the lives of animals have inherent value. I don't like killing for the sake of killing. I try to avoid killing animals just because they are annoying. I believe the right to life should not just be about humans.

The bears out here in the woods are a long way from planning resistance. Lucky for us.

STEVE HOCHSTADT
Springbrook WI

Hunting is one of those human activities that inspire passionate argument on all sides. In the suburbs, where I grew up, shooting guns meant crime and human danger. In Maine and Wisconsin, where I have spent much time, hunting is normal outdoor life, as is fishing, with the same twin explanations, food and sport. Living with hunting has educated my suburban mind.

Where we live and what we see shapes our thinking, and thus our politics. But the reality of our surroundings is only one input to political thinking. Ideologies based on deep unprovable convictions also play a determining role, shaping in turn what we see, especially when real knowledge is lacking about an important subject. For most Americans, and a higher proportion of American voters, poverty fits that mold. American political discussions about poverty often seem less reality-based and more ideological than is healthy.

We know all about the rich. From local papers to the finest national journals of news and opinion, from HGTV to the Kardashians, from reality TV to public TV, the rich are a subject of constant fascination. One defense might be, that's what the public wants. But how does anyone know what the public would think of media which did more than dip in and out of poverty? Maybe a series about a normal poor American family wouldn't qualify as a sit-com, because it's not easy to laugh at people who are struggling. I don't think it will be necessary to find some special "deserving" family to observe. Find a normal family that is poor, of which there are too many millions in America, and show us reality.

How Do We See the Poor?

AUGUST 25, 2015

Last week I attended the Illinois Democratic County Chairmen's Association annual brunch at the Springfield Hilton. I know what the Republicans said in their presidential debate. I wanted to hear what Democrats say as we gather steam for election year 2016.

People handed me stickers for candidates; candidates wandered around shaking hands. Then came two and half hours of speeches. Political speeches tend to sound alike. But they tell you what concerns the speaker most, what they want to accomplish with your vote. At the Democrats' brunch, I heard over and over again the imperative to help "the most vulnerable" in our society.

Susana Mendoza, the City Clerk of Chicago who is running for Illinois Comptroller, worried about how the current budget crisis would lead to cutbacks at Illinois social service agencies, hurting "the most vulnerable". Mike Frerichs, the Illinois Treasurer, told us what he is proud of since he barely won election in 2014: financial measures to help the poor, like college savings accounts, retirement plans, and the Able Act, helping families with a disabled dependent. He also talked about "the most vulnerable".

Four Democrats are running for the US Senate seat held by Republican Mark Kirk. In their brief speeches, they all spoke of the imperative of helping poorer people. Congresswoman Tammy Duckworth said, "We have to be there for the voiceless. We are better off as Americans when we don't leave anyone behind." Richard Boykin, Cook County Commissioner, will advocate for "those who have been left out". Andrea Zopp gave us the image of "people working hard to pull themselves out of poverty".

Napoleon Harris went to school with the same clothes every day, before his talent carried him to an NFL career and now to the Illinois Statehouse. His life demonstrates that getting out of poverty requires effort by many individuals, which is what Republicans focus on. But Harris also stressed the importance of collective help from the surrounding society.

The contrast between what these Democrats said and what Republican presidential candidates say about poverty is striking. Little has changed since Mitt Romney said that 47% of voters "believe that they are victims, who believe the government has a responsibility to care for them, who believe that they are entitled to health care, to food, to housing, to you-name-it. I'll never convince them they should take personal responsibility and care for their lives."

Only one of the ten men at the Republican debate, Ohio Governor John Kasich, discussed poor Americans at all. For Republicans, poor people are mainly targets of abuse, not help. Donald Trump said in June that poor people "sit back and say we're not going to do anything. They make more money by sitting there doing nothing than they make if they have a job." Jeb Bush has criticized poor families, proposing a model he doesn't think they follow: "A loving family taking care of their children in a traditional marriage will create the chance to break out of poverty far better, far better than any of the government programs that we can create". Wisconsin Governor Scott Walker blocked the expansion of Medicaid in his state, asking, "Why is more people on Medicaid a good thing?" The health insurance plan he outlined in the debate to replace Obamacare would cut subsidies to poor people.

There is nothing new about Republicans blaming the poor for their own predicament. Long before Ronald Reagan used stories about welfare fraud to characterize poor people in America, conservatives created a distinction between the "deserving" and the "undeserving" poor. Republican candidates don't propose to help people in poverty, because Republican voters believe poverty is poor people's own fault. 51% of Republicans in a 2014 Pew survey thought that poverty is caused by "lack of effort". Republican politicians helped to create the image of the poor as undeserving. Now Republican voters demand it. Economic data, census surveys, or social scientific research are not useful here.

The Republican unwillingness to use government resources to help the poor is just what the richest people want. That's one reason why donations of $1 million or more have benefitted Republican candidates 12 times as much as Democratic candidates.

I don't feel that way. Conservatives imagine all kinds of explanations for why I might not think the poor are undeserving: I'm a liberal, a socialist, a communist, a Jew, a New Yorker, a college professor. I would blame my parents. They managed to communicate two ideas. It was important to look upwards, to try for better, and to work for that. Equally important was to look down the scale of success, but not to look down on less successful people. I learned from them to see how the system of power and wealth promulgates the idea that those who don't have it don't deserve it.

I wouldn't have been able to hold down a brunch with the Republican presidential candidates. When Republicans turn their evil eye on the poor, I get sick. The Democrats made me feel at home. They see the system and want change it. We can argue about how much. But we won't argue that the poor deserve what they get.

It doesn't do Democrats any good to advocate for the poor. They don't make the giant political contributions that keep the Republican machine going. They don't vote as often as the people who make those contributions. They don't staff the offices of lobbyists in Washington. They don't hobnob with candidates at fancy dinners. There is no quid pro quo for helping "the most vulnerable", except the feeling that it's the right thing to do.

STEVE HOCHSTADT
Jacksonville IL

The ideology that sees poor people as undeserving often claims justification from the idea of a free market. Just as businesses rise and fall on their merits and at their own risk, so people should just do for themselves, rather than depend on government to help them. Today's free marketeers are both hypocritical and radical. They are adamant about how government help to those they assume are undeserving is pernicious. Taxpayer subsidies and tax breaks to all manner of businesses they like, such as fossil fuels, are to be protected, at all costs to the climate.

They go far beyond the prescription of their founding hero, Adam Smith, who would find no home in today's Republican Party.

The Great Myth of the Free Market

OCTOBER 27, 2015

In 1776, in "An Inquiry into the Nature and Causes of the Wealth of Nations", Adam Smith developed a new theory of economics, which we now call the theory of the free market. He wrote that a man should be "free to pursue his own interest his own way.... By directing that industry in such a manner as its produce may be of greatest value, he intends only his own gain, and he is in this...led by an invisible hand to promote an end which was no part of his intention." That useful end was economic progress for the whole nation.

Smith was an economic genius who realized that the restrictions placed on their economies by 18th-century European monarchies stifled productivity and the creation of wealth. If people were allowed to seize opportunities that they perceived, to assess risk and seek reward, the larger economy would grow more rapidly than if rulers dictated how commerce should proceed.

The moral superiority of free choice over monarchical fiat was indispensable to Smith's argument. As a partner to the demand for more political freedom, the promotion of the free market was inherently democratic.

Since then, no economic system has equaled capitalism in creating wealth, for nations and individuals. The "free market" is such a sweet phrase that it has become a magic incantation, a panacea for every economic problem. The free market as an idea appears to have attained religious status. Proponents of an unfettered market invoke their version of God's will in favor of their political position against any government regulation, for example, laws protecting the environment. The lineup of conservative presidential candidates has nothing good to say about any economic regulation.

The people who raise the unregulated market to a religious commandment support political advocacy with mythical stories, beginning with Adam Smith. Smith did not have absolute faith in the "invisible hand". He openly preached that governments must play a significant role in the economy.

Governments should provide roads and bridges and other public works which individuals or private enterprises are not likely to build. He praised regulation of the labor market, but only when it supported workers.

"When the regulation, therefore, is in favour of the workmen, it is always just and equitable; but it is sometimes otherwise when in favour of the masters.... Masters are always and every where in a sort of tacit, but constant and uniform combination, not to raise the wages of labour above their actual rate." Smith distrusted the motives of employers, who sought, he believed, to keep wages as low as possible, "always and everywhere".

He not only supported taxation, but favored a progressive tax system. "The subjects of every state ought to contribute towards the support of the government, as nearly as possible, in proportion to their respective abilities; that is, in proportion to the revenue which they respectively enjoy under the protection of the state.... It is not very unreasonable that the rich should contribute to the public expence, not only in proportion to their revenue, but something more than in that proportion."

By obscuring these uncomfortable elements of Adam Smith's theory, free market absolutists offer another myth: regulation has only costs, not benefits. Every regulation increases rather than decreases the costs of doing business, otherwise businesses would undertake these measures themselves. But modern life is dependent on the greater benefits of regulation: food products free of disease, rivers with live fish, and air healthy to breathe. Regulations took the lead out of gasoline and paint. Regulations keep harmful drugs, like thalidomide, off the market.

Regulations put seat belts and air bags into cars, saving countless lives, a good example of their value. Every state but one legislates that adult drivers must wear seat belts. That state, New Hampshire, has the lowest usage of seat belts in the country. Live free and die.

Car manufacturers were successful in delaying the deployment of the air bag, costing thousands of lives. In 1983, the Supreme Court ruled 9 to 0 in favor of government-mandated air bags, writing: "For nearly a decade, the automobile industry waged the regulatory equivalent of war against the airbag and lost — the inflatable restraint was proved sufficiently effective."

The writers of our Constitution, 13 years after Smith published "The Wealth of Nations", enshrined the mutual necessity of freedom and regulation into Section 8, "The Congress shall have Power...To regulate Commerce with foreign Nations, and among the several States".

We can joke about the conservative effort to deregulate our economy. "How many conservatives does it take to screw in a light bulb?" Answer: "None. If the government would just leave it alone, it would screw itself in."

But saving lives is no joke.

STEVE HOCHSTADT
Jacksonville IL

Saving lives is a science. How do you build an air bag that we could require automobile manufacturers to install? How do we test proposed medicines to ensure that they work?

Could anyone make the argument that the automobile industry would make safer cars if they had been left alone by government? I don't hear any serious voices saying that there should be no government testing of new drugs, because Big Pharma would do a more reliable job. How do we create a national science structure that will make human life better in the future?

The only science that is explicitly in the people's interest is government science. University science, which overlaps government science considerably, pursues a different goal: discovery of reality without regard to immediate usefulness, believing that is also ultimately in the people's interest. A lot of money and effort is expended on private industrial science, usually accomplished by good scientists. But the purpose of those labs and the people way up high who direct them is to make money. We need government science to find out when private science is used against the people's interest.

I'm not a scientist, although I almost became one. Before settling on history as my life's work, I considered math and chemistry. I can only understand the rudiments of today's scientific discoveries, but I cheer for science as the path to progress. When politicians seek popular support by attacking university and government science, when they accuse scientists of wholesale cheating, I feel targeted myself.

I believe in government as the collective construction of the whole society. That vision, much broader than the male-dominated, white supremacist version of democracy embraced by America's founders, has not yet been fully realized and continues to be contested by the forces of the right. In historical terms, real American democracy is still an infant. That explains some of the enduring weaknesses of our governing system, one of which is policing.

On the screens that seem to dominate our modern lives, we can watch two kinds of interactions between the police and "suspects". The endless cop shows, many of which I enjoy, display carefully chosen scenes of violence involving police, nearly all following precisely written regulations about when and what violence may be deployed. Occasionally, a good cop smacks a suspect during interrogation, but we are made to know that's exceptional behavior. Unrestrained violence against the presumed innocent is reserved for the very few bad cops, who always get their comeuppance.

Then we can watch the real world, thanks to inconvenient unofficial and official videos, when police break their rules and brutalize, or even kill, ordinary citizens. These are rare occurrences among the millions of police actions every day. But shouldn't they be rarer? Is just asking that question being anti-police?

Cops Out of Control

NOVEMBER 24, 2015

I just watched a fuzzy video of two policemen beating an unarmed man with batons while he lay on the ground. One cop hit him at least 20 times, the other at least 15 times. They kept on hitting him after other policemen arrived. The most appropriate word in my vocabulary for this scene is sadistic.

This happened on November 12 in San Francisco. The man is a criminal, who had apparently stolen a car, led police on a chase at high speeds, and injured another policeman in attempting to flee. But the beating had nothing to do with arresting him. It was about inflicting pain.

I had seen this video before, but forgotten the particulars. When I searched for it by Googling "police beat man", I found many similar videos of police brutalizing people they had caught.

In Inkster, MI, in January, Floyd Dent was pulled over on a traffic stop, yanked from his car and punched at least 16 times while being held in a chokehold. He was shocked three times with a taser. At the police station, he was stripped and made fun of, with no attempt to treat his injuries.

In Philadelphia in April, two officers beat an unarmed man who had been riding his bike on the wrong side of the street. Eventually 11 police cars and 26 officers gathered to deal with this one man.

In Salinas, CA, in June, a man who had been fighting with his mother was whacked many times with a billy club by a policeman. He was on the ground, and the policeman was standing over him, waiting for him to move, swinging the club with both hands like a baseball bat, then waiting and whacking again. Another policeman stood by and watched. There was no attempt to handcuff him. This was simply a beat-down. After three other police arrived, he was beaten further with a billy club, still lying on the ground.

That's a selection among a longer list of incidents of violence by police this year, that happened to be recorded on video, including others in Brooklyn, San Bernardino, CA, and Chester, PA. In most cases, the victim was doing something illegal. In each case, multiple policemen beat up the victim with weapons or fists while he was unarmed and defenseless. Although one of Floyd Dent's police assailants was charged with assault, in most cases nothing happened to the violent officers.

None of these victims was killed. Media attention to violent police tactics has become much more intense recently because of a number of deadly incidents in 2014, such as the choking of Eric Garner in New York in July, and the shooting of Michael Brown in Ferguson, MO, in August. The *Guardian* has tried to list every person killed by police during 2015, tallying 202 unarmed victims.

In May, a 39-year-old woman led police on a high-speed chase in Wyoming. Her tires were deflated by spikes, and she emerged from her car with a knife, confronting five police. She was shot with a taser, but still did not drop the knife. Then she was shot twice and killed. Ten women armed only with knives were shot and killed by police in 2015.

I wonder about shooting to kill in those circumstances. As in the Wyoming case, often more than one officer was involved. How dangerous is a woman with a knife versus several police with batons? What about shooting in the leg?

The violence in these cases appears grossly excessive. It was not necessary to beat Floyd Dent, or any of the other victims mentioned above, before handcuffing them. It was not necessary to kill Michael Brown or Eric Garner. It was not necessary to kill all 10 women or the 125 men armed with knives who were killed in 2015.

Racism means that in all of these situations, African Americans are more likely to be victims of excessive police violence, more than twice as likely to be killed as whites. But twice as many whites were killed as blacks in 2015. The problem is larger than racism. When a group of heavily armed and highly trained police confront a suspect, even one armed with a knife, death should not be the result. Police should never hit someone multiple times with a club when they are down.

Policing is a dangerous business, every day and every night. Excessive police violence, now caught increasingly on camera, does not make it less dangerous. These incidents reduce the trust between police and the people they are paid to protect. The reluctance of police administrators and courts to get rid of violent cops makes policing less effective.

There are about one million police in the US. These incidents do not reflect normal interactions between citizens and police. But if we can watch a new video every month of groups of police brutalizing unarmed citizens, then we have a police problem.

STEVE HOCHSTADT
Jacksonville IL

Later that day, I received an email from the local deputy chief of police. He didn't like my "lack of knowledge of police tactics." My discussion of five police surrounding and shooting a woman with a knife "couldn't be further from the truth." He tried to be polite, but couldn't help writing that I "know nothing about the law." He claimed to know nothing about the incidents I discussed.

He invited me to participate in "simulated critical incidents", and another officer phoned to invite me to take part in the Citizens' Police Academy, so I would be "a little bit more informed." I offered to meet any representative of the police, under the condition that they watch the videos I discussed. I wondered what they thought was uninformed about my opinion that

"Police should never hit someone multiple times with a club when they are down."

I never heard back. Two days later, the dash-cam video of Laquan McDonald was released, showing him walking away from Chicago police as he was shot 16 times.

That's the life of an opinion columnist. People find it easy to say that you don't know anything, but avoid confronting the issues you bring up, and then disappear.

Thanksgiving had arrived. The juxtaposition of violence and feasting, of injustice and thankfulness, is a staple of most cop shows, as it is typical of the modern world. Many Americans are shielded by geographical privilege from the most dangerous manifestations of American life. We are all confronted with their reality every day by a media environment still following the motto, if it bleeds, it leads.

We ought to be more thankful just to be alive and secure.

Thanks at Thanksgiving
NOVEMBER 29, 2015

We have a tradition at Thanksgiving dinner, probably like many families, when we all say what we are thankful for. It's good to think about the good things in our lives, to dwell on what makes us happy, especially in these perilous times when bombs and bullets seem to threaten us wherever we look. Right now I am thankful that when our Christmas tree, that we had just put up and decorated, crashed over, nobody was hurt.

But something is often missing in these recitations: whom we are thanking. We can be thankful for food on the table or family togetherness without thinking too hard about who might be responsible. So I'll say a little about the people I wish to thank for the life I enjoy.

I should start with my parents. Of course, without them I would not exist, but they did much more than conceive me. My mother showed me how to play ping-pong and pool, taught me tennis and golf. My father, who grew up with soccer rather than baseball, played endless games of catch until I threw a ball better than he could. They showed me how to play fair to win. Sports always demonstrates wider ideals. Their love for the Dodgers and Jackie Robinson was my first lesson in civil rights. They nurtured and taught me, modeled values and created a personality.

My brother is younger, and didn't teach me much until we were both adults. Over these last few decades, he has taught me much about myself just by being himself. I look to him to connect me with my first family.

My wife taught me about feminism. Creating gender equality takes much more than repeating slogans or wishing the world were different. I had to give up male privileges, in exchange for which I gained a partner, someone whose life is as interesting as mine, whose ideas are as weighty, whose opinions as valuable.

I thank my children for showing me how to be a father. My own father was a good model, but imitation is not enough. These days they teach me more than I teach them, from cooking vegetarian dinners to making computers work to thinking clearly about life's difficult problems.

I thank my teachers. Some went beyond their prescribed lessons, designed for all students, to see me and what I needed, transforming teaching from a job into a calling. They inspired me to follow in their footsteps as well as I can.

I thank my editor, who has literally given me space here to think out loud, without regard for whether we agree.

Much more distant, but still important in my life, are the founders of our nation. They risked their lives to conceive something new, a political system based on neither tradition, religious dogma nor inherited status, but on ideals of equality and democratic power. Since then, many generations of founders have ignored conventional prejudices and improved that system, stretching equality and democracy to include more people, always risking much to fight those who claimed superiority for themselves. Our system was not nearly perfect when I was born, and remains imperfect. But the American life I enjoy would not have been possible without their struggles and sacrifices.

I thank many people whose names I don't know, who bring my mail and take my trash, who arrange for electricity and water and gas to be delivered to my house, who do their jobs so I can do mine. We don't think of them often enough. If you try to fetch your own water, chop your own wood and create your own heat, their contribution to our lives becomes apparent.

I thank government workers. As a group, they take a lot of heat from people with political axes to grind. Most earn middling salaries and deal with every kind of citizen, day after day, providing services without which we could not drive our cars, fly in airplanes, vote, or organize our communities. Some of them have risky jobs. I have never needed a firefighter or a cop, but I sleep better at night knowing that I can call them up at any time for help in situations far beyond my control.

I thank the writers who don't know me, but have provided me with their wisdom, their flights of fancy, their strings of words which enrich my life. I try to do the same for my readers.

I thank my friends. Some I have known nearly all my life; others I met only recently. Friends forget my mistakes and forgive my excesses. They are willing to give more than they get, because we are not keeping score.

None of us is an island. Whatever goodness comes to us is brought by others. Whatever we achieve has been helped by others. I should have thanked more people more often for what they have given me, but this is the best I can do now to catch up.

STEVE HOCHSTADT
Jacksonville IL

Gratitude toward others is precisely the human quality that Donald Trump most conspicuously lacks. Well before he became President, before any Republican primary votes, when he was merely the front-running candidate, his incessant bragging about his own abilities and denigration of everyone else angered me. Only much later did we learn from enterprising NYT reporters that he never publicly thanked the person he was most indebted to, his father. Trump said many times that he had used a small loan from his father to start his very big business. In fact, he was being paid $200,000 a year at age 3, and received over $400 million in all from his father. That would be worth several billion today just through inflation, about what Trump is worth. Thanks, Dad, do you mind if I lie about it?

It's a Bird! It's a Plane! It's Superman!
DECEMBER 20, 2015

Superman was the great savior during my childhood, along with a few other heros with seemingly superhuman abilities to dodge bullets and fight evil, like Wyatt Earp and Matt Dillon. It's thrilling to know that a real, live Superman now flies among us, fighting evil and saving America. Of course, I mean Donald Trump.

The earlier comic Superman hid his vast strength under a meek disguise, but when it came time to rescue us, he boldly displayed his awesome powers. Trump has never toyed with humility, but only recently has he thrown off all disguise to reveal the truly superhuman Trump.

Trump attended a military-style boarding school for 5 years in the early 1960s. He "always felt that I was in the military". School gave him "more training militarily than a lot of the guys that go into the military." That explains why he showed no interest in earthly war in Vietnam: he knew everything already. His military experience must have come from other planets. He told an Iowa audience, "I'm good at war. I've had a lot of wars of my own. I'm really good at war. I love war, in a certain way." Doesn't everybody?

Today he is a military expert without equal. "You know the thing I'll be great at? And I do very well at it. Military. I am the toughest guy. I will rebuild our military. It will be so strong and so powerful and so great, that we'll never have to use it. Nobody's going to mess with us, folks. Nobody. Nobody. Nobody's going to mess with us." He said, "I will be so good at the military, your head will spin." He told Bill O'Reilly, "There's nobody bigger or better at the military than I am."

Superman is tougher than anyone, but always fair. So is Trump. In 2011, he said, "I am the least racist person there is." In November, he reported that he was the "least racist person on Earth". This month, he told Don Lemon, the black CNN newsman, "I am the least racist person that you have ever met." That is why "I have a great relationship with the blacks. I've always had a great relationship with the blacks."

Superman had great physical powers. Trump also has great mental power. "I went to the Wharton School of Business. I'm, like, a really smart person." "I was a great student." His memory is other-worldly. He remembered graduating first at Wharton in 1968, when none of his classmates could remember him at all, and the commencement program did not list him as getting any honors.

Trump is really smart, and most of the rest of us are dummies. On Republican Congressional leaders: "These people are babies.... They're babies. They're babies." On other presidential candidates: Jeb Bush is "dumb as a rock" and Marco Rubio is a "clown". He told it like it is in Fort Dodge, Iowa, when he came in second in an Iowa poll: "How stupid are the people of Iowa? How stupid are the people of the country?"

These intellectual abilities enabled him to write a fantastic book. "I write a book called *The Art of the Deal*, the No. 1 selling business book of all time, at least I think, but I'm pretty sure it is." Other business books have sold 10 times as many copies here on Earth, like Stephen Covey's *The 7 Habits of Highly Effective People*, but Trump is adding in sales from all over the galaxy.

Put those superpowers together and you have an out-of-this-world negotiator. At the 2015 Values Voter Summit in Washington, he guaranteed the audience that after he is elected President, but even before he takes office, the Americans who are prisoners in Iran will be back. "I'll tell you what, I'll tell you what, I'll make this statement, if I get elected President, before I ever get to office, I guarantee you, they will be back, I guarantee you, 100%, 100%."

That's just a selection of his superpowers. Women are irresistibly attracted. "All of the women on The Apprentice flirted with me, consciously or unconsciously. That's to be expected." "I love beautiful women, and beautiful women love me." "I'll be the greatest jobs president that God ever created." "Teachers love me, every one of them". "The Hispanics love me." In fact, "People love me. I've been very successful. Everybody loves me."

Wow.

Add in one more super-power, his invisible shield that protects him from rays of knowledge from the outside world which he doesn't like.

I think he is super-fooling all of us. Here is what he is using all of his powers for: "It's very possible that I could be the first presidential candidate to run and make money on it."

That would be super. For him.

STEVE HOCHSTADT
Jacksonville IL

Here's what Trump's Superman complex means in real life. One of the first Trump books of 2020, *A Very Stable Genius*, by *Washington Post* reporters Philip Rucker and Carol Leonnig, revealed his concept of the Commander-in-Chief soon after he took office. The top military and foreign affairs advisors in our government, whom he had appointed, were so alarmed at his ignorance about our postwar alliances and military policies, that they scheduled a special seminar at the Pentagon to teach him the basics. The chair of the Joint Chiefs of Staff, the leaders of all the branches of our military, and other lower-level military and civilian men and women watched the Secretaries of State and Defense, Rex Tillerson and Gen. James Mathis, offer lessons. Trump got angry at the contradiction between what they were teaching and what he believed. He startled the entire room: "You're all losers. You don't know how to win any more. You're a bunch of dopes and babies."

Christmas came later that week. Although many evangelical Christians appear to worship Trump as their savior, it's hard for me to imagine Trump and Christmas in the same sentence. But even with all his superpowers, he can't overpower the good feelings of the holidays, spanning Hanukkah, Christmas, and New Year's Day.

Christmas is Always and Never the Same

JANUARY 5, 2016

I learned about Christmas from my wife Liz's parents, Janet and Roger. My own Jewish parents had put on a few Christmases for us, mainly as an excuse to give us presents. I can't remember if we had a tree. Those occasions left no permanent memories for me.

When my generation were all young marrieds, Christmas took place at my in-laws' house, around their tree, under their control. Every year the same foods were served and rituals were enacted, annually reproducing the Christmases my wife and her two sisters had grown up with.

I discovered there that Christmas is a family moment like no other, a universal celebration transformed into family customs, spiced with surprise and generosity. Everyone was welcome and I jumped right in.

Soon the next generation appeared in a flood, 6 cousins over 5 years. The needs of young families scattered across the country sometimes interfered with tradition. We had a Christmas in Maine one year with a tiny live tree, still growing these days as a towering spruce in our former front yard.

Gradually more control migrated to my generation, whether by default or assertion, it's hard to say. I felt empowered to express my wish that chipped beef on white toast, the notorious SOS, would disappear from the Christmas morning menu by demonstrating that a whole loaf of Wonder bread could be balled up and put into my pants pocket. The tomato aspic at Christmas dinner, a relic of a long dead generation which became the source of risqué humor among the youngest generation, disappeared.

Family never stops changing with time, and now my children's generation are in charge of their Christmases, shared, or more accurately, divided between families near and far. This year, Jack, the first child of a new generation, has joined us, a grandchild to my generation, to others a great-grandchild or a nephew. Jack's parents decorated their own tree and negotiated their Christmas celebration among competing sets of families. We became guests. The traditional rituals of our extended family were not abandoned, but reshaped into new circumstances.

I realize only now that Janet and Roger had not always created Christmases. They had grown up with the Christmases of their elders, then gradually took control, not in a struggle for power, but as part of life's inevitable progression. By the time I learned about Christmas from them, they were in the middle of their phase of temporary control.

I miss their raucous family gatherings, organized by two generations of adults for the benefit of our children. I haven't stayed up late on Christmas eve putting together a Barbie ice cream shop for many years. Those delightful Christmas mornings are unforgettable, when our children and their cousins gathered excitedly at the top of the stairs, waiting for the signal to dash down toward the presents under the tree.

Those were high points during one stage in all of our lives. Those Christmases were shaped by the unique circumstances of three generations, all in agreement that these celebrations must go on forever, but unable to alter the passage of time. They have given way to a more patient brewing of coffee and tea before unwrapping stocking gifts.

As in many other things, my generation of post-war babies has had our day. We played our role as teachers of Christmas. What our children choose to take into their own Christmases will eventually tell us how we did. Baby Jack is the first of a new generation of kids, for whom Christmas will be recreated and repeated until they are old enough to know how they want to celebrate family and tradition.

Trees will still be decorated, presents wrapped and stockings filled. Well-loved ornaments will reemerge from their boxes. The repetition is comforting, and the not entirely predictable changes will remind us how exciting Christmas is for everyone.

STEVE HOCHSTADT
Springbrook, WI

★ ★ ★

CHAPTER 7

Heroes and Rebels: 2016

It's only in retrospect that 2016 turns out to have been the year of Trump winning more Electoral College votes than anyone thought. It began as the eighth year of the Obama presidency, which had settled into a political routine. Republicans in Congress would do nothing that Obama proposed, and tried to undo everything he had accomplished. On January 8, he vetoed the Restoring Americans' Healthcare Freedom Reconciliation Act, passed by the Republican Congress on party-line votes to undo Obamacare and suspend federal funding for Planned Parenthood. Republicans did not have a two-thirds majority in the House or Senate, so the bill was simply one of dozens of symbolic gestures to demonstrate their unrelenting hostility to Obamacare.

Both the booming economy, the best since the 1990s, and Republican intransigence against governing with Barack Obama, had become normality by 2016. The year's events demonstrate that Trump's hatred for Obama and everything connected with him stood fully in the Republican mainstream.

Normal American life in 2016, as in any year, includes countless individual family dramas, of great importance to a small number of people, and a handful of national dramas, which everyone knows about. January's drama grew out of the persistent struggle between reactionary conservatism and government liberalism, staged on the wide open spaces of the American West, reminiscent of the range wars of the 19th century. Quoting God and the Constitution, carrying long guns, and disdaining everybody but themselves, the Bundy gang turned naked greed into a political crisis.

Western Stand-Off

JANUARY 24, 2016

Over three weeks ago, armed men occupied the Malheur National Wildlife Refuge in eastern Oregon. The stand-off between illegal occupiers of a federal reserve and everyone else turns on a fundamental disagreement about democratic government and public property in America.

Malheur is located in a lightly populated section of the huge Northern Great Basin in the West. Once this area was home to millions of large nesting birds, including egrets and greater sandhill cranes. In the late 19th century, hunters seeking feathers for hats nearly killed off these flocks. In 1908, Teddy Roosevelt established the Lake Malheur Reservation, one of 51 wildlife refuges he created as President. In the 1930s, over 1000 men in the Civilian Conservation Corps built stone buildings, miles of roads, bridges, camping facilities and lookout towers in the Refuge. They connected local communities with telephone lines. Jobs provided to local craftsmen, and purchases of food and supplies for the CCC enriched the economy of Harney County during the deepest Depression.

The Malheur Refuge is part of a system of wildlife refuges run by the US Fish and Wildlife Service within the Interior Department. Over 560 refuges across the country provide access to wildlife within an hour's drive of most metropolitan centers. More than 45 million people visit the refuges every year for hunting, fishing, photography, hiking, or just watching. There are seven wildlife refuges in Illinois, including the Emiquon National Wildlife Refuge at the confluence of the Illinois and Spoon Rivers, wetlands for thousands of migratory ducks only 40 miles north of Jacksonville.

The angry men who have taken over the Malheur Refuge don't care about the democratic public uses of federally owned lands. The occupiers disdain the idea of public property. They want the US government to give up control of the wildlife refuge to private uses. They asked local people to sign documents repudiating the U.S. Bureau of Land Management's authority.

A list of people who are occupying Malheur perhaps provides a sketch of the militia movement. Most have criminal records. Most went to Cliven Bundy's ranch when he defied federal officials in 2014. Many have failed economically and owe money to the government they are protesting. Many had participated in another destructive demonstration of their disdain for public use in May 2014, when they drove ATVs through a canyon closed to motorized vehicles because it houses thousand-year-old ruins of dwellings and burial sites of Native Americans.

The occupiers thought local people would welcome them. The opposite is true. The ranchers whom the occupiers claimed they wanted to protect from arrest have criticized them. The Harney County Sheriff condemned their intimidation of local law enforcement. A group of sportsmen, Backcountry Hunters & Anglers, tore down a makeshift sign put up by the occupiers, and denounced their taking of public lands. A few days after the occupation began, the Sheriff asked hundreds of local residents at a public meeting at the Harney County Fairgrounds if the occupiers should leave. Nearly everybody raised their hands.

Like Cliven Bundy, their spiritual and political godfather, they want these lands, improved by a century of public investment, to be used for private economic benefit. In 2014, Bundy had concocted arguments about why the Constitution allowed him to have free grazing rights on public land, which every court rejected. He continued to graze his cattle on public land, but stopped paying. He used the language of the "sovereign citizen" movement to defend his right to ignore all government authorities. Ammon Bundy, his son and one of the stand-off leaders, rejects the authority of the FBI.

It's not always useful to listen to a movement's loudest mouths. But the Bundys have rallied this small occupation, and the wider movement of armed opponents of our democratic government, behind their expression of basic ideas.

They all wave the Constitution, along with "history books" that allege some connection between our founding document and their current politics. They reject all forms and manifestations of national government authority. That's not a Constitutional interpretation that anyone else shares. It doesn't derive from the document, it precedes it. The basis of this interpretation was made abundantly clear by Ammon Bundy: "I did exactly what the Lord asked me to do." Cliven and Ammon Bundy in 2014 and now Ammon Bundy again cited passages from the Book of Mormon to justify their actions.

The sovereign occupier movement is a religious rebellion against the political structure of our country. All the nation's authorities about that structure, from local law enforcement to state judges to the Supreme Court, plus the accumulated wisdom of generations of historians, reject the occupier movement's claim to be supported by the Constitution. Leaders in the Church of the Latter Day Saints said they "are deeply troubled by the reports that those who have seized the facility suggest that they are doing so based on scriptural principles."

In a 2014 survey, law enforcement agencies said sovereign citizen groups pose the greatest threat to their communities, more than radical Islamists. Economists, on the other hand, might applaud their tactics. If I wave the Bible and the Constitution and my gun and my cowboy hat enough, we won't have to pay what we owe. So far it's worked.

STEVE HOCHSTADT
Jacksonville IL

Amazing to my way of thinking about justice and rule of law in America, Ammon and Ryan Bundy were later acquitted and walked free. Imagine if the armed occupiers of Malheur had proclaimed that Black Lives Matter.

Big Republican names, including Rand Paul, Ted Cruz, Ben Carson, and, of course, Donald Trump, had praised Cliven Bundy and his family. That's a sharp contrast from the way Republicans talk about peaceable professors going about our business of teaching and research. We appear to be more dangerous to Republican ideas about government than armed lawbreakers.

The Trump administration's attempt to get science out of government has become a crusade to eliminate all restrictions on business activities that are based on medical, biological, geological and meteorological science. What seems unprecedented is in fact the logical outcome of years of normal Republican attacks on the discoverers and promoters of modern science, American professors. If the news is bad, slander those who report it.

The Republican Assault on Higher Education
FEBRUARY 16, 2016

Republican politicians are angry about public higher education in America. The ideas they and their conservative supporters cherish are repeatedly demonstrated by academic experts to be false.

While every Republican presidential candidate argues that creationism should be taught, either alone or alongside evolutionary biology, biologists at every state university dismiss creationism as nonsense. While every Republican presidential candidate argues that climate change is a hoax, or a natural occurrence, or anyway nothing to worry about, physical scientists in every field at every state university have overwhelming evidence that human-caused global warming could lead to a global disaster.

These are just the most obvious examples of how unhappy Republicans are with the work of America's professors. Scientists across the disciplines keep demonstrating that industries create health hazards and that fossil fuels contribute to warming. Social scientists around the country discuss how we should deal with the continuing legacy of racism and sexism. Political scientists cast doubt on the Constitutional interpretations Republicans use to justify their political preferences.

Historians keep digging up incidents in our past which discredit the dreamy illusion of America as God's country and Americans as God's people. They put words like "race" and "gender" into their book titles and courses, when conservatives would rather not think in those categories. They disparage the publications of Ted Cruz's favorite historian, David Barton, head of Cruz's super PAC. Barton claims that it is a myth that the Constitution insists on separation of church and state, and his "historical" research is devoted to proving that the US was founded as a Christian nation.

How can the collective wisdom and work of the best educated people in American society be dismissed as unworthy of attention? The Republican answer: America's professors advocate these ideas because we are both liberal and dishonest.

It's not hard to find statistics that show the great majority of professors to be liberal or worse. There must follow another logical step: we pursue our liberal agenda by ignoring evidence, cooking the numbers, and making things up. Ted Cruz's father Rafael says that evolution is a communist plot. Donald Trump offers a different reason why science isn't scientific, but political: "The concept of global warming was created by and for the Chinese in order to make U.S. manufacturing non-competitive." The extraordinary claim that the world's climate scientists are engaged in an international conspiracy to tell a big lie is one part of their broader argument that academics are liars.

Across the country Republican politicians are attacking public universities. Governor Scott Walker sought to promote his presidential ambitions by trying to cut the funding of the University of Wisconsin and to repudiate its fundamental intellectual mission. He proposed to remove the phrases "search for truth" and "improve the human condition" from the University's charge, replacing them with "meet the state's workforce needs". The Republican-dominated Board of Governors of the University of North Carolina voted to close UNC's Center on Poverty, Work, and Opportunity because it advocates for the poor, and the Institute for Civic Engagement and Social Change at historically black North Carolina Central University, because it promotes voter empowerment. The Board is hiking tuition and capping financial aid, after years of state cuts to higher education spending.

While attacking public universities, Republicans lavish attention on Liberty University, founded by Jerry Falwell in 1971. Liberty University promotes a "Christian worldview" that "leads people to Jesus Christ as the Lord of the universe and their own personal Savior." Cruz announced his candidacy there, and Jeb Bush, Ben Carson, and Donald Trump also spoke there.

Another favorite is Bob Jones University, whose ban on interracial dating lasted into the 21st century. Cruz, Carson, Bush, and Marco Rubio appeared there this month, Cruz and Carson for the second time. BJU scientists say that "claims which contradict scripture cannot be true", such as that the Earth is more than a few thousand years old.

Republican politicians deliver to the American public the idea that every field of knowledge is dominated by political interest, that there is no "science", only advocacy. Republican know-nothingism has led to the assault on vaccines, one of the greatest public health triumphs of the 20th century. Trump has repeatedly claimed that vaccines lead to autism. Ben Carson equivocated about vaccination, saying "we are probably giving way too many in too short a period of time". Carly Fiorina argued against mandatory vaccination, as did Rand Paul, who also claimed that vaccines cause mental disorders.

Public education decreases public ignorance. The Republican attack on institutions of higher learning whose budgets they control, their slandering of our nation's professors, and their dismissal of the Enlightenment idea that better science means a better society are a comprehensive political strategy to maintain and even increase public ignorance.

Combined with the much more vicious attack on private and public media as politically biased and unreliable, the Republican Party seeks to rule a dumbed-down America. Are we dumb enough to support that?

STEVE HOCHSTADT
Jacksonville, IL

The fact-checking website PolitFact called Trump's entire campaign the 2015 Lie of the Year. Everyone was writing about Trump's lies, which tormented my moral sense. Equally outrageous to me was Trump's pose of manliness. His public persona deliberately embodied all that I define as toxic masculinity, without showing any evidence of courage or strength. I was deeply offended.

Donald Trump the He-Man

MARCH 6, 2016

Who is Donald Trump? Now that Trump has taken a commanding lead in the Republican presidential race, this question is being debated across the country. What kind of person is he? Why does he behave as he does?

Whatever Trump may be like at home, in public he deliberately projects the image of a thoroughly masculine character, a man's man, as the now outdated saying goes. Here are some traits which are typically associated with masculinity: competitive, forceful, aggressive, independent, willing to take risks, assertive, acts as leader. These are all qualities which Trump displays at every opportunity, which he brags about in interviews and in his books, and which he tries to personify.

Rarely has anyone outside of the sports world talked so much about winning. Trump believes every aspect of life is a contest that he must win. In September, he said at a rally on Capitol Hill: "We will have so much winning if I get elected, that you may get bored with the winning." After he won in Nevada in February: "We weren't expected to win too much and now we're winning, winning, winning the country. And soon the country is going to start winning, winning, winning." He admits to no losses in his past and he constantly calls others "losers": Ted Cruz, editor Graydon Carter of *Vanity Fair*, columnist S.E. Cupp, Republican consultant Cheri Jacobus, Karl Rove (4 times in the past few months), all of ISIS, the *New York Daily News*, and *Politico*.

Trump's aggressiveness takes his political opponents by surprise. Any criticism of him is met with amplified aggression. His Twitter account is filled with nasty remarks about the incompetence and low intelligence of anyone who has noted his past failures or present prevarications. His debate performances display verbal aggression unprecedented for a presidential candidate.

One traditionally masculine trait is bragging about sexual power. Soon after Princess Diana was killed in an auto accident, Trump said on radio that he could have slept with her. In *Trump: The Art of the Deal*, he repeatedly wrote about his many affairs with "beautiful women". In *Trump: The Art of the Comeback*: "If I told the real stories of my experiences with women, often seemingly very happily married and important women, this book would be a guaranteed best-seller." In *Trump: How to Get Rich*: "All the women on The Apprentice flirted with me — consciously or unconsciously."

In response to Marco Rubio's irrelevant and crude remark about his "small hands", Trump felt it necessary to assure everyone about his genitalia: "I guarantee you there's no problem. I guarantee you."

When he criticizes others, he uses the language of inadequate masculinity. "Weak" is one of his favorite taunts, directed at Jeb Bush, Ben Carson, Hillary Clinton, Marco Rubio (many times), Barack Obama, European leaders generally, the Democratic Party, the Republican National Committee, and the United States. He thinks of his opponents as "lightweights" — Bush, Rubio, and Megyn Kelly. Most insulting for the super-masculine Trump, he gleefully repeated one of his supporter's comments about Ted Cruz: "He's a pussy."

One quotation that Trump recently retweeted exemplifies this hyper-masculinity: "It is better to live one day as a lion than 100 years as a sheep." Benito Mussolini was the author, which didn't seem to bother Trump, perhaps confirming his similarity to a quintessential strong man.

Trump aggressively displays the opposite of the traits which are often described as feminine: sympathetic, sensitive, compassionate, loyal, gentle, understanding.

One stereotypical masculine trait which Trump does not openly display is physical strength. Arnold Schwarzenegger and Jesse Ventura used their imposing bodies to attract attention to their political campaigns. But Trump wants us all to know how powerful he is. He released a letter from his family physician in December claiming that his health is "astonishingly excellent" and "extraordinary". The doctor wrote that Trump would be "the healthiest individual ever elected to the presidency."

In December, Fox News host Andrea Tantaros said that American men could "get their masculinity back" by voting for Trump. Trump's he-man pose, combined with his attacks on women aimed at their sexuality, might well energize some men, especially white men, who feel they have lost their dominance in the modern world. One could suspect, however, that a man who can't stop touting his masculinity might be less certain than he proclaims.

STEVE HOCHSTADT
Jacksonville IL

By April, Trump was far ahead of all his Republican rivals, all men, polling over 40%. Only Ted Cruz and John Kasich remained in the race, falling behind in the competition for delegates. I thought he could win the Republican nomination. But I assumed that the feelings at the foundation of my political morality were American feelings, broadly shared. They seemed to me self-evident, needing only the persuasion of facts like those I had just outlined. I made the pundit's error of mistaking my wishes for reality.

I was still optimistic about American voters.

Later in April, Trump broke through the 50% barrier, winning over 55% of East Coast primary voters. Conservatives were not like me at all.

Except perhaps for our love of sports. Even in terms of athletics, though, partisan politics distorts perceptions. Many conservatives believe that liberals, especially liberal men, are "wimps", feminized "soy boys" in the latest right-wing insult to follow "quiche-eaters". In fact, most NFL fans are Democrats. I've never seen any evidence that conservatives are better athletes than liberals. Apart from such nonsense, sports is infected by politics, not so much among athletes, but among those who control sports organizations.

The most obvious struggles between conservative sports bureaucracies and liberal political activists occur around race and gender. Prejudiced judgments by the white male leaders of athletic organizations are still apparent today: black coaches are a rarity in the NFL and world champion women soccer players have to fight for reasonable financial rewards.

The "scientific" judgments that women are not physically capable of strenuous athletic effort and that blacks are not intellectually capable of team leadership are an American tradition.

Women in the Boston Marathon

APRIL 26, 2016

My daughter-in-law ran the 120th Boston Marathon last week. She was one of 13,000 women in the world's oldest yearly road race.

The very first marathon race, part of the revival of the Olympics in 1896, was won appropriately by unheralded Greek water carrier Spyridon Louis in under 3 hours. Eight of 17 runners finished, seven Greeks and one Hungarian.

The Boston Marathon was initiated the next year, April 19, 1897, to celebrate Patriots' Day, which had been invented in Massachusetts in 1894 to commemorate the battles of Lexington and Concord in 1775, as well as the first bloodshed of the Civil War in the Baltimore riot of 1861. The Marathon was added to the patriotic holiday to link the American struggle for independence with Athenian ideals of democracy. The newly formed Boston Athletic Association was well organized: alongside each of the 15 runners rode a militiaman on a bicycle with water, lemons, and wet handkerchiefs.

Over the next 70 years, the race was transformed into an international event for men. The field ballooned from its usual 200 before 1960 to nearly 500 in 1965.

But women were banned in Boston. Into the 1960s, athletic authorities claimed women were incapable of running that distance. The longest AAU-sanctioned race for women was 1.5 miles. Women could not compete further than 800 meters in the Olympics.

By that time, Roberta Gibb was in her 20s. Accepted ideas about what women could and couldn't do were no longer universally believed. Gibb watched the 1964 Boston Marathon and thought she could try it. She trained on her own for two years, including a trip across the US which combined driving and running. By the time she reached the Pacific Ocean, she could run 40 miles.

But she couldn't run Boston in 1966. The race director wrote: "Women aren't allowed, and furthermore are not physiologically able."

Gibb took a bus from San Diego to Boston, arrived the night before the race, hid behind a forsythia bush near the start, and blended into the crowd of male runners as they passed by. She had worn a hooded sweatshirt to hide her illegal gender, but soon got too hot. She was worried that taking it off would get her in trouble, but the men around her said not to worry. "We won't let anyone bother you." The news that a woman was running spread quickly. As the runners passed through Wellesley, thousands of extra spectators cheered her. Fifty years later, Gibb remembered, "The women of Wellesley College knew I was coming and let out an enormous scream. They were jumping in the air, laughing and crying." Her feet bled in her new boy's size 6 running shoes. There were no shoes made for women. She finished in 3:21 in the top third of the pack, faster than average finish times for men today.

The press was excited by her story, but unable to understand her motivations. She was asked whether she had some axe to grind against men. Photographers followed her to her parents' home, where they wanted to take pictures of her cooking. The BAA released an official statement: "There is no such thing as a marathon for women."

All around her, Gibb had found acceptance and encouragement from runners and spectators. The authorities, the experts, the people in charge said women couldn't do that. They meant that women, their idea of women, shouldn't do that. After she did it, they said she was an anomaly, a freak. We won't let you do that. Roberta Gibb was a freak in a sense — she was willing to reject their thinking and violate their rules.

That wasn't enough, though. The next year, Gibb ran again unofficially. Jock Semple, the race director, ran into the street to tear the bib number off Kathrine Switzer, who had entered incognito as K.V. Switzer. Switzer's running partner, a hammer thrower, body-blocked Semple, and other racers protected her.

In the years after Gibb's first Boston marathon, the idea that women could do it, too, whatever it was, bubbled through American society. It took a movement to crash through the walls authorities had built around women.

Gibb ran again in 1968, beating four other women. In 1972, women were finally allowed to enter — 8 women started and they all finished. Title IX, opening all forms of school sports to women, was passed in 1972. That year women were allowed to run 1500 meters in the Munich Olympics. The first Olympic women's marathon was held in Los Angeles in 1984.

The 2016 program of the Boston Marathon celebrates 50 years of women in Boston. Gibb was the Grand Marshall of Boston this year. My daughter-in-law did not have to hide or feel alone when she ran. She didn't have to be an activist or a freak. She just had to be a runner.

STEVE HOCHSTADT
Jacksonville IL

Athletes who wave the American flag at Olympic events are celebrated. Those who protest American racism are punished. Mixing politics and sports is outlawed, unless the politics is conservative nationalism.

The history of American black athletes protesting racism is long. Jackie Robinson never protested on the field, but he used his celebrity to support the civil rights movement in the 1950s. Bill Russell and other black players on the Boston Celtics boycotted an exhibition game in Lexington, Kentucky, in 1961, after they were refused service at a restaurant. The American Football League All-Star game was scheduled to be played in New Orleans in January 1965, but the 21 black players on both teams encountered discrimination as soon as they arrived at the airport. They refused to play, and the game was moved to Houston. Muhammad Ali raised the stakes later in the 1960s.

He Was the Greatest

JUNE 7, 2016

Muhammad Ali is dead. His life at the end was severely restricted by the consequences of repeated blows to his head. The debilitating effects of concussions are now a national topic, beyond boxing, even beyond hockey and football. Ali was a shadow of his former self, better known for his daughter's boxing successes than for anything he could do or say.

He is universally known for his joyous insistence that "I am the greatest," an outrageous boast that he first made when he was 18, right after winning the gold medal in the Rome Olympics in 1960. Typically it was combined with a taunt to a rival boxer, Floyd Patterson: "Hey Floyd — I seen you! Someday I'm gonna whup you! Don't you forget, I am the greatest!" He repeated that boast after defeating Sonny Liston in 1964.

For a long time he was the greatest. He was undefeated as a professional until Joe Frazier beat him in 1971. He won back the heavyweight championship twice. But in his prime, Ali transcended his sport by insisting loudly that sports, politics and race were inevitably intertwined. He used the outsized personality he created as a boxer to turn the spotlight on racism.

As Cassius Clay, he had felt the lash of American racism as it was still practiced in the postwar South. His mother remembered a time when her little son was refused a drink of water in a store. A decade later, returning to Louisville after winning the gold medal at the Rome Olympics in 1960, he was refused service at a whites-only restaurant.

Although Cassius Marcellus Clay had been an abolitionist politician, who published an anti-slavery newspaper before the Civil War in Lexington, Kentucky, the young Clay changed his name right after defeating Liston, as he joined the Nation of Islam. He had been moving closer to the Black Muslims since meeting Malcolm X in 1962.

Ali became a much more prominent political figure when he was drafted in 1966. He had failed the written induction test earlier, but the needs of the escalating Vietnam War led the Selective Service to lower the standards, and Ali was reclassified 1-A. He refused induction.

His heavyweight title was taken from him, he lost the right to fight in the US, he was convicted of draft evasion and sentenced to five years in prison. He had won 29 fights in a row since turning pro in 1960. He did not fight for over three years, between age 25 and 28, prime years for a boxer. Rarely has taking a principled political position caused someone to lose so much.

His opposition to fighting in Vietnam was not only rooted in his religious belief. It was also about race, not just about him, but about all African Americans. In February 1966, he said: "Why should they ask me to put on a uniform and go ten thousand miles from home and drop bombs and bullets on brown people in Vietnam, while so-called Negro people in Louisville are treated like dogs and denied simple human rights?" On a campus speaking tour to support himself in 1967, he said to white students, "My enemies are white people, not Viet Congs or Chinese or Japanese. You my opposer when I want freedom. You my opposer when I want justice. You my opposer when I want equality. You won't even stand up for me in America for my religious beliefs, and you want me to go somewhere and fight, but you won't even stand up for me here at home." "They never called me nigger. They never lynched me. They didn't put no dogs on me."

That same year Martin Luther King, Jr., came out against the Vietnam War, and referred to Ali: "Like Muhammad Ali puts it, we are all, black and brown and poor, victims of the same system of oppression." Ali inspired other athletes to connect sport and racism. When Juan Carlos and Tommie

Smith raised their fists at the 1968 Olympics, one of their demands was "Restore Muhammad Ali's title." Eventually the Supreme Court overturned his conviction in 1971, on the grounds that the government had not given any reason for disallowing his claim to be a conscientious objector on the basis of his religion.

These days we hear another outsized personality constantly proclaiming that he is the greatest. Donald Trump was a friend of Ali, but when he advocated banning Muslims from entering the US, Ali responded immediately in a statement entitled "Presidential Candidates Proposing to Ban Muslim Immigration to the United States". "We as Muslims have to stand up to those who use Islam to advance their own personal agenda. They have alienated many from learning about Islam."

Ali devoted years to becoming champion. But he was willing to give up his personal agenda to defend his principles. That was great.

STEVE HOCHSTADT
Jacksonville IL

Ali was not alone. The most famous black athletes of his era supported his refusal to fight in Vietnam: Lew Alcindor, Jim Brown, and Bill Russell, among others. Ali was never silent. But even silent gestures of protest by black athletes earned punishment. That was true when Tommie Smith and John Carlos took off their shoes and raised their fists in Mexico City in 1968, and when Colin Kaepernick knelt in 2016.

Athletes are presented to us as heroes, whose number jerseys we should proudly wear. We should admire them for winning. Ali was a great winner, but I did not admire him for beating up other men in the ring. I was inspired by his willingness to give up winning in order to make a political statement.

I admire other athletes just for their persistence in competing. The story of the Paralympics offers many individuals to admire, athletes and others.

Inspiration from the Paralympics

SEPTEMBER 13, 2016

Right after the Nazis took power in 1933, Ludwig Guttman, one of the top neurosurgeons in Germany, was fired from his position at a public hospital, because he was Jewish. In 1939, he and his family fled to England, when they realized their lives were in danger.

Guttman convinced the British government to start a new center for veterans with spinal injuries, and he became the first director of the National Spinal Injuries Centre at Stoke Mandeville Hospital. Guttman wanted to reintegrate his patients into society. Physical rehabilitation was only the first phase of his treatment. One of his patients wrote, "One of the most difficult tasks for a paraplegic is to cheer up his visitors!"

Guttman believed in athletic activity, both to improve a patient's physical health and to aid in integration into the community, by increasing self-respect and competitive spirit. Some of his paraplegic patients would roll their wheelchairs along the hospital halls and hit objects with sticks. Guttman developed team sports, which became the first Stoke Mandeville Games, when 16 ex-servicemen and -women competed in archery on the day that the 1948 Olympics opened in London. In 1952, a team of Dutch war veterans joined in, creating the first international games for the disabled, with 130 participants.

In 1958, Guttman and the Director of the Spinal Center in Rome, Antonia Maglio, started preparations for the 9th Annual International Stoke Mandeville Games to be held in Rome in 1960. Only athletes with spinal cord injuries competed. The competition took place six days after the Rome

Olympic Games, and besides archery included swimming, wheelchair basketball and fencing, and track and field.

The Rome Games were a tremendous step for all athletes with physical impairments. Later that year, an International Working Group on Sport for the Disabled was created to consider sports for other kinds of disabilities: the blind, amputees, and persons with cerebral palsy. In 1961, Guttman founded the British Sports Association for the Disabled, and national organizations began to proliferate. Acceptance for the legitimacy of international games for the disabled grew, and eventually in 1988 in Seoul the word Paralympic came into official use.

The Games have expanded to include 20 different sports and over 4000 participants from nearly every nation in the world. In 1976 in Toronto, different disabilities were included for the first time, expanding the games beyond athletes in wheelchairs. American athletes won the most medals at each meeting until Sydney in 2000. The Chinese made their first significant appearance then, and in the next meeting in Atlanta in 2004 won the most medals, which they have done each time since. In London in 2012, volleyball, cycling, and judo were added. In Rio, athletes will compete for the first time in sailing and triathlon.

Many types of disabilities from birth, disease or accident can distort the normal functioning of the human body: missing limbs, limited range of motion of joints, decreased muscle power, visual or intellectual impairment. The Paralympics movement has developed a complex system of classifications to ensure "fair and equal competition".

In order to include as many athletes as possible, there are multiple versions of the same event. In the 100-meter dash, 15 gold medals can be won by women in different classes depending on degree of visual impairment, or whether they are missing legs or arms.

The Rio triathlon exemplifies the complexities of creating inclusivity among athletes with different disabilities. Blind athletes can compete with a guide accompanying them in all phases. Paraplegics use wheelchairs for the run and handcycles instead of bicycles. Race bikes with adaptations are used by those with partial use of their legs. Men and women competed for three gold medals in triathlon in Rio, including 10 blind women in class PT5, each accompanied by a guide.

Looking for inspiration from athletic success? Watch a one-legged high jumper from China clear the bar at 6′ 5″ at https://www.youtube.com/watch?v=_FoUNuTGFzg. That's not a world record, though, because the Canadian Arnie Boldt, who lost a leg in a grain augur accident at age 3, jumped 6′ 8″ outdoors and 6′10″ indoors in 1981. Or watch the women's 100-meter final from London in 2012, when 9 runners with 7 full legs among them competed, and Martina Caironi set a new world record of 15.87 seconds.

Ellen Keane from Ireland used to wear long sleeves to cover up the fact that she was born without a left arm. Now she proudly dons a swimsuit to compete in the 200-meter individual medley, in which she won a bronze medal at the 2015 International Paralympic Committee World Swimming Championships in Glasgow. She says, "Sports taught me to accept my handicap. I now find it okay to have only one arm. I wouldn't have it any different."

Dr. Guttman's vision has been realized on a world scale. The athletic performances of the thousands of Paralympic athletes in Rio, far exceeding what most "normal" athletes could accomplish, make the word handicapped seem inappropriate. None of them can earn a living from professional sports. They have achieved much more: pride in what their bodies can do, rather than shame for what they can't.

STEVE HOCHSTADT
Berlin, Germany

Maybe I watch too much sports. Maybe athletic contests bring out unhealthy feelings of national pride, home team favoritism, my team is better than your team partisanship. Maybe sports is given too much emphasis in educational institutions and professional athletes earn too much money.

Okay, but I've loved sports all my life and played sports as long as I could, from Little League to old men's basketball. But not as an escape from "real life". Sports is part of our real lives, and that means that politics in the widest sense is ever present, even if talking trash about Trump has no place during the game.

A surprising study of the political leanings of sports fans shows how athletic preferences can mirror political choices. Everyone likes the Olympics. Republicans like NASCAR and the PGA tour. Democrats like the NBA and tennis. Women's sports attract the most one-sided fans, and the WNBA lies at the extreme: liberals support female athletes.

Women as Second-Class Athletes

OCTOBER 4, 2016

The other night I saw women play basketball, a sport I love to watch and used to love to play. These were not ordinary women. Most were over 6 feet, several over 6'6". Many could dunk, although dunking is not a significant part of the women's game, as it is for men. They were extraordinarily skilled with the ball, hitting shots from beyond the 3-point line, dribbling in traffic between their legs and behind their backs, and controlling the ball with one hand. Their team play was terrific.

The Minnesota Lynx beat the Phoenix Mercury in the second game of their semi-final playoff for the Women's National Basketball Association championship. About 12,000 fans did the usual professional basketball things: waving little towels, standing up and sitting down, distracting Mercury foul shots, mugging for cameras, and trying to catch T-shirts propelled into the stands with a slingshot. Since then, the Lynx won one more game and will play in the finals.

The average attendance for the men's NBA team in Minneapolis, the Timberwolves, was 14,500 in 2015-2016. Their record was terrible, 29-53, placing 13th out of 15 teams in the Western conference, and missing the playoffs for the 12th consecutive season.

That's the weakness of women's sports in America. Fans prefer to see a losing men's team over a winning women's team. Average attendance at WNBA games is less than half of NBA games.

American women have dominated the basketball world for the past 32 years. Since winning Olympic gold for the first time in 1984, the US women have won nearly every international game they played. They missed one Olympic gold medal out of eight and two World Championships out of eight. Their record is 126-3.

But professional opportunities here are limited. The first women's professional league, the WBL, lasted only from 1978-1981. Salaries barely reached $5000, and were not always paid. The Women's American Basketball Association existed only for the 1984 season, and FOX Sports bought the Women's Basketball Association after a few seasons in the 1990s and disbanded it.

The WNBA is now celebrating its 20th year. It was a creation of the NBA, which owned the league for its first years. Only recently have teams gotten individual ownership. For its first 11 years, the WNBA was unable to get a network agreement to pay teams television rights.

Maya Moore dominated the scoring in the game we saw, one of best players in America. She was the first WNBA draft pick of 2011. She also won the Euroleague title in 2013 with a Spanish team and has led her Chinese team to league titles since 2013. Moore describes women's professional sports in America: "We go from amazing AAU experiences to high school All-American games to the excitement and significant platform of the collegiate level to this. Less coverage. Empty seats. Fewer eyeballs. Somewhere up the chain of command — in companies that, in many ways, dictate what is 'cool' — people are making choices not to celebrate the WNBA and its players." Moore lays the blame on "cultural influencers and partners in corporate America".

Women play WNBA ball because they love the game. The economics of women's sports in America continues the inequality of salaries, press attention, endorsements, and fan excitement.

I rooted against Phoenix's Diana Taurasi, but I've loved watching her play since she led UConn to 3 national championships in 2002-2004. Lucky for me she was playing this year, after sitting out the last WNBA season. Taurasi's real professional life is in Russia. Phoenix made her the first WNBA draft pick in 2004, but by 2005, she was also playing for Dynamo Moscow. She switched to Spartak Moscow in 2006 and led them to 4 consecutive Euroleague championships, twice winning Finals MVP.

After a couple of years in the Turkish basketball league, she switched to UMMC Ekaterinburg, 900 miles east of Moscow. She earned $1.5 million for a season at Ekaterinburg, compared to $107,000, the top WNBA salary. When she broke her hand in 2014 league play, she had to sit out the championships. To ensure her health, Ekaterinburg offered to add her tiny WNBA salary on top of theirs, if she skipped the 2015 WNBA season. She took the deal.

Brittney Griner, another number 1 WNBA draftee, made less than $50,000 in her first year, but collected $600,000 from a Chinese team. The men's first draft NBA pick made over 100 times what a comparable woman makes in the WNBA.

Check your local paper for coverage of women's sports. Local high school teams might get nearly equivalent coverage, but men's college teams and especially men's professional teams crowd out stories about women athletes. WNBA scores are hard to find out from papers like this one.

Chicken or egg? Will corporate America change its bottom-line mindset only when the real America buys more tickets to see professional women play? Will that only happen when public media, from cable giants to local papers, pay more attention to professional women?

Progress is slow. But if you want to see great ball, check out the WNBA finals coming in a few days.

STEVE HOCHSTADT
Springbrook, WI

As I write this, the WNBA has just signed a contract with its players to double their salaries and grant them paid maternity leave. Welcome to the 21st century!

Dogs like sports, too. Fetch the ball, race other dogs, and tug of war are favorite canine sports. It doesn't matter who wins, pure fun lies in the playing. There's a lesson for adults that children instinctively grasp, but we can't seem to learn.

Walking With Dogs
NOVEMBER 1, 2016

This crazy election is only a week away. I need relief and find that my dogs ease political stress. Their simpler lives are not affected by politics and they help me recognize what is important in this life.

I like to let my dogs, two Boston terriers, run free. Dogs on leashes are terribly constrained to go where their owners go, to walk a narrow path through their lives. Modern extension leashes give them a bit more latitude, but not any more freedom. I don't like them, because dogs don't learn how to heel, one of the most important disciplines for our canine friends.

I believe in a combination of strict training and free running. I want my dogs to come when called, to behave around other people, to sit or stay or lie down when I tell them. I have trained a series of Bostons to walk with me (heeling) without a leash. That effort has not been so successful now that I have two brothers, because they distract each other, so I have to use leashes when we are around other people.

What happens when dogs run free? I don't go to the tiny "dog parks" which have recently proliferated, because they usually provide little room for exercise. Wherever I live, I find places where I can walk and dogs can run.

Every breed is different. Boston terriers like to stay relatively close to their human companions, so Homer and Hector stay within sight as I walk, but run backwards and forwards, stop when and where they want, and chase each other. They make their own decisions about what to do and where to go, but we can walk for 10 minutes without my saying a word. I get to observe dogs doing their own thing.

My dogs listen to me, but think mostly about each other. Homer and Hector have been together since the day they were born and they pay close attention to what the other is doing. When one stops at an interesting spot, usually marked by another dog, the other comes running and their heads come together to smell the fine aromas. But they have their own personalities. When Homer rounds a corner, he stops and stares ahead, searching the landscape for prey (I think). When I let him out the back door of our house, he insists on going through the door first, but then stops immediately to survey the back yard. Hector just runs past him, less interested in other animals, following his own path. He tends to wander further afield, so I have to call him occasionally to come closer. They sleep next to each other or on top of each other, keeping warm contact since they were puppies.

People often assume that the way they do things is the only possible way. German dogs and dog owners behave differently, at least what I have observed in cities. Leashes are unusual. People walk crowded streets with dogs nearby, following the same general path, but their own way. Dogs accompany diners in restaurants, sitting quietly at their feet.

I think we underestimate canine intelligence. As I watch my dogs running around, I wonder what they are thinking about, what is important to them. We often say that dogs are smart when they obey commands. That's a human perspective on dogs. More interesting to me are dog decisions. We know little about how dogs make decisions — go left or right, stop and smell, run or walk, pee here or there.

Dog researchers believe that our best friends are particularly good at figuring out what we mean by our communicative gestures. I have seen my dogs figure out what I mean by various gestures that I repeat in similar situations. They want to know what I am doing and going to do, and the gestures help them make sense of their world. I had to be disciplined about using particular gestures to mean always only one thing and to reward the dogs for figuring out what they mean.

This communication goes the other way. Hector and Homer try to tell me what they want, because I control so much of their lives — let me out, feed me, pet me. I need to figure out what they want and respond, even if it's not what I want, because that encourages their efforts at communication.

The more we observe our animals, the more freedom we give them to make choices, the deeper our relationships. Dogs are not just pets. They can be our partners in life.

STEVE HOCHSTADT
Jacksonville IL

A week later, Trump won. I avoided writing about him until January by focusing on my daily life for the next two months, thinking about what government means every day.

Dogs in my house make me feel good. Poisons would make me feel angry, but they usually remain unnoticed. Yet we have been poisoning ourselves for centuries with "useful" products that can kill us. In an old house like mine, layers of lead and asbestos lurk beneath newer surfaces. Many coats of lead-based paint were used for decades outside and inside. Asbestos floor tiles were common until the 1960s. That's better living through chemistry.

Get The Lead Out!

NOVEMBER 22, 2016

I have been stripping many layers of paint from the columns on my porch. The most recent layers come off easily, but underneath are more stubborn coatings of old lead-based paints. They take more work and require more care, because lead is one of the most pervasive poisons in our environment. I wear a mask to protect against the lead dust.

Ingesting lead can harm every organ and system in our bodies. It is dangerous for adults, who can suffer from damage to the nervous system, increases in blood pressure, anemia, and weakness in the extremities. Exposure to lead for pregnant women can cause miscarriages. Children are especially vulnerable, because lead can injure their developing minds and bodies permanently.

Problems with lead exposure are of such concern, because lead was a common additive to paint until very recently. Lead speeds up drying and increases durability. Lead was used to make white paint by the ancient Greeks. The dangers of working with lead have been known for hundreds of years. The monthly newsletter of the Sherwin-Williams Co. noted the dangers of lead in white paint in 1904. In 1886, German law prevented women and children from working in factories that processed lead paint, and Australia banned lead paint in 1914.

Yet toys and furniture in the U.S. continued to be painted with lead-based products. Water pipes and gasoline contained lead. Older homes were covered with lead paint. Children put lead into their mouths every day. Public health researchers wrote, "By the 1920s, virtually every item a toddler touched had some amount of lead in or on it. Toy soldiers and dolls, painted toys, bean bags that were tossed around, baseballs, fishing lures, the porcelain, pipes and joints in the sparkling new kitchens and bathrooms of the expanding housing stock — all were made of or contained large amounts of lead."

Our federal government was slow to prevent continued lead poisoning in America. Baltimore prohibited the use of lead paint in interiors in 1951. In 1955, the paint industry adopted voluntary standards which excluded lead from interior paints. The use of lead paint was already in decline due to health concerns by then. Yet it was not until 1971 that the federal government passed the Lead-Based Paint Poisoning Prevention Act, which prohibited lead paint in new homes.

The Consumer Product Safety Commission finally banned lead paint for consumer use in 1978. That agency was created by the Consumer Product Safety Act of 1972, passed with overwhelming bipartisan support and signed by President Nixon. Congressional Republicans and conservative Democrats had tried to prevent the creation of the independent Commission, and to gut the Act's enforcement provisions, but narrowly lost.

In 1986, the California legislature said that lead exposure was the state's greatest childhood environmental health problem. Lead is so dangerous that nobody would allow children to ingest lead. Unless those children are poor inner-city blacks in Flint, Michigan. This impoverished, majority-black city was devastated by the closing of General Motors factories in the 1980s. When the water supply was changed to the Flint River in 2014, residents immediately began complaining about pollution. Less obvious were the elevated levels of lead, which systematically poisoned the city's population.

Michigan state officials, including those in the Michigan Department of Environmental Quality, dismissed the residents' concerns and repeatedly claimed the water was safe. Republicans and Democrats participated in creating and prolonging the crisis, because they didn't want to spend the money to deal with it. Now several Michigan officials have been convicted of crimes and a generation of Flint children have been poisoned with lead.

The story of lead poisoning of the water supply in Flint, Michigan, is complicated and controversial. Lawsuits will seek to find those to blame for years to come. But the lessons from Flint are obvious now. Bad environmental decisions can damage enormous numbers of people. Regulation of the poisons which abound in our society are necessary for public health. Governments are responsible to protect our lives.

The demonization of "regulations" that has been a hallmark of Republican politics for decades and that was one of Donald Trump's signature campaign issues means less protection from all kinds of dangers to our lives, from unscrupulous banking practices (Wells Fargo), to outrageous payday loan interest rates, to unsafe foods, to pollution of our air and water.

The story of lead poisoning in America shows government acting too timidly, permitting industry lobbyists to block safety legislation, while adults and children suffer long-term health problems that could have been prevented. Flint is the tip of an iceberg of water supply problems across the nation's cities. Minority inner city residents are the most likely to suffer.

It will take lots of money to replace the lead in old water pipes around the country. It will take strict government regulations on lead and other environmental hazards to keep Americans healthy. Conservatives say regulations are "job killers". I say they are life savers.

STEVE HOCHSTADT
Jacksonville IL

Who could believe that after Flint the Trump EPA would propose new rules that reduce federal protections against lead poisoning? In October 2019, Andrew Wheeler, the EPA chief whose qualifications for the job consisted of working on Senator Jim Inhofe's staff and lobbying for coal magnate Robert Wheeler, proposed to "update" the 1991 Lead and Copper Rule. Updating doesn't mean lowering the level of lead in drinking water that triggers federal action. It means greatly extending the time for fixing lead pipes that deliver water to homes.

Hardly anyone noticed this little alteration of federal regulations. Hardly anyone notices that water has too much lead. Everyone notices when their child displays brain damage from lead exposure, but then it's too late.

We need government to notice what we don't or can't. Modern life is too complex for ordinary citizens to evaluate the products delivered to us by the "free market". The self-interested, bottom-line-first, keep-doing-it-until-we-get-caught attitude of big corporations requires even bigger government to act in our interests. Ronald Reagan's greatest crime against the American people was his pithy sentence from 1986: "the nine most terrifying words in the English language are: I'm from the government and I'm here to help." Like much for which Reagan gets credit, he didn't create that phrase. Democrat Edmund Muskie told it to the conference of mayors in 1976, as part of a Yankee joke about common lies, along with "I put your check in the mail yesterday." It was widely repeated in the media that year. Reagan used the idea to justify the Republican attack on federal laws that regulate business to protect consumers.

Whom does help from the government terrify? Victims of floods and tornadoes? The poor or the unemployed? People injured by con men or con businesses? No, it's the businesses that are terrified that they will be held accountable for their choices to put making money over our safety and security. That's why we need all the help we can get.

We Need Help Fighting The Banks

DECEMBER 13, 2016

The other day I got a letter from my credit card bank, Citibank. It began, "We're replacing your existing Card Agreement with a new version, which is enclosed." They claimed that "It's designed with you in mind," but I doubt that.

The new Agreement is described in detail, without any indication of what is new, so I don't know what they have changed. What hasn't changed is the tilt of the Agreement toward Citibank. Interest rates for loans are very low these days. Rates for mortgages range between 2.5% and 4%. Auto loans are even cheaper, between 2% and 3%. My home equity loan from my local bank is 3.5%. When big banks borrow money, they pay close to zero interest.

But don't borrow money from your credit card bank. My new Agreement, like the old Agreement, lists huge rates for money I "borrow" from Citibank. If I owe money on my card, the rate is 14.24%. If I get a cash advance, the rate is 25.49%, beginning the moment I get the money. There are also fees. A cash advance costs 5% of the amount, in addition to the interest.

These are the costs of having a credit card. We might think they are unreasonable, but getting a card means agreeing to one-sided Agreements like this one. If I didn't like any of the changes to my Agreement, whatever they were, I could close my account.

But on one new provision in my new Agreement, I was given a choice. Citibank wants any disputes about my account to be subject to arbitration, meaning that the dispute is settled by an arbitrator, without recourse to the courts. Here's why Citibank and other credit card companies like this idea.

An arbitration is an individual case, so consumers can't band together in a class action suit. The result is purely monetary, so if the dispute is caused by fraud or other illegal action by the bank, they are not subject to legal penalty. The cost of arbitration is picked up by the bank and they typically select the arbitrator (do you know one?), steering lots of business to arbitrators who deliver verdicts they like. One big arbitration service, the National Arbitration Forum, had to get out of the business of consumer arbitration because it was so cozy with the banks that it was being sued by many city and state attorneys.

Wells Fargo, the current Dishonest Bank of the Year, defrauded countless customers by creating millions of fake accounts in their names. Now it is killing lawsuits filed by its customers by moving the disputes to arbitration. If successful, the bank might have to repay fees they charged to the customers, but would not be liable for penalties due to fraud. Although some judges have ruled that Wells Fargo's fraud should be adjudicated in court, other judges have forced customers to go to arbitration.

The dishonesty of Wells Fargo over many years, cheating millions of customers for many years, and thus far escaping with no jail time for any employee, shows how insignificant we consumers are when we come up against giant corporations. Even well known people, like the Los Angeles music star Ana Bárbara, get crushed by their power. A Wells Fargo employee created sham accounts and credit lines in her name, took out more than $400,000 of her money, then regularly went to her house to steal her Wells Fargo statements from her mailbox. She had to cancel appearances, costing her hundreds of thousands of dollars. Instead of her day in court, Bárbara will have to go to arbitration.

Protection for the consumer can only come from the government. The Dodd-Frank Wall Street Reform and Consumer Protection Act of 2010 takes its name seriously. Dodd-Frank does not let banks force consumers into arbitration for the biggest loans we take out, mortgage and home equity loans. It created the Consumer Financial Protection Bureau to write regulations to implement that change. It also asked the CFPB to study credit card arbitration agreements and report to Congress.

The government effort to examine credit card "agreements" about arbitration is why my bank offered me the chance to opt out of arbitration. All I had to do was write a letter to them saying I rejected the arbitration provision of my "updated Card Agreement". I did that. Thank you, Dodd-Frank.

Republicans have fought against Dodd-Frank since it was first discussed in Congress. They tried to prevent the CFPB from ever being formed. Donald Trump has said he would dismantle Dodd-Frank, saying, ""Dodd-Frank has made it impossible for bankers to function." Trump's selection for Secretary of the Treasury, who will oversee banking regulations, is Steven Mnuchin. Mnuchin worked for Goldman Sachs, a financial firm that got a $10 billion bailout from the federal government in 2008. He made billions by foreclosing on homeowners during that financial collapse. His main qualifications for running Treasury is that he was Trump's campaign finance chairman.

Dodd-Frank makes it less possible for the big banks to push us into tilted arbitration when the banks act like Wells Fargo. It's an equalizer for the little consumer dealing with the big banks. Without it, we're at their mercy.

STEVE HOCHSTADT
Jacksonville IL

So another year ends, a normal American year, maybe the last normal year for a long time. But who knew? Obama was still President, soothing our souls with his measured cadence, thoughtful words, and smiling presence. Trump lurked in the near future, but informed opinion agreed that being President would make him presidential. So let's watch "It's a Wonderful Life" and "Miracle on 34th Street", and imagine that goodness triumphs in the end.

Our Family's White Christmas
DECEMBER 26, 2016

We had a white upper-middle-class Christmas this weekend. I don't mean that we did the same things as all the other white upper-middle-class families, or that there exists a single model for a white Christmas in our tax bracket. I mean that our Christmas is shaped by the facts of our economic status and racial privileges.

As thirteen of us gathered around the dinner table, our commonalities were striking. Everyone around the table has a college degree, with quite a few advanced degrees. We all have good and interesting jobs or had them before we retired. Although we all are anxious about money some of the time, none of us worry about where the next meal is coming from or paying the rent. In fact, nearly all of us live in our own homes. Our celebration was determined by benefits accumulated over generations.

So there was nothing unusual for us when we exchanged more than 40 books, with lots of exclamations of "I've read that," "Her other books are great," and "Can I have that book after you?"

Although none of us are artists, we value artistic creation. We gave each other paintings, prints, ceramic tiles, and framed photographs, passing them around the circle, admiring the skill and vision behind them. All those gifts will be displayed in our homes, adding beauty to our daily lives.

The phrase "artisan foods" labels the contemporary desire for individually designed and carefully crafted foods of all kinds. We exchanged dried Michigan cherries and artistically decorated chocolates. "Homemade" hardly does justice to the foods created by my relatives: I got spicy coated nuts and mustards from my niece, sauces from my sister-in-law, and jam from my brother-in-law's mother.

Food is always central to life, and modern American culture has radically transformed eating conventions in ways that showed up on our table. A staple of our Christmas breakfast had long been chipped beef on toast, what my father and father-in-law would have called SOS from their WWII days. Now that and the Christmas turkey are only memories. Our meals were meatless and much more imaginative and varied than the famous Norman Rockwell image of a holiday meal.

The new foods exemplify the gradual changes in our family Christmases each year. We remain comfortable with the familiar, but over many years small changes accumulate. Some are voluntary, like the abandonment of tomato aspic after years of mocking complaints by children. Others represent the inevitable passing of family time. Forty years ago, I was brought into this family's Christmas by marriage, adding a bit of eastern European heritage to a northern European gathering. Now all the younger generation around the table have partners. A new generation has just made its appearance, although this year only virtually by instantly transmitted pictures.

Generations arrive and others pass. My family's Christmas has long been defined by the December 24th birthday and grand personality of my father-in-law. A long struggle with Alzheimer's that took away his personality now nears its end. He gave many gifts to all of us. We have given him the collective love and care that only family can offer. Around our table, hope for peaceful endings surrounded by family was a universal Christmas wish.

In our world, that is a luxury. Everything I've described is a luxury. We are so lucky to need nothing and be able to give everything.

We all recognize our good fortune. We worked hard for what we have, and owe much to previous generations who paid for our educations and could afford to help us financially at crucial moments. A new element in our family Christmas is the explicit recognition that we should use this occasion collectively to share our good fortune with others who have more unfulfilled needs. Many gifts were made to organizations who use our money to provide food for the hungry, medicine for the sick, and legal protection for the

unjustly targeted. The dozen 30-somethings in my children's generation decided that their gifts to each other would be charitable donations to causes
they shared. That new idea makes a parent proud.

What's white about our Christmas? I can't be sure, because I have never
experienced Christmas with a black family. I imagine that many minority
families have celebrations like I have described. So our white privileges
can seem invisible and thus easily overlooked.

But I know that our whiteness has made certain things much more likely
for us in America. Our families could buy and grow up in homes in good
neighborhoods. Grandparents and parents and children could get good
jobs, earn good salaries, pay for fine educations, and then get another set
of good jobs. None of us has been harassed by authorities, been passed
over for promotions, been ignored or insulted or humiliated or threatened
for being the wrong color.

My penniless immigrant father could move past Americans who had been
here for centuries because he was white. Nobody challenged my right to
succeed because of the way I looked.

I'm lucky, but I'm not thankful for that. It's just what I, and everyone else,
deserve.

STEVE HOCHSTADT
Minneapolis, Minnesota

The American crisis was coming, but I didn't see it.

CHAPTER 8

An Education in Partisanship: The Trump Presidency 2017

What would the Trump presidency be like?

An official Republican response was offered by Paul Ryan, Speaker of the House, Mitt Romney's Vice Presidential candidate, just after Trump was elected. Speaking on CBS "60 Minutes", Ryan characterized what the Party wanted by imagining Trump's attitude: "He feels very strongly, actually, that, that, that, under President Obama's watch, he stripped a lot of power away from the Constitution, away from the legislative branch of government. And we want to reset the balance of power, so that people and the Constitution are rightfully restored."

Ryan couldn't have been more wrong, and he declined to run for Congress again in 2018.

Out with the Old, In with the New
JANUARY 3, 2017

I'm writing this on New Year's Day, an obvious moment to think about the past year and wonder about the next. The calendar makes it seem like an ending and a beginning, but the New Year happens at different times around the globe, and different seasons in different traditions. The calendar is an evolving and arbitrary social creation, yet it offers a convenient moment to satisfy our human need to think about beginnings and ends.

Every year has its sad endings. My father-in-law died a few days after his Christmas Eve birthday. His years of struggle with Alzheimer's were perhaps longer than most, because Roger Tobin kept his athletic body going long after most people have given up. We hoped his end was a relief to him.

My son-in-law's father died earlier in 2016. He was about my age, still vigorous, still working, still strong in every way. He had much left to do, but cancers strike at much less predictable times than Alzheimer's, meaning they take the young and old.

In the future, those endings will be different. Human science has cured so many afflictions and made so many others more livable. Fighting disease is one of the most successful international collaborations that modern society has developed. Beware of those who would say that work is unnecessary, too expensive, too cooperative.

It seems like many cultural heroes died last year, people of the most varied and individual talents: David Bowie, Prince, Carrie Fisher and her mother, Debbie Reynolds, Muhammad Ali, and Elie Wiesel. Some deaths became important news, although the lives were virtually unknown. Black Lives Matter began in 2012, but burst into prominence in 2016, because the ending of some ordinary black lives, such as Philando Castile and Alton Sterling, finally penetrated public consciousness. Perhaps that kind of ending will also become less common in the future.

Some more metaphorical deaths occurred. The long political career of Hillary and Bill Clinton, stretching back to Bill's election as class president at Georgetown University in 1964, is over, landing with a thud in November. The 8-year presidency of Barack Obama is over. I believe he will be remembered and revered long after his numerous opponents have earned their deserved insignificance. He will accomplish much more over the next decades.

Some are lamenting the "death of democracy", but that seems pessimistic to me. Not outrageous, because apparently strong democracies have been killed in the past by people with many resemblances to Donald Trump. But I don't predict the death of American democracy, because Trump is much more interested in himself than in any authoritarian program and is not smart enough to actually lead an organized movement.

2017 will certainly be the start of a new political era in America, characterized by changes that are still unpredictable. Trump will cause some, but others will come from real social movements, born to oppose him. Those movements will define the newest version of American democracy, ever changing, usually improving. Martin Luther King, Jr., said, "The arc of the moral universe is long, but it bends towards justice." I share his optimism.

A New Year's baby symbolizes beginnings. Babies point us all forward. My nephew's family added a second child in the fall, one of millions of babies whose feelings about 2016 will have nothing to do with politics. The wisdom of children helps us get beyond the regrets of the past, because the whole idea of regret is foreign to little children. My nephew told us about driving his older son, not yet two, on the day after the election. He was too bummed to notice the song that was playing for little Jack, "If You're Happy and You Know It". The singers said, "If you're happy and you know it, say hooray!" Jack put up his hands and shouted "Hooray!"

It's a lesson to us all. Too bad about 2016, but it's over. There is much to do in 2017.

Hooray!

STEVE HOCHSTADT
Springbrook, WI

The laments about the "death of democracy" are now louder than ever. I maintain my belief that Trump is not smart enough to lead an organized movement. But I see that he is narcissistic, vindictive, and dishonest enough to get nearly all Republican politicians to dismantle American democracy themselves.

I am no longer as optimistic as I was in January 2017. Progressive social forces that have been germinating for a long time have mobilized themselves openly and forcefully, not caused but sparked by Trump. The forces they oppose are not merely the obvious targets, the banks, Big Pharma, and fossil fuel producers. It's not only about money. The Republican Party commands the support of nearly half of Americans, no matter what it does. Trump is venerated, not matter what he says or does. The clash in November 2020 will be epic. But whoever wins, we must still persevere, we still need to be able to say "Hooray!"

Trump began ignoring the promises with which he won election before he was inaugurated. I was one of a legion of commentators who spread that message across the country. Maybe some Americans listened to us, or just paid attention to the contrast between what he promised and what he did, as Trump's approval ratings fell below 40% by May. But some people were professionally delighted about Trump.

The World is Laughing at America

FEBRUARY 21, 2017

On a Sunday at the end of January, a Dutch television program aired a satirical video with a voice-over pretending to be Donald Trump. The TV host, Arjen Lubach, began by showing a clip of Trump saying at his inauguration, "From this day forward, it's going to be only America first." Lubach said about Trump, "He had a clear message to the rest of the world: 'I will screw you over big time.'" Then he played the video, supposedly an official Dutch government introduction of the Netherlands, in English, to the new

American President. "We speak Dutch. It's the best language in Europe. We've got all the best words. All the other languages failed. Danish — total disaster. German is not even a real language. It's fake." The video shows a Dutch dike: "This is the Afsluitdijk. It's a great, great wall, that we built to protect us from all the water from Mexico." The video made fun of the crowd at Trump's inauguration, his negative comments about NATO, and his attitudes toward blacks. The Dutch politician Jetta Klijnsma is shown using a walker: "We also have a disabled politician for you to make fun of."

The video ends, "We totally understand it's going to be America first. But can we just say, the Netherlands second? Is that okay?" The clip was downloaded 42 million times from the show's Facebook page.

A German late-night TV host reacted to the viral video about a week later. Jan Böhmermann said he was furious that the Netherlands wanted to be second. "Stop, Holland! We want to be number two. Germany wants to be second, because we are strong, we are big. And who, if not us, deserves a third chance?" So he presented a similar video, saying he wanted to make it as simple as possible for our President, who "reads nothing". "Mr. President, this is for you."

The German video is more pointed. There are photos of Hitler, who "made Germany great again. Steve Bannon absolutely loves him." "Germany hosted two world wars in the last 100 years. They were the best world wars in the world, and we won both of them. Bigly. Anyone who says anything else is fake news." "We built a great German wall. And we made the Russians pay for it." The video referenced Trump's comments about being backstage at the Miss Universe pageant and about grabbing women. It's very funny.

By that time, similar videos were being produced by late-night shows across Europe. They all poked fun at their own nation's histories and politics, and at their neighbors, by references to Trump. Most of them are not as funny, perhaps because they are less subtle. Serbia: "Mr. President, just like you, we also like to grab women by the genitals." Poland: "You want to destroy the

EU, we're already doing it from the inside." Switzerland said the KKK were Trump's friends. "We also love to treat our women badly. Love it. We didn't let them vote until 1971. In some places, even until 1990. We grabbed them by the civil rights. And they let us do it. It was great." Norway: "We might even award you the Nobel peace prize. You've already done more than Obama to bring people of the world together. Against you."

Soon the viral video craze spread beyond Europe. A version from India said, "We know you love grabbing women by the [a cat meows]. We have an ancient manual, the Kamasutra, which lists more than 245 ways to grab someone by their [cat meows]." Mexico: "We build walls. Nobody builds walls better than us." An Israeli one was very funny, saying that Jews controlled Hollywood, but that Alec Baldwin was not Jewish. It contained frequent references to sexual assault and making fun of the handicapped. The website collecting the videos displays 29 of them, mostly from Europe, but ranging to Australia and Namibia. A bit of web surfing reveals many others.

The idea seemed so good that non-nations got into the act. A video from the 566 sovereign nations of the USA, meaning Native American tribes, said, "We know all about cleansing, immigrants coming in, destroying your communities, taking your water, taking your land, taking your women." Others came from Mars, Mordor (the evil empire in the Lord of the Rings trilogy), the Galactic Empire, former East Germany, and the North Pole, which stresses all the different white animals there. "Everybody is white for sure."

These videos typically make fun of insignificant issues, like the size of Trump's hands or the way he combs his hair. But they all address in a joking way much more serious issues. His most important policy ideas, his demeaning behavior towards the handicapped, and his prejudices about blacks, Mexicans and Muslims are treated in his own words, seemingly in his own voice. Trump's comments about grabbing women come up in all of these videos.

The whole world is invited to laugh at, and simultaneously disdain, the American President. After showing the video, Böhmermann said in English: "When the whole world is standing up to make fun of you, you really achieved something truly great."

America has become the laughingstock of the world. That's not so great.

STEVE HOCHSTADT
Berlin

That was written in Berlin, as were the next three pieces. Retirement from paid employment allowed us to move into an apartment in Berlin that we had owned for 10 years. We decided to spend three months a year there, and began our experiment with the worst season of the year, the dark, damp, chilly Berlin winter.

There is much to say about the son of a Viennese refugee living in the former capital of the Third Reich. I emphasize here how living abroad supplies an outside perspective on America. Everyone we talked with, everyone who talked on TV, saw the US from the outside, and none of them was persuaded by "America first".

More important than a new view of the US, though, is the insider's view of other places. It is remarkably easy to fall into Trump's constricted global image, thinking that all that matters is America, because that same image is pervasive throughout American culture. We appear to care mostly about the goods that foreign people send to us. What they think and do while they're at home hardly ever appears on our screens, in our papers, in our heads. Immersing ourselves in Berlin life for a few months every year is a daily education. And the coffee is better.

Museums and the Power of Facts

FEBRUARY 28, 2017

A unique collection of museums sits on an island in the center of Berlin. Beginning in 1830, Prussian Kings and German Emperors built four large museums on the so-called Museumsinsel, Museum Island, now designated as a World Heritage Site by UNESCO. A fifth museum was added in 1930.

These great neoclassical buildings displayed the enormous art collections of German monarchs, demonstrating their wealth, power, and cultured taste. Showing off vast collections of painting and sculptures was one means of competing with the other ruling families of Europe, proud of their self-appointed status as god-like rulers of the most civilized human societies.

In the 19th century, Germany was a world leader in scientific research and discovery. The German model of universities as scientific centers of teaching and unbiased research uniting the arts and sciences influenced higher education across Europe and the US. In the first years that Nobel prizes in science were given, from 1901 to the beginning of World War I, Germany won more than any other country.

At this moment of German leadership in the pursuit of knowledge, interest in the long history of human societies developed into new scientific disciplines in the Western world. The study of human history became systematized into the fields of archaeology, ethnography, and anthropology. One of the museums on Museum Island, the Neues Museum (New Museum, opened in 1855), was devoted to organizing and displaying the ethnological and archaeological artifacts that German scientists were busily digging up where ancient cultures had thrived around the eastern Mediterranean. Heavily damaged during World War II, the Neues Museum was closed for 70 years until it reopened in 2009. Once again, its halls display remarkable objects of human creation during the past 5000 years.

As a teenager, I was fascinated by the story of Heinrich Schliemann (1822-1890), who was determined to find the site of Homer's Troy on the Turkish coast. His excavations and those of other Europeans contributed to the understanding of the development of human cultures. European scientists in the late 19th century used such artifacts to formulate the so-called Three Ages system, dividing human history into the Stone, Bronze and Iron Ages.

The comparative study of thousands of artifacts unearthed on Cyprus from the millennium before Christ's birth allows us to understand the successive waves of settlers, conquerors, and traders in the eastern Mediterranean, where the most advanced human societies outside of China developed. The Neues Museum holds one of the world's most important collections of documents written on papyrus, whose study by linguistic scientists revealed the succession of languages in ancient Egypt.

At the same time, German historians reshaped the writing of history from the glorification of great leaders, powerful nations, and military victories to a scientific investigation of what happened in the past. Leopold von Ranke (1795-1886) moved the historical profession toward the study of archival documents in order to understand "how things actually were".

The fundamental principle upon which both science and history were founded was the reliance on the understanding and interpretation of empirical information, in short, facts. While there may be disagreement about what data means, scientists of all kinds, physical and social, all over the world, came to base their work on reliable evidence.

After the Nazis took over in 1933, these hard-won scientific insights were rejected. Human history was rewritten to demonstrate the superiority of white northern Europeans. Racist beliefs became state policy, unwelcome science was disparaged as a Jewish conspiracy, and modern art was labeled "degenerate". Journalism based on real events was branded as lies and replaced with a state propaganda of alternative facts. Eventually the big lies at the heart of Nazi ideology led to their own destruction, but not before they did unprecedented damage to Europe and its people.

There are always those who insist on mythical understandings of history and who reject science if it conflicts with their ideologies. A racist dictatorship must suspend a population's belief in the value of facts and the primacy of evidence in order to sustain the myths which legitimize its inhumanity. Seekers of illegitimate power always create distorted narratives to justify their dominance. Freedom and justice depend on popular insistence on learning the truth about themselves, their world and their rulers.

Science, history and journalism are the means of discovering those truths, figuring out what they mean, and communicating that to everyone. A society which does not protect these fundamental human tasks from the enemies of truth risks losing its freedom.

STEVE HOCHSTADT
Berlin

If I'm still articulate on the day I die, I'll insist a final time on the importance of facts. I loved science fiction and mythology as a young reader, and still thrill at the inventions of filmmakers and mystery writers. But I rely on non-fiction when I want to know what really happened. As my intellectual interests shifted in my twenties from math and the sciences to history and the social sciences, I retained my faith in facts, my quest to discover them, and my delight in fitting them together. The only opinion writing worth reading is firmly founded in observable reality.

Observing Berlin life inevitably brings new ideas. Patriotism that transcends nationalism is hard to imagine in America. But Trump has impressed upon Berliners, Germans, and Europeans that they are part of something wonderful that is not American.

Europe is Alive and Well

MARCH 28, 2017

On Saturday, 4000 Berliners gathered at the Brandenburg Gate to make a political statement — Happy Birthday, Europe! They let loose blue balloons, carried blue flags with yellow European Union stars, and trampled a "wall" made of cardboard cartons. Saturday was the 60th anniversary of the Rome treaty among 6 nations which created the European Economic Union, the first step towards today's European Union of 28 nations.

Not long ago, such a celebration would have been unlikely. United Europe has many problems. The economic difficulties of some southern countries, especially Greece, required international financial assistance. Unemployment and sluggish growth persist in many countries. Refugees from northern Africa and the Middle East have put enormous pressure on the more prosperous countries of western Europe.

Nationalist, so-called "populist" politicians and parties have won new popularity and power in the last few years by attacking the EU. The British vote to leave the EU was the heaviest blow against European unity. Marine Le Pen of the National Front in France is one of the front-runners in the presidential election next month, whom recent polls give about 26% among four major candidates. Her platform is anti-immigration, anti-Muslim, and anti-EU. Geert Wilders, a Dutch politician who hates Muslims and is against non-white immigration and the EU, appeared on his way to winning their presidential election earlier this month.

Nationalist politicians have recently gained power in Poland and Hungary, and are part of coalition governments in Finland and Denmark. In the April 2016 Austrian presidential election, the Euro-sceptical and anti-immigration Freedom Party won the most votes in the first round.

Alternative für Deutschland (AfD) was founded in 2013 as a critic of the pro-European policies of the German government, and has gradually moved further and further right towards opposition to immigration, homophobia, Islamophobia, and denial of climate change. It is the only German party which talks about leaving the EU. The AfD got 4.7% of the national vote in 2013 and 7.1% in 2014. National support in 2016 reached 12-15%, and seemed to be heading higher.

The election of Donald Trump, who made disparaging statements about Europe and selected advisors who have promoted the break-up of the EU, was a turning point in European politics, but not in the direction he favors. His apparent withdrawal of American support for a united Europe pushed Europeans to a more vigorous defense of their unprecedented international alliance and the values it promotes: tolerance, human rights, fluid borders.

Just after Trump's election, a married couple from Frankfurt, Germany, decided with some friends to demonstrate support for a united Europe. In February, 600 people came to a meeting. On March 5, there were public demonstrations in 35 cities under the name "Pulse of Europe". The first theme listed on their website is "Europe must not fail." Their method is also clear: "Let us become louder and more visible!" That is exactly what Europeans have done recently. The Pulse of Europe website now lists 53 German cities and 14 others, where every Sunday a pro-Europe demonstration takes place.

The tide has turned against the right-wing parties. The Austrian Freedom Party lost to a Green politician in the presidential run-off in December 2016. Wilders' support in the Netherlands peaked and fell, and his second-place finish and lower than expected vote totals have been cheered across Europe. Support for the AfD in Germany has been dropping since January, and they won just 6% in a provincial election this weekend.

A major survey in 2015 of European public opinion shows majority support for the EU: 71% of citizens wanted their country to remain in the Union.

Within the 28 nations of the EU, 59% preferred more integration, 16% were satisfied with current levels, and only 24% wanted less.

A few nights ago, I saw a big poster in the center of Berlin: "Only those who don't value freedom can cast doubt on Europe." It's part of new advertising campaign for Berlin called "#FreiheitBerlin" or "Freedom Berlin". The quotation comes from Nicol Ljubić, a novelist with Croatian background, who lives in Berlin. Like many people across Europe, he associates freedom with a united Europe.

Of course, everyone has some complaint about the EU, some criticism of policies hammered out among 28 nations. But the threats to European integration, from outsiders like Trump and insiders like Le Pen and Wilders and the AfD, have made people here in Germany and all over Europe more willing to become louder and more visible, saying not only "Europe must not fail," but also "Europe is good."

Europe is good. Three times as many Europeans as Americans trust their national legislatures. One-sixth as many Europeans as Americans are in jail, probably related to the fact that one-fifth as many murders occur. Health care is universal and Europeans live longer. According to the "World Happiness Report", Europeans are the happiest people in the world. Americans do pretty well, too, ranking 14th, about the same as Germans.

Such comparisons are not meant to prove that Europe is better than the US. But they do show that Europe, more and more united over the past 60 years, is not a failure, as American conservatives often assert. United Europe has created peace and prosperity across the continent for 60 years.

Happy birthday, Europe!

STEVE HOCHSTADT
Berlin

The rise of the right on every continent is a mark of the early 21st century. Like the parallel wave of reactionary ideologies in Europe in the early 20th century, at their heart lies the rejection of the Enlightenment ideals of universal human rights, democracy and science.

I have the hardest time understanding how Republican parents and grandparents can ignore the dangers that threaten the well-being of their own families. The "family values" that the right has arrogated to itself for decades disappear when more important ideological considerations intrude. While some Republicans in Florida and other coastal states are responding to the real effects of global warming at home, the national Party continues to attack climate change science as political propaganda.

I see politics as one means to protect my family, and all families, from the dangers of modern life, to make their lives better and happier. There is no more important job for a father.

Thinking like a Father
JUNE 20, 2017

I'm writing this on Father's Day. I like Father's Day, despite the commercialism that overwhelms all of our special days. Children should honor their fathers every day, but it's nice to have a day set aside to think about fathers, just as for mothers.

Although celebrating Father's Day in June was an American invention, a day honoring fathers has been a Catholic tradition for many centuries. St. Joseph's Day celebrates the idea of fatherhood.

The first attempt to create a secular day for fathers was the result of a terrible mining disaster, an explosion in the mines of Monongah, West Virginia, on December 6, 1907, which killed at least 360 men, and possibly as many as 500. Grace Golden Clayton, who lived nearby, was at the time mourning the loss of her own father, a preacher, and she suggested honoring the hundreds of dead fathers to her pastor. Another influence was the very recent inauguration of a Mother's Day celebration in May in another West Virginia town by Anna Jarvis, who wanted to honor her mother, a Civil War peace activist. But it wasn't until President Lyndon Johnson proclaimed the third Sunday in June as Father's Day in 1966 that it became official.

Besides inspiring Grace Clayton to honor all fathers, the Monongah mining disaster led to a public clamor for government oversight of the dangerous mines. In 1910, Congress created the U. S. Bureau of Mines to reduce mine explosions with a system of inspections by field officers. Father's Day and Mother's Day are linked to peace activism and government regulation.

My children are grown up and ready to have children of their own. My hands-on fathering is intermittent and often long distance. No use in trying to raise my children any more — advice on dealing with life's challenges is now more appropriate.

But one way I can be a good father is to try to ensure that my children, and their children, can achieve their dreams in a healthy world. My generation has not done well in preserving the world, probably being responsible for more pollution of the air, land and sea than any other generation. On the other hand, baby boomers also contributed to the public efforts to control pollution in countless ways, from regulating automobile exhaust, to recycling, to cleaning up our rivers.

Those efforts continue, but a new threat, recognized only within the most recent decades, could make our children's lives harder, more dangerous, and less enjoyable. Climate change is already creating human problems around the US. In northern Alaska, some villages will have to be moved inland as the sea rises. In the Rocky Mountains, some of the country's largest forests are dying from heat and drought. In Louisiana, the residents of Isle de Jean Charles are being offered $48 million to move from their homes, because rising seas have already washed away most of their island. In

California, the worst drought in a thousand years cost farmers billions in lost income. Western wildfires are expected to expand as temperatures rise.

Thinking like a father means recognizing these threats to our children's happiness and doing everything we can to protect them. Instead, many men are doing the opposite. They refuse to believe any evidence about the existence of climate change, its causes, and the damage it is doing to human life already. They apply their intelligence to obfuscation, misdirection, and outright lying, because they don't like the political consequences of global warming. Except for those who have been deluded by this anti-environmental campaign, these men are only hoping for delay.

Five years ago, one of the world's leading climate scientists appeared before Congress to tell our political leaders that climate change will produce more severe droughts, wider wildfires, bigger storms, and rising sea levels. Republican Senator Jim Inhofe from Oklahoma responded, "The global warming movement has completely collapsed." Since then, 2014 was the hottest year on record, then 2015 broke that record, then 2016 got even hotter.

But Inhofe, and the others who say they know better, still sing the same tune. They are not thinking like fathers, but like sons. They are rooted in the past, denouncing everything that points to changes in our world, repeating forever that we don't need to do anything in the face of this unprecedented threat.

When the weatherman forecasts rain, a good father sees that his children wear protective clothing. When the weatherman forecasts a thunderstorm, a good father keeps his children safe inside. When the weatherman forecasts a tornado, a good father leads everyone to the basement.

Now the world's weathermen and weatherwomen forecast rising seas, more severe storms, more frequent drought and heat waves. Yet those poor fathers ignore their children's futures. They don't deserve to be honored on Father's Day.

STEVE HOCHSTADT
Jacksonville IL

Everywhere one looks, religion affects political choices. Better would be to say, certain interpretations of religion influence political policies. Under the wide tent of Christianity, social movements that emphasize a gospel of liberation and love of one's neighbor gather next to opposing movements which proclaim exclusion of the sinful, meaning people not like them. Jews divide similarly, likewise dependent on precisely which passages of scripture are taken as literal truth. Some passages are virtually ignored by everyone, such as Jesus' invocation to his disciples: "It is easier for a camel to pass through the eye of a needle, than for a rich man to enter the kingdom of God." Jesus emphasized that clear statement, "Again I tell you," which appears in three places in the New Testament: Matthew 19:24, Mark 10:25, and Luke 18:25.

No matter how often that might appear, its exact opposite was proclaimed by the Calvinists during the Reformation and by the promoters of the prosperity gospel today, including televangelists who do become quite prosperous by their preaching.

Few religious controversies have so divided modern Christians as the proper way to view homosexuality. The United Methodist Church, with over 10 million members worldwide, just broke into two pieces by the disagreement over whether the practice of homosexuality is consistent with Christian teaching. The majority of American UMC leaders support changing the Church's stated discipline to include LGBTQ people, but the majority outside the US is opposed. This rethinking of traditional Christian doctrine has been led by young Americans. In historical terms, the shift has been startling. July 4 seemed an appropriate day to celebrate this revolution.

Gay Equality Is Coming Quickly

JULY 4, 2017

Usually public opinion on important and emotional subjects shifts gradually. The realization that discrimination against African Americans and
women was wrong came very slowly. For more than a century, Americans
spoke out against sexism and racism. In the 19th century, they were considered radicals, advocating unpopular political positions against traditional
beliefs in white male superiority. By the 20th century, opinion in America
was split and some discriminatory laws were changed, but common practices based in prejudice persisted.

Only after World War II did majority public opinion shift away from en-
trenched discrimination, but even then progress was halting. The two Supreme Court decisions that declared school segregation (1954) and laws
against mixed-race marriages (1967) unconstitutional were 13 years
apart, and they were just way stations along a much longer journey toward equality. In both cases, defenders of discrimination used religious arguments to oppose equal treatment for blacks and women, citing Biblical
verses written thousands of years ago to claim that God had declared the
superiority of white men for all time.

Change comes more quickly in modern society, as we can see in the tech-
nological innovations which replace each other with bewildering rapidity.
In 1999, Ray Kurzweil proposed the "The Law of Accelerating Returns"; he
believed that change in a wide variety of evolutionary systems, including
technology, would come with accelerated speed. We might see this "law"
operating in the third great shift in public opinion about traditional discriminatory practices, the acceptance of homosexual people as normal and
deserving of equal rights.

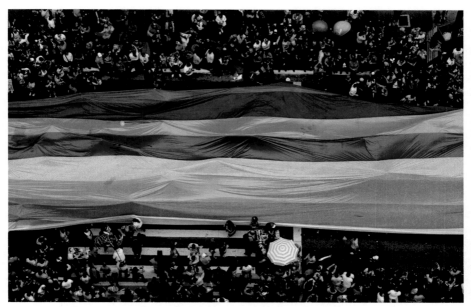

Gay pride parade in Sao Paulo, Brazil, 2018

Data from the Pew Research Center shows a dramatic recent shift in American public opinion on same-sex marriage, which may be taken as an indicator of more general attitudes about homosexuality. After years of relative stability, in the last 8 years the proportion of Americans who oppose gay marriage dropped from 54% to 32%, as the number who favor it rose from 37% to 62%. That same amount of opinion shift on inter-racial marriage took about twice as long.

The popular shift has been rapid, but not smooth. After Massachusetts became the first state to legalize same-sex marriage in 2003, 12 states passed constitutional amendments outlawing it in the next year alone, and eventually 30 states passed such backlash legislation. The Supreme Court decision in 2015 that rights guaranteed by the Constitution to all citizens included the right to get married came four years after support for same-sex marriage reached majority status.

Like many shifts in social attitudes, this was led by young people. The latest Pew survey shows 18- to 29-year-olds against discrimination by 79% to

19%, while Americans over 72 remain opposed to this change by 49% to 41%. But every demographic group, whatever their attitudes were a few years ago, has shifted towards acceptance. Opposition remains concentrated among white evangelical Protestants, conservative Republicans, and the oldest Americans, groups which considerably overlap. Those who demonize their neighbors who have a different sexual orientation continue to use arguments derived from Christian tradition as justification.

What caused this rapid shift in public opinion? When Pew asked why people had changed their minds, the most common answer was that they knew someone who is homosexual. Visibility has been a significant factor in the increasing acceptance of gays in America. While race and gender are usually obvious, homosexuality was not.

I grew up in an America where homosexuality was queer, meaning strange and unnatural. It was dangerous for a gay person to reveal their orientation, which could cost them their jobs. Homosexual relations were criminal across the country, until Illinois was the first state to decriminalize same-sex relations in 1962. So I didn't know any homosexuals. I, like most Americans, had no evidence from life experience that gay people were not as they were portrayed in medical practice (sick), in official propaganda (dangerous), and in common talk (weird).

Over the course of 30 years, the proportion of Americans who said that someone they knew revealed to them that they were gay rose from 24% in 1985 to 75% in 2013. Since it is unlikely that the incidence of homosexuality has changed significantly, what did change was the realization that there are gay people in everyone's social circle.

The end of discrimination against homosexuality is determined by changing public opinion and political practice, which differ from country to country. Germany, in many ways more officially opposed to discrimination of all kinds than the US, just legalized gay marriage last week. A recent poll showed that 83% of Germans approved of same-sex marriage, much higher than in the US. But the politics of the conservative party, the Christian

Democrats, who have led the government since 2005, prevented any vote on the issue until now.

Bigots will keep using religion as a cover for prejudice, as in the so-called religious freedom laws. But the shift toward acceptance of homosexuality will continue, as older opponents are replaced by younger advocates. Because our gay relatives and friends do not fit the prejudicial stereotypes, discriminatory impulses will lose their persuasive power. Happy birthday, America.

STEVE HOCHSTADT
Springbrook, WI

The fight over gay rights seems mainly based on warring principles. The revolution occurred as a shift in the popular adherence to the principle of sin versus inclusion. I think that shift was caused by the force of family love, an emotion that transcends intellectual principles.

Although there are principles which I think are misguided, I generally applaud people who stick to their principles. We use the adjective "principled" to mean honorable, honest, moral, regardless of the actual principles involved. "Unprincipled" means deceitful, unethical and unscrupulous. The history of American democracy has often been a struggle between principles, but all too often the principles have been smokescreens for baser motives. Opponents of civil rights framed their argument around the principles of "states' rights" and local control. For most of my life, conservatives have argued against the expansion of centralized power and the growth of the federal government. This happened to fit nicely with their opposition to the particular policies that liberals wanted the federal government to enforce: racial and gender equality, environmental protection, welfare for the poorest Americans.

The Republican Party has abandoned some of the core governing principles that it has proclaimed for decades. In order to prevent communities from legislating policies conservatives don't like on environmental and labor issues, Republicans have used state and federal power to simply eliminate local jurisdiction. "Let's do it if it helps us" was a working anti-principle among many in the Republican Party even before Trump came on the scene. Their principle appears to be unlimited Republican government.

The politics of health care, how to distribute or not distribute billions of government dollars across the American economy, seems like a heated argument about principles. On TV, health care also means big bucks, as every imaginable unpronounceable medicine can save our lives, except for those inconvenient federally mandated warnings. To me and the people I know, health care is an immediate, daily concern.

Conversations About Health Care

JULY 25, 2017

Everybody's talking about health care. But it's not because of the incompetent ideological circus playing in Congress. That offers a fascinating look into the Republican soul, but few of my conversations about health care mention politics. Talk about health care is mostly about the health of my family, my friends, and my friends' families, and the care they need.

As a healthy youngster, my input to health care discussions at home was usually, "I'm fine." I probably said that to my mother while I was soaking in a tub full of hot water after playing touch football. She didn't believe me, so I got on the operating table soon enough to stop the bleeding from my ruptured spleen.

In college, I remember a lot of conversations about whether we should do something that was obviously bad for our health. I leaned toward caution, not popular then, but looking better in retrospect.

Then my parents and my friends' parents got old. Then we got old. Now most conversations with friends and family begin right after "hello" with talk about health care. "How are you?" is not a meaningless greeting, it's an earnest question.

There's no cure for old age, and I don't care. I do care about how many people close to me are dealing with forgetfulness, blood tests, pain, and walkers; with health problems of mothers and fathers and ourselves; with nurses, doctors, hospitals, and insurance companies.

Longer-lived women are taking care of men who are sinking, along with many but fewer cases the other way around. Baby boomers like me turn into caregivers, managing doctors' visits and prescription drugs, making nursing homes a second home.

Times have changed, too. The earnest TV commercials for cough medicine and aspirin and "Preparation H" have turned into ubiquitous ads for medicines that might make you sick or kill you; for lawyers who will sue your doctor; for hospitals that will treat you, and insurance companies that might pay them.

It's hard not to think constantly about health. Those thoughts can be difficult, confusing, and inconclusive. Joys are recovery from illness, the kindness of health care professionals, health scares that are false alarms. The sad stuff can last a long time, changing into something different but permanent at the end.

And we talk about money. It costs money to live and maybe more to die. Whose money will pay for the health care of people I love? That's not the first thing we talk about. It's not the most important thing most of the time. But it's one of the most perplexing.

When I get a bill from a doctor, I have no idea who is going to pay what. Will Medicare pick up the tab? How much will my insurance company pitch in? What will I pay at the end? How much of my deductible have I used up?

Should I get long-term care insurance? Or should I have gotten it 10 years ago? Should I save money on insurance premiums by taking a high deductible? Or is that a risky bet?

Nobody can take away such worries. Ignorance doesn't help, either from those who shouted "Keep your government hands off my Medicare," or from our President, who says he doesn't care what happens to the rest of us, now that he didn't get his way.

I believe that we have a right to get help with our health care from our government. We need that help every day, to prevent con artists from lying to us about miracle cures, to prevent the pharmaceutical industry from selling untested drugs, to prevent insurance companies from kicking the sickest off their rolls, to sponsor research which can save lives.

Our government got into the health care business to save lives, and it has been doing that, more or less successfully, for nearly two centuries. In my home town, Jacksonville, the state of Illinois long ago created institutions to care for people with health problems: a school for the deaf in 1839, a school for the blind in 1849, a hospital for the mentally ill in 1851.

Progressives around Teddy Roosevelt advocated for universal health coverage before World War I, at the same time that our government began to try to prevent disease by inspecting meat packing plants, and prohibiting adulterated drugs and false therapeutic claims.

The creators of our nation believed that "Life, Liberty and the pursuit of Happiness" were the most important universal rights to be protected by government. It's not clear what led Thomas Jefferson to elevate the pursuit of happiness to an inalienable right. If that phrase means anything, it must include government participation in our efforts to stay healthy. How can anyone be happy who can't pay for health care they need?

There's no such thing as a right to good health. But as Americans, we have a right to get collective help, if we need it, to stay healthy. That means government protection from poisons in our food, air, and water (see Flint, Michigan), from false claims by drug producers, and from medical malpractice. In today's world, it must also mean assistance in paying for medical treatment for those without resources.

So says the Declaration of Independence.

STEVE HOCHSTADT
Springbrook WI

I would like our government to ensure the health of all Americans. That also means being tough on crime. I want state and federal governments to work harder to investigate, capture and punish criminals. In 2017, when I wrote the following indictment, and now in the wake of more than dozen Goldman Sachs executives being accused of siphoning billions of dollars from a Malaysian development fund and Big Pharma executives entangled in promoting opioids, criminals get away with murder.

As I write in 2020, Americans are finally rejecting the laws and legal procedures that targeted minorities for petty offenses. The passage of The First Step Act in 2018 significantly reduced the prison population by reversing the disproportionately harsh sentences given for crack cocaine offenses. This was a rare moment of bipartisanship, as every Congressional Democrat and most Republicans in both Houses sent the bill to Trump. Both sides now argue over who gets the credit.

The other half of social injustice that needs reform is the leniency which is showered on the white men in suits, who break bigger laws in bigger ways and do much more social damage. If a single burglary earns a year in jail, shouldn't the stealers of millions, even billions, get 10,000 years?

White Collar Crime at Wells Fargo

SEPTEMBER 12, 2017

Wells Fargo was the world's most valuable bank until 2016, when it slipped into second place behind JPMorgan Chase. It may also be one of the biggest criminal enterprises in American history.

I'm not the only one who thinks so. Harold Meyerson, executive editor of the *American Prospect*, began an op-ed in the *Los Angeles Times* last month: "What's the biggest criminal enterprise in California? MS-13? The remnants or successors to the Crips and the Bloods? The Mexican Mafia? If we're talking about the sheer volume of offenses, the answer is clear: Wells Fargo."

Not just journalists. New York Congressman Gregory Meeks told CEO John Stumpf at a Congressional hearing a year ago that Wells Fargo "basically has been a criminal enterprise". Meeks said, "I've got individuals right now on the street, they're not back in their homes," because of fraudulent mortgages. Would Wells Fargo put his homeless constituents back in their homes? Stumpf had no answer.

Wells Fargo employees created 3.5 million fraudulent accounts in customers' names without their knowledge. The bank signed up 500,000 customers for online bill payment services without their knowledge, some of which carried fees. It charged military personnel illegally high interest on loans and then seized vehicles from soldiers who fell behind on their payments. It charged half a million auto loan customers for insurance that they did not need. About 20,000 people could not pay these extra fees, went into default, and had their cars repossessed.

The bank didn't only cheat its customers. Wells Fargo paid $100,000 to settle a class action suit in 2009 by its employees in Nevada, who were mislabeled "managers" so they would not have to be paid overtime and then forced to work unpaid "call nights" to drum up more business. A branch manager was fired in 2010 when he reported these criminal actions to his supervisors. The bank was ordered this year to pay him $5.4 million in back pay and compensatory damages. One manager notified the bank's confidential ethics hotline about fraudulent activity in September 2011 and was fired later that month. A banker in Pennsylvania also called the hotline and sent an email to human resources about the unethical practices he was told to perform in September 2013. Eight days later he was fired.

Wells Fargo has committed these crimes for at least 15 years. And company leaders knew it. Internal complaints were made as early as 2005. In 2009, six fired employees sued, alleging unethical practices. Employees wrote directly to CEO John Stumpf as early as 2011. In 2013, the New York Times reported that Wells Fargo employees were under intense pressure, including threats of getting fired, if they did not meet ambitious goals by opening accounts and starting credit cards without permission. Complaints were made to managers and nothing was done.

If somebody uses someone else's personal information to open a credit card account, the penalties are severe. Ordinary crime. Our customary language puts Wells Fargo's actions in a different light: white-collar crime, which the FBI defines as "characterized by deceit, concealment, or violation of trust and are not dependent on the application or threat of physical force or violence." The escape from any jail time or criminal record of every participant except one banker after the bank collapse and financial crisis of 2008 shows how our society excuses big crimes when they are committed by rich, usually white men in fine suits.

But some other definitions might be more appropriate for Wells Fargo's actions. The crimes of so-called "organized crime" are defined clearly. Extortion, a time-tested endeavor of organized crime, is the acquisition of property through the use of threats or force. Didn't Wells Fargo threaten homeowners and car owners with seizure of their property if they didn't pay illegally created charges? And then make good on those threats?

Loan-sharking is the provision of loans at illegally high interest rates accompanied by the illegal use of force to collect on past due payments. Didn't Wells Fargo charge illegal interest rates to soldiers and then forcibly take their property?

Wouldn't Wells Fargo fit the FBI's definition perfectly? "The FBI defines a criminal enterprise as a group of individuals with an identified hierarchy, or comparable structure, engaged in significant criminal activity."

What price has Wells Fargo paid for their millions of individual crimes? Virtually none. The few hundred million dollars that Wells Fargo has paid in fines or has promised to pay customers who were cheated are a tiny fraction of the $11 billion in profits for just the first six months of 2017. Wells Fargo says it will refund nearly a million dollars to customers who had been signed up for online bill payment — that's less than $2 per fraudulent transaction.

Wells Fargo's chief executive after 2007, John Stumpf, was publicly rebuked in a congressional hearing in 2016, had to resign, and forfeited $41 million in stock options. That left him with Wells Fargo stock worth almost $250 million. Carrie Tolstedt, leader of the community banking division, where these criminal actions occurred, had to "retire" at age 56, and lost $19 million. She had made $27 million in her last three years, and took with her a mere $125 million in stocks. Earlier this year, four second-level executives were fired. Nobody has done a day of jail time.

After years of intense pressure on employees to get new accounts any way they could, Wells Fargo fired 5300 employees for unethical behavior. The company leaders walked away with millions of dollars.

That criminal enterprise was too big to jail. Our political and judicial systems seem inadequate to protect ordinary Americans from corporate crime or to punish criminals when they are caught.

Can we, the people, do something? Wells Fargo customers could simply switch banks. There is no big advantage in using a giant global bank. My local Jacksonville bank performs all the services I need, whether I'm at home or across the world.

A survey in October 2016, just after the scandal made headlines, showed that only 14% of Wells Fargo customers had decided to leave. It's not so easy. Most people get multiple services from their bank, including loans, automatic bill pay, and credit cards. Switching takes time and money, and many customers don't have either. One third of Americans with savings accounts have a zero balance. Although the number of new credit card and checking accounts fell by half earlier this year, that still means that thousands of people were opening new accounts with Wells Fargo.

Other corporations are happy to take tainted money from Wells Fargo. The bank will now be a sponsor of the annual football rivalry between Oregon and Oregon State. Wells Fargo signed an extension of its deal as official retail bank of Major League Soccer, and became an official partner of the NFL Los Angeles Rams.

Since the beginning of 2017, Wells Fargo stock has fallen about 10%. Don't buy their shares. TV viewers could tune out the Wells Fargo golf championship, broadcast every May, forcing the tournament organizers to find another sponsor, and avoid other sporting events and programs sponsored by Wells Fargo.

Not very satisfying. But if we don't say no to white-collar criminals, who will?

STEVE HOCHSTADT
Springbrook WI

My newspaper said "no" to me. David Bauer, the editor, wrote that "there are some worries about the column." He consulted the attorney for the Illinois Press Association and they agreed that the "column as a whole opens us up to a potential defamation action." I can't say that Wells Fargo was a "criminal enterprise" or even write the phrase "white collar criminals of Wells Fargo". It made no difference that Rep. Gregory Meeks of New York had called Wells Fargo a "criminal enterprise" in Congress the year before, or that an op-ed in the *Los Angeles Times* called Wells Fargo "the biggest criminal enterprise in California".

I'm not sure whose freedom of the press was curtailed, but the Wells Fargo criminals got a pass. Although criminal charges may still be brought against some high-level Wells Fargo executives, so far thousands of low-level employees have been fired and no executives have gone to jail.

That's enough to get a normal person angry. But political anger is easily overwhelmed by family joy. Not only do little children make us forget the troubles of the outside world, they can teach us about proper human priorities — do I have enough to eat? will someone pick me up? would you play with me?

Perfect Love in a Tiny Package

NOVEMBER 7, 2017

I've become a grandfather.

My granddaughter Vera is a month old. My wife and I are getting to know her by singing silly songs, carrying her around, and watching her rapid development at this very young moment.

Everyone who hears the news congratulates me in a different way than new parents are congratulated. The lives of new parents are forever transformed by new responsibilities. That's long ago in my past. This time, experienced grandparents tell me how much fun I will have.

Connecting as a grandparent has been transformed by social changes over the past few decades. The increasing geographic mobility of American families means that many grandparents live too far away for regular visits. But even though we were over 1000 miles away when she was born, we could see Vera every day via a video chat. Keeping in contact with family across generations has never been easier.

Naturally new technology brings new dilemmas. Coming from a generation where party lines were still common and there was only one screen in a household, grandparents of my age are likely to disapprove of young children carrying video games and movies around in their pockets.

Social change creates the potential for generational conflict centered on grandchildren. Grandparents visit and then go away. We cuddle and sing songs and read books, but we don't take on the heavy daily duty of parenting. We follow the parents' lead, help rather than make big choices. We change diapers, but don't decide whether cloth or paper. We feed, but don't pick out what baby eats. We don't decide how to decorate the nursery, whether or not to follow the traditional gendered color choices for clothing, or how much screen time will be allowed. After each visit, we go back to our own lives, eagerly anticipating the next visit.

One of the delights and pitfalls of grandparenting is highlighted in a how-to produced by the *Guardian* newspaper, called "10 ways to be a fabulous grandparent". They advise: "stick to the parents' rules when you're looking after the children...mostly." Experienced grandparents often say that "spoiling" the child is a great joy. The child soon learns that grandparents often have license to allow forbidden things, like sweets or later bedtimes. But differences in rules can bring conflicts with the parents. The *Guardian* advises grandparents: "Accept that you have no control: The hardest thing about parenting is being responsible for everything. And the hardest thing about grandparenting is accepting that you're not."

The real fun of grandparents is their difference, but that doesn't have to include extra leniency. What I treasured about visiting my grandparents were the new card games they taught me, the exotic foods my grandmother prepared, the different conversations we had, the strange magazines lying around, the unfamiliar TV programs they watched.

Becoming a grandparent changes familial relationships. A child becomes a parent, assuming responsibilities and making decisions once reserved for the grandparent. Those decisions inevitably become comments, positive or negative, on the grandparent's parenting. Some of these choices are socially determined by evolving conventions of good parenting. Fathers in the delivery room and breast-feeding are no longer uncommon. Putting baby to sleep on her stomach under a blanket is now taboo. These shifts can appear to represent rejection of the grandparent's child-rearing practices.

How one acts as a grandparent is not entirely a matter of choice. Not all grandparents can afford to view grandparenting as a series of fun visits. About 1 in 10 grandparents in the US live with their grandchildren. About 6% of children under 18 live with their grandparents and that percentage is dependent on race: 12% of African American children live in grandparent-headed households, but only 4% of white children.

Historical social shifts have changed the relationships among generations. Rising divorce rates and increasing numbers of families where both parents work encourage more regular grandparental care for children. Economics play a key role. The recent depression increased by 20% the number of children mainly cared for by their grandparents. Of the 20 million pre-schoolers in the US, about a quarter were cared for regularly by their grandparents, about a third of children under 2. Typically grandparents provide care when mothers are employed full-time, and are more likely to jump in as caregivers for single mothers in poverty.

Even when parents are capable of taking care of children by themselves, grandparents are invaluable. A friend told me that parenting is a humbling experience, placing young adults before difficult decisions: should I feed now or later? should I let the baby cry itself to sleep? which bit of contradictory advice from books, friends and internet should I listen to? Grandparents don't have all the answers, but we can bring extra hands, patience and skill to the most important human task — bringing up baby.

Vera doesn't care about conflicts between parents and grandparents over who makes the rules. She doesn't care about rules. Right now she single-mindedly seeks warmth and love and a dry diaper. I can provide those.

That's the best thing grandparents can do.

STEVE HOCHSTADT
Missoula, Montana

Changing diapers and voting. Caring for a tiny being and thinking about national politics. We multi-task throughout our lives, jumping among activities with different levels of significance. Sometimes it's hard to see how these levels relate to each other.

Election 2017: Repudiation of Republicans
NOVEMBER 14, 2017

Several million Americans voted last Tuesday in the first nationwide election since Donald Trump became President. In the 4-year cycle, this year has the fewest significant election results: two governorships (36 next year) and three state legislative chambers (87 next year) were decided. The media repeated constantly the idea that this was a referendum on Trump's performance, which is true, but only part of the story. Every race concerned local issues and local personalities, yet we can learn much about our national mood from these statewide and local elections.

Most results are easily predictable from previous elections, because fundamental voting patterns remain dominant. The only Congressional election, replacing Utah Republican Jason Chaffetz who had resigned to become a FOX commentator, was won by another Republican with 58% of the vote. In New York, Democrat Bill de Blasio won overwhelming reelection as mayor, but lost Staten Island, typically a Republican stronghold, to his Republican challenger. In elections for NY City Council, 41 of 42 incumbents won and the last incumbent was in a race too close to call. All seven NY big city mayors won re-election, including the Republican mayor of Binghamton. Only 2 incumbents lost in the 40-seat New Jersey Senate. Democrats picked up one seat in the Senate and one in the NJ House.

Exit polls in Virginia show how demographic differences in voter preference stayed relatively stable. Just as in the Clinton-Trump contest, voters over 45, men, and whites were more Republican, and women, under 45, and voters of color were more Democratic. The western mountainous regions went Republican and the Washington DC suburbs went Democratic.

But small shifts within these groups had major consequences for the outcome. Democrats slightly increased their percentage of votes in all demographic groups over previous years. For example, Trump won 52% among men and 59% of whites, but the Republican candidate for Governor, Ed Gillespie, won 50% and 57%. Clinton won 56% of women's votes, but the Democrat Ralph Northam won 61%. The biggest shifts toward Democrats were among young voters 18-29 and middle-class voters with incomes of $50-100,000. The movement toward Democrats repositioned the Virginia House of Delegates, where Republicans held a huge 66-34 seat majority and all 100 seats were in play. Democrats defeated 10 Republican incumbents and picked up at least 15 seats, with 3 Republican seats still too close to call. Control of the Virginia legislature remains in doubt.

The deciding factor in this major legislative shift in Virginia may have been turnout. In the 15 districts that Democrats picked up, turnout increased by 26%.

A different sort of small shift occurred in Washington state, where only 5 state Senate seats were up for election. Two Democratic and two Republican incumbents won huge victories in safe districts, but one open seat in a formerly Republican district was won by a Democrat, switching control of the Senate from a one-vote Republican majority to a one-vote Democratic majority. Three other state legislative seats were flipped, all from Republicans to Democrats, in New Hampshire and Georgia.

Dissatisfaction with Trump and Republican politics since his election is certainly one reason for Democratic gains through higher turnout in these local elections. Another change that exhibited renewed liberal energy was the success of new candidates from previously under-represented groups. Trump's sexism brought out an army of female candidates who won historic victories. In Newton, MA, and Manchester, NH, the first women were elected mayors. Seattle elected its first woman mayor since the 1920s, and the number of female mayors in larger Washington cities rose from 11 to 27. Women increased their numbers on city councils in Massachusetts to nearly half in Boston and Newton, and doubled their numbers in Cambridge, including the first Muslim woman. In Atlantic City, NJ, 32-year-old Ashley Bennett, who had never held public office, defeated 58-year-old John L. Carman, well-known in local politics for 20 years, for county commissioner.

Non-whites won election firsts: the first black female mayor in Charlotte, NC, and a majority of people of color on the Seattle city council. At least 7 cities elected their first black mayor, including Wilmot Collins, a refugee from Liberia, who was elected mayor of Helena, Montana. Elizabeth Guzman, an immigrant from Peru, trounced a retired Army colonel who has served in the Virginia legislature for 15 years in a traditionally Republican-leaning DC suburb.

Openly transgender candidates won unprecedented victories: first to win election to a state legislature — Danica Roem in Virginia; first to win election to a city council seat in a major city — Andrea Jenkins in Minneapolis; first to win any election in Pennsylvania — Tyler Titus in Erie school board.

The *Washington Post* wondered whether "the Trump era will one day be remembered as the last gasp of white male privilege." That will only happen if Trump continues his descent into national disapproval and the energy of liberal voters can be sustained through more election cycles.

STEVE HOCHSTADT
Boston MA

Again the trees obscured my view of the forest. The shift from 2016 to 2017 favored the Democrats across the country, who then won a more consequential shift in 2018 and took back the House. But the idea that Trump and Trumpist Republicanism were in retreat was just a dream.

Trump's "descent into national disapproval" had reached bottom at 37% approval and soon began a long slow climb back up to the low 40s, where it has remained until today, despite his coronavirus incompetence. Nothing more that he did won new converts or pushed his fans away. The giant tax cut that put the lie to every economic promise Trump the candidate had made may have cost the country dearly, but it didn't hurt him at all.

This Tax Cut Is Not For You

NOVEMBER 21, 2017

The news is all about tax cuts. For corporations, the news is good — both the Senate and House plans cut corporate taxes by nearly half. For real people, not such good news, unless you are rich. These plans are complicated and subject to change, but one thing is clear. This is not a middle-class tax cut.

It's not a tax cut for teachers, whose $250 deduction for classroom supplies is eliminated.

It's not a tax cut for middle-class and working-class families who work for colleges and universities, because the House bill classifies their children's free tuition as income. They would get a tax increase of thousands of dollars on tuition costs of $10,000 to $40,000 a year.

It's not a tax cut for middle-class families in states with high taxes, like New York, New Jersey and Illinois. The Senate bill eliminates deductions for property taxes and state income taxes; the House bill allows a deduction for up to $10,000 in property taxes. About 30% of all taxpayers claim these deductions, including half of middle-class taxpayers who make $50 - $100,000 a year.

It's not a tax cut for families with high medical expenses. People who have to spend more than 10% of their income on health care could no longer deduct that amount, according to the House bill. About 9 million people, with average income of $55,000, take that deduction every year. People in nursing homes and families with disabled children often need that deduction to make ends meet.

This is not a middle-class tax cut. It will only lower some middle-class families' taxes for a few years. But Republican leaders won't say that. Two weeks ago, House Speaker Paul Ryan said: "according to the Joint Committee on Taxation — which is the official scorekeeper of these things — every single person, every rate payer, every bracket person gets a rate cut."

But he was doubly lying. First, while every category of taxpayers would see an average reduction of taxes, not everybody in each category gets a cut. If the House version becomes law, 10% of taxpayers in the middle income range would pay $1000 more in taxes next year and every year.

Second, the cuts for the middle class don't last long. Senate Republicans made the tax cuts for individuals temporary, expiring in 2025, while the tax cut for corporations is permanent. Whatever benefit middle-class families gain disappears in a few years. That is clear from an exhaustive analysis by Ryan's own scorekeeper, the Joint Committee on Taxation. By 2025, the Senate bill would increase taxes for Americans whose income is under $50,000 and collect about the same from those with incomes between $50,000 and $500,000. Only those making over $500,000 a year will still see a tax cut by then.

President Trump has broken the promises about taxes made by Candidate Trump. Candidate Trump said, "the hedge fund guys, they're going to be paying up," meaning they would no longer get a special low rate for their income. He repeated this many times, saying they are "getting away with murder." Both the Senate and House bills leave that tax break intact.

The most important promise Trump made was that the tax cut was for the middle class. Just two months ago, he said his tax plan was "not good for me, believe me" and "there's very little benefit for people of wealth." Don't believe him. This month he urged a cut in the rate for the richest Americans and an end to the estate tax for inheritances over $11 million.

But you can believe that Trump is still trying to kill Obamacare. With his encouragement, Senate Republicans eliminated the Affordable Care Act's requirement that everyone have health insurance. As we learned during the health care debate, this means insurance premiums will go up for millions of Americans, wiping out any tax cut they might get.

What would a real middle-class tax cut look like? Reduce taxes on Social Security benefits. If you receive other retirement benefits, then you'll probably pay taxes on some or most of your Social Security income. Only if your total family income is less than $32,000 is your Social Security income free of tax. Millions of middle-class retirees would benefit if that threshold were raised. Pay for that by ending the tax boondoggle for hedge fund managers.

The Republican tax cut is not about economic policy and is certainly not for the middle class. It is political legislation about economic issues: cut corporate taxes to satisfy Republican donors and try again to kill Obamacare.

Mainly it is a backwards reduction in the size of government. First create a giant deficit, much larger than the deficit that Republicans have been saying for years would bankrupt the country. Then later start screaming about deficits again and cut government spending to fit reduced revenues by slashing the programs that most Americans need to keep afloat — Social Security, Medicare, and Medicaid.

Only 25% of Americans approve of the Republican tax bills. The more Republicans know about the details, the less they approve. Trump, Ryan and company are trying to pass this giant bill so fast, that most people won't realize what is happening to them.

STEVE HOCHSTADT
Jacksonville IL

The Republican tax cut was a remarkable boondoggle for the rich, sold as a benefit to all Americans. Trump notched an "accomplishment" about which he will be bragging until the 2020 election, while average taxpayers will balance gains and losses, and wonder what the fuss was all about. That's why Trump is now recycling the promises he made before the tax bill was written. He said in November 2019, "We're going to be doing a major middle-income tax cut, if we take back the House." The same old lies to drum up votes from the people he lied to before.

Keeping the Blacks Far Away
DECEMBER 12, 2017

I grew up in Carle Place, a new suburban town on Long Island, outside of New York City. Young families lived in inexpensive but well-constructed houses in quiet residential neighborhoods with good schools. When I get together with my classmates at reunions, we all agree that our little town offered a wonderful place to grow up.

I never thought about black kids, because I never saw one in my neighborhood or at my schools, right up through high school. I knew black people lived in other towns, and sometimes we faced black kids in athletic contests. I never wondered why they didn't live near me.

Now I know. I've been reading a book titled *The Color of Law* by Richard Rothstein, who explains how residential segregation happened in America and in my home town.

In response to the government-created Jim Crow discrimination in the South, millions of African Americans moved north in the Great Migration after World War I. At the same time, the nation's population doubled from 1900 to 1950.

Facing growing population, American cities used zoning laws to direct new construction and to control where people lived. Across the country, zoning was designed to keep black and white apart, to protect white neighborhoods against black people. For example, in St. Louis zoning guided liquor stores, polluting industries, bars, and rooming houses into African American neighborhoods, preserving real estate values in white neighborhoods and creating black slums.

Private business supported segregation. The National Association of Real Estate Brokers adopted a code of ethics in 1924 warning its members that "a realtor should never be instrumental in introducing into a neighborhood members of any race or nationality whose presence would clearly be detrimental to property values."

In the midst of the Depression, the federal government used its enormous resources to promote home ownership. In 1934, the Federal Housing Administration, part of the New Deal, created affordable mortgages and made loans to encourage home ownership based on color-coded maps of every city, where black neighborhoods were colored red, meaning no help for residents. After World War II, the newly created Veterans Administration offered mortgages to returning servicemen with no down payments and low interest rates, but only for whites.

Collaborating with private developers, banks, and realtors, the federal government helped create the new suburbs which mushroomed around America's cities. I lived in a suburb built by William Levitt, whose name has become synonymous with suburbanization. His signature project was Levittown, a development with 17,500 mass-produced two-bedroom homes a few miles from where I lived. He repeated this success in Pennsylvania, New Jersey and Maryland. Behind him stood the FHA and the VA, which financed Levittown on the condition that it be all white. In 1953, the 70,000 residents of Levittown represented the largest all-white American community.

Carle Place was a microcosm of postwar America. Young white men and women could begin their long climb into affluence, security, and respectability through the American dream of home-ownership. Realtors would guide families into the mushrooming modern neighborhoods. Banks offered more favorable terms than ever before. And everybody depended on governments to allocate local spaces for new construction, advise the new projects, and guarantee the loans that bought the houses.

For white people. Not for black people.

So I grew up with no relationships with black Americans, whom I first met in college during the tumultuous years of the civil rights movement. By that time, for me and my suburban baby-boomer peers, getting to know African Americans was awkward and uncertain. We were all, black and white, deprived of the natural development of friendships across lines of race.

Blacks were deprived of much more than that. As I was growing up, Carle Place and much of Long Island embodied a futuristic landscape of tens of thousands of identical houses in geometric patterns on plowed over, treeless ground. Today shady streets, mature landscaping, and countless home expansions and improvements have transformed the aesthetics. The houses that cost about $10,000 to buy now sell for $400,000 to $700,000. Accounting for inflation, the white families like mine, that bought in the late 1940s and early 1950s, tripled or quadrupled their wealth through home ownership.

Instead, black families were forced to live in urban neighborhoods, where discriminatory zoning rules kept home values down. At least into the 1990s, toxic waste facilities continued to be built in minority neighborhoods. Urban highways were typically built in minority neighborhoods. It is still common in American cities to use zoning laws to place businesses that deal with alcohol, firearms, pornography, and now marijuana into low-income neighborhoods, preventing minorities there from building up equity as fast as in residential white neighborhoods.

The end of slavery in 1865 represented the beginning of other forms of government-enforced discrimination for another century. By helping white families to build up wealth through home ownership and preventing black families from doing the same, federal, state and local governments have contributed to today's racial disparities in wealth.

As Richard Rothstein wrote, "Government and private industry came together to create a system of residential segregation." All Americans have suffered from this history of racism.

STEVE HOCHSTADT
Jacksonville IL

When I grew up in segregated America, race and gender were rarely subjects of public concern. White male supremacy was so fully ingrained into our society that just questioning it was a radical act. In the 1950s, a few radicals did raise the issues of racism and sexism, but there was no clue that pervasive and open discrimination would explode into political controversies in the 1960s. My ignorance about race and gender as political issues in the 1950s mirrored America.

Now half a century of turmoil has upended the comfortable certainties of (white) fathers know best, but the real meanings of subordination and discrimination are still emerging as cultural shock waves. The pervasiveness of male sexual assault of women was only fully realized when the #MeToo movement liberated women to talk about experiences they had kept to themselves. Hollywood's dirty secrets, known to many but not publicly discussed, now shock the world. The dirtiest secret of all, that the regular assaults of women by men in power were winked at by those around them, might explain why #MeToo has not yet transformed gender relations. Twenty-five women have reported Trump's inappropriate behavior, including assault, but his approval among men has consistently been 10% higher than among women. The nonsense spouted by male chauvinists about masculinity being about protecting weaker women was merely a cover for their real belief that masculinity means the right to grab women.

The Politics of Sexual Assault

DECEMBER 19, 2017

Men of all political persuasions have been grabbing, fondling, propositioning and assaulting women for a long time. Occasionally a particularly flagrant perpetrator gets caught in public, sometimes with unpleasant consequences for him, sometimes with none at all. Suddenly we face an avalanche of news about the hidden gropers among us.

It's not just creeps like Harvey Weinstein who are now suffering for their sins. A number of famous "good guys" turn out to have systematically abused women: of course Bill Cosby, but also Dustin Hoffman, Matt Lauer, and Kevin Spacey. The list keeps growing.

The national attention to victims of sexual abuse and punishing perpetrators is new, but it's been a long time coming. When Anita Hill said in 1991 that Clarence Thomas repeatedly harassed her, even Democratic Senators did not take her accusations seriously. The Me Too slogan was started 10 years ago by Tarana Burke, a black woman incensed by sexual abuse, who began the organization Just Be Inc. to help victims. When the actress Alyssa Milano sent out her famous tweet, "If you've been sexually harassed or assaulted write 'me too' as a reply to this tweet," just two months ago, she did not know that Burke had used the tag before.

Harassment happens everywhere and has been kept a dirty secret everywhere. After the movie industry and television and journalism, problems have surfaced in the hospitality industry and state politics. Institutions of higher learning are just now being forced to come to grips with serial harassers.

The grabbers come in all political flavors: four Republican and three Democratic Congressmen have resigned or have announced the end of their careers in the last two months. Both NPR (Charlie Rose) and Fox News (Bill O'Reilly) have lost big personalities.

But the national outrage over bad male behavior does have a significant partisan tinge. That partisan nature of sexual assault politics was brought out into the open by two recent polls. In a Quinnipiac survey, there is only a slight difference between Democrats and Republicans about whether sexual harassment is a "serious problem": 94% of Democrats and 82% of Republicans said yes.

A TIME poll showed more significant political differences. Democrats are more likely than Republicans to believe female accusers, 93% to 78%. Republicans are much more likely to think the media treat the men unfairly, 52% to 20%. The power of Republican partisanship over issues of character was revealed by questions about what should happen if a Congressman is accused of sexual harassment. While over 70% of both Republicans and

Democrats agreed that this Congressman should resign if he is a Democrat, only 54% of Republicans said he should resign if he is Republican.

The issue of immoral and illegal sexual behavior became deeply politicized by the case of Roy Moore, which shows how partisanship can distort ideas of morality. Republicans at the national and state level gyrated wildly, trying to come up with a reasonable response to an accused sexual predator and child molester who might be a crucial vote in the divided Senate. Because Moore constantly quotes the Bible and represents all the right political positions of evangelical conservatives, the "family values" and religious moralizing crowd were faced with a dilemma. While a few prominent Republicans took the moral side, like Senators Richard Shelby of Alabama and Jeff Flake of Arizona, and House Speaker Paul Ryan, many equivocated (Mitch McConnell) and many put politics first, notably Donald Trump.

Thus questions about politicians and sex were implicitly questions about Alabama and control of the Senate. Questions like this one: "If a political candidate has been accused of sexual harassment by multiple women, would you still consider voting for them if you agreed with them on the issues?" Only 12% of Democrats, but 43% of Republicans would consider voting for such a candidate.

The Roy Moore problem for Republicans has gone away, but an even bigger problem remains — Donald Trump. Republican politicians and voters decided last year that multiple accusations of sexual assault and some open bragging by Trump about grabbing women, caught on tape, were not enough to disqualify him as a presidential candidate. Now when asked what should happen if Trump were proven to have harassed women, 88% of Democrats but only 28% of Republicans said he should be impeached.

Sexual harassment and assault are about power, the power of men over women, and sometimes the reverse, which permits holders of power to commit crimes of personal behavior in the belief that they are safe from consequences. Harvey Weinstein's assertion, "You know what I can do," stands for the threat that has forced victims into silence and others into complicity.

The silence is now broken. Every day another creep is outed, another powerful man loses his power to humiliate, shame, and demean women.

Our culture is still far too focused on women's bodies and men's appetites to expect that harassment will stop. But creeps like Moore, Weinstein, Cosby, and even Trump can no longer expect to get away with a lifetime of hunting and abusing women. That's progress.

STEVE HOCHSTADT
Jacksonville IL

Oops. Kevin Spacey harassed young men, not women. It's easy to make mistakes about harassment, although that's no excuse for mine. Joe Biden appears to have thought his physical touches were welcomed by women, but so do men whose touches were much more forceful and sexual. Tara Reade says Joe did that, too. Will we ever know what happened? Maybe that's less important than making physical harassment as taboo as racial harassment.

CHAPTER 9

Personal Losses and Political Disasters in 2018

2017 was an awful year in American politics, and 2018 looked to be even worse. But at the beginning of a new year, I wanted to express optimism to my neighbors, my local readers. Who wants to read repeated descriptions of the worst President ever? I didn't want to write them. My family background in the Holocaust, just a few years before I was born, warns against any sense that this, now, is terrible. Things can be much worse, and they are in many places in the world.

In 1956, at the end of the Montgomery bus boycott, Martin Luther King, Jr., paraphrased a century-old sermon by the abolitionist minister Theodore Parker, when King said, "the arc of the moral universe, although long, is bending toward justice." If at those times and places, King and Parker could express such far-sighted hope, so can I.

Arcing Toward Equality in 2017
JANUARY 3, 2018

Conservatives might celebrate 2017 as a year of triumph. I'm not sure, because I don't understand the current American conservative mind. Having a man represent you as President who is a constant liar, an abuser of women, and an incompetent manager of people might outweigh the few conservative pieces of legislation he has signed, even if one is a big tax cut for rich people. But most conservatives rallied around an apparent pedophile in Alabama, so ideology seems to be more important than character on the right wing.

What I do know is that American liberals have been thrown into despair by the new nastiness of American politics, as Republicans have given up the principles they defended for so many years in order to force a few political gains over the objections of the majority of voters. The daily news about Trump's latest tweet, about the real nature of the tax cut, about the desertion of science in the federal bureaucracy, about the attempts to blind the public to the necessity of an informed media, all make each day's headlines another affront to liberal values. Even worse, truth seems to have been redefined as a liberal value.

But behind the headlines, our country has been evolving in directions that liberals could find encouraging.

Public disdain for homosexuality and discriminatory behavior against homosexuals have a long history. Opinion surveys show an unchanging and strong majority believing that homosexual sex was "always wrong" until about 1990. Over the past 20 years that disapproval, expressed as opposition to same-sex marriage, has been gradually declining, from about 68% in 1997 to 53% in 2007, until approval finally won out over disapproval in 2012. That trend continued in 2017, as support for gay marriage was expressed by nearly two-thirds of Americans.

There are significant differences among sub-groups, with white evangelical Protestants and older Americans showing the least support. But all groups show increasing acceptance of the right of gay people to fully enjoy their lives, and the jump in 2017 from 27% to 35% among white evangelicals and from 18% to 41% among conservatives (these groups overlap considerably) means that 2018 might continue this trend.

Similarly, public acceptance of transgender Americans is rising, although there have only been surveys over the past few years. Since 2015, the Human Rights Campaign's surveys show positive feelings about transgender people rising from 44% to 47%. In 2017, the proportion of Americans who said that transgender people should be able to use the bathroom of their choice jumped by 10 percentage points. The Boy Scouts of America both reflected this growing acceptance and pushed it further by announcing in January that transgender boys would be allowed to join. Joe Maldonado, who had been rejected in 2016, became a Boy Scout in February 2017.

The most notable cultural shift of 2017 was the public outrage over male sexual abuse of women, symbolized in December by TIME Magazine making female "silence breakers" the Person of the Year. The public naming and shaming of many egregious abusers was the culmination of the gradual shift in public opinion opened by Anita Hill's testimony against Clarence Thomas in 1991, and accelerated by the prosecution of Bill Cosby beginning in 2015. 2017 may become known as the year in which sexual harassment became publicly unacceptable.

Discussion of the continuing racism in American society was heated in 2017, but it is harder to discern how much progress was made in the struggle for racial equality. On the positive side, the public glorification of the Confederate defense of slavery, which has been a fundamental feature of the way American history has been told since the late 19th century, may be coming to an end. Controversy over statues was the most conspicuous flashpoint of violence, but the reconsideration of the content of history textbooks and the naming of buildings at prominent universities point to a more lasting shift in the place of our painful racial history in American self-consciousness.

The public protests by black athletes at the beginning of the NFL season caused a significant backlash, as such protests did at the Olympics in 1968 and 1972, and in many less notable moments since then. In most cases, the athletes were severely disciplined, and Colin Kapernick's 2016 protest was probably the reason for his continued unemployment as a professional football player. But in 2017, the protesters were not punished, perhaps a signal that public protests of racism, while not acceptable to many Americans, are now seen as within everybody's democratic rights.

All of these long-term transformations in American culture and public opinion were condemned by conservatives, with Donald Trump in the lead. Backlash against the movement toward racial and sexual equality may have helped him win election, but even the power of the presidency has not been sufficient to stop it. 2017 was a difficult year for Americans committed to equality for all, but the long arc of the moral universe still bent toward justice.

May that continue in 2018.

STEVE HOCHSTADT
Boston

The holiday season certainly contributed to my cheerful mood. We helped our son and daughter-in-law welcome Leo, the best possible Christmas present, and spent New Year's Eve with our granddaughter Vera.

I consider it a privilege to be able to give family such a large portion of my attention and energy. It's easy to forget how few people on this Earth can put aside all thoughts of political structures and economic inequalities, to focus inward, without anxieties about what's happening outside. Writing about my family is as close as I get to writing about myself.

At the New Year, my wife and I were faced with an intractable problem and agreed on a difficult solution, drawn from our deepest feelings about pets. In 1989, I had returned exhausted from China to face an immediate decision — what kind of dog should we get? Liz, 5-year-old Mae and 8-year-old Sam brandished a guide to dog breeds with the finalists marked out. Since then, we've had Boston Terriers. Magically, Liz and I, both with lots of dogs in our pasts, agreed on the place of dogs in our lives, something few couples hash out on the way toward partnership. Decisions about pets, like decisions about children, are drawn from the core of human identity, and display our deepest feelings.

I didn't seek affirmation of our choices by writing about our dog. This essay was mainly a gift to my family and friends. Now it stands as an expression of our identity as a dog owners, a phrase that not everyone accepts.

Homer Tobin-Hochstadt 2008 - 2018
FEBRUARY 6, 2018

Dogs don't usually get an obituary. I may think that Homer was an extraordinary dog, but every dog owner believes that about their dogs. Obituaries are mainly for people who knew the deceased, and many people were acquainted with Homer, and many more know of our family's obsession with Boston Terriers. So this is for them. And for me.

Homer had the best doggy life we could provide. Homer spent every day with his brother, Hector. In fact, nearly every minute. They went everywhere together, inside and out. They slept on the same bed, usually touching, sometimes with one's head on the other's body. They came with me to my office every day. On the few occasions they were separated, for example when one went to the vet, the other was confused, hanging near the door. I don't know how Hector will deal with Homer's absence.

That's another reminder that our understanding of our pets is limited. We may be able to predict what they will do, but we can't penetrate their little minds. Unless they display their emotions with sounds or actions in some obvious way, their thinking is a mystery.

Dogs' minds are much simpler than ours, but they certainly do think. They decide what to do in the situations that they confront. They obey our commands, not like robots, but more like little children, who wrestle with the conflict between what they are told to do and what they want to do.

Homer (left) and Hector 2010

Every dog wants to jump up and this is one of the most important things to teach a dog not to do. Our dogs' jumping was always about being friendly. While it may be fine for the family, jumping up on children, the elderly, or people who are worried about dogs is not good. We always trained our dogs not to jump, but they still did it, especially when someone crouched to pet them. I have witnessed many amusing moments, when someone leaned down to pet one of our Bostons, who then raised up and licked them in the face. Very friendly, but not always welcome.

We have lived with four Boston Terriers and none of them barked. Our first two, Hermes and Ajax, never barked. I mean that literally — I don't think Hermes ever barked and I believe that I heard Ajax bark once. Not much good as guard dogs, but very peaceful. Neither Homer nor Hector barked for their first 7 or 8 years, then started occasionally to bark when someone came to the door. These barks were not aggressive — as soon as anyone came in the door, both dogs would wag, greet, lick, and sometimes jump up.

Like people, as dogs get older, their behavior changes. Some changes represent learning. Homer learned that when we let the dogs out in the backyard, and then forgot about them while watching TV, he could come around to the front of the house and put his paws up on the window sill. Barking here might have helped, but see previous section about barking. Homer also learned how to tell us that he was desperate to go out. He would sit down in front of us and stare silently for as long as it took to get our attention. It took us a while to figure out his meaning, but this was an unmistakable signal about what he wanted. People can train dogs, but dogs can also train people.

One change in Homer's behavior became a problem. At age 8 or so, he began to get aggressive, a trait that is unusual among Boston Terriers. He would occasionally nip at dogs who crowded him, or came near his food or his bed. Homer and Hector had always engaged in play fighting, accompanied by fearsome noises and bared teeth, but never with any intent to harm. Recently Homer seemed to be less playful in these doggy arguments.

Worst of all, Homer began to nip at children. Our earlier Bostons were delightful with little kids, but Homer and Hector entered our lives when our children were grown, and therefore rarely encountered babies or toddlers. That became a problem when babies began to appear in the lives of our children's generation. Homer did not like animals his size other than Hector crawling onto his bed or getting near to his face. It's hard to know what he thought about babies. Did he think they were other dogs? Was he trying to send a message about keeping a distance?

He didn't growl or bite, just nip. But nipping a baby's face can be dangerous and is completely unacceptable. He nipped our nephew's son and our daughter's friend's son. Both of our children now have babies who will soon be crawling around. He began to nip at other dogs. Sometimes he seemed unfriendly to Hector.

That brought a painful decision, but a necessary one. We tried neutering Homer, but it had no effect. It seemed to us that there was only one alternative. Biting dogs, in my opinion, have no place in human society.

How will Hector react to Homer's disappearance? He may be even sadder than we are.

STEVE HOCHSTADT
Berlin

Hector got over any sadness quickly, but showed that he remembered his brother. That summer, Hector became clumsy and confused while we were living in the Wisconsin woods. By the time we got him to a vet, the deadly disease blastomycosis was too far gone to cure. He went blind, fell down, and was miserable. We've been dogless since then, an emptier nest than ever. Daily walks with my dogs had been doubly therapeutic, against creeping age and creepy politics.

I wish my dogs, or my friends, or anyone could help me understand Trump voters. I never understood Trump either — I can't imagine how anyone can act that way for a lifetime. That's actually a common historical problem. Some historians spend their lifetimes trying to explain the minds of a few "great men", often concentrating on the worst of them. Yet the countless psychological studies of Hitler and Stalin still don't enable the rest of us to understand what motivates a mass murderer.

We have to judge leaders by what they do. Trump is not a mass murderer, but his all-around evil makes him equally impenetrable. The worst are the hardest to figure out, partly because they create a dense smokescreen around their actions, while impersonating an imaginary normal person.

No evil ruler can manage alone. Trump couldn't do nearly as much damage to our country without his "base". If more Americans would simply follow the principles they have been announcing their whole lives, Trump's power would melt away.

The part of his "base" who show up at rallies prepared to worship their political Messiah may be beyond my understanding, but I've seen them before in my historical studies of democracies under siege. I would like to understand a second group, the "base" who merely tell themselves, and then tell families, friends, pollsters and election officials, that they prefer Trump to anyone else. I want to write something that will change their minds. But I don't get their motivation — why vote for a jerk who tries to screw you at every turn?

President Trump Versus Trump Voters

FEBRUARY 20, 2018

Donald Trump became President because millions of Americans believed him when he promised to protect their financial health. Social Security, Medicare and Medicaid keep the budgets of most Americans, especially the elderly, above water. Trump promised over and over again not to cut them.

He did this loud and clear, as a way of differentiating himself from other Republicans. Even before he officially announced his candidacy, he told the conservative "Daily Signal" in May 2015: "I'm not going to cut Social Security like every other Republican and I'm not going to cut Medicare or Medicaid. Every other Republican is going to cut, and even if they wouldn't, they don't know what to do because they don't know where the money is. I do." His announcement that he was a candidate the next month included "Save Medicare, Medicaid and Social Security without cuts. Have to do it."

In July 2015, he said, "The Republicans who want to cut SS & Medicaid are wrong." In October 2015, he said, "I am going to save Medicare and Medicaid." In February 2016, he said, "We're gonna save your Social Security without making any cuts. Mark my words."

Trump's promise not to cut Social Security included explicit statements that he would not raise the retirement age, as he said in the Republican debate in March 2016. "And it's my absolute intention to leave Social Security the way it is. Not increase the age and to leave it as is."

In fact, that was never his intention. In his book "The America We Deserve" in 2000, Trump compared Social Security to a Ponzi scheme and suggested that the retirement age be raised to 70. In a private conversation with Paul Ryan after he won the nomination, Trump responded to Ryan's plans to cut Social Security: "From a moral standpoint, I believe in it. But you also have to get elected. And there's no way a Republican is going to beat a Democrat when the Republican is saying, 'We're going to cut your Social Security' and the Democrat is saying, 'We're going to keep it and give you more.' "

And that's what happened. Trump convinced voters he would protect government programs which ensured that average Americans would be able to get health care and retire with some financial dignity. Once he was President, he returned to his "moral standpoint", the exact opposite of what he had promised.

As soon as he was elected, he appointed former Dallas mayor Tom Leppert as his Social Security advisor. Leppert is in favor of privatizing Social Security and Medicare. Trump's budget director Mick Mulvaney also favors privatization. In May 2017, Trump's budget plan for 2018 proposed drastic cuts in Medicaid. In June, he supported the Republican Senate health care bill, which made big cuts to Medicaid.

Now the White House has released a new Trump budget, which makes huge cuts in Social Security, Medicare and Medicaid. Under the heading "Reform disability programs", Trump proposes cuts in Social Security programs which support poor and disabled Americans, totaling $9 billion over the next four years and $72 billion over the next ten years. On the issue of how people will be affected, nobody could be clearer than budget director Mulvaney. When asked in the White House press room, "Will any of those individuals who receive SSDI receive less from this budget?" Mulvaney replied, "I hope so."

Funding for Medicare will be cut by $266 billion, mainly for patients who still need care after being discharged from hospitals. Medicaid will be cut by $1.1 trillion over ten years, by putting a cap on how much will be spent on individual patients.

Other cuts in Trump's budget: Meals on Wheels, home heating assistance, and teacher training. He wants to eliminate the Corporation for Public Broadcasting, the National Endowment for the Arts and National Endowment for the Humanities.

Every poll shows that most Americans are opposed to cutting Medicaid, Social Security, and the other welfare programs that Trump wants to cut or eliminate. So why is Trump ditching his promises not to cut these programs?

A poll of voters before the 2016 election showed that Republicans, even more than Democrats, said they wanted a leader with honesty, and that was most true for voters with incomes under $50,000 a year. After the election, over 90% of Republican voters believed that Trump was "a strong and decisive leader" who "keeps his promises".

It is hard to imagine a leader who is less honest than Trump. He has broken his promises about issues which hit Americans right in the wallet and pocketbook. It does take a "strong and decisive" person to repeatedly promise Americans that he will protect their interests in order to get elected, when he had no intention of doing so.

Will Trump's so-called "base" ever wake up? Does he have to shoot someone in the middle of Fifth Avenue before his supporters recognize who he is? Or was he right that even that won't hurt him?

STEVE HOCHSTADT
Berlin

The answers to those questions fall into two piles — 1) white Americans in Trump's base are motivated by anger at the "system", the attraction of simple answers, and ignorance imbibed from FOX News; or 2) they are racist. That latter alternative upsets me, because it can't be fixed with words.

My life has spanned the greatest improvement in race relations in American history. Every year seemed to deliver another blow to the white supremacy threading through our past, culminating in Barack Obama's election, at the time I began to write columns. The possibility that a racist electoral movement could win the Presidency is now a profound disillusionment.

Trump's racism is obvious from a lifetime of behavior. He was so outraged by Obama's election that he branded himself the chief "birther", an idea he has never given up. But what does it mean that nearly all conservative Republicans told pollsters that black Americans themselves are mostly responsible for their own condition, not discrimination? That more than half of Republicans think whites suffer from discrimination in the US? That Republicans believe that evangelical Christians are the most discriminated against religious group in America?

Trump promised he would make life better for those Americans aggrieved about their economic place in society. His efforts toward exactly the opposite haven't moved his disapproval scores a bit. The only promise he has kept is to hold up his white evangelical and racially angry base as the best Americans.

There is another movement in America that offers hope, defining itself as public opposition to Trump's base. Barely a quarter of adults under 30 approve of him. Young people have the longest future, but the least patience. 2018 might have been the year of politicized youth in Western democracies. Greta Thunberg began to skip school in August to stand outside the Swedish parliament with a sign "School strike for the climate". She said she had been inspired by American high school students, who were also afraid for their lives because of political inaction.

Kids Against Guns

FEBRUARY 27, 2018

Once again thousands of Americans poured into the streets to express a clear political position. This time it was high school students horrified at the mass murders of other students and at the unwillingness of politicians to do anything about it.

Students lay down in front of the White House last Monday. Survivors of the attack at Marjory Stoneman Douglas High School in Florida rallied at the state Capitol and urged legislators to change gun laws. Thousands of students across the country walked out of school last Wednesday to protest gun violence.

A nationwide school walkout is planned for March 14, lasting 17 minutes for the 17 Florida victims. Then come a march in Washington, called March For Our Lives, on March 24, and a National High School Walkout on April 20, the 19th anniversary of the Columbine shooting.

We never know what incident will provoke a mass social movement. Wikipedia conveniently lists all school shootings with 3 or more deaths over the past two centuries. There were 3 in the 19th century, one in the first half of the 20th century, 6 more before 1990. Then there were 9 in the 1990s, 5 in the 2000s, and 11 since 2010, more than one a year. Before Columbine in 1999, only one incident involved more than 7 deaths; since then, six with 10 or more deaths. In the past year, three school shootings have left 26 dead. If we widen our gaze to all shootings at schools, then there was one every other day in January, mostly without deaths.

After Columbine and Sandy Hook there were protests about how easy it is for those who plan mass murders to get powerful weapons, but they didn't last long enough to force politicians to listen. Will this time be different?

Days after the Florida massacre, Republican state legislators there voted not to consider a bill to ban large-capacity magazines and assault weapons. Instead, as school shootings increase, the Republican response has been "More guns!" Republican state lawmakers recently decided to bring guns onto college campuses in Arkansas, Georgia, Texas, Ohio, Tennessee, Kansas, Wisconsin and other states. Two Republican candidates for Congress, Tyler Tannehill in Kansas and Austin Petersen in Missouri, are giving away an AR-15 as part of their campaigns. Donald Trump's call to arm teachers and spend millions training them fits neatly into the Republican policy of arming everybody.

It's useful to stand back and think about whether this idea has even been proposed for other similar situations. Dylann Roof murdered 9 people at the Emanuel African Methodist Episcopal Church in Charleston, SC, on June 17, 2015, with a Glock .45-caliber handgun. On November 5, 2017, Devin Patrick Kelley killed 26 people at the First Baptist Church in Sutherland Springs, Texas, with an AR-15 pattern Ruger AR-556 semi-automatic rifle. These mass killings are the most horrific of a growing wave of church shootings.

Dallas Drake and his team of researchers at the Center for Homicide Research in Minneapolis counted 136 church shootings between 1980 and 2005, about 5 per year, but 147 from 2006 to 2016, over 13 per year. Should we arm priests and rabbis and ministers?

Right now, the political engagement of young Americans for gun control is very high. Can the kids accomplish politically what generations of adults have not be able to do — prevent further school massacres?

The political protest of youngsters can move national politics in particular circumstances. In May 1963, schoolchildren marched in Birmingham, Alabama, to protest segregation and discrimination. That Children's Crusade had political effect mainly because of the violent response of Commissioner of Public Safety Bull Connor and his policemen, and the bombing a few months later of the 16th St. Baptist Church, killing four little girls. Politicians learned that attacking children with fire hoses and batons is stupid. Now they politely listen and then ignore the youngsters' message.

The Australian response to a massacre in 1996 is sometimes brought up as a model for the US. The government not only banned further sales of semiautomatic weapons, but confiscated 650,000 guns. Since then there have been no mass killings. But an Australian gun owner and supporter of restrictions argues persuasively that Australians, with their very different history, don't like guns and offered no opposition to this revocation of their right to own weapons of mass killing. Too many Americans love guns for this to work here. Our culture accepts, even glorifies gun violence.

But it is not necessary to transform our culture to deal with guns in America. Most of the kids may not be able to vote yet, but persistent political action could shift the small number of votes needed to defeat the small number of state and federal legislators who stand in the way of majority votes for banning assault rifles and large capacity magazines, for tightening rules about who can own guns.

We'll see if students can keep up the pressure all the way to the elections in November. That would require behavior uncommon among teenagers — long-term political engagement. It may save their lives.

STEVE HOCHSTADT
Berlin

Tyler Tannehill withdrew from the Kansas Republican primary. Austin Petersen won 8% of the Republican primary vote in Missouri. Americans under 30 nearly doubled their voting turnout in November 2018, and they picked Democrats by 2 to 1. And some of them came out into the streets.

Often, what I choose to write about one week shapes the next week's choice. The unpredictable flow of my life sometimes impels me toward a subject that I think others may care about. Occasionally these two pointers align with each other.

We spent the winter in Berlin, observing American politics though a telescope anchored in German history, a subject we have studied for most of our lives. The week after thinking about American kids against guns, a movie showed us German kids against dictatorship. Writing about them brought me right back home.

Off With Their Heads!

MARCH 6, 2018

An historical film is attracting audiences in Berlin. "The Silent Classroom" offers a fictionalized version of a remarkable protest in East Germany and the more remarkable government reaction. In 1956, thousands of Hungarians fought to free their country from Soviet domination and one-party dictatorship. A class of seniors preparing for final exams heard of the revolt from the American radio station in West Berlin, which the East German government had forbidden its citizens to listen to. Hungarians asked people in other countries to stay silent to protest Communist oppression. One student, Dietrich Garstka, told his comrades, "We'll do that too!" In class, everyone was silent for five minutes.

The government went crazy. The Hungarian revolt of 1956 had installed a democratic socialist government before Soviet tanks crushed the uprising three weeks later. The Soviets and the other Communist governments in eastern Europe defined the revolt as counter-revolution and asserted that Western spies were behind it. The Western news media who reported the Hungarians' program for freedom and human rights were spreading false propaganda. Students who silently honored the uprising were counter-revolutionaries, too.

Specialists interrogated the students. The Minister of Education insulted and threatened the students: unless they named the ringleaders, the whole class would not be allowed to take the exams which qualified them for university. The class displayed extraordinary solidarity and refused to give in to government pressure. They were all thrown out of school.

Garstka soon crossed the border into West Germany, which was still relatively easy in 1956, and was followed by 15 of the other 19 students in his class. They took their exams there and pursued their careers, cut off from family and friends.

The system that transformed their silence into subversion was a perfectly self-contained organism. All media were monitored and controlled. Information about internal problems, weaknesses, and injustices was propaganda, fake news designed to weaken the system, and thus counter-revolution. Anyone who taught uncomfortable facts about history or politics was labeled an accomplice of Western enemies, a hater of the system, and punished with the weight of the state. Science was not allowed to contradict political ideology.

East German communism had very different intentions and assumptions than the Nazi government which it replaced. But both systems shared this enclosed structure of self-protection, where deviation was treason, where facts were subordinated to rigid ideology, where questioning was punished by exclusion. Both saw only black and white, and jailed people who realized there was grey.

Those structures are the opposite of democracy. But the forces of arrogant ideology, of undoubting righteousness, of hatred for difference can exploit the tolerance of democratic systems to disrupt them from within. The extraordinary democracy of the German Weimar Republic in the 1920s allowed the Nazis to grow strong enough to overthrow it. Or I should say that too many people in Germany, people with power and influence, through weakness, self-interest, and political expediency, let the Nazis come to power by not opposing them strongly enough.

Now in America we saw armed men, who disdain our elected government, take over a public installation at the Malheur National Wildlife Refuge, threaten government officials and then escape without punishment. We heard a presidential candidate encourage his supporters to beat protesters and disbelieve any news he doesn't like. We see virtually all leading Republican politicians accept Trump's vilification of the press, self-enrichment in office, and smearing of the judiciary.

Americans who report on these events are attacked with verbal violence. I have been called seditious, a traitor. Activists for civil rights are called communists and anarchists, whose political activities are thus illegitimate. The whole progressive movement, whose candidate, Bernie Sanders, almost won the Democratic nomination for President, is identified as hating America. Thousands screamed that the losing candidate in the last election should be put in jail. They say that journalists who report uncomfortable information about politicians they like are spreading lies. Many people have urged this newspaper to stop publishing my articles, because they don't like the facts I write about.

Listen to the radio, scroll around the internet, or go to rallies for the President, and you'll find many people with these attitudes. Instead of lurking on the fringes of the American political system, these people are brought into the White House. The President has called journalists "sick people" who hate our country and the other party "un-American" and "treasonous". Telling the truth and defending democracy means being bombarded with insults and threats from the small far right minority, who only see black and white.

What if they had full power in our government? What would they do with me, the traitor? Or our journalists, professors, scientists? Or you?

We must prevent that, to avoid repeating the naive complacency of other peoples who have allowed their freedoms to be taken away. Asserting your right to think and act freely can be dangerous, as the East German students realized. But they demonstrated solidarity, courage, and determination in the face of naked shameless power.

We have to do that, too.

STEVE HOCHSTADT
Berlin

Shameless power exists in America, too, in less dangerous forms, and perhaps not quite so naked. The children's crusade against gun violence inevitably provoked the National Rifle Association to wield its power more overtly. Most people only see the mask of patriotism and constitutional virtue that the NRA leadership uses in its public sound bites. Less obvious and much more threatening is the propaganda they feed to their members. As I wrote earlier, wider political motives often lie behind discussions of the Second Amendment. Those motives are more frightening, because they have me and people like me in their sights.

The Extremism of NRA Politics
APRIL 17, 2018

For reasons we will puzzle over for decades, the high school shooting in Parkland, Florida, provoked a mass political movement of young Americans, when all the other horrific school massacres did not. Gun politics is, at least now, big news.

Whenever public discussion of guns breaks into our daily lives, the NRA raises its voice, ostensibly to protect its interpretation of the Second Amendment. The NRA leadership must be especially concerned this time, since they are paying for a nationwide TV campaign, "NRA: Freedom's Safest Place". Executive Vice President Wayne LaPierre says the NRA's political ideology "evokes the patriotism, freedom, history, traditions and struggles of 'we the people'."

I have no argument with the right of the NRA, or anybody else, to proclaim its interpretation of American law about guns. But gun rights are not the main subject of the NRA's current political intervention. Below the surface of public statements about gun legislation, the NRA sells its members a disturbing critique of our society. Under the title "Standing Guard | Colleges Spread Anti-Gun Sentiment" on the NRA website, LaPierre says this about American higher education. Every sentence is worth notice.

"American freedom faces no greater threat than from our academic institutions, where the most basic fundamental principles upon which our nation was founded are aggressively attacked by extreme socialists posing as honest professors. Principles upon which America has become the greatest nation in the world — constitutional freedom, free-market capitalism and individual responsibility — have been replaced with Marxism, socialism and a perverse culture of politically correct societal collectivism. We know that, at the end of the day, the wave of socialism we face threatens all of our freedoms and could very well destroy our nation. Make no mistake. Their goal is not just to create a campus of socialism. They lust for a nation of socialism. They'll warp every young mind they can get their hands on, to pervert the American values we hold dear to create a brand new, socialist voter to send to the polls. If their socialist takeover is successful, they'll do everything they can to render Trump ineffective, with an end goal to replace him with a screaming socialist in 2020. And then they'll come for us...for our freedom and for our guns. That is the tsunami of socialism that threatens every law-abiding gun owner and freedom-loving American in this country."

In the NRA's magazine, "American Hunter", this statement of principle appears under a more threatening title: "Our Colleges are Breeding Grounds for Socialists Who Will Take Our Guns". This is not mainly about guns. LaPierre's America is mortally threatened by organized socialists and brainwashed youth, echoes of Joseph McCarthy in 2018.

During the 1950s, politicians who doubted McCarthy's crazy charges, but who thought their personal political interests could be served by being quiet, created a federal government that embodied exactly what McCarthy and his ilk supposedly warned about: an ideological state which ignored the Constitution and used the law to punish political opponents. By the time a few courageous politicians raised critical voices, government had damaged the lives of civil rights activists, labor leaders, filmmakers, and teachers.

Are we repeating a terrible history? Our Republican-dominated government takes the NRA's cash and praises its stance on gun rights. The biggest Congressional recipients of NRA money are all Republicans: 51 Republicans in the Senate and 41 in the House get more NRA dollars than any of their Democratic colleagues.

Politicians who praise the NRA also implicitly endorse LaPierre's extremist rejection of American society. They support the accusation that college campuses, including those in their districts, teach revolutionary socialism and hatred for American institutions. They believe that "academic elites are brainwashing our youth like never before." They agree that "every freedom-loving American" is endangered by a home-grown socialist conspiracy.

My congressman, Darin LaHood, is running for reelection this year. He proudly announced that the NRA gave him an A-rating, saying, "I am grateful for the NRA's support." He accepted $1000 from them, as did all of the other six Republican congressmen from Illinois.

Mr. LaHood, please tell the voters in our District whether you support the NRA's political ideology, as announced by its spokesman and published in its official media.

Do you think that socialists have "hijacked" the institutions of higher learning in Illinois? Do you believe that Illinois faculty are promoting communism out of a "lust for a nation of socialism"? Will a "wave of socialism" "destroy our nation"? Or do you think that NRA propaganda is itself dangerous?

Are you willing to defend the men and women who teach in our state's and our nation's colleges and universities from NRA accusations? Or do you give NRA politics an A-rating?

Republican and Democratic politicians who oppose restrictions on gun rights, also need to be clear about their stance on NRA political extremism. If your congressman is supported by and supports the NRA, does he (nearly all are "he") also endorse the NRA's radical rejection of contemporary American life?

The NRA is not protecting the Second Amendment, it is attacking America. Do they agree?

STEVE HOCHSTADT
Jacksonville IL

I got no answers to this public request from any NRA-defending politician. None of them, not even my own Congressional representative, offered any support for academics or the academy. Whatever they might believe about higher education, allowing this attack on us as traitors to go unanswered weakens the nation.

That's my opinion. I think that "We the People" includes me and everyone else here within our borders. I distrust claims by any "freedom-loving" group that "real Americans" are threatened by a dangerous "them" in our midst, defined by ideology and color and origin. That apparently makes me a dangerous promoter of a "perverse culture".

What could be more perverse than admiring Karl Marx? I grew up with anti-communism as normal American life. One of the first shocks to my system of political understanding was the film "The Russians Are Coming", released just as I was about to graduate from high school in 1966. The portrayal of sympathetic Russians and silly Americans caught in the storm of the Cold War was made for laughs, and featured some of my favorite Jewish comedians, Carl Reiner, Theodore Bikel and Alan Arkin.

Reading European, especially Russian and Soviet history as a graduate student in the 1970s made a much deeper impression, pushing my internal political dial to the left. Wayne LaPierre is right that education, especially the study of history, can explode the reactionary "traditions" of American anti-left politics.

I encountered Karl Marx, not as the evil genius behind Stalinist genocide, but as a historian himself, struggling to understand the mechanisms and direction of political and economic change all around him. Unlike me, he took his ideas to the barricades, physically taking part in every democratic revolt he could join against repressive monarchies. Most influential for me was his argument that politics and culture were shaped by transformations of everyday material life, the basis of the new social history that shoved its way into historical thinking as I was pursuing a PhD. I've never been the same.

Happy Birthday, Karl Marx

MAY 8, 2018

Saturday was Karl Marx's 200th birthday. It's dangerous to even wish Mr. Marx a happy birthday, because his name has become so closely associated with dictatorship and mass murder in the 20th century. But Marx killed nobody and never advocated killing anyone. He spent his life fighting against repressive monarchies in the 19th century.

Marx criticized the governments and societies he experienced in Europe, because they limited the freedoms of the majority. Hereditary monarchy, surveillance of political meetings, censorship, and banning of labor unions were discriminatory against the working class.

Marx's political program for workers was remarkably progressive in the middle of the 19th century and includes ideas that should be familiar to Americans. The "Demands of the Communist Party in Germany" in the Communist Manifesto of 1848 included: the right to vote for everyone (probably he just meant men) over 21; a free justice system; "universal arming of the people"; universal free education; strongly progressive taxes; and separation of church and state.

Marx signed a letter by the International Working Men's Association congratulating Abraham Lincoln on his 1864 reelection, which ended: "it fell to the lot of Abraham Lincoln, the single-minded son of the working class, to lead his country through the matchless struggle for the rescue of an enchained race and the reconstruction of a social world." Marx died in 1883, long before anyone who called himself a "Marxist" entered the political arena.

Marx experienced capitalism in its rawest form. The painfully detailed descriptions of the lives of early English industrial workers by Marx's collaborator Friedrich Engels led them both to see the social, economic and moral flaws in a system where some own property and others work for them for wages. In today's economically wealthy Atlantic world, where their demands for political change have been met for a century or more, their criticism of economic inequality as the basis for political inequality is still valuable.

Besides critiquing the world's economic system based on the system's own statistics, and calling for its overthrow, Marx occasionally imagined what real personal freedom for everyone would be like, with no company and no government telling people what to do. In the "German Ideology" in 1845, he wrote:

> ...each can become accomplished in any branch he wishes, society regulates the general production and thus makes it possible for me to do one thing today and another tomorrow, to hunt in the morning, fish

in the afternoon, rear cattle in the evening, criticize after dinner, just as I have a mind, without ever becoming hunter, fisherman, herdsman or critic.

He argued that such many-sided activity was most likely to produce happy and fulfilled people, willing to cooperate with each other, rather than compete against everyone.

There are strong resemblances to the extreme libertarian wing of Republican politics in America, but they won't admit it. Marx is an emphatic punching bag for the right, because his writings lay bare the poverty of their appeal to people without property.

Every idea has dangerous possible consequences. Medieval Popes and critics of the Papacy like Luther both thought the Bible admonished them to demean and even kill Jews. People who called themselves Marxists killed millions during the 20th century.

Thoughtful, courageous, honest and ethical Marxists were inspired by the vision of a free society of free individuals to oppose Lenin, Stalin, and Mao, and their versions of Marx's ideas, often losing their lives in the process. Marxists, both intellectuals and workers, became leaders in the deadly struggle against fascism in Europe, along with certain religious Christians. Christians who risked their own lives to hide Jews from the Germans, and sometimes their own police, demonstrated the hopeful humanitarianism of the Christian message. Does it make sense to toss them in the same pot as Torquemada?

Blaming Marx for the history of the Soviet Union or Communist China is like blaming Jesus for the Crusades or the Spanish Inquisition.

On Marx's birthday, as I do most days, I spent a few hours in my office, dug in my garden, read, and amused myself sharing the NBA finals with my wife. The productive, creative and self-regulated life appeals to me. I don't like being told what to do or need a boss to tell me to how be useful to society. I like collaborations among equals. I see honor in all types of honest labor and don't think that the work of executives is worth more than 300 times the work of average employees. I believe that humans become stunted intellectually and morally by a lifetime of one-sided dependent labor. We flourish best when we are able to do many things, develop many talents, control our own destinies.

For those ideas and others for which there is no space here, I am grateful to Marx. I wish the ideologues who perverted his ideas in order to justify becoming political tyrants had paid closer attention to what he meant.

STEVE HOCHSTADT
Jacksonville IL

In the white and black world of American conservatives, any compliments to Marx put me on the black side. In the multi-colored world we actually inhabit, it's also possible for me to say that I love private property. I would not be happy if I could not possess my own wool shirts, our vehicles and our home. I cherish the choices we can make about where to plant trees, what color to paint, and how to care for our house. The attempt to abolish private property was one of the deadliest errors of politicians who called themselves Marxists.

I also love public property. We all use public property every day, every time we get into a car, stroll along the sidewalk, cross a bridge, or enjoy a park. Those who attack either private or public property, from the extremes of the political spectrum, are dangerous. Finding the proper balance between private and public has been a dominant thread in American history.

Today's conservatives hate that kind of thinking. Historians, economists, sociologists and political scientists in American universities teach facts and ideas that challenge conservative dogmas and puncture conservative myths. Extremists like the NRA leadership regard all reasoned discussion of what that balance should be as treasonous leftist politics. They sound like the John Birch Society of my youth, railing against fluoridation and civil rights. Anti-intellectualism has long lurked at the edges of conservative thought. But then broad attacks on the entire higher education enterprise accelerated after the 1980s, as women's studies and African American studies contributed an expanded knowledge of historical and continuing discrimination.

In the Trump era, the methods of acquiring knowledge through research and analysis that I practiced every day became illegitimate, as facts themselves became objects of right-wing scorn. Online commentators on my columns used my title of "Professor" as a curse.

Why Do Some People Hate College?
MAY 15, 2018

I went to a college graduation on Sunday. Graduations are festive events, when everybody dresses up, smiles a lot, and congratulates everyone else. They are called "Commencements" because the ceremony represents the beginning of a new life as an educated person.

A college education in America is expensive, nearly $100,000 for students at public universities in their home states and over $200,000 at smaller private colleges. But as an investment, that expensive education is clearly worth it. College graduates earn on average nearly twice what those with only a high school diploma earn, which adds up to over $1 million in lifetime wages. The unemployment rate for college graduates is about one-third that of high school graduates.

Some Americans sneer at the idea that a college degree is worth anything. They do not argue with these numbers. Instead they criticize the entire American higher education system as fraudulent brain-washing. I doubt that these critics of American universities and colleges have any idea what actually happens on college campuses.

The distrust of political conservatives for intellectuals and higher education has been a feature of our politics for half a century. Before that conservatives had wielded their political power to shape education in their image, to prevent it from challenging the myths which supported their ideology. When I went to school and college in the 1960s, our lessons and instructors supported the status quo. The subject of history, the most politically dangerous of all disciplines, was written and taught to prevent questioning of political traditions.

James Loewen, and many others, have shown how conservative myths dominated history textbooks which were used then in high schools and universities. Slavery, the antecedent of Jim Crow discrimination, was transformed into a humanitarian effort by well-meaning whites to care for inferior blacks, who were happy in their bondage. Women were portrayed as best realizing their limited potential as home-bound caregivers. They, too, were pleased with their limitations. White men taught these myths, assigned textbooks written by white men, in courses selected and organized by white men, and made sure that when one white man retired, another one was found to take his place.

The few men and women who challenged these ideas and the structure that had created and propagated them had been struck down with the powers of the state during the lengthy postwar period of political repression, lasting long after Joseph McCarthy had been repudiated.

The protests of the 1960s targeted not only segregation and the Vietnam War, but also conservative power in American higher education, initiating a fundamental transformation of both knowledge and teaching that have alarmed conservatives.

American conservatives have been infuriated by the gradual dismantling of that whole system since then. The stories that confirmed their historical worldview and their contemporary politics were shown to be whitewash. African Americans and women demonstrated with their bodies that they were not happy with a rigidly subordinated place. The composition of history departments changed and so did their teachings. Studies of race and gender by a gradually diversifying faculty revealed uncomfortable truths about white supremacy and male domination in American history.

Crude conservatives like Wayne LaPierre say this all represents the hostile takeover of our universities by communists. The Heartland Institute, ostensibly embodying loftier intellectual aims, says that college is useless: their "policy advisor for education" Teresa Mull mocks today's graduates as "ignorant and inept", because "most college courses...are a waste of time." Revealing what really bothers American conservatives, the example of "brainwashing" she provides concerns teaching about racism.

I don't know how much experience such people have on American campuses. Their claims are not descriptions, but propaganda in the conservative war against knowledge they don't like. The majority of conservatives who say that American higher education damages the nation really mean that it damages the propagation of their myths about American racial history, about the proper roles of men and women, about the effects of human society on the natural environment.

Decades of conservative attacks on higher education have succeeded in creating an image of the college teacher as radical, elitist, unpatriotic, and intellectually dictatorial. The students who marched in their robes across the Illinois College campus Sunday, and tens of thousands of students marching across America, know better. They know that no course and no professor is perfect. They know about the flaws and achievements of institutions. But they know that they have been challenged, not brainwashed, encouraged, not repressed, coached and tutored and prepared for useful lives. They say the word "professor" with respect.

The real students I met are thrilled to graduate, because they appreciate how their college years and college teachers have transformed them. They are wiser, more knowledgeable, more skilled, more expressive, and more confident. They know themselves better — what they are good at; what they want; how to use their personal skills to achieve their goals.

At Commencement they're doubly happy — happy to be done and happy for what they have gained. Good for them and good for us all.

STEVE HOCHSTADT
Jacksonville IL

I fear that the efforts of a conservative war on college will persist long after these particular conservatives have passed on. A society which disdains knowledge, turns history into fairy tales, and substitutes lies for facts cannot exert world leadership.

I was not a politicized youth. Even going to college in the late 60s only mildly affected my general political disinterest. Living in Washington DC from 1971 to 1973 politicized me. Woodward and Bernstein, their secretive source "Deep Throat", and the honorable journalistic ethics of the *Washington Post* are to blame. They provided a model I strive to follow.

My articles are driven by my daily encounters with American life. I try to reach my readers by putting my personal experiences into the broad context of the society we live in. Only a few people care about my health, but we all live with a health care system that is determined by national politics.

Health Care Politics Are Scary

JULY 24, 2018

I just got over a health scare. I don't mean a big splinter under my fingernail or a stuffed nose. To me a health scare means believing that some serious bodily problem might ruin or end your life.

The "might" is important. It's scary to be unsure if this bad health moment might have disastrous consequences. So much of health care recommended by doctors and practiced for ourselves by all of us is about probability.

Some things are certain. The doctor was certain I had ruptured my spleen playing football when I was 17 and certain that the internal bleeding had to be stopped right away. That was a health scare I didn't know about until afterwards, when the surgeon told me, "You could have died." He was just trying to cheer me up.

Lots of medical issues are more speculative. Doctors consider the probabilities that particular symptoms mean this specific disorder and that certain medical and pharmaceutical steps will help this patient. We the patients weigh our options, based on what we know and don't know, using our own set of intuitive needs, beliefs, and probabilities.

My doctor helped me recover from this current scare by telling me, "Something else will probably kill you." He and I both understood the value of frank talk about the future.

My scare was not at all about money. I knew I'd have to pay something for the visits and tests and more visits and tests. But I knew it would be affordable, because I have good health insurance. Like nearly everyone my age, Medicare is my primary insurer, the biggest health insurance organization in the US. Medicare is bureaucratic, but reliable. They will not go bankrupt, like my parents' long-term care insurance provider did.

Medicare is incredibly cheap. In fact, coverage for hospital visits, so-called Part A, is free, with a deductible of about $1300 for each hospital stay. Not bad when the average hospital stay costs about $10,000. You only have to pay something per day if your hospital stay is longer than 60 days, meaning the total cost has probably gone well above $100,000. Medicare coverage for doctor visits, tests, and other services, so-called Part B, is not free — that costs about $1600 per year for anyone with an income under $85,000, that is, for most people. That's cheap, too.

All my probabilities would change if I didn't have good health insurance that I could count on until something else kills me. That puts me in the minority of Americans. Health problems become health crises for most Americans when they worry, "How are we going to pay for this?"

My doctors' recommendations were based on careful scientific studies of tens of thousands of cases over many years. My political representatives' recommendations about health care are based on self-interest and dogmatic political ideology, designed to misinform me and everyone else. The discussion of health care and health insurance in this country is worse than useless, it is often deliberately misleading. How can average Americans judge health probabilities when our politicians constantly threaten to upend our health insurance system?

Democratic politicians created an imperfect system which drastically reduced the probability that an American family would be uninsured. I think that's great. Democratic politicians have been arguing for a long time over whether some version of "Medicare for all" would be even better for most Americans. We need that debate.

The Republican contribution to our national health discussion has been, "We will destroy that system and tell you about a much better system later." If they really had developed another system, we would know about it by now.

Conservatives hated Medicare when Democrats created it in 1965. They have never stopped complaining about it and have never done anything to make it better. House Speaker Paul Ryan announced in December that Republicans wanted to cut spending on Medicare. A few months ago, the White House budget proposed cutting $554 billion from Medicare over the next 10 years. In June, the trustees of Medicare, who are mostly Republicans, like Treasury Secretary Steven Mnuchin, reported that Republican policies have hurt Medicare's financial prospects.

Nobody knows what our President, Cabinet, or Republican majority in Congress will do about American health care tomorrow, next year, or any time in the future. That makes all of our health care probabilities worse by increasing the financial uncertainties of all Americans. Nothing they have done so far has made anyone's health better. That is a national health scare.

I hope that something else kills me before any Republican health care plan goes into effect.

STEVE HOCHSTADT
Jacksonville IL

When I was growing up, my father brought home the tabloid and often sensationalist *New York Post* every night. *Newsday*, the biggest suburban Long Island newspaper, was delivered to our house. On Sundays, we settled in with the massive *New York Times*, bought mainly so my father could do the crossword puzzle. Three different kinds of newspapers, which shared a fundamental discipline — investigate and report what is happening. At grocery store check-out counters, you could buy things that looked like newspapers, led by the *National Enquirer* and the *Globe*. Their discipline was entirely different — use sex and sensationalism to sell printed words designed to be entertaining. The distinction between newspapers and supermarket tabloids was the same as the gulf between TV news and daytime soaps.

The "mainstream media" was decidedly conservative. In the 1960s, Republican candidates for President got twice as many newspaper endorsements as Democrats. In the 1980s, they got four times as many. But since 2000, Democrats have gotten a few more, led by the most influential papers, the *New York Times* and the *Washington Post*. Sarah Palin built a national following after 2008 by claiming the entire "lamestream media" was biased and untruthful. As I watched the impeachment hearings, it was clear that the whole Republican Party had turned against the press, led by Trump. That is one of the most fateful trends in our current and future political life.

How to Kill the Free Press

AUGUST 7, 2018

Anti-democratic rulers always try to prevent a free press from reporting what they are doing. Authoritarian governments past and present have developed a model for eliminating independent news reporting. Donald Trump and his allies are creating a different model, with disastrous long-term effects for American democracy.

The common model has been to shut down unsupportive newspapers and to create their own "news" outlets spouting official "truth". When the Bolsheviks took power in Russia in October 1917, they were uncertain about how much press freedom they would allow. During the New Economic Policy period from 1921 to 1928, limited freedom to publish was given to sympathetic non-Communists. After Stalin took power, however, every word published in the Soviet Union had to conform to strict government guidelines.

When the Nazis came to power in 1933, there were 4700 newspapers in Germany, but the Nazis took control over the published word much more quickly than the Soviets had. Leftist parties were outlawed and their newspapers seized. Two Jewish publishing empires owned by the Ullstein and Mosse families were destroyed within a year. Critical journalists fled the country. Joseph Goebbels' Propaganda Ministry issued detailed daily guidelines about what could be printed, with the threat of arrest and concentration camp for those who disobeyed. By the end of the Nazi regime, there were only about 1000 newspapers, and those owned by the Nazi Party outsold independent organs 5 to 1.

Violent repression, censorship and news written by the government were the hallmarks of the Nazi and Soviet destruction of press freedom. This model has been followed by many repressive regimes since then, and extended to news media on radio and TV.

The connection between control of journalism and development of authoritarian government is demonstrated most clearly today in Recep Erdogan's Turkey. As Erdogan jailed political opponents and reconstituted the government to consolidate personal power, he initiated a wide crackdown on the press. Turkey has jailed more journalists in the past two years than any other country.

Trump's war against the free press is often compared to the methods of Hitler, Mussolini, and other dictatorial rulers. But I think these comparisons are misleading. The Republican Party in no way resembles the monolithic parties which violently suppressed opponents. Trump's administration does not have the broad powers to deploy force against the press. Closing newspapers or arresting journalists would cause a constitutional crisis in the US.

Instead Trump has used another model for reducing the ability of our free press to describe and criticize his government. First, he has spread distrust of the mainstream media, so that their reporting about his words and his administrative actions is not believed by his supporters. He goads those who attend his rallies to shout "CNN sucks", calls journalists "horrendous people", and lately uses the phrase "enemy of the people" to describe the mainstream media in general. Attacks on the major national news outlets are part of nearly every speech he gives.

Trump did not initiate conservative attacks on mainstream news reporting. The objective reporting of news was Sarah Palin's primary political target in the 2008 campaign and afterwards, but she was following an already conventional conservative complaint about media bias against the right. In 2014, before Trump began his campaign, Pew surveys showed that "consistent conservatives" distrusted the major national newspapers, NYTimes, Washington Post and USA Today, and the national TV news organizations, except FOX.

Second, Trump supplements attacks on responsible media with unprecedented support for the irresponsible reporting of pretend journalists. Again, the far right media establishment predates Trump. Already in 1995, FAIR reported on a "right-wing media machine" based on personal attacks, fabricated stories, and thinly disguised white supremacy. But Trump gives respectability to what used to be a lunatic media fringe. His anti-free-press model uses existing right-wing media organizations to circulate the "news" he likes.

Alex Jones disseminates made-up conspiracies on his website "Infowars", designed to create distrust of our government: that the mass murders at Sandy Hook, the Boston Marathon, and Oklahoma City were government-perpetrated hoaxes. Trump appeared on his program as a presidential candidate, praised him as "amazing", and repeated many of his wild and untrue ideas. The White House granted Infowars official press credentials in 2017.

Trump's promotion of Steve Bannon, the director of "Breitbart News", to be his campaign director and then special advisor in the White House, put the leading voice of alt-right disinformation at the center of his administration.

Recent polling shows that more than two-thirds of Republicans think traditional major news sources make "fake, false, or purposely misleading" reports "a lot". That is true for only 42% of independents and 22% of Democrats. Most Republicans think the *NYTimes* (74%) and the *Washington Post* (65%) are biased, but only 19% distrust Breitbart.

Trump's model is designed to subvert democracy from within without violence. Responsible news sources will continue to report Trump's constant lying and his political failures, while Trump will continue to call these reports "fake news". Unless FOX decides to start reporting in a "fair and balanced" manner, conservative voters will continue to prefer the fantasyland of right-wing media to the real world of factual journalism.

STEVE HOCHSTADT
Springbrook WI

Without newspapers, we are left in the dark about what is happening in the world around us. Could we measure the slow rate of inflation by collecting a year's worth of grocery receipts? How would we know how big a raise the CEO's of big corporations gave themselves? Who else would tell us if our water was clean or dirty? From Ida Tarbell's investigative scoop about the corruption and monopolistic practices of John D. Rockefeller's Standard Oil Company at the beginning of the 20th century, to Watergate, to the revelations about National Security Agency spying on American citizens published in the *Washington Post* and the *Guardian* in 2013, newspapers have been our crucial source of information that people in power would rather keep secret.

My column allowed me to use the freedom of the press to discuss issues that did not otherwise appear in our small-town paper. The few daily pages of news could only offer a small sample of American news and a bit of world news. It was a privilege for me to occasionally bring something unfamiliar from the world outside Jacksonville to my readers. Sometimes I used my platform to uncover what had been right in front of us.

Unless one counts the daily customers at the Central Illinois Foodbank and similar institutions across the country all year, most Americans won't know how the poorest Americans are surviving. It's all too easy for the great majority to ignore the plight of the least fortunate among us.

The Poor Are Invisible

SEPTEMBER 25, 2018

Go shopping at the grocery store. Order a burger or a taco. Buy clothes at the department store. Go about your normal life.

There are no poor people. Or just a few, as you drive by the homeless shelter, where a few people might be smoking outside. Or you see someone in ragged clothes shuffling around downtown. Maybe someone asks you for a quarter.

So there's a few poor people, but not many, not enough to make more than fleeting impressions on your day.

The newspaper doesn't show poor people, either. There's no poor person explaining how they get along on page 1, no reports on policies in Washington that take poor people seriously. Poor people don't make the sports or culture or society pages and are even unlikely to appear in the obituaries, which cost money.

Students at prestigious universities won't see poor people in their classes. Most poor young Americans, aged 19-22 and in the bottom 20% of incomes, are not in college. Those who are don't show up at the famous private universities, where, for example, all our Supreme Court justices were educated. Many of those schools enroll more students from the top 1% than from the bottom 60%.

But you have been surrounded by poor people all day. More than 1 in every 8 Americans lives below the poverty level, over 40 million Americans. The greeter at Walmart, the young woman taking your food order, the shopper looking for day-old bread — they might all be poor.

You just don't know they are poor. You don't know about their struggles to put food on the table for their families, about how poverty causes health problems, about how they choose between paying rent and getting health insurance. You don't see them buy clothes at the thrift store, because you only ever go to the side entrance to drop off things you don't need. You don't see them at the emergency room, because you can schedule an appointment with a doctor and pay a quarter of what an uninsured person would be charged. You only see their neighborhoods through car windows and don't have to think about how they got that way.

Adding to their invisibility, the poor are more concentrated in rural America than in cities. One-quarter of rural American children live in poverty, somewhat more than the one-fifth of urban children.

Poverty has many causes. Some are personal choices, like drug use, while others are bad luck, such as an accident. But the level of poverty in a nation is a consequence of political choices. The United States has more poor people than all other countries with similar economies, because of decades of political choices. More than 1% of Americans, that's over 4 million people, live on less than $1.90 a day. Among the 10 countries with the highest per capita income in the world, the United States has by far the highest proportion of very poor people, more than twice as many.

Poverty is an inherent part of the American economic system. Over the past 40 years, the American economy has boomed, but the number of people living in poverty has grown steadily with our population. The boom helped the rich, not the poor. In that period, the incomes of the top 1% doubled, while the incomes of the bottom fifth grew a total of 4%.

Conservatives have made poverty into a liberal cause. Anyone could advocate for the poor, but conservatives in America have chosen to blame the poor for their plight, depicting the poor as venal, lazy spongers. Ronald Reagan picked out a singular woman con artist as a "welfare queen" to illustrate his view of everyone who was on welfare. FOX News regularly offers "evidence" that the poor live comfortably from welfare. Paul Ryan compared the safety net to a "hammock that lulls able-bodied people to lives of dependency and complacency".

Americans who are conservative tend to blame the poor for being poor. More than half of Republicans believe that people are poor because of a lack of effort, true for only 19% of Democrats.

Poverty is more than twice as likely for blacks, native Americans and Hispanics, than for whites. So white Americans tend to greatly overestimate the connection between poverty and race, which feeds into the conservative tendency to blame poor people, who are assumed to be minorities, for their poverty. Those attitudes explain Republican efforts to cut holes in the safety net for the neediest Americans. The Republican tax reform paid for huge cuts for the wealthy by reducing health care funds for the poor.

It's easy to ignore the poor, to pretend there aren't very many of them, that they get what they deserve, that they have nothing to do with us. None of that is true. No child deserves to get poor medical care or to have to miss meals every day. The poor do the jobs we don't want and their low wages mean we can afford more of what we don't need.

The poor don't live off of us — we live on them.

STEVE HOCHSTADT
Springbrook WI

I began writing these columns in November 2009. By this point in 2018, the column shaped the flow of the week, especially my weekends. If I didn't have an idea by Friday, I needed to find one. I could do research, try out phrases, and think about where I wanted to go on Saturday. By Sunday evening, I had to have a piece that satisfied me, meaning it had undergone rewrite after rewrite before I emailed it to my editor.

In September, I received a brief unexpected email from my editor.

"Please pardon the informality of an email, but I wanted to let you know we will be discontinuing your column after Oct. 16.... This has nothing to do with the subject matter or quality of your column; it is a budget decision. We appreciate the insight you have brought to our readers all these years."

Suddenly I was no longer a weekly columnist. If the $15 per week I earned was too much, there were serious problems at the paper. The other weekly local columnist, Jay Jamison, was also fired. For whatever reason, a piece of my identity was cut away, and I had to rethink my vocation. For the first time in years, my editor was very concerned about exactly what I wrote in my farewell.

Last Column: An Unexpected Farewell

OCTOBER 16, 2018

This is my last column for the *Journal-Courier*. A few weeks ago, the editor, David Bauer, informed me that my column was being discontinued as of today. He said the decision was "a budget decision". I don't know what other changes have been made.

These are hard times for newspapers. Newspapers large and small have suffered in the recent past. Circulation for daily newspapers across America has fallen by about half since 2000. Advertising revenue for newspapers has fallen over 75%.

This has hit newsrooms particularly hard: the number of news journalists has dropped by half. While national newspapers are weathering this storm, many local newspapers are closing. Since 2004, about 1,800 local papers have closed or merged. The smaller the paper, the more likely it would close.

The new tariffs imposed by the Trump administration raised costs suddenly. The tariff on paper from Canada greatly increased costs for all papers. In September, the US International Trade Commission found that American paper mills were not hurt by Canadian imports and canceled the tariffs. But David Bauer told me that the tariffs on imported aluminum, used to create plates for printing presses, mean that printing costs have jumped.

I was very lucky to be given the opportunity to write opinion pieces for the *Journal-Courier* during remarkable times. For me, "freedom of the press" captures the sense of intellectual and political freedom I was given at the end of my working life. An example of that freedom is the word limit within which most op-ed writers must operate. David let me gradually push the length of my articles from the standard 650 to 850.

Probably more important, for me and my readers, was the freedom of subject I was given. Although I was a local columnist, I could write about any
place or any subject. Over 9 years, I never heard one negative word from
my editor about my subjects or my opinions about them. I could go wherever I wanted in my Tuesday columns.

I will continue to write. I feel a need to comment on life and current events.
Writing columns means going beyond my immediate reactions and opinions to read what other people have written, to put together relevant facts,
to think again and to put my thoughts into a coherent argument. I learn
something every week about the world and about myself.

But I think that something is lost in this shift away of local columnists commenting on national issues, especially political issues, occurring here and
elsewhere. There are many writers across the country who write from perspectives similar to mine or to Jay's. The internet allows anyone with a computer to access countless opinion columns on any issue every day.

The difference is that they are not here in Jacksonville. They are not neighbors. They don't share the life of this community. You will never see them
in the grocery store or at a concert or eating at a restaurant. There is no
chance of developing a relationship with them.

My writing will no longer seep into a single community, not just as single pieces, but as a regular injection by a person who is familiar, who
sees the world from the same place as my neighbors, although not with the
same eyes.

A newspaper is an experience shared across a physical community, trying,
these days desperately, to appeal as broadly as possible. So we all read
the same obituaries and advertisements, the same sports reporting, the
same advice columns, and the same opinion pieces. Some local people,
who would never go to any website that featured my writing, who would
never seek out the well-known liberal media voices on the internet or on TV,
did more than glance away from my Tuesday op-eds. I know that, because

some of them repeatedly wrote nasty messages to me, ostensibly provoked by what I had just written, but often simply outraged by my existence.

I have talked with enough people in Jacksonville to know that some who hated my politics learned to respect me and my opinions, perhaps shifting their political perspective ever so slightly.

The demise of newspapers in America may put an end to the kind of interactions between writers and audiences which bridge partisan gulfs, which challenge partisan certainties. When people search on the internet for reading material, they usually look in familiar places where their views are shared. Internet opinion tends to reinforce what we already believe.

I will miss the sense that I am writing mainly for people I see every day. After eating breakfast at Norma's the other day, when I went to pay, I was told that someone had picked up my tab. The internet cannot provide such personal connections.

Perhaps this change will lead to new thoughts about how to distribute my essays more widely, most likely through social media. In the meantime, my articles will be posted each Tuesday on my website stevehochstadt.blogspot.com. I will be happy to send them by email to anyone who wishes to get them — just let me know by writing to me at shochsta@ic.edu.

Thank you for allowing me into your homes and into your minds.

STEVE HOCHSTADT
Bloomington, IN

Sadly the end of my column was only one piece of a greater shift in the *Journal-Courier*. All the local columns, whatever their subject or frequency, were cancelled. The daily editorials were now copied from newspapers located elsewhere. The reporting staff shrank.

That was just the beginning. Copy-editing became hit or miss. Articles were printed in two places on the same day. The number of pages shrank. We just got a letter to subscribers informing us that the paper will no longer by delivered to our door in the morning, but by the Post Office, thus no papers on postal holidays and Sundays. A tradition of local journalism stretching back before the Civil War is ending with a whimper.

I said I would keep writing. What would the transition from print journalist to internet journalist mean for me and my readers?

CHAPTER 10

Freedom from the Press: The Death and Rebirth of an Opinion Columnist

I didn't die. In fact, my firing from a $15 per week job as a newspaper opinion columnist had only minimal effect on my well-being. The death was metaphorical: a bit of my identity disappeared, but only the part about being published, not the part about writing. My public promise that I would keep writing Tuesday articles for my family, friends and others on my email list was a recognition that the writing was good for me. I often told myself, when I thought about the laudable political activism of people I admire, that my activism lay in writing. Among possible political activities, writing felt the most comfortable, profited most from my knowledge and experience, and best expressed myself.

I don't think anyone knows what the efficacy of opinion columns is, where we try to persuade distant and unknown readers. By offering to send weekly columns to anyone who asked, I discovered one thing I had accomplished. Many people in Jacksonville thought my writings were honest, thoughtful, full of information they wanted to know, and unlike what they found elsewhere. Dozens of local readers asked that I send them my columns.

So I kept going. I did not know yet how a different audience and different rules would shape my writing. I was happy about one obvious new freedom from the press that I had gained — freedom of language.

A Man For All Men

OCTOBER 23, 2018

Suppose you just met a man at a party, in a bar, at a meeting, or at a ball game. He talked only about himself. He told amazing stories about how wonderful and rich he was. He said he was a genius, one of the most successful businessmen in the world, and superior at everything he does. He commented on how attractive or unattractive the women around him were and bragged about his sexual exploits. He laughed about getting away with groping women he encountered. He made fun of the intelligence of well-known people. He made fun of the handicapped. Although flabby and overweight, he puffed up his chest praising men who were "tough" like him.

Then later you found out that his stories about himself were lies. That he cheats at golf. That he had cheated everyone he worked with and conned his customers. That he had cheated on his wives. And that his wealth was not earned, but given to him by his very wealthy father.

What would you say about this man? A man you would not trust with a dollar. A man from whom you would want to protect the women in your life. There's one word which sums up this personality — asshole.

Even assholes can be nice sometimes. Maybe such a man could show compassion in his interactions with others and empathy for those less fortunate. Maybe with more public responsibility, he could become more responsible. Maybe he would show another side of his personality.

But we have observed Donald Trump for two years since his election, and he has escalated his repellent behavior. His lies have multiplied, even about facts that can be easily checked. He mocks women, their bodies, and their stories of abuse by men. He refuses to believe people who know more than he does. He encourages people to hate the press, to hate his political opponents.

He is now the most famous asshole in the world.

Some people support the political policies Trump pushes and some people don't. But nobody could argue that Trump the man is anything but an asshole. And that means that it is worth taking a second look at those policies, because such a man cannot be trusted to do what he says. A clear example is secretly using a heartless policy of separating children from their parents as a way of dealing with asylum seekers, then denying it ever happened, then blaming it on Democrats, then imprisoning children in barracks without sufficient facilities, then defying court orders to reunite families, then admitting that they had not kept track of what they were doing.

That's what it means to have an asshole as President.

American women have recognized how Trump's true nature contaminates his policies. Nearly two-thirds of women disapprove of Trump. Although 84% of women who identify as Republican say they support Trump, fewer and fewer women identify as Republican now that Trump is President.

What about men? Men split nearly evenly between approval and disapproval of Trump. It's not black men or Hispanic men, but white men who support Trump.

Men who want to protect the women in their families from guys like Trump, men who believe in honesty, who dislike braggarts, who don't think worrying about getting venereal disease is comparable to fighting in Vietnam, who don't accept a draft-dodger's claims that he knows more about war than our generals — they still applaud Trump.

Conservative white men overwhelmingly support Trump. Don't conservative values count for anything?

Trump isn't on the ballot anywhere, but he says over and over again that this election is about him.

White men, what are you doing? Don't vote for a sleazy liar, for an abuser of women, for a con man. Pay attention to what women around you think. Have some pride in being a man.

Send this message to every man you know. Proclaim it from the rooftops.

Don't vote for the asshole!

STEVE HOCHSTADT
Boston

An online commenter wrote once that he still favored Trump, even if he did "acknowledge his faults and indiscretions." The unwillingness to admit that Trump's behavior has always gone and continues to go beyond such euphemistic labels typifies his supporters.

The evidence couldn't be more public. But it makes no difference, because personality is seen through a purely partisan lens. Just as the right wing vilified one of the most decent men in our public lives, Barack Obama, it ignores or excuses the real Trump.

Yet I continued to believe that more personal columns might persuade potential opponents to pay attention to my political writings. The yearly Christmas columns were part of this effort. I gradually grew more comfortable allowing my words to reflect feelings, especially about my family. Politics and analytical thinking are never absent, but I am also happy to follow the other side of my brain to subjects I care about.

The Humanity of Patience

NOVEMBER 6, 2018

It's Election Day! We are all overwhelmed with news about the immediate present. Certainly the next two years of our nation's life will be shaped by the election results. How about our own personal lives?

To some of my relatives, today's politics don't matter. Vera, 13 months old, and Leo, 10 months old, remain blissfully unaware of Democrats and Republicans, Congress and the President, who's winning and who's losing. They are in the middle of a uniquely human phase of life — extended childhood.

Humans develop very slowly. Humans are the slowest of animals to learn to walk: a newborn horse can walk within an hour after birth. My granddaughter has just learned to walk at one year and running will come much later. She can't talk, although she can communicate many simple desires.

Human brains are much less developed at birth than the smaller brains of other animals, because the human birth canal is too narrow to allow fully developed big brains to pass through. Much of our brain development comes after birth, allowing us tremendous adult brain capacity, but requiring years of dependence on adults.

Years will pass before Vera and Leo are ready for school. Most human societies across the globe plan a dozen years of schooling before we assume that our young are ready to be self-sufficient. So-called advanced societies plan another 4 years or more of schooling to prepare for more complex professions. Years and years of slow development and preparation to become physically, mentally and psychologically ready to be adult humans.

We might say that humans develop at a snail's pace, but some snails are sexually mature at 6 weeks old. Humans must develop skills far beyond what any other animals are capable of, such as speech. Both the complexity of human society and the biological nature of the human animal contribute to the long years of development. This slow maturation is uniquely human.

We make an enormous investment of time into the growth of our children. Observing my granddaughter and her parents day after day, I realize how important is patience to human life. Nothing seems to change from day to day. The same tasks and lessons are repeated countless times before they appear to have any effect. Negative lessons, like not touching hot things or pulling men's beards, have to be repeated hundreds of times before they are learned. The whole process depends on unending patience.

It's ironic that good parenting depends on patience, but our constant efforts to urge patience on our babies are useless. When they are hungry or tired, when they want to be picked up or put down, get out of their strollers or clothes, or generally do that thing that is inconvenient for adults, we say "Wait a minute. Have patience. Soon." But the words are meaningless. Patience is the long game and babies can only think of now. Like other adult qualities, patience develops very slowly.

Patience is not just useful in dealing with children. It also helps us deal with the world's problems. To build a better world for Vera and Leo and all of our babies, we must patiently find good solutions.

But patience has its limits. Sometimes patience is a code word for doing nothing. During the Civil Rights era, after centuries of white tyranny over black Americans, whites in power kept saying, "Not so fast. Patience." In that case, reasonable patience had long ago run out.

Our children will face a difficult world, if we don't take action now to counteract climate change. We have let the time for patience slip by. If we keep doing nothing, by the time that Vera and Leo are ready to have children of their own, rising seas will have inundated our coasts, storms of unprecedented power will have battered our homes, crops will fail around the world, people will die of the heat.

We need patience to raise the next generation of human beings. We need action to ensure that their lives are as good as they can be.

STEVE HOCHSTADT
Jacksonville IL

I'm a summarizer. We now have access to so much information, that it is easy to construct evidence-based arguments that are nonsense. Synthesizing impossibly varied evidence to find its gist, its center, its weight, is part of the training of a historian. Every class I have taught, every talk I have given, everything I wrote were summaries of far more widely varied information that needed summarizing.

Often that involves numbers, a discovery I made in graduate school, which I welcomed as a former math major. It's only when we don't know or want to hide the real numbers, that we say "many", or "a lot" or "some". After a national election when there are millions of data points, I think it's especially important to develop a summary that covers as much as possible. Behind every summary are individual, personal choices that betray our ideal of objectivity. The best check on my subjectivity, here and elsewhere, was my hope to reach a wide local audience. I needed to think about how my summary would speak to everyone else.

Any worthwhile summary of a national election needs detail. This piece is 1100 words, far more than my newspaper would have allowed. My freedom from the press opened new possibilities of description and analysis for me.

Where Is Our Country Now?

NOVEMBER 13, 2018

On Tuesday, millions of voters selected among thousands of candidates to run our country. Now thousands of people are telling us what these elections mean about America. So it's easy to find claims that every side won.

Trump won.

Democrats won.

Women won.

Minorities of all kinds won.

It's important to say over and over again that a person looking for truthful analysis and clear explanation can find them in profusion in American media. The *New York Times* is a national treasure, but newspapers that I have lived with in Boston, Chicago, Minneapolis, Providence, and Washington make a powerful effort at non-partisanship and objective research. The tiny newspaper I wrote for didn't cover much and was shrinking before my eyes, but it was reliable and truthful.

TV news, on the other hand, has been taken over by showmanship and bipartisanship, which is displayed by letting people from both camps say whatever they want and calling it news. Television employs countless spin doctors, who only care about reducing the pain for their own partisans. They tailor their claims to the needs of their party at the moment. Tomorrow they'll say something entirely different. Mingled in are useful commentators, whose biases are subordinated to their professionalism, but they often end up sounding just like the hacks they appear next to.

FOX News can only be trusted to seek market share by telling its viewers what they most what to hear. What FOX promotes most is the most biased. Its star, Sean Hannity, explained what he does: "I'm not a journalist jackass. I'm a talk host." FOX put its partisan purposes into practice by blaming liberals and Democrats for sending pipe bombs to themselves.

MSNBC annoys me with their repetitive gleeful reporting of whatever makes conservatives look worst. But they don't make anything up. Their content is researched, insightful and reliable. They were as good at interpreting the election in real time on Tuesday night as anyone else. I've been putting all kinds of sources together to outline the election results and explain what I think about it all.

Who voted last week? The *Washington Post* delivered a fine graphic overview. Voters in all age groups picked Democrats in House votes at the highest rates in over 10 years, including two-thirds of 18- to 39-year-olds. Suburban voters preferred Democrats by a wide margin, except in the South, where the parties were even. 60% of women preferred Democrats, while men narrowly preferred Republicans, better for Democrats among both genders than at any time in the last 10 years. Democrats got more votes from college-educated men and women than at any time since 2006: two-thirds of women who had gone to college voted for Democrats. Many voters who did not go to college had jumped away from Democrats in 2010, but have been coming back since then.

Across America, Democrats received 5 million more votes in House races than Republicans, winning 52% to 47%.

Women did win. There will be over 100 women in the House next year, many more than ever before. The first female Senators from Tennessee and Arizona will take their seats.

Minorities won. In Congress, we'll see the first two Native American women, the first two Muslim women, the first Hispanic women from Texas. The first openly gay man was elected as Governor, among other LGBTQ winners.

Trump did not win. He was not on the ballot, although he told his supporters to act as if he were. Of the 75 House and Senate candidates he endorsed, who were in heavily Republican-leaning districts, only 21 won. He made public appearances for 36 House and Senate candidates in heavily Republican-leaning districts, and 21 won. He endorsed 39 other candidates, also in Republican districts, and they didn't win.

Some combination of Trump's unpopularity among people who had voted for Republicans in the past, the positive appeal of new candidates, among them many women and people of color, and the desire of most voters to entrust Democrats with taking care of their health and education created a wave of Democratic victories in districts held by Republicans.

Was it a big wave or a little wave or a ripple? Who even knows what those words mean applied to national elections? Numbers are better. The Democrats gained at least 36 seats in the House, flipped 7 governorships, and 8 state legislative chambers.

Here is what did not change and what will continue to animate political controversy. It is hard for many Americans to vote. Republicans profit from suppressing the vote. The numerous court judgments that they have done this unlawfully have not stopped them yet.

Republican gerrymandering has been dented, but not yet defeated. Voting in North Carolina proceeded in districts that were declared unconstitutional twice: although Republicans barely won there in terms of total votes 50.3% to 48.4%, they won 10 of 13 seats in the House. But voters approved ballot measures that would eliminate partisan gerrymandering in 4 states, with 3 of those decisions overwhelming. When they had a chance to register an opinion, voters were in favor of making voting easier.

White men are still in charge in America. Their hold on power has been weakening for decades, and 2018 was an important milestone on the path toward more equality. But everywhere you look, from the White House to

Congress to elected officials at every level to company board rooms, white men are mostly in charge.

The Republican Party is the party of white evangelical men. 60% of white men voted Republican and 75% of white evangelical Christians. White men made up 46% of Republican voters, white women 39%, and minorities only 16%. Minorities were 40% of Democratic voters, white men 26% and white women 34%.

Less than half of Democratic Congressional candidates were white men, but 77% of Republican candidates. White men were 76% of the much more numerous Republican candidates for state legislatures, a proportion that has remained unchanged since 2012.

Americans who think that sexual harassment is not a serious problem, that it is not important to elect more women and racial minorities to office, that Roe v. Wade should be overturned, and that stricter gun control laws are a bad idea are all reliable Republican voters.

Lots of electoral commentators are comparing this "blue wave" with past waves, often to prove that their side did extraordinarily well. It's more important to think about the future. Will the overwhelming liberalism of young Americans gradually replace the self-interested conservatism of my generation? Will women keep moving in a liberal direction? Will they take the men around them along?

Women didn't just win races. They shoved American politics to the left by running and donating and voting and winning.

American government has many new faces. We'll see if they can produce better results.

STEVE HOCHSTADT
Jacksonville IL

Suppressing the vote is as old as voting. We equate voting with democracy, in honor of the political systems of some Greek cities over 2500 years ago. The Greeks suppressed the vote of women, slaves, and foreigners. The great majority of men couldn't vote in England before 1867. Any woman who voted before 1900 was exceptional. Our Constitution did not specify which men could vote, but most states limited the franchise to white male property owners. A few states, like New Jersey, allowed men of all races to vote on ratifying the Constitution. The Jim Crow system of repression of African Americans that lasted for a century after the Civil War was created and maintained by preventing blacks from voting, even where they were a majority.

We have never experienced a national election in the US that was free and fair across the land. The power of states to determine who can vote, the ultimate states' right, allows deliberate electoral injustice to taint our democracy.

Free and Fair Elections

NOVEMBER 20, 2018

The bedrock of democracy is the free election of those who govern. Our founders created the world's first constitutional democracy in 1789, but only white men with property were allowed to vote at the beginning. Although some highly undemocratic states allow everyone to vote under very restrictive conditions, democracy has become synonymous with universal suffrage. The United States only achieved universal suffrage because of the protests of the 1960s, after which Jim Crow laws excluding African Americans from the franchise were gradually dismantled.

Voting is complicated. Two weeks ago, over 116 million Americans voted for thousands of political offices, the highest proportion of eligible voters in a midterm election since 1914. Hundreds of jurisdictions across America set their own rules, make their own ballots, and supervise their own elections.

The rules for voter registration, absentee ballots, and the possible need for identification are all over the map.

My wife and I decided to be election judges in our county in central Illinois. Judges here perform the official functions of insuring that someone who wants to vote is registered and votes in the proper precinct, and then documenting that the person has voted. But the unofficial work on Election Day is just as important: helping people to vote who are confused about some element of this system. At my polling place, which included three precincts, we helped voters find the proper precinct or told them where to go if they were at the wrong place. We guided new voters to the county courthouse if they were not yet registered, because Illinois allows voters to register on Election Day. Voters who had recently moved, who had changed their names, whose polling place had moved since the last election, or who had made a mistake in filling in their ballot were all handled with courtesy and care. It was a long day, from 5 AM to 8 PM, but everything went smoothly. Nobody had to wait more than 5 minutes to cast a ballot. Democracy in action.

That was not the case for all American voters.

Voters had to wait for hours in Georgia and other states. Voters in big cities, like New York and Philadelphia, reported very long lines. The likelihood of unusually heavy turnout had been discussed for months, but many polling places were unprepared for large numbers of voters.

There were problems across the country with voting machines. Most states use voting machines that are more than 10 years old, and 43 states have machines that are no longer manufactured. Inadequate numbers of outdated machines, some of which broke down almost immediately, caused long delays for thousands, maybe hundreds of thousands of voters. We had two machines at my polling place, which broke down several times during the day, once at the same time. A technician who came from the courthouse to fix them said there were many machine problems across the city. Fortunately, we had paper ballots for anyone who wanted them.

Not so easy to fix are the structural problems that make it hard to vote. Inadequate staffing at many polling places caused preventable delays. Siting of polling places far from where voters live reduces voting.

The Republican legislature in North Carolina recently passed new rules which resulted in the closure of one-fifth of all early polling places. That came after a federal court ruled that the legislature's 2013 law, which reduced early voting by a week and eliminated same-day registration, was designed to reduce African American voting with "surgical precision".

Racial vote suppression has been a permanent feature of American democracy, even after the end of Jim Crow. Democratic and Republican Congresses felt the need to reauthorize the Voting Rights Act of 1965 for nearly 50 years. In Shelby County v. Holder in 2013, the Supreme Court eliminated that federal scrutiny of local electoral behavior, when it decided that systematic racial discrimination no longer existed. Suppression of the black vote, and of other non-white Americans, had become more subtle.

The placement of voting machines in Ohio in 2004 led to long lines in black districts. A thorough analysis of the 2012 elections showed that most voters there waited only a matter of minutes to vote. But in some communities, the average wait was almost two hours. The only way to explain these differences was race: African Americans had to wait twice as long as white voters.

Where polling places are located can encourage or discourage voting. My polling place was over one mile away from one of the precincts we covered.

Purging people from lists of registered voters has been another tactic used by Republican state officials to tilt the results. In Ohio, two million voters were purged between 2011 and 2016, overwhelmingly low-income, black Democratic voters. Voter purges have been used recently in many states, eliminating millions more, always predominantly Democrats.

Democrats did it, too. American history provides a gold mine of notorious examples of every political party cheating about elections by gerrymandering the geography of electoral districts. But Republican officials across the country developed such extreme methods to target their most persistent electoral foe, African Americans, that the same Supreme Court admonished them to stop.

The justices rejected Pennsylvania's gerrymandered electoral maps, designed to prevent Democratic victories. Republicans had won 13 of 18 congressional districts in 2016 with only 54% of the popular vote, but only 9 two weeks ago.

Federal judges struck down the North Carolina electoral map engineered to ensure that Republicans won 10 of 13 congressional districts, but that map was still used in this election, and 10 Republicans won again. The vote totals show how the Republicans had concentrated all the Democrats they could into a few districts. In all three districts that Democrats won, the margin was more than 40%. In four of the districts that Republicans won, the margin was 10% or less.

Republicans don't even try very hard to hide the purpose of their voting "reforms". North Carolina Republican consultant Carter Wrenn told the *Washington Post* in 2016, "Look, if African Americans voted overwhelmingly Republican, they would have kept early voting right where it was." The map creator himself, Republican state rep. Dave Lewis, said, "I think electing Republicans is better than electing Democrats, so I drew the map to help foster what I think is better for the country." He explained, "I propose that we draw the maps to give a partisan advantage to 10 Republicans and three Democrats, because I do not believe it's possible to draw a map with 11 Republicans and two Democrats."

Legal proceedings will only catch the worst electoral criminals. Voters this time had a chance to voice an opinion about how voting should proceed. Voters in Colorado (71%), Michigan (61%), Missouri (62%), and Utah (by a hair's breadth) passed proposals to put the drawing of district lines in the hands of non-partisan authorities, as did Ohio (75%) earlier this year. Ballot measures passed in Nevada and Michigan to automatically register as voters anyone who proves their citizenship while obtaining an ID card.

There are many ways to cook an election. We must always ensure that our governers are not cheating. The methods are new, but the targets are the same. As long as Republicans believe that their power depends on preventing some Americans from voting, we will have to fight for the basis of our democracy.

STEVE HOCHSTADT
Jacksonville IL

Bad politics can be based on good historical evidence. The forms of voter suppression practiced by Republican state governments are rooted in careful analysis of who voted for whom in the past. Only in the computer age could North Carolina Republicans have achieved 10 out of 13 Congressional victories, when they won only half of the votes.

But bad politics is most often justified with bad history. The "history wars", whose outcome determines what public school students learn about our history, broke out over new arguments about how to rewrite that history. The American history taught in our schools had been white-washed and sanitized to reflect the proper dominance of white males. The expansion of African American, Native American, and women's history in academia in the wake of the civil rights movements threatened conservatives, who fought a determined resistance to these changes. They lost the battle in higher education, where good history counts, but were more successful in public schools, where political power matters. A clearer look at our past is necessary if we hope to move forward.

The Persistence of Bad History

DECEMBER 11, 2018

The thousands of monuments to the Confederacy and its leaders scattered across the South have become a national political controversy that shows no signs of abating. The decision of the City Council of Charlottesville, Virginia, to remove the statue of Robert E. Lee, mounted on his horse on a 20-foot high pedestal in the center of town, prompted three public rallies of white supremacists in 2017. At the Unite the Right rally in August last year, James Alex Fields Jr. drove his car into a crowd of counterprotesters, killing one woman and injuring dozens of people. He has just been convicted of first-degree murder. The statue still stands.

Of the approximately 1700 public memorials to the Confederacy, less than 100 have been removed in the past few years. These visible symbols represent the persistence of a cherished historical myth of American conservatives, the honor of the "Lost Cause" of the Civil War. Developed immediately after the defeat of the South in 1865, the Lost Cause relies on two claims: the War was caused by a conflict over states' rights, not slavery, and slavery itself was an honorable institution, in which whites and blacks formed contented "families". Thus the political and military leaders of the Confederacy were engaged in a righteous struggle and deserve to be honored as American heroes.

This interpretation of the Civil War was a political tool used by Southern whites to fight against Reconstruction and to disenfranchise and discriminate against African Americans. Northern whites generally accepted this mythology as a means to reunite the nation, since that was more comfortable for them than confronting their own racial codes.

During most of the 160 years since the end of the Civil War, the Lost Cause reigned as the official American understanding of our history. The glorification of the Ku Klux Klan in the film "Birth of a Nation" (originally titled "The Clansman") in 1915 was a landmark in the nationalization of this ideology. The newly formed NAACP protested that the film should be banned, but President Woodrow Wilson brought it into the White House, and the KKK sprang to life again that year in both North and South.

Not as overtly supportive of white supremacy as "Birth of a Nation", "Gone With The Wind" in 1939 reinforced the Lost Cause stereotypes of honorable plantation owners, contented slaves unable to fend for themselves, and devious Northerners. It broke attendance records everywhere, set a record by winning 8 Academy Awards, and is still considered "one of the most beloved movies of all time".

Generations of professional historians, overwhelmingly white, transformed the Lost Cause into official historical truth, especially in the South. Textbooks, like the 1908 *History of Virginia* by Mary Tucker Magill, whitewashed slavery: "Generally speaking, the negroes proved a harmless and affectionate race, easily governed, and happy in their condition." This idea prevailed half a century later in the textbook *Virginia: History, Government, Geography*, used in seventh-grade classrooms into the 1970s: "Life among the Negroes of Virginia in slavery times was generally happy. The Negroes went about in a cheerful manner making a living for themselves and for those for whom they worked." A high school text went into more fanciful detail about the slave: "He enjoyed long holidays, especially at Christmas. He did not work as hard as the average free laborer, since he did not have to worry about losing his job. In fact, the slave enjoyed what we might call collective security. Generally speaking, his food was plentiful, his clothing adequate, his cabin warm, his health protected, his leisure carefree. He did not have to worry about hard times, unemployment, or old age." The texts were produced in cooperation with the Virginia state government.

The Civil Rights struggles of the 1960s not only overturned legal segregation, but they also prompted revision of this discriminatory history. Historians have since thoroughly rejected the tenets of the Lost Cause. All the leaders in the South openly proclaimed that they were fighting to preserve slavery, based on their belief in the inherent inferiority of the black race. Both official and eyewitness sources clearly describe the physical, psychological and social horrors of slavery.

But the defenders of the Lost Cause have fought back against good history with tenacious persistence. In the international context of the Cold War, the local journalists and academic historians and forthright eyewitnesses, who investigated and reported on the real race relations in American society, became potential traitors. These "terrorists" of the 1950s cast doubt on the fiction of a morally superior America, as it battled immoral Communism. The dominance of white Americans in every possible field of American life was also threatened by a factual accounting of slavery before, during, and after the Civil War.

Bad history persists because those in power can enforce it by harassing its critics. It was easy for the FBI and conservative organizations to pinpoint those academics, journalists, and film directors who dissented from the Lost Cause ideology. They could then be attacked for their associations with organizations that could be linked to other organizations that could be linked to Communists. These crimes of identification were made easier to concoct because of the leading role played by American leftists in the fight against racism during the long 20th century of Jim Crow.

Thus did Norman Cazden, an assistant professor of music at the University of Illinois, lose his job in 1953. The FBI had typed an anonymous letter containing what Cazden called "unverified allegations as to my past associations," and sent it to the University President. Cazden was among 400 high school and university teachers anonymously accused by the FBI between 1951 and 1953.

The defenders of the Lost Cause switched parties in my lifetime. Shocked by the white supremacist violence of the Civil Rights years, popular movements and popular sentiment forced both parties to end Jim Crow, using historical and political facts to attack all facets of white supremacist ideology, including the Lost Cause.

The shift of Dixiecrat Democrats to loyal Republicans is personified in the party shift of Strom Thurmond, Senator from South Carolina and most prominent voice in favor of segregation, from Democrat to Republican in 1964.

It still seemed appropriate in 2002 for the Senate's Republican leader, Trent Lott, to toast Thurmond on his 100th birthday by saying he was proud to have voted for Thurmond for President in 1948, and "if the rest of the country had followed our lead, we wouldn't have had all these problems over the years, either." None of the major news outlets, the "liberal media," reported the remark, dwelling instead on the pathos of the old famous rich racist. Only a groundswell of criticism forced the mainstream media to recognize Lott's words as a hymn to white supremacy.

By then, generations of Americans, both in the South and in the North, had absorbed the bad historical lessons that remain the basis for racist beliefs today.

The Lost Cause lives on in the South, supported by federal and state tax dollars. An investigative report published in Smithsonian magazine revealed that the official sites and memorials of the history of the Confederacy still "pay homage to a slave-owning society and serve as blunt assertions of dominance over African Americans." During the past decade, over $40 million in government funds have been spent to preserve these sites, originally created by Jim Crow governments to justify segregation. Schoolchildren continue to be taught Lost Cause legends.

Politics keeps bad history alive, because of the political expediency of the false narratives it tells. American white supremacists have been created and encouraged by this version of American history.

So the struggle over history goes on. Most recently, several dozen graduate teaching assistants at the University of North Carolina announced a "grade strike" to protest the University's plan to spend $5 million constructing a new building to house a Confederate monument that protesters had pulled down in August. They are refusing to turn in students' grades.

The Lost Cause story itself deserves an "F", but it will persist as long as po-litical leaders find its fictions convenient.

STEVE HOCHSTADT
Jacksonville IL

At this moment, it appears that the attempt to preserve Confederate mon-uments across America as proper public displays of history is a lost cause. Notably it is a particular cause adopted by conservatives who believe that more truthful history is a liberal invention. The whiteness of American conservatism is nowhere more evident.

In my opinion, white is a boring color. My preference for red and black is certainly unpopular among the influencers who push white houses and white kitchens. To me, white evokes anonymity.

Except at Christmas. The physical properties of snow make it white to our eyes. A Christmas that is not white on the ground is always a disappointment.

Christmas

DECEMBER 25, 2018

This year I'm thinking about what makes the Christmas season such a spe-cial time. The seemingly obvious phrase, "Christmas comes but once a year", does capture the uniqueness of this holiday.

I believe that more family members reliably come together at Christmas than at any other time, except at weddings and funerals. Schools of all kinds make this possible by closing for uniquely long vacations. Organi-zations and institutions shut down or offer more holiday time for staff. Both my children and their families, including my two one-year old grandchildren, are here together with us for the only time this year. That alone makes Christmas a uniquely joyous time.

Of course, there are many elements of Christmas that are deliberately unique. I'm looking at our spruce tree, covered with colored lights and ornaments collected over decades, even generations. This year a family friend with a chain saw and tree-felling experience and I cut our own tree in a county tree farm, for which I paid a $2 fee. The tree is not symmetrical like the trees that can be bought outside grocery or home improvement stores, but it is the best tree we have ever put up. The many small lights in our living room provide a unique atmosphere, something like the flickering candles of Hanukkah, but more playful.

Under the tree are presents, more presents for more people than at any other time of the year. We have struggled against the commercialization of this celebration, which is certainly encouraged by commercial interests, but is enacted by us in our desire to be generous and appear generous. But there is no doubt that giving and getting presents is immense fun. Among family who know each other well, gifts can be meaningful, useful, desired and perfectly appropriate.

Our family has Christmas traditions, as I assume each family does, some common, some unique. We watch "It's a Wonderful Life" and "Miracle on 34th Street". Reading "The Night Before Christmas" and "The Polar Express" began when our children were little, but continued when they were past 30, and now will gradually again take on new meaning with the youngest generation.

Certain foods appear only at Christmas time, although this changed over the years. Liz's family had long served creamed chipped beef on white toast on Christmas morning, which always reminded me of my father's reminiscences about S.O.S., an abbreviation that Army veterans will recognize. Never a fan of white bread, one year I was sent out to buy a couple of loaves on Christmas Eve. I bought an extra one, so that I could demonstrate that a whole loaf could be crushed into a ball small enough to fit into my pocket. That was the last year we did that. This year we are planning bagels for Christmas brunch, which might demonstrate the religious syncretism that often occurs in mixed marriages.

The way Christmas is celebrated can depend on the venue. When our children were small, Christmas took place at my in-laws' two-story home with the families of Liz's two sisters. On Christmas morning, six kids gathered behind a gate at the top of the stairs until my father-in-law was ready. Their collective anticipation of being released to dash downstairs is a fond memory. After that house was sold, we celebrated at my in-laws' apartment on a beach in Venice, Florida. This year we are in a cabin in northern Wisconsin, where wood fires provide heat and a focal point.

The idea that this season should encourage generosity, charity, joyfulness and kindness adds a public moral element to private celebrations that goes beyond Christian traditions. This idea has long animated cultural creations, from the negative apparitions that frightened Dickens' Ebenezer Scrooge to the more modern kindness of Kris Kringle, which convinced Mr. Macy and Mr. Gimbel to recommend each other's wares in "Miracle on 34th Street".

The stress of shopping for gifts, preparing for relatives, and traveling can interfere with getting into the spirit of the season. A focus on presents within the family can obscure the plight of families, so many families, who cannot afford the extra spending that Christmas seems to demand.

We cannot solve our society's social problems in one holiday season, nor should we try. If the Christmas spirit is an admirable motivation, if Kris Kringle is a character to emulate, if life is to be wonderful for everyone, we have to learn from the holiday experience about how to behave throughout the year.

Whether one says "Merry Christmas" or "Season's Greetings" matters less than the exchange of positive emotion that should accompany our encounters with family, friends and strangers, this season and all seasons. We could solve many seemingly intractable problems with simple good cheer.

Merry Christmas!

STEVE HOCHSTADT
Springbrook, WI

The calendar that puts Christmas at the end of the year was probably produced by an elite conspiracy to get people to feel good about the past year and forget about political corruption and economic inequality. That happened when the Romans changed the New Year from March to January about 2500 years ago. There's no sense to this idea, but facts are irrelevant to conspiracy theorizing. Aliens may have had something to do with it.

Despite the good feelings flowing outward from the holiday season, it's useful to take a hard look at the last year, good and bad. We won't make the proper resolutions for the future, if we don't know the past.

2018: The Year in Review

JANUARY 8, 2019

New Year's Day brings inevitable reflections about past and future, about 2018 and 2019. Pundits' predictions about 2019 abound, few of which are worth repeating. I'm an historian anyway, less interested in guessing about what might happen than trying to understand what already happened.

I won't say anything about popular culture, because I don't know enough about its current version to distinguish Britney Spears from Miley Cyrus or to care about either. The last time I was familiar with pop culture, doo-wop was playing on my transistor radio. As you already know, political economy is what I care about.

2018 was a bad year for investors. The Dow Jones index bounced around during the year, peaking over 26,000 in January, reaching an even higher record 26,800 in October, then plummeting to 23,000 now. No other kinds of investments made money in 2018, either, including the faddish Bitcoin, which lost 80% of its value. But 2018 was merely a minor dip after years of incredible steady growth: the Dow had more than tripled since 2009, the longest uninterrupted bull market in history.

The stock market only gives a partial reflection of the economy. Only about half of Americans have any stake in the good or bad news about stocks. Nearly all rich Americans are invested in stocks, but few poor Americans. That inequality extends throughout the economy. The profits from stocks and from the wider economic growth since 2009, and in fact over the past 50 years, have overwhelmingly gone to the wealthiest Americans. Since 1970, the share of the nation's income earned by the poorer half of the American population has fallen by nearly half, while the share for the top 1% has nearly doubled. The "middle class", rhetorically beloved by politicians of both parties, has also lost ground. The long economic growth in the last half century and the recent boom since 2009 have fattened the wallets of the top 10%. The very, very rich may have suffered slightly in 2018, but no crocodile tears for them: their after-tax income has multiplied by 6 times in 50 years. That was before the massive Republican tax cut enacted this year, which further benefitted mainly the wealthy and big corporations.

But 2018 was a pretty good year for normal working Americans, because the economic number that matters most, the minimum wage, is heading upwards. Legislatures in 6 states raised the minimum wage and voters approved wage hikes in 6 other states. Millions of workers will get pay raises in 2019.

2018 was a bad year for Donald Trump. His personal lawyer, his first National Security advisor and his campaign manager, along with many other figures near to him, were convicted of crimes, Cabinet secretaries had to re-sign for unethical behavior, his Defense Secretary and several other close advisors resigned because they could not accept Trump's erratic behav-ior. His legislative accomplishments with a Republican Congress were nil, until the bipartisan criminal justice reform just enacted, which was mainly a Democratic initiative. His public approval rating remained underwater, since nearly as many people strongly disapprove of his presidential perfor-mance as approve. His family foundation was revealed as merely a family bank account. In November, voters decisively rejected him, when Demo-crats won 7 million more votes than Republicans and decisively took over the House. At least a dozen scandals surround Trump, and 17 separate investigations, including those by Mueller, menace his future. And the pros-pect of Democratic House investigations of everything Trump loom ahead.

We might believe that a bad year for Trump is a good year for America, but that's too simple. Our beautiful land will be poisoned, our air dirtier, and our water less drinkable due to the dismantling of the environmental regulations by those Cabinet secretaries who turned out to be too corrupt even for Trump. 2018 was a bad year for the Earth.

2018 was a bad year for men who abuse women in corporate offices, on movie sets, and in doctors' examining rooms. Manohla Dargis in the *New York Times* wrote about the "torrent of truth-telling" by brave women who have had enough. On that issue, it wasn't yet a good year for women, which will happen when there is less need for truth-telling because there is less abuse. But it was a good year for women in politics, and for other minorities, who made terrific gains with voters in November.

2018 was a good year for me. Two grandchildren turned one year old and are surely the cutest babies ever. My pensions, both public and private, support our freedom in retirement to do what we want. We don't want the expensive, thoughtless, wasteful and exhibitionist lifestyle that character-izes most of those people whose faces appear in our media. We can afford what we do want: a comfortable home, good health care, two 13-year old vehicles, the ability to visit our children and vacation with them, good meals out and good meals at home. And the belief that we can keep on going this way as long as our health holds out. We'll have good years ahead.

2018 was not so good for some of those I am close with. We all know people who are happy just to stay alive or to recover from some difficult health problem. Nobody I am close to got arrested or physically attacked, a result of good luck and of my social class and the relative safety of our small-town life.

But 2018 was tough for half of Americans. Departing leader of the House Paul Ryan said a year ago that half of Americans are living paycheck to paycheck. Then he shepherded through Congress the tax cut he's been pushing for years, which benefits the other half. Any bad luck could have made 2018 a bad year for someone in the paycheck half.

Making political decisions based only on what benefits him is why Trump is such a dangerous political leader. It's not enough to just think about what was good for one's small social and familial circle. We have to consider our whole diverse population.

Individually we can't make good things happen for large numbers of people, but we can be part of collective movements that are outward-looking, compassionate, generous and humane. We can focus part of our energies and good fortune on doing for others what we do for our families: use our best selves to create bright futures.

So here we are, looking forward to 2019 with the tendency toward optimism that might be one of humanity's most endearing traits. We can hope for an American politics that addresses our worst social problems rather than exacerbating our greatest cultural divides. We can hope that the environmental leadership of European nations can show the way toward healing our damaged planet. We can hope that #MeToo and justice reform and more renewable energy and voter registration drives and broader health insurance will make our country a better home for all of us.

2019 won't transform the world or our lives. But it can be a good year, if we make it so.

Happy New Year!

STEVE HOCHSTADT
Springbrook, WI

I think the ultimate message of my columns is that we can make our future. The vast bureaucracies of government and commerce may seem unstoppable. Some determined individuals have moved nations, but most people ask, "What can I do?" It's a good question, because each person can do good, as neighbor, as consumer, and as worker to make our society better. But in politics, it's the wrong question. "What can we do together?" While her contemporary intellectuals focused on a few great men, Margaret Mead said, "Never doubt that a small group of committed citizens can change the world. Indeed, it is the only thing that ever has."

Often what appears to be the influence of one man was actually created by several or many. My awe for Jackie Robinson is no secret. Let me here recognize the roles played in his racial breakthrough by some other favorites of mine, Branch Rickey and Pee Wee Reese. Robinson was a great man, whose achievements depended on many others.

Robinson was a local model for peaceful social change in my early youth. He's still bringing people together. I bonded with a Peoria trustee at Illinois College over our fascination with Jackie and the Dodgers. He gave me a "42" jersey to wear every January 31. Thinking about Jackie at least once a year is rewarding and therapeutic.

Happy Birthday, Jackie!

FEBRUARY 5, 2019

January 31 was Jackie Robinson's 100th birthday. Thinking about him always brings tears to my eyes. Let me try to figure out why.

I was born a Brooklyn Dodgers fan. Like most kids, I didn't have much choice about whom to root for. My parents were Dodgers fans, and so was I. I was born in Manhattan, spent two years in Queens, then moved out to the Long Island suburbs. I never asked them why they didn't root for the great Yankees or for the Giants.

Was it my mother's choice? She grew up in Queens, a girl athlete before girls were allowed to be athletes. She taught me how to throw a ball, play golf and tennis and ping-pong, and shoot pool. I don't think she ever was allowed to be on a team, until she became captain of adult women's tennis teams in California in the 1970s. Did she learn to root for Da Bums, just a couple of miles away at Ebbets Field, who had not won a World Series since 1890 and sometimes presaged the clownish ineptitude of the early Mets, who inherited many of their fans? She never explained her Dodger love.

It might have been my father, who probably had never heard of the Dodgers until he arrived in New York alone at age 18 in 1938, just escaping when the Nazis took over his home in Vienna. He grew up playing soccer and never was able to smoothly throw a baseball. Did my father hear of Jackie's college exploits when he sold men's hats in Los Angeles in 1939 and 1940? Jackie led the NCAA in rushing and in punt returns on the undefeated 1939 UCLA football team. He also lettered in basketball, baseball, and track, the first athlete to letter in four sports in UCLA history. He won the NCAA championship in the long jump in 1940, and would have gone to the Tokyo Olympics that year if they hadn't been cancelled due to the outbreak of war.

I was born the year after Jackie played his first game for the Dodgers in 1947. By the time I understood anything about baseball, he was already a superstar with a super team: Rookie of the Year in 1947, MVP in 1949, All-Star every year from 1949 to 1954, leading the Dodgers to six World Series in his ten-year career.

My brother and I have puzzled over many of our parents' ideas since they died. But I don't think that their fondness for the Dodgers was about success. Although they never talked about it, I believe race was at the heart of their preference.

I doubt if my father ever met a black person growing up in Vienna. But the Nazis taught him about the evils of white supremacy as he was growing up and later when he returned to Europe with the US Army, interrogating prisoners of war and seeing concentration camps. In our home, Jackie Robinson was a moral hero, as was Branch Rickey, general manager of the Dodgers, for signing him in 1945. We were excited to watch catcher Roy Campanella, who entered the majors in 1948, and pitcher Don Newcombe, who was Rookie of the Year in 1949. When most major league teams were still all white, the Dodgers fielded three black men, all of whom played in the All-Star game in 1949.

I must have seen Jackie play in many games on our little black-and-white TV and listened to Vin Scully's play-by-play on the radio. But Jackie retired when I was 8. I remember him more vividly in connection with Chock full o' Nuts, that "heavenly coffee": "better coffee a millionaire's money can't buy." Another enlightened white businessman, William Black, hired Robinson as vice president for personnel right after his baseball career ended. Chock full o' Nuts was the Starbucks of the mid-20th century, with 80 stores in New York, most of whose staff were black. Robinson's political activism for civil rights was fully supported by Black.

I understood little about the civil rights struggle and was too young for coffee, but I knew about Jackie's role as business executive.

Jackie Robinson was a Republican. He supported Richard Nixon against John F. Kennedy in 1960 and worked for Nelson Rockefeller's 1964 presidential campaign. My parents were Democrats and I've wandered further to the left since then. But partisanship mattered much less in those days than morality, and Jackie came to represent for me the high moral calling of activism for equality, not just in politics, but in life. I was born into a family that assumed that racial discrimination was immoral. It was immoral in Europe against Jews and immoral in America against blacks.

When I was young, I didn't know about Jackie Robinson's life before the Dodgers or about my father's life before he left Vienna. I didn't learn in school about either the Holocaust or segregation. I grew up in an antisemitic and anti-black society in the 1950s and 1960s, but barely realized it until I went to college. Even at an Ivy League university in the late 1960s, lessons about American prejudice and discrimination were not a regular part of the curriculum. Over the past 50 years, life and the study of history have taught me the facts behind my family's moral certainties. Jackie Robinson has accompanied me along the way, as inspiration, role model, hero.

To see 100 photos of Jackie's life, go to: https://www.nytimes.com/2019/01/31/sports/jackie-robinson-photos-100th-birthday.html. If you're like me, have a handkerchief ready.

Happy Birthday, Jackie.

STEVE HOCHSTADT
Berlin

I don't think that being a grandfather made me a better op-ed writer, but it changed me. The new lives in our family revealed wonderful strengths in our children, added unexpected joys, and shifted my focus. The facts of the world are the same. But now I ask a new question. For me there is only one answer, shocking me more when I wonder about those whose ideology seems not to care at all.

How Much Do We Care About Our Grandchildren?
FEBRUARY 26, 2019

I have two one-year-old grandchildren. They are happy and healthy, learning to talk and feed themselves and make their desires known to the adults who control their world. I am lucky, but it wasn't just luck. Their parents were thoughtful about changing their lifestyles to give the babies the best possible chances at healthy lives — less alcohol, less caffeine, heathy diets, paying attention to doctors' advice. Good luck and good care.

In 2050, Vera and Leo will be 32. They may just be starting their own families. They might become great parents, but what if the world is collapsing around them?

Vera and Leo discovering corn on the cob, 2019

By that time, unless we make great changes, the Earth will be hotter. Where I live in central Illinois, summer temperatures will be 6 degrees warmer than in 2000, and 4 degrees warmer in winter. After 2050, the Central Plains states may suffer from droughts much worse and much longer than the 1930s Dust Bowl. Each year, Chicago will have a month of days when the heat index reaches 105 degrees, compared to four days in 2000. Peoria and St. Louis are among the 25 cities that have warmed up the fastest in recent decades.

Each region in the US will face different combinations of severe hazards due to the warming climate. The greatest hazard on our coasts will be rising sea levels. More and more powerful storms will especially threaten Florida. Some cities in Texas will see the heat index rise over 105 degrees for more than half the year. Droughts in the Southwest and in Indiana, insufficient rainfall in much of the Midwest, but heavier precipitation from Maine to Alabama represent the most significant dangers.

Climate hazards translate into human suffering. Heat waves cause increased heart and respiratory problems. Drought leads to more intense wildfires. Floods cause contamination of water supply, and thus spread of water-borne diseases. Pregnant women exposed to increased smoke from fires or contaminated water give birth to less healthy children.

Heat waves, floods, fires, droughts and storms also damage agricultural land. Warming oceans harm fisheries. In California, the source of over a third of the country's vegetables and two-thirds of our fruits and nuts, the severity of summer drought will triple by 2050.

Wealth can protect some humans from the immediate effects of climate hazards. More expensive food, the need to purify water, increased medical attention, even moving away from storm-threatened coasts, dried out forests, or hot cities present little problem for those with extensive personal resources. Economic inequality within the US and across the world will translate even more forcefully into unequal life chances. The infrastructures of poorer countries in Asia, Africa and Latin America are much weaker, meaning that severe climate events have much greater impact. The World Bank predicts that more than 140 million people will be displaced in developing regions of the world by 2050, mostly in Africa. In wealthier countries whose populations will not suffer as much directly, heightened pressure will result from increased immigration, more expensive raw materials, and more violent conflicts.

Our planet is now nearly 2 degrees warmer than in the early 20th century. The economic effects thus far have been staggering: the number of extreme weather events that cost over $1 billion in economic losses has quadrupled since the 1980s. Continued burning of fossil fuels, contributing to warming and air pollution, will cost the US economy $360 billion a year in the 2020s.

My life will barely be affected by climate change. By the time the accumulated results of human activity create disastrous effects in America, I will probably be in a nursing home. But Vera and Leo will not be so lucky. Wherever they live, the climate will be unfriendlier, the infrastructure will be overburdened, the costs of coping with severe hazards will be higher, and the economic inequalities will be deadlier. The future for them and their children will be bleaker. People will be angry.

I am angry now. Angry at the professional liars who have claimed for years that nothing was happening. Angry at the politicians who pretend to believe them. Angry at the corporations who care only about this year's bottom line.

I'm angry at the self-proclaimed Christians who say they are pro-life, but put the lives of all future generations in danger by denying climate change; who quote the Bible at every turn, but ignore those passages they violate every day: "You shall not defile the land in which you live."

I am angry at those who want responsibility, but are irresponsible, who not only do nothing to preserve the Earth for the future, but do everything to further pollute our planet.

We have already gone past the point of no return. More carbon dioxide was released into the atmosphere from burning fossil fuels in 2018 than ever before. Glaciers are melting, seas are rising, storms are getting stronger. It will take more than recycling, more than a few electric cars and wind turbines, more than the kind of minimal lifestyle changes recommended by trendy columnists.

In order to prevent climate catastrophes by 2050, the nations of the world must cut fossil fuel use in half within the next 15 years and nearly eliminate their use by 2050. That means no more gasoline engines, no more heating homes with oil, complete restructuring of manufacturing plants. No more throwaway economies.

We have to change our lifestyles now. That will be uncomfortable, even scary. Do we care about our grandchildren enough to do that?

STEVE HOCHSTADT
Berlin

How can anyone say "no"?

I was in Berlin when I wrote the previous two pieces and the next two. Living there for three months every year since we retired in 2016 doesn't push my American life into the background. I write to Americans as an American. Immersion in Berlin adds new information, new insights, and new interests. Every new thought somehow involves America.

International Women's Day and Gender Equality
MARCH 12, 2019

Last Friday, March 8, was International Women's Day. You might not have known that, since little notice is given to this date in the US, even though

Theresa Serber Malkiel (1874-1949), socialist labor organizer

American women initiated it. Here in Berlin, one could not help but be aware of this special day, because the city government had declared it a holiday, and everything was closed except restaurants and museums.

A "National Women's Day" was first declared by women in the Socialist Party of America for February 28, 1909. It was proposed by Theresa Serber Malkiel (1874-1949), whose story exemplifies the history of the uneasy connection between leftist politics and women's rights in Europe and America, and the continued relevance of a "women's day".

As part of the emigration of 2 million Jews from the increasingly antisemitic Russian Empire between 1881 and the beginning of World War I, the Serber family moved from Ukraine to New York in 1891. Theresa went to work in a garment factory. At age 18, she organized the Woman's Infant Cloak Maker's Union of New York, mostly Jewish women workers, and became its president. Like many trade unionists, she gradually came to believe that socialism was the only path to liberation for workers and for women. She led her union into the Socialist Labor Party, the first socialist party in the US, the next year. Angered at the authoritarian tendencies of the SLP leader, Daniel De Leon, she and others joined with Midwestern socialists Eugene Debs and Victor Berger to form the Socialist Party of America in 1901.

At that time, both in the US and in Europe, socialists were the only political group to openly advocate women's equality. In contrast to suffragists, socialists argued that gaining the vote was only the first step in creating an egalitarian society. But Theresa Serber almost immediately attacked the tendency of socialist men to say they favored gender equality, but to do nothing to bring it about, even within their own ranks. She formed separate women's organizations to reach out to women workers and discuss their particular issues. She denounced the relegation of women in the Party to traditional women's roles: women were "tired of their positions as official cake-bakers and money-collectors." In 1909 she published an essay, "Where Do We Stand on the Woman Question?" criticizing her socialist "brothers" for their attitude toward female colleagues: "they discourage her activity and are utterly listless towards the outcome of her struggle."

That year, Serber was elected to the new Women's National Committee of the Socialist Party, and she promoted the idea of a "National Women's Day" on February 28. In 1910, she published "The Diary of a Shirtwaist Worker", a novel about the 3-month strike by about 20,000 mostly Jewish women factory workers in New York, the largest strike by women to that point in American history, which won better pay and shorter hours.

In 1910, German socialist women at the International Socialist Women's Conference in Copenhagen proposed creating an annual Women's Day to promote equal rights. By 1914, March 8 was established as the day for demonstrations across Europe and America. The importance of this event grew when a women's strike on March 8, 1917, in St. Petersburg began the Russian Revolution.

Women won the vote across Europe and America over the next few years: Russia 1917, Germany 1918, United States 1920, England 1928, although many individual American states had already given women the vote. Some nations moved slowly toward women's suffrage: France and Italy only granted women voting rights in 1945.

But as socialist women had argued for decades, neither one celebratory day a year nor the right to vote brought equal rights. March 8 was declared a national holiday in many communist countries, but women continued to occupy secondary social, economic and political roles. Even after feminists in the US began in the 1960s to use the day to protest their continued subordinate status and the United Nations declared International Women's Day in 1975, equality was still far away.

The socialist origins of a day devoted to women's rights exemplifies the long-lasting political controversy over gender equality. The idea of equal rights was heretical for conservatives: a German poster calling for the vote for women on March 8, 1914, was banned by the Emperor's government. Issues of equal rights continue to be marked by partisan political division in the US. The Lily Ledbetter Fair Pay Act was passed in 2009, supported by Democrats in the House 247-5 and in the Senate 56-0, and opposed by Republicans 172-3 in the House and 36-5 in the Senate. Democrats support the #MeToo movement and Republicans mock it. The Republican Party itself, as represented in Congress, is overwhelmingly male: 93% in the House and 85% in the Senate. Democrats are represented by a more equal, but not yet equal gender division: about 62-38 male in both chambers.

The same differences exist in Germany, but with more women overall. From left to right, the percentages of women delegates in the Bundestag, the federal legislature, are: Left 54%, Greens 58%, Social Democrats 43%, Free Democrats 24%, Christian Democrats 21%, and right-wing Alternative for Germany 11%.

A major point of discussion in German politics is the introduction of a gender quota system to ensure equal representation in legislative assemblies. The Left Party proposed in November a law that would raise the proportion of women in the Bundestag, but it was voted down by a majority led by the Christian Democrats and Free Democrats. The far right Alternative for Germany was most vehemently against any effort to raise the proportion of women.

In the state of Brandenburg, ruled by a leftist coalition of Social Democrats, Greens and Left Party, the first German law requiring all parties to put forward equal numbers of men and women in their lists of candidates starting in 2020, the Parity Law, was passed this January.

The Social Democrats in Berlin proposed at the end of 2018 that March 8 should be a new holiday, and this was passed in January with the support of the Left and Greens. A coalition of activists used the March 8 holiday as a *Kampftag*, day of struggle, including a demonstration of about 10,000 people. Their demands included that abortion be fully legalized, pay be equalized, and more action be taken against sexism in daily life, especially violence against women.

International Women's Day serves to highlight the remaining gender inequality in our society. The #MeToo movement exemplifies the much more vigorous public discussion of how to keep moving toward equality and the need for significant behavioral changes for both men and women to make that possible.

The goal is to make International Women's Day superfluous.

STEVE HOCHSTADT
Berlin

I taught about antisemitism at home, but I see its physical traces in Berlin. As the capital of Nazi Germany, Berlin directed an unfathomable human slaughter. As the capital of reunified Germany, Berlin proclaims, "We did this. Never again." There is Holocaust history on nearly every street, literally true since Gunter Demnig began laying his brass *Stolpersteine* (stumbling stones) in the cobbled sidewalks of German cities in 1992.

Antisemitism still exists in Germany, as it does around the world, and may be more openly expressed these days, as racism is in the US. The whole subject is much more present in Berlin than in small-town America, and more thoughtfully addressed.

What is Antisemitism?

MARCH 19, 2019

Antisemitism is alive and well these days. In Europe and America, the number of antisemitic incidents are increasing every year, according to those who try to keep track.

News about antisemitism has recently wandered from the streets and the internet into the halls of Congress. The presence of two newly elected young Muslim women in the House, who openly advocate for Palestinians against Israel, has upset the strongly pro-Israel consensus that has dominated American politics for decades. Accusations of antisemitism are especially directed at Ilhan Omar from Minneapolis, who has used language that is reminiscent of traditional antisemitic themes in her criticism of Israeli policies. Her case demonstrates that it can be difficult to distinguish between unacceptable antisemitism and political criticism of the Jewish government of Israel and its supporters.

Some incidents seem to be easy to label as antisemitic. For example, when a large group of young people physically attacked Jewish women while they were praying. Many women were injured, including the female rabbi leading the prayers. The attackers carried signs assailing the women's religious beliefs, and the press reported that the women "were shoved, scratched, spit on and verbally abused".

An obvious case of antisemitism? No, because the attackers were ultra-Orthodox Jewish girls and boys, bussed to the Western Wall in Jerusalem in order to attack the non-Orthodox Women of the Wall, who were violating misogynist Orthodox traditions about who can pray at the Wall. This incident fulfills every possible definition of antisemitism. For example, the International Holocaust Remembrance Alliance offers the following description of public acts that are antisemitic: "Calling for, aiding, or justifying the killing or harming of Jews in the name of a radical ideology or an extremist view of religion." The ultra-Orthodox leaders who encouraged the assault would argue that they were protecting, not attacking Judaism, and that the Women of the Wall were not really Jewish anyway.

Acts of antisemitism are political acts. Accusations of antisemitism are likewise political acts, deployed in the service of the political interests of the accusers. Many, perhaps most accusations of antisemitism are made in good faith for the purpose of calling attention to real religious prejudice. But such accusations are often made for less honest political purposes.

The Republicans in Congress who demand that Democrats denounce Ilhan Omar are cynically using the accusation of antisemitism for political gain. Many Republicans have themselves made statements or employed political advertisements that are clearly antisemitic. The rest have stood by in silence while their colleagues and their President made antisemitic statements. But they saw political advantage in attacking a Democrat as antisemitic.

Supporters of the Israeli government's policies against Palestinians routinely accuse their critics of antisemitism as a means of drawing attention away from Israeli policies and diverting it to the accusers' motives. Sometimes critics of Israel are at least partially motivated by antisemitism. But the use of this rhetorical tactic also often leads to absurdity: Jews who do not approve of the continued occupation of land in the West Bank or the discrimination against Palestinians in Israel are accused of being "self-hating Jews".

This linking of antisemitism and criticism of Israeli policy has worked well to shield the Israeli government from reasonable scrutiny of its policies. In fact, there is no necessary connection between the two. Criticism of current Israeli policy is voiced by many Jews and Jewish organizations, both religious and secular.

Supporters of the idea of boycotting Israeli businesses as protest against Israeli treatment of Palestinians, the so-called BDS movement, are sometimes assumed to be antisemitic and thus worthy of attack by extremists. But the pro-Israel but also pro-peace Washington Jewish organization J-Street argues that "Efforts to exclude BDS Movement supporters from public forums and to ban them from conversations are misguided and doomed to fail." I don't remember that any of the supporters of boycotting and divesting from South Africa because of its racial policies were called anti-white.

Those who advocate a "one-state solution" to the conflict between Israel and the Palestinians are sometimes accused by conservatives of being antisemitic, with the argument that this one state will inevitably eventually have a majority of Muslims. The Washington Examiner calls this equivalent to the "gradual genocide of the Jewish people".

The absurdity of equating anti-Zionism with antisemitism is personified by the denunciations of Zionism and the existence of Israel by the Orthodox Satmar, one of the largest Hasidic groups in the world.

On the other side, the most vociferous American supporters of Prime Minister Netanyahu's government have been evangelical Christians. Although they claim to be the best friends of Israel, the religious basis of right-wing evangelical Christianity is the antisemitic assertion that Jews will burn in hell forever, if we do not give up our religion. Robert Jeffress, the pastor of First Baptist Church in Dallas, who spoke at President Trump's private inaugural prayer service, has frequently said that Jews, and all other non-Christians, will go to hell. The San Antonio televangelist John C. Hagee, who was invited by Trump to give the closing benediction at the opening of the new American Embassy in Jerusalem, has preached that the Holocaust was divine providence, because God sent Hitler to help Jews get to the promised land. Eastern European nationalists, who often employ antisemitic tropes to appeal to voters, are also among the most vociferous supporters of Netanyahu and Israel.

Political calculations have muddied our understanding of antisemitism. Supporters of the most right-wing Israeli policies include many people who don't like Jews. Hatreds which belonged together in the days of the KKK may now be separated among right-wing white supremacists.

But no matter what they say, purveyors of racial prejudice and defenders of white privilege are in fact enemies of the long-term interests of Jews all over the world, who can only find a safe haven in democratic equality.

STEVE HOCHSTADT
Berlin

Antisemites say that too much attention is paid to the Holocaust, just as racists say too much attention is given to black history. The level of continuing ignorance about the Holocaust proves them wrong. In a recent poll, one-third of Europeans said they know little or nothing about the Holocaust. Two-thirds of American millennials do not know what Auschwitz was.

It's easy for a teacher to say there should be more teaching. After teaching more than a thousand college students about the Holocaust, I wholeheartedly believe that. I witnessed students widen their eyes and rethink their assumptions when presented with historical reality. More knowledge would help Americans to recognize the dishonest use of the Holocaust to score political points, as in the Harris County (Texas) Republican Facebook message on Holocaust Remembrance Day, "Leftism Kills", and other Republican leaders' claims that gun control caused more Jews to be killed.

The fluid boundary between conservative Republicanism and white Christian supremacy would not be such a problem if other Republicans would denounce the overlap. Trump's involvement and wider Republican silence ensures that American Jews will overwhelmingly vote for Democrats, including Bernie Sanders, not because he is Jewish, not because they support his "democratic socialism", but because of Republican antisemitism.

I should not find it remarkable that the greatest patriotism, the most fervent love of America, is claimed by those who appear to hate many kinds of Americans and the American government. The right-wing movements that caused so much destruction in Europe in the 20th century offered their political "solutions" in the name of great patriotism.

I see patriotism in other places.

Another Kind of Patriotism

JULY 23, 2019

I went to a patriotic rally on Sunday. There was a lot of talk about flags, which were shown with great reverence. Military veterans were honored as heroes, due great respect. It was colorful and loud.

The rally had nothing to do with Trump. The event was a traditional Ojibwe, or Anishinaabe or Chippewa, Pow Wow, celebrated every year at the Lac Courte Oreilles reservation in northwestern Wisconsin. The Honor the Earth Homecoming Pow Wow is the opposite of the "patriotic" rallies that Trump is holding as the beginning of his re-election campaign.

On the way to the site, signs were posted along the road urging everyone to think of themselves as unique and worthy persons. Inside, the focus was entirely on the celebration of Native American traditions, wisdom, and culture, without any hint of comparison to other cultures. Members of the local tribe were joined by tribes from across the region, each of whom could sing and drum their own songs. There were no enemies, just friends.

Ojibwe veterans from all service branches were named and honored for their service to the American nation and to the Ojibwe nation. But no weapons were displayed, except ceremonial versions of traditional hunting weapons displayed by brightly costumed dancers.

Politics was conspicuously absent, as was any complaint about how the Ojibwe and all other Native Americans have been treated by white settlers who invaded the lands they lived in and took them for their own. The only historical hint I heard from the announcer, who was also broadcasting over the reservation's radio station WOJB, was his brief mention that the Anishinaabe had been defending their land for hundreds of years, long before the appearance of whites.

The messages of the Pow Wow were clear: "We are patriots. We love our land and our unique culture. We love America and have defended it in every war. We welcome and respect all Americans."

Donald Trump's rally in North Carolina, and his whole constant campaign about himself, send the opposite messages. "We are patriots, better patriots than you. We love America and therefore we hate you. Hating you is true patriotism."

I find the implicit violence of the crowd in North Carolina to be just a few steps away from the real violence of the white supremacists in Charlottesville. What if a woman in a hijab had walked in front of that crowd as they chanted "Send her back"? That is the new Republican model of patriotism.

What could love of America mean? It could be love of the land, the amazing lands of our 50 states, encompassing beautiful vistas of mountains and lakes and prairies and desert that might be unmatched anywhere else. The Ojibwe love their land as a sacred trust from previous generations, the little bit that has been left to them after centuries of white encroachment. They wish to preserve it forever.

Love of America could be allegiance to the principles at the foundation of our political system. Those principles have not been consistently followed, and a truly democratic and egalitarian nation is still a dream to be realized, rather than a reality to be defended.

It could be reverence for American history, our unique national story of the creation of a new democracy by European immigrants and the evolution of the United States toward a more perfect union by embracing the lofty principles set forth in our founding documents. That story has many dark chapters, but we could say that American history is a narrative of overcoming — the struggle to overcome regional division, racism, sexism, homophobia, poverty, a struggle that may continue long into the future.

Love of America could be affection for Americans. I think of my own tendency to root for American athletes when they compete against athletes from other nations at the Olympics, the World Cup, or in tennis Grand Slams. Americans are incredibly diverse, and it is not easy to put into practice a love for all Americans, no matter ethnic, economic, educational, regional and personality differences. At the least, it should mean that one practices good will toward another American until proven wrong by inhumane behavior.

I don't see any of these forms of love for America in contemporary conservative politics. Conservatives support digging up American land rather than preserving it and fight against every attempt to preserve clean water and air. They taunt conservation organizations who worry about global warming, deny the science of climate change, and oppose all efforts to prevent our own land and the whole globe from becoming less friendly to human habitation. The Trump campaign now sells Trump-branded plastic straws as a deliberate sneer at attempts to save ocean life from being overwhelmed by plastic. For today's conservatives, American land is a source of financial exploitation: don't love the land, love the money you can make from it.

Today's conservatives, preceding and following Trump, don't respect the democratic principles that America has at least tried to embody. From blatant gerrymandering to vote suppression to attacks on the free press to praise for dictators and criticism of foreign democracies, principles have been entirely replaced by temporary political advantage as the source of conservative action.

Conservatives hate American history, instead trying repeatedly to substitute myths for facts. They deny the historical realities of racism, the "patriotic" excesses of McCarthyism, the expropriation of Native American lands. They attack historians who simply do their job of uncovering evidence about how Americans behaved in the past, good and bad. And they celebrate some of the worst Americans: the Republican state government in Tennessee has now named July 13 as "Nathan Bedford Forrest Day", honoring the Confederate general who became the first Grand Wizard of the Ku Klux Klan.

Conservatives don't like most Americans. Again led by Trump, and operating as his megaphone, Republican politicians attack Democrats as enemies of America, despite that fact that Democrats represent the majority of American voters.

I didn't see any Trump hats at the Ojibwe Pow Wow, and I doubt that any Native Americans cheered for Trump in North Carolina. These very different rallies represent opposing ideas about patriotism and America. In my opinion, one expresses a beautiful vision of land and people that has stood for America for hundreds of years. The other is an incoherent reverence for a cult figure of dubious value.

I never liked cults.

STEVE HOCHSTADT
Springbrook, WI

What could be more patriotic than fighting to preserve American land and American people from looming disaster? The highjacking of "patriotism" by the right means that it is forcibly welded onto other conservative positions, like rejection of climate change and of the whole concept of environmentalism.

On the most important issues confronting Americans, I believe that Republicans are wrong. But what is right? How do we solve our real problems? I admit to the ignorance that we all share. Ignorance is not bliss. Admitting our ignorance is necessary, but hard, because the spreaders of lies use such admissions to lie even more. As we desperately tinker with the machinery of modern life, we are distracted from recognizing what we still don't know, which is profound. The unforeseen coronavirus pandemic has demonstrated again how much we don't know.

We Don't Know What We Are Doing

OCTOBER 1, 2019

We don't know what we are doing about poverty. The Great Society programs reduced the poverty rate during the 1960s from 22% to 12%, but since 1970, rates of poverty in the US have remained between 10% and 15%. The proportion of children living in poverty is higher, perhaps as high as 21%. The poverty rate in the US is higher than nearly all other highly developed countries, and about twice as high as most countries in western Europe. The wide variety of federal and state programs for the poor have simply managed to maintain poverty rates at the same level for 50 years. Our policy-makers, Democrat and Republican, have been tinkering around the edges of poverty, but have not found a set of policies which can make an impact. Raising the minimum wage significantly, say to $15 an hour, would slightly reduce poverty, but not eliminate it.

We don't know what we are doing about homelessness. Since the great recession of 2008, homelessness has dropped slightly in the US from about 650,000 to 550,000 in 2016, as poverty levels, the main cause of homelessness, fell. Since 2016, homelessness has again risen.

We don't know what we are doing about the invasion of our lives by the internet. Misinformation and disinformation, transferred to us instantaneously and constantly, pollute our brains. Young people are not only addicted to their phones, for too many their ambitions are entirely tied up in hopes of becoming "influencers" in virtual space. Impenetrable corporations demand to know our private information, and then collect, exploit and sell it.

We don't know what we are doing about climate change. Scientific experts warn us about how much damage we have already done to the environment by lifestyles that few people are willing to change. Rising temperatures in the Earth's oceans have already caused irreparable damage to aquatic life and to the human lives that depend on it. No nation has put into place policies that are sufficient to eliminate further warming. No scientific warning has been able to move enough people to demand the changes that are necessary. Nearly half of Americans continue to vote for a party which officially denies that climate change is a problem.

We don't know what we are doing about the corruption of our society and our politics by money. This is nothing new. Despite centuries of agonizing about how to prevent those with money from amassing the power to suck up more money through illegitimate means, in democratic and authoritarian societies, we are no closer to a solution.

We don't know what we are doing about the widening social chasms, the hollowing out of the middle, the growing anger, not just at the system or "the man", but at each other.

We don't know what we are doing about the linkage among all these problems. For the millennia that humans have walked the Earth, it didn't matter if we didn't know what we were doing. The carefully balanced global natural systems that supported an incredible variety of life were impervious to the local activities of bands of humans. But now, with nearly 8 billion people digging up the Earth, consuming everything we can get our hands on, spewing waste in every direction, and accelerating the speeds of these processes every day, we have thrown the Earth out of balance. As our world apparently hurtles toward ecological, political, and social disaster, we have created problems for which there are no solutions in sight.

Now is the tipping point. And we don't know what we are doing.

STEVE HOCHSTADT
Jacksonville IL

Impeachment took over our public lives in the fall and winter of 2019. It was useless to try not to talk about impeachment. Running away from impeachment conversations or impeachment news didn't stop the swirling in our heads. The facts were in dispute, even though they were clearly revealed, confirmed, and repeated. I perceived a moral emergency, and was free to write about it in the most direct way.

Take Back Our Lives

OCTOBER 29, 2019

There is evil in our land. Men with power, put in office to protect us, lie and scheme to benefit themselves. They conspire to pollute our air and our water and our food, to put poisons in the products we use every day. They ignore the law, and use their money and power to corrupt our court system. They attack the tellers of truth, the reporters of reality, and substitute fictions for the facts of their deeds. They pervert our democracy to keep themselves in power. They seek out sycophants to do their dirty work, never lacking for toadies who sing their praises, embellish their lies, defend their attacks on the general welfare, and pretend that heaven blesses their immorality. Every day brings new evidence of their malice toward the people they have sworn to serve, their disdain for those who do not join them. They rely on distractions, count on our apathy, and believe they can exhaust us.

They are powerful and clever, but we can stop them. We cannot wait for others to defeat them, we must take action now. We must defend the virtues they scorn — solidarity, empathy, honesty, kindness, charity, justice.

Use the laws to confront their dishonesty. Use the press to uncover and trumpet their corruption. Use our speech to protest loudly and repeatedly. Object to their actions each day in every way we can. We must employ the gifts that our democratic system provides to defeat them, or that system itself will be debased.

They will fight back, lying about anyone who exposes them, attacking our truthfulness, our patriotism, our families. There is no limit to their viciousness. They have billions of dollars, but we have millions of voices. Use them.

By resisting their evil, we will rediscover our nation and ourselves.

STEVE HOCHSTADT
Jacksonville IL

Recognizing evil is useful, because it makes goodness more apparent. One of the ways to rediscover our nation is to examine the past for the beams of goodness that the culture usually ignores in favor of the flash of mayhem. Hollywood films are designed as escapist entertainment, but they sometimes slow down enough to show us a way out.

Curing Ourselves

NOVEMBER 26, 2019

I find it hard not to be upset all the time about American politics, and the American society underneath. For me, things have been getting worse for a long time. Often, I find out that things had been even worse than I thought earlier, but I didn't know the facts until they were uncovered by some journalist prying into our secretive government. The good news that honest investigations can reveal what powerful people want to keep secret doesn't quite outweigh the bad news that these investigations reveal.

I don't mean that I am upset all the time. At many times every day, I rejoice at my grandchildren and the children who are raising them, I root for some team on TV, I puzzle over a murder mystery, I accomplish do-it-yourself things all around our old house trying to recapture the past, or I kneel in the gardens pulling up weeds. Thoughts about America as a nation are swamped by the joys of one person's everyday life.

But when those thoughts peek through, or take up all the air when we watch the news at night, they are unhappy ones. In the 15 years I have been writing columns about politics, I have identified all the big problems we face now. The names have changed, but the political ideas and underhanded methods persist. What is new is that those problems all seem more upsetting to me lately. I can identify when this condition began four years ago, as Trump came down the escalator to announce that he was campaigning for President.

I think the diagnosis is evident: I suffer from T.I.A.D., Trump-Induced Anxiety Disorder. There may be some help; please see this video for the wonder drug Impeachara:

https://www.youtube.com/watch?v=QXUlhT3-r0c

Even if the drug doesn't work, or exist, just thinking about it provides some temporary relief.

I think a longer-lasting cure may be available, one that's been in front of us all the time. Liz and I joined lots of local baby boomers to see "It's a Beautiful Day in the Neighborhood". Fred Rogers was news to me. I had never watched his program and I only knew of his reputation, not him.

All the evidence I can find says that Mr. Rogers was just as he was portrayed by Tom Hanks: a lover and inspired teacher of children; impossibly nice to everyone around him; willing to talk to children about the most difficult subjects, like divorce and nuclear war; clever but transparent about using television to spread his message of love and tolerance.

Less well known is that he was a determined advocate for public television, was an ordained Presbyterian minister, and that he wrote all the songs for

Mr. Roger's Neighborhood. However far you dig into Fred Roger's life, he was a remarkably good man who spread goodness all around him.

Instead of stressing about Trump's latest idiocy or the decline of American politics, about which we can do very little, we could try to emulate Mr. Rogers. We could see the world as an opportunity to make a difference in people's lives and devote our energies to doing that.

I'm no Fred Rogers. Coming from New York, I could never talk that slowly. The rest of us are just not so good so much of the time. But that doesn't matter. We can all inch our way toward goodness by thinking more about the real people right in front of us and less about the personalities we see on the screen and the news we get from people we don't know.

That is really the message of my whole collection of articles. The way to take back our lives is to focus more on the immediate, to practice the principles we believe in, to wrest more control by being intentional whenever we can.

Mr. Rogers can't save us, even though Esquire did put him on the cover of an issue about heroes. He wasn't trying to save the world himself. He was doing his part as less than a billionth of humanity. If we want to be cured of T.I.A.D. without danger of remission, we all have to do our parts, for our own lives and for others.

STEVE HOCHSTADT
Jacksonville IL

Mr. Rogers and Mr. Trump, symbols of the contradictory impulses of Americans. Trump nicknamed Dan Coats, his Director of National Intelligence for two years, "Mr. Rogers", to symbolize his supposed weakness.

Will the most brutish forms of power win out over quiet goodness? What will happen in 2020?

CHAPTER 11
Not The End

I don't think I'll ever write a memoir, but this book may be the closest I'll come. My own story is defined by writings, the many I read and the fewer I produce. I write because I must — every week, I have felt the need to offer readers ideas and information that I believe are worthy of consideration. After a decade, it is clear than I love the craft, although my possible influence is more like a dripping faucet than a gushing river. Some op-ed writers are seen and heard and read everywhere, while many more like me are known only to smaller overlapping, essentially local circles.

These essays are about a particular time in our country's life and my life. Everything here represents the public side of my life, seen through my commentary on the most public sides of our collective lives. My writing is not my whole life, but is shaped by it.

I haven't given up on taking back our lives. I recognize the naiveté with which I began this quest in 2009. I understand how difficult it is to win political battles with facts and logic as the main weapons. I learned that the prejudiced and gullible segments of our population are much larger than I thought. I discovered how many and clever are the deliberate purveyors of lies and how nasty their acolytes are.

But the quest still seems worthwhile. Perhaps that conviction stems from my confidence in history, where the liars are eventually revealed, the cheaters identified. Historians I'll never know will look more deeply at our times, armed with much better information. They will create fuller, truer, less subjective narratives.

I write from within, hemmed in by restricted vision and imperfect knowledge, observing from the peculiar vantage of a Jewish New Yorker, an early baby boomer, a descendant of refugees, son of my idiosyncratic parents, raised in a suburban utopia.

What could be more subjective than my decision to organize these essays so that many chapters end with Christmas? No matter how discouraging politics and public American life have been recently, Christmas focuses my attention on the smaller and happier circle of my family. Not without challenges, sadnesses, and reverses, but more immediate, more real, and more important. Christmas is one of many examples of how the calendar shapes our lives. Every human society pauses to celebrate the new year, an arbitrarily varied moment across the globe. There is comfort in the special foods and lengthy readings of the Seder, practiced for more than 3000 years.

The yearly sequence of significant moments is artificial, created by human history and liable to change rapidly. The peculiar American celebration of our two most revered presidents in February has been squashed into one Presidents' Day sale opportunity. Perhaps eclipsing their birthdays is the brand new Martin Luther King Day, made an official federal holiday by Ronald Reagan in 1983, celebrated in all 50 states for only the last 20 years.

Like Black History Month, MLK Day offers an easy fix for continuing racial problems — celebrate, then go back to normal life. Since that normal life will not reach racial equality in my lifetime, MLK Day helps me think about how much further we need to go.

A Special Time

JANUARY 21, 2020

I went to the annual city-sponsored celebration of Martin Luther King, Jr., on Monday. Jacksonville's Mayor, Andy Ezard, inaugurated these yearly breakfasts a decade ago. Every year a speaker helps us think about what MLK said, what he wanted to happen, and how he lived. There is often music, and we sing "Lift Every Voice and Sing", a hopeful song: from "the dark past", "the gloomy past" "that with tears has been watered", to the present, "the place for which our fathers sighed", to the future, "Let us march on till victory is won."

Some years, that song and the celebration around it do lift hope, because the present is evolving to a brighter future that is joyous to imagine. But not today.

Today hope means believing that we will soon stop going backwards, that this moment is just a hesitation on the journey toward the unity we seek. Sometimes hope makes way for despair about how things might get worse.

What American governments since the 1960s have created in order to undo centuries of prejudice, discrimination, and persecution, the Republican Party is dismantling. I don't say that Trump is doing this, even though his name is on every new policy of his administration, because he is not alone. Republican politicians across the country are doing this work themselves, defending the work of their colleagues, and pledging allegiance to the man who is leading the charge backwards.

Two authors of distinguished books on the history of race in America just wrote articles for the *New York Times* for Martin Luther King Jr.'s birthday, which tell us where we are and what is being done in our names. Michelle Alexander published *The New Jim Crow: Mass Incarceration in the Age* of *Colorblindness* 10 years ago, when Trump was just a glittery real estate con man. She showed how the explosion of the number of Americans in jail in the wake of the "war on drugs" was at its heart "another caste system — a system of mass incarceration — that locked millions of poor people and people of color in literal and virtual cages."

The numbers must be printed to make their proper impression. These are careful estimates only, because fuller data does not exist, but they are the best estimates we have. Between 1980 and 2010, the proportion of Americans in prison tripled to 1%, but the proportion of African Americans in prison also almost tripled from 1.3% to 3.1%. The racial disparity remained about the same, as American governments imprisoned so many more Americans. In 2010, one out of three black men had a felony conviction in their past, and one of every ten were in prison or on parole. That was true for only one in fifty of the rest of the population.

This happened in Boston, where African Americans were subject to police observations, interrogations, and searches at seven times the rate of the rest of the population. It happened in Charlottesville, Virginia, in 2017, when African Americans were nine times as likely to be subject to police investigative detentions. And so on.

Alexander shows that both Democratic and Republican political leaders gave the US the dubious distinction of having more than one fifth of the world's prisoners and the highest incarceration rate in the world: 756 per 100,000, while most countries imprison fewer than 150 per 100,000. Both Boston and Charlottesville were dominated by Democrats.

Now she delivers a shorter message: our nation must move back to the path toward racial justice from the detour we are taking. Obama and the national Democratic Party did not do enough to reverse those trends. But that is a long way from what has happened in the past 3 years. She is clear that the transition from Obama to Trump moved us from a hopeful discussion of racial reform to an era of white supremacy, clothed as returning to greatness.

Richard Rothstein published *The Color of Law: A Forgotten History of How Our Government Segregated America* three years ago. He also covered the long history of discrimination that Alexander described, but this time from the point of view of housing segregation. In fine detail, Rothstein explained how the federal government throughout the 20th century, under Democrats and Republicans, used its vast financial powers to promote further residential segregation, notably in the new postwar suburbs. Where I grew up, in the giant Levitt developments on Long Island, the federal government insured his loans on the condition that African Americans would be excluded from buying his houses.

This has been the American way for centuries, putting an unfair economic burden on African Americans. 1968 appeared to put an end to federal complicity in the segregation of American housing. Through the Fair Housing Act, included in the Civil Rights Act of 1968, groups who are discriminated against in anything to do with housing can use the legal system to demand redress. That Act was passed in the wake of MLK's assassination.

But discrimination continues, taking less obvious forms. An example of how this occurs out of our sight comes from Syracuse. Since 1996, property has not been reassessed in the city, which seems like merely local government incompetence. But since then, the values of homes in white neighborhoods have risen much faster than homes in black neighborhoods. Reassessment would shift some of the weight of property taxes toward those much more valuable white homes. Not doing anything means that black homeowners have been paying an increasingly disproportionate share of property taxes. The city government in Syracuse is dominated by Democrats.

Rothstein's article in the *NYTimes* shows how Secretary of Housing and Urban Development Ben Carson is directing his vast bureaucracy and billions of dollars away from the process of desegregation. Since he was a candidate for President in 2016, he has argued that efforts to fix racial segregation are bad "social engineering". Now HUD is trying to make it impossible for residents in a community like Syracuse, where government or business policies discriminate against racial minorities, to prove that in court. One of the far-reaching policies of the Trump administration which makes fighting discrimination more difficult.

These are pieces in today's national puzzle of race. Martin Luther King has missed more than 50 years of change in race relations, in party politics, in the American landscape. But his yet unrealized dreams can still inspire hope.

Hardly anything is more worth fighting for.

STEVE HOCHSTADT
Jacksonville IL

I have used the word "truth" hundreds of times in this book. I know the truth is not a single hard, well defined thing that we can look at and grasp. I also know the difference between truth and lies. I have lived through the academic deconstruction of truth, and yet maintained a traditional belief that truth is a most worthy goal, even if unattainable.

Sometimes I write untruths. I learned that it was Mayor Ezard's predecessor who had initiated the MLK breakfasts. The quest for truth is a process. As I write, I always ask myself, "Can that sentence be truer?" The truth feeds nobody, nor does it set anyone free. Like democracy, pursuing truth may be the worst form of apprehending reality, except for all the other forms that have been tried.

Can We Save the Truth?
FEBRUARY 4, 2020

Is there truth? During the late 20th century, the humanities became enmeshed in esoteric discussions about truth. Deconstructionists argued that all writing was relative to the writer, whose identity and biases created work that might be true for the writer, but not for other people with different identities. This argument came out of a radical critique of Western white male hegemony, which has since been expanded to the analysis of all forms of hierarchy. White supremacy, male chauvinism, homophobia, and all other kinds of discrimination lead to claims by dominant groups that they possess truth, when they are actually only expressing their self-interest.

This line of thinking was taken up especially by literary scholars, who argued that every text has multiple, perhaps infinite meanings. There is no true interpretation of a piece of writing. When this was expanded into other disciplines, it became more confusing. Some historians argued that it is impossible to make a true historical statement. Every statement can have multiple, even contradictory meanings. Excellent examples of this would be statements that really do depend on the position of the author: Wikipedia's article on Fort Seybert in the Allegheny Mountains is mainly about fighting at the Fort in 1758, and includes the phrase "the Indians massacred 17 to 19 people". Such statements were assumed to be truths until recently, as long as the number of dead were accurate. Yet the attackers were not "Indians", but members of the Shawnee and Delaware tribes; "massacre" implies mass murder, when this was one battle in a war begun by white invaders of Native American lands; etc.

Much historical writing had to be rewritten to remove what turned out to be obvious biases in language and meaning. Much remains to be done.

Scientific ideas also were criticized as claiming truth when there was none. An example that has upended many social assumptions is the idea of gender, a seemingly biological concept. How do we tell the difference between a man and a woman? We should not simply adopt traditional ideas, supposedly scientific, which are merely social ideas put into scientific language. In athletic contests that question has led to many controversies about who may compete against whom. The relativists' argument would be that gender is a matter of self-definition, not truth.

Does this mean that there is no truth? That any statement can be shown to be untrue by people with a different point of view? Objectivity is impossible, so there is no objective truth.

I always have regarded these questions as irrelevant to my work as an historian and political commentator. I recognize that every historical statement can be attacked as not precisely true. Six million Jews were killed during the Holocaust. Well, certainly not exactly six million, which is an estimate, the best one we have. Many of the people the Nazis murdered as "Jews" did not consider themselves Jewish. Many more millions were killed by the Nazis using the same methods in the same places — they should not be left out of the concept of Holocaust.

I'm sure that nearly every sentence I have ever written could be taken apart and shown to be not as true as some other much more complicated formulation.

Please pardon this lecture on abstruse intellectual arguments. They were all the rage when I was a graduate student, and tended to make doing historical writing difficult. For my own writing, I have settled on a method of writing and rewriting in which I seek to improve places where I use imprecise categories and labels, where I slide over gaps in my knowledge with vague phrases, where my ignorance leads to false statements. I find and fix many such places in the process of revising. I hope to produce writing which is as close as possible to being objective and true. That I have such goals indicates that I do not accept the idea that there is no truth. I do believe that truth is very hard to reach, that nearly every proposition in history or science can be improved by more work, that we are imperfect seekers of truth. So we can approach truth, but perhaps never reach it.

At last we arrive at my point. When these arguments were raging in the academy, conservatives were greatly annoyed. Conservative historians asserted that relativists were ruining everything, that truth did exist. They criticized post-modernism as a mask for moral relativism, connected this immorality with the popular movements of the 1960s, and asserted their own moral primacy (the Moral Majority).

I was prompted to write this because of the great irony that the political conservatism, which once argued for objective truth, now relies on the broadest attack on truth that we have ever experienced. Political lies are nothing new and nothing inherently conservative. President Lyndon Johnson's lie about a North Vietnamese attack on American ships in the Tonkin Gulf in 1964 led to a disastrous expansion of the war, which was extended by years of lying laid out in the Pentagon Papers. But today we suffer from a multiplication of lies as a Republican tactic to win elections.

The platform of the Republican Party about climate change and health care, two of our most pressing issues, is just one big lie. The use of a fabricated story about Ukraine and Joe Biden is a set of lies, that then led to one of the greatest scenes of collective public lying in American history, the response of Republican Representatives and Senators to the impeachment.

We are being bombarded with carefully crafted lies throughout cyberspace, designed to distort the results of the 2020 election. False stories about Joe Biden and Ukraine have already spread virally to millions of people. Fighting them takes enormous effort and resources, well beyond anything that will be deployed this year.

Disinformation spread by bots can come from anywhere on the globe. The technology is non-partisan. But the use is not. Russia's online campaign in 2016 was designed to help elect Trump. The Trump campaign is now using one of these Ukraine stories in various media. CNN refused to run it, but it's up on Facebook.

The intersection of a Republican Party which sees no value in distinguishing between truth and lies and an emerging technology that makes spreading lies incredibly easy is a great political danger. Is there truth? Not if those in power in America don't care.

STEVE HOCHSTADT
Jacksonville IL

In politics these days, everything leads to Trump. As I write now, the questions taking up the most airtime and column inches focus on whether he will win in November. That's not a proper op-ed question, since opinions on that issue are just guesses.

I prefer to offer an opinion on where we are now. By the time you read this, a hundred news cycles will have come and gone. Wherever we end up, where we were in February 2020 shaped where we have gone and will go.

Trump the Great and Powerful

FEBRUARY 18, 2020

Donald Trump's legal troubles have had an unexpected result — the proclamation of a view of the Presidency, in which Trump is legally untouchable and newly all-powerful. The head of the party of limited government has proposed a theory of American democracy, the unlimited Presidency, and the rest of his party has fallen into line.

The district attorney of Manhattan is trying to obtain Trump's financial records, including tax returns, in the case about whether the payments to Stormy Daniels by his former lawyer, Michael Cohen, then reimbursed by Trump, were legal. William Consovoy, Trump's lawyer, told the 2nd Circuit Court of Appeals that as President, Trump is immune from the entire judicial system. Consovoy said that if Trump shot someone on Fifth Avenue, he could be charged with a crime only after he is out of office.

After the hearings about the Mueller investigation, Trump said in a speech about the Constitution in July 2019, "Then, I have an Article II, where I have to the right to do whatever I want as president."

Trump's impeachment defense team based their case on a belief that the Presidency is much more than one of three separate and equal powers. Alan Dershowitz argued during the impeachment trial in the Senate that anything a President does to help his re-election is in the public interest, and thus not impeachable.

In a tweet about the recent legal case of Roger Stone, Trump insisted that he has a "legal right" to intervene in criminal cases.

Trump often asserts that he has the "absolute right" to do what he likes. Last April, he said he had never "ordered anyone to close our southern border," but he could do it if he wanted. After he was criticized for revealing classified information to Russian officials in 2017, Trump said he has an "absolute right" to release such material to foreign powers.

The Associated Press has counted at least 29 times since his election that Trump has said he has an "absolute right" to wield executive authority. One example is his claim that he could end birthright citizenship by executive order, even though it is assured by the 14th amendment to the Constitution.

In June 2018, Trump tweeted a new absolute right in his Presidential theory: "As has been stated by numerous legal scholars, I have the absolute right to PARDON myself, but why would I do that when I have done nothing wrong?" Why would he bring it up if he had done nothing wrong?

Trump's absolute right is tolerated with silence by the same Republicans who screamed "dictator" when President Obama issued an executive order offering deportation relief to DACA children. "Why is @BarackObama constantly issuing executive orders that are major power grabs of authority?" Trump tweeted in 2012. Gov. Chris Christie of New Jersey said, "He's not a king, he's not a dictator, he's not allowed to do it himself." House Speaker John Boehner said Obama was acting like a "king or emperor." He said Republicans "will not stand idle as the president undermines the rule of law in our country and places lives at risk." Now Republicans are nervously standing by as Trump declares himself above all law.

Trump appears to argue that he can exercise absolutely all powers that are not specifically denied to the President in the Constitution. But he goes further. Two key powers are explicitly vested in the Congress by the Constitution: power of the purse and power to declare war.

When the Congress did not appropriate funds for Trump's beautiful wall, he ignored their decision, declared a national emergency, and then diverted funds which the Congress had appropriated for other purposes. Although majorities in House and Senate voted for a resolution to end the "emergency", only a dozen Republican Senators out of 53 voted to reject Trump's arrogation of new powers. One of those Republicans, Susan Collins of Maine, co-sponsored the resolution. She said, "The question before us is not whether to support or oppose the wall, or to support or oppose the President. Rather, it is: Do we want the Executive Branch — now or in the future — to hold a power that the Founders deliberately entrusted to Congress?" But she didn't believe that idea strongly enough to vote for Trump's impeachment.

Last week, the Senate passed the Iran war powers resolution that limits Trump's ability to wage war against Iran. Eight Republicans voted with Democrats to pass the bill 55-45. The House passed a similar bill last month 224-194, with only 3 Republicans voting for it. Only a small minority of Republicans is willing to challenge Trump's theory of the unlimited presidency.

The other modern example of a President asserting absolute rights in instructive. When David Frost interviewed Nixon in 1977, three years after he had resigned, he asked, "Would you say that there are certain situations - and the Huston Plan was one of them - where the president can decide that it's in the best interests of the nation, and do something illegal?" Nixon famously replied, "Well, when the president does it, that means it is not illegal." The so-called Huston Plan was the plan hatched by Nixon and his advisors after he had been in office for 2 years and the bombing of Cambodia in 1970 had unleashed massive popular protests. Here's the Plan: "The report recommended increasing wiretapping and microphone surveillance of radicals - relaxing restrictions on mail covers and mail intercepts; carrying out selective break-ins against domestic radicals and organizations; lifting age restrictions on FBI campus informants; and broadening NSA's intercepts of the international communications of American citizens." FBI Director J. Edgar Hoover and the National Security Agency, who would have to carry out the illegal activities, convinced Nixon to abandon the Plan. But according to Nixon years later, those illegal actions cannot be illegal if he initiates them.

That appears to be where Trump is heading. The most illegal Presidents wish to abolish the possibility that the President can commit a crime.

It is not surprising that a president so unconcerned about Constitutional norms would try to add to his powers. It is disturbing and dangerous that the Republican Party as a body supports Trump going far beyond what they harshly denounced just a few years ago. Republican Congressmen and -women are sitting by while Trump amends the Constitution by fiat.

STEVE HOCHSTADT
Jacksonville IL

It is neither coincidence nor clairvoyance that gives the three 2020 essays above a special significance in assessing the effects of the coronavirus. At this moment, I am locked down, hiding from the virus in my home. Every day brings new knowledge about COVID-19, new dangers to worry about, new ideas about how to protect our lives, new guesses about when and how the crisis will end. There will be many stories in the future about the way the coronavirus has changed our lives. The three issues I wrote about in this chapter should be part of every story, because they lie at the heart of the American pandemic experience.

The lingering racial inequalities that make MLK Day so important have become deadly differences. The disease has struck black Americans more than twice as hard as whites. The deficit in life expectancy for African Americans has been a permanent feature of American life and death. But now the doubled or tripled death rates for blacks puts our society's racism in our faces.

The Republican disdain for truth has been on display across the country, in wild forms of preposterous conspiracy theories (Dr. Anthony Fauci and Bill Gates are trying to spread the disease) and in official forms in the response of elected Republicans to medical facts. At every stage over the past few months, Republicans have painted rosy pictures of how America, unique among nations, would skate around the disease, then been proven wrong, only to come up with a new set of dangerous ideas that put American lives at risk. Stephen Colbert's 2006 quip that "reality has a well known liberal bias" was meant to provoke laughs, but has become a deadly truth.

Above it all, Donald Trump's egomania and the wider Republican toadying to his infinite self-regard have defined the national pandemic experience.

Ideology Versus Life
MAY 12, 2020

Every President and every Congress in my lifetime has tried to improve our physical environment: make it cleaner, better-smelling, and less likely to make people sick and die. After nearly a century of industrial poisoning of our air, waters, and land, accomplished with a heedless disregard for long-term consequences, Americans realized what we had lost and the need to get it back. At every stage, industrial polluters fought new regulations, slowing down but never stopping the gradual clean-up of the environment and the increasing protection of our natural resources. Republicans as a Party may have been less enthusiastic about this work than Democrats, but the concern for environmental and human health was bipartisan.

The election of Donald Trump appears to have suddenly reversed decades of progress, but the reversal began earlier within the ranks of Republican elected officials. As soon as they controlled the key federal agencies in early 2017, a new 21st-century Republican policy has taken over, attacking environmental protection instead of environmental polluters.

Pollution costs money, too

The NY Times has again done the world a service by collecting every environmental regulation that the Trump administration is reversing. Environmental regulations, which consider a future decades away, may seem less important in this time of immediate existential crisis. I think Trump's single-minded reduction of environmental protections also explains his seemingly confused coronavirus policies, and the larger ideology of the elected Republican Party, which stands, or perhaps hides, behind him.

The Times article is not a story, but a list, an accounting of every intervention the Trump administration has made and is trying to make on the environment. There is a link to a story on each of 98 separate efforts to reverse direction. Those stories begin repeatedly with words like "Revoked", "Withdrew", "Replaced", "Cancelled", "Weakened". The new rules fall into basic categories: air pollution and emissions; drilling and extraction; infrastructure and planning; animals; toxic substances and safety; and water pollution. It's an encyclopedia of disdain for human life.

The deep motivations of contemporary Republicanism can be found in three exemplary efforts by the Trump White House, with full support by Republicans in Congress.

The agency most vigilant about threats to the health of American workers, the Occupational Safety and Health Administration, OSHA, alerted by doctors and scientists across the world, long ago recognized a novel workplace danger. Since the 1990s, the popular trend toward using manufactured stone for countertops greatly increased the number of American workers who inhaled silica dust on the job. More and more of the men who do the cutting and polishing, often Hispanic men, had developed silicosis. OSHA had been created by the Democratic Congress in 1970 and signed into law by Republican President Richard Nixon. Within months, OSHA issued a rule limiting the permissible amount of silica dust in the air at workplaces. Because the dangers have recently increased, OSHA issued a "warning" in 2015 about the dangers of silica dust and a new rule in 2016, reducing by half the permissible levels of dust in the air at workplaces. The Trump administration cancelled this special emphasis on silica dust, ending the ability of OSHA to inspect countertop fabrication plants.

Congress had been concerned about reducing deadly chemical accidents since 1990, and established a new Chemical Safety Board to oversee the industry. The Environmental Protection Agency, EPA, was also created by President Nixon in 1970. It first promulgated regulations to prevent industrial chemical accidents in 1996. In 2013, the whole country heard of the explosion of a fertilizer factory in West, Texas, that killed twelve first responders and two members of the public, and injured 180 workers. As one of its final acts under President Obama, the EPA mandated less risky practices at chemical factories, to go into effect in March 2017. The new Trump EPA immediately delayed the new "Chemical Disaster Rule" so they could reconsider it, and many states sued the EPA. In court, Trump's EPA cited costs as justification, "the rule's substantial compliance and implementation resource burden". But the US Court of Appeals ruled decisively against further delay. In its 2018 opinion, the Court wrote about the history of environmental protection as a "cooperative effort by federal, state, and local governments" to "protect and enhance the quality of the Nation's air resources so as to promote the public health and welfare." The justices ruled that the EPA delay was "arbitrary and capricious", "makes a mockery of the statute", and "has delayed life-saving protections." Taking another tack, Trump's EPA wrote a revised rule in 2019 that rolled back most of the new requirements of the 2017 rule.

The crisis of lead in the water pipes in Flint, Michigan, shocked the nation and may have damaged a generation of children there. The rule about removing lead from water pipes had been written in 1991, requiring that a water system that exceeds maximum allowable lead levels must replace 7% of its faulty pipes every year until the level is reached. The Trump EPA has proposed a new rule reducing the repair to 3% per year, greatly extending the time that ordinary citizens would be exposed to unsafe lead levels.

I had to dive deeply into a chain of internet sources to put together those brief summaries of actions by Republicans in our government. They typify the other 95 narratives: quick reversals of decades of life-saving regulations after Trump took office, led by industry representatives, who had long been arguing about rolling back regulation, that he then put in charge of environmental positions in his administration.

In each case, the long history of bipartisan agreement about promoting the health and safety of Americans is being repudiated. Instead, the relative weights of saving lives and the "substantial compliance and implementation resource burden" have been shifted. Industrial finances now trump human life, a decision perhaps made easier by the disproportionate burden that industrial poisons put on the poor and the non-white.

The news these days about Trump, Republicans in Congress, and many Republican governors hastening to restart the economy before the most basic protections against spread of the coronavirus are in place is simply a continuation of this calculation. A week ago, Trump explained the Republican balancing act: "Will some people be affected, yes, will some people be affected badly, yes, but we have to get our country open and we have to get it open soon."

The Party that preaches "right to life" has fully embraced an ideology that puts economic considerations in front of the lives of Americans. Our lives have been systematically devalued since 2017. I have not seen all of Trump's televised briefings, but I have seen many and read about others. Completely missing is any sign of sympathy for those who have died, are dying, and will die. Today the official number of deaths is over 83,000, and the Party of Death is in charge.

STEVE HOCHSTADT
Jacksonville IL

That's stronger language than I have used in these essays. The stakes are higher now. Trump is a cancer on America, multiplying parasitic cells every day that threaten our collective lives. While his origin story is personal, his reign of greed and incompetence was carefully prepared by leading Republicans and conservative influencers. Republican politicians have lined up behind him, because he so successfully exemplifies their ideology. Every day he is in office, he and his Party multiply the suffering of some group of Americans. COVID-19 has transformed suffering into mass death.

When Trump said in 2016, "I could stand in the middle of Fifth Avenue and shoot somebody and I wouldn't lose any voters", that seemed to be his typical hyperbole. But his incompetent response to the pandemic has cost thousands of lives, and his supporters still defend him.

He has always been clear that he prefers not to know about people getting sick. In May, he said, "When you test, you have a case. When you test, you find something is wrong with people. If we didn't do any testing, we would have very few cases." He was even clearer about why he disdained testing: "by doing all of this testing, we make ourselves look bad."

Testing or no testing, America looks bad these days. The United States no longer leads the advanced world in anything but climate change denial, coronavirus deaths, homelessness, and gun violence. We are now just another rich nation, attractive for our material wealth, not our ideas.

But the story I have been telling is not over. It's never over. The coronavirus is writing an unexpected chapter in the history of 2020. The most important election in our history will come and go, and then there will be another. The daily crisis that is Trump will end, to be replaced by other crises. His exploits will move from front pages to best sellers to scholarly journals. The underlying ecological crisis of our planet is less obvious and only sporadically reported, although it threatens our human survival on pieces of its surface. The Earth will live on for billions more years, warming and cooling its drifting land masses and dirtied oceans. But the societies we inhabit, all politically unique, may be forced to fight for their survival. Our American society faces an existential choice: some Green New Deal or multiplying disasters.

I am not a reporter. I never could keep up with breaking news in my years as a print journalist. Even now when my freedom from the press allows me to communicate instantly about today, I don't try to do that. That's not my job — people of great skill and professionalism put much more effort into doing that than I could. They provide the basis for my effort to put the news in some context that reaches back in many directions as a way of understanding.

Not *the* way of understanding, *my* way. The topics I chose, the contexts into which I put them, the phrasing and emphasis, beginnings and endings, are all my choices. Our paths of thought are so individual, the means of expression so characteristic of our personalities, that I recognize the futility of attempts to convince or persuade.

I hope that these sketches of the many paths I have taken are useful for the creation of your own paths. May your lives be in your own possession.

Acknowledgments

Every writer gets help from friends and relatives. My wife, Liz Tobin, has shaped these essays in countless ways, from inspiring subjects, to providing space for me to write, to proof-reading this book. The life I describe here has been shared for 42 years — we shared our teaching job, child-rearing, and opinion-making.

A larger circle of relatives, from children to distant cousins, offered encouragement about my weekly essays. By telling me when I had done well and remaining silent when I had not, they subtly shaped my practice. The same is true of a larger group of friends, some from my high school days and others more recent. When I found American politics depressing, their continued interest in what I had to say kept me writing. My friend Nancy Gerth contributed the index, and saved me from a number of errors.

Just before I became a regular newspaper op-ed writer, Dick Price of LAProgressive offered what every prospective columnist wishes for, a forum for putting opinions in front of the public. He has adorned every column since 2009 with an appropriate image and placed me in the company of a community of progressive writers.

I thank David Bauer, my editor at the *Journal-Courier*, for taking a chance on my opinions and sticking with me, even when he was bombarded with outraged calls for my termination. I don't blame him for the slow demise of that newspaper.

The enthusiastic people at Atlantic Publishing—Katie Cline, Jack Bussell, Nicole Sturk, Jessie Ranew, and Douglas Brown—enabled me to achieve a dream, to put my collected work in front of a larger public in the most attractive form.

I thank you for opening this book and trying me out.

Index

Note: An *italicized i* following a page number indicates an image.

Dodgers, Brooklyn, 47, 118-121, 223, 244, 384-387
donations, 170, 265–266
"Don't Ask, Don't Tell" repeal, 92
draft-dodger, 359
draft lottery (1969), 204
driving while black, 156
drought, 281, 282, 389
drugs, harmful, 216, 217, 290, 291

E

Earth, 89, 382, 405. *see also* climate change (global warming); gardening; pollution
Easter, 162
East Germany (former), 272, 328–331
economic disasters, 31, 44, 95, 96
economic factors. *see also* banks and bankers; capitalism; class, economic and social; corporations; free market, myth of; home ownership; income and wages; poverty and poor people; private business; recession of 2008; taxes; throwaway economies
  Bundy's gang and, 233, 234
  climate change and, 180, 390
  conservative ethnic views and, 177
  Europe and, 277
  grandparent responsibility and, 298
  health care and, 289–290, 344–345
  Illinois Republicans *versus* Democrats and, 184–185
  inequality, 149, 151, 336, 381, 389–390
  lives of Americans *versus,* 427–428
  media and, 288
  Obama and, 231
  poverty and, 351
  segregated housing and, 415
economic recovery, 185
education. *see also* higher education and professors; history and historians; teachers
  American history and, 372

  bad history and, 375
  Christmas and, 377
  conservatives/Republicans and, 135, 138, 235–238, 340
  Germany and, 274
  ignorance and, 237–238
  Marx and, 336
  racism and, 62, 175, 177
  Trump supporters and, 151
  wars *versus,* 207
Ehrhart, W.D., 205
Eisenhower, Dwight, 200
election of 2006, 21–22, 37
election of 2008, 27–28, 33, 37, 76, 85, 96
election of 2012, Ch. 3
  climate change and, 68–71, 99
  energy and, 85–90
  entitlements and, 83–84
  facts and information and, 63–64, 97–98
  food-stamp receiving voters and, 134
  foreign policy and, 82–85
  health care and, 71–74, 99
  Hochstadt's nonpartisanship and, 63–64
  overviews, 63–64, 97–101
  policy and, 98–100
  racism and, 121
  regulation of banks and, 64–68
  Republican ideology and, 79-82, 91–97, 100
  "secession movement" and, 106
  Trump compared, 82, 85
  2020 election and, 64, 89, 100
  voter responsibility and, 77*i*
  voter suppression and, 74–79
election of 2014, 183–186
election of 2016, 144, 170, 211–212, 231, 241
election of 2017, 299–302, 313–314
election of 2018, 360, 364, 365–367, 368, 382
election of 2020, 64, 89, 100, 151, 158, 419–420

About the Author

Steve Hochstadt grew up on Long Island, earned a BA and PhD at Brown University, and taught history at Bates College in Maine for 27 years and at Illinois College in Jacksonville 2006-2016. His early research measured migration in Germany: *Mobility and Modernity: Migration in Germany 1820-1989* won the Sharlin Prize of the Social Science History Association. The Holocaust became his focus: *Sources of the Holocaust* is a documents collection used across the country in Holocaust courses. His grandparents escaped from Vienna to Shanghai in 1939, and two books reveal the refugee experience: *Shanghai-Geschichten: Die jüdische Flucht nach China* and *Exodus to Shanghai: Stories of Escape from the Third Reich*. He has spoken widely about the growing interest in the history of Jews in China, and he sits on the International Advisory Board of the Shanghai Jewish Refugees Museum. He is the treasurer of the Sino-Judaic Institute, a pioneer in the scholarship of and support for Chinese-Jewish relations for the past 30 years.

His explanations of political issues rely on historical background, careful logic, clear writing, and social scientific evidence, from the perspective of a Holocaust historian, Jackie Robinson fan, child of a Jewish refugee, and believer in American liberalism. Because he wrote for a downstate Illinois audience, his language appeals to readers from many backgrounds.